CHILD PROTECTION PRACTICE:
PRIVATE RISKS AND PUBLIC REMEDIES

A study of decision-making, intervention and outcome in child protection work

ELAINE FARMER and MORAG OWEN
University of Bristol, School for Policy Studies

STUDIES IN CHILD PROTECTION

LONDON: HMSO

Contents

Table Index

Acknowledgements

This research was funded by the Department of Health. We are very grateful for this assistance and for the help of our research liaison officer Dr Carolyn Davies.

We are indebted to the three local authorities and their staff who enabled us to undertake the research. It is not easy to have one's work scrutinised by outsiders, but in spite of this we were met with cooperation and an interest in what we were doing. We are also extremely grateful to the parents, young people and social workers who talked to us at great length.

Brenda Henson gave us useful assistance with the early analysis of the case conference data. Rajinder Ghotaora and Velma Cooley helped with the interviewing in our third local authority. A number of colleagues at Bristol and elsewhere have commented on our drafts but we are particularly grateful to Phyllida Parsloe, to Michael Little and other members of the Dartington Social Research Unit, and to the members of our Advisory Group, that is, June Thoburn, David Berridge, David Quinton, Jane Aldgate, Peter Marsh, Michael Power, and Jo Tunnard from the Family Rights Group.

Finally we would like to thank two members of our own team. We are very grateful to our consultant, Professor Emeritus Roy Parker, who gave us sound advice and patient encouragement throughout the project. He also wrote the chapter on the historical background to the study. To him our warmest thanks. We are also deeply indebted to our research support officer Patricia Lees, who helped to analyse the material, contributed substantially to the writing of chapter 16 and typed the manuscript with exceptional care and skill.

PART I

The Background

Chapter 1

A brief history of child protection
by Roy Parker

What today is referred to as the 'system' of child protection has been in existence for little more than a hundred years and was only recently regarded as a system at all. This is not to say that children had not been protected, sheltered or their lives safeguarded in earlier times. Various historical studies have now made that clear. Boswell's *The Kindness of Strangers* (1989), for example, has obliged us to look again at assumptions about the nature and extent of infanticide and the abandonment of children in the Roman Empire and later. Likewise, Shahar's enquiry into *Childhood in the Middle Ages* (1990) has alerted us to the fact that in those times 'the king, and every feudal lord and knight, was expected to act as a protector of orphans' and that 'the obligation to defend them was an important component of the knightly ethos'. Furthermore, both feudal lords as well as peasant parents had a keen interest in the survival of healthy children as future workers and economic contributors. Looking at a somewhat later period (from the sixteenth century until the end of the nineteenth) Pollock, in *Forgotten Children* (1983), undertakes a critical examination of the widely accepted view that 'the majority of children were cruelly treated in the past', particularly from the seventeenth century onwards. She argues persuasively that the sources upon which this conclusion is based are suspect and that they do not provide a sound foundation for general theories about the nature and condition of childhood in the past. In particular, she warns us not to confuse the parental care of children with public policy towards them. These are, as she says, two different issues. In a telling elaboration of the distinction she writes:

> 'It is important to realise that, although the state may not have strategies and laws for the protection of children, and though it may even at times sanction such things as child employment, this does not mean that parents will also abuse and exploit their offspring. It is as absurd to claim that as it would be to claim that, once the rights of children are safeguarded by law, they will no longer be ill-treated.'

Thus, to regard a child protection system, located within the realms of public policy and law, as having emerged in this country in the late 1880s is not to assume either that no protection existed for children before then nor that thereafter most children were satisfactorily protected from exploitation, ill-treatment or neglect. Nevertheless, the establishment of a child protection system did reflect important social and economic changes which it would be foolish to ignore. The pattern of these changes might be better appreciated by dividing the recent history of child protection into seven stages or periods, dividing the recent history of child protection into seven stages or periods, two of which occurred before the crucial legislation of 1889, the time from which we would date the 'modern' system for safeguarding children.

Extra-familial protection: the nineteenth century up to the 1870s

As the nineteenth century unfolded a certain amount of protection for children gradually became established. However, at least two characteristics of that protection need to be emphasised. First, it was in all senses of the word, rudimentary. Its application was erratic, often inconclusive and sometimes counter-productive. Secondly, it dealt almost wholly with children in situations *outside* their families. Legislation was introduced, for example, to protect apprentices, to limit the labour of children with respect to the hours that they worked and the conditions in which they did so. Within the penal system children began to be offered a measure of protection from the severest forms of punishment and, through separate treatment, from the contaminating effects of imprisonment alongside adult offenders. The industrial schools and reformatories that began to proliferate in the 1860s were important steps in this direction, but they also reflected the deep-seated concern that society should be protected against the transformation of juvenile offenders into hardened adult criminals. A somewhat similar set of concerns led to separate provisions being made for children in the care of the Poor Law. Here too it was seen as imperative that they did not become the long-term adult paupers of the future. To that end they were increasingly 'protected' against the ill-effects of daily association with the adult workhouse population and given an education and training sufficient to ensure that they could earn an independent livelihood (Parker, 1990 a). Children also had to be protected from the dangers of the streets. Before, and later alongside the industrial schools, night refuges and ragged schools were to be found in the poorest and most crowded areas of the cities, gathering in hungry and homeless children.

What is significant about these aspects of the history of child protection is that they went hand-in-hand with the often stronger concern to protect society *from* children and from what children might become. That is an enduring theme but one which has become implicit rather than explicit: we remain much exercised, for example, about the likelihood that the abused child of today will become the abuser of tomorrow.

The other outstanding feature of this early stage of 'organised' child protection was its formal disregard of what went on in the child's own home. Certainly, there was concern about brutal parents, but no legal framework existed (except criminal sanctions) through which children could be protected against either neglectful or cruel parents. Children had virtually no rights as children within the context of the parental home. More specifically the rights of fathers over them were almost absolute.

There were, of course, other practical problems in contemplating inter- vention in these matters, but above all there was the problem of identification. With high levels of infant mortality, malnutrition, overcrowding and the common practice of harsh punishment, it was difficult to separate out what was wilful and deliberate from what was the consequence of poverty and appalling living conditions. How, for example, was neglect to be distin- guished from destitution? And how was infanticide to be proved in the face of widespread stillbirth, with thousands upon thousands of unattended labours and no registration of live births until 1840 and no compulsory registration of *all* births until 1874?

The campaign against parental cruelty: the last decades of the nineteenth century

The problems discussed in the last section continued well into the final quarter of the nineteenth century, but a movement for action to be taken against parental cruelty did materialise in the 1870s. Some would argue that its origin was to be found in the heightening of public concern about child suffering that occurred with baby-farming scandals, in particular that which led to the execution of Mary Walters and indirectly to the Infant Life Protection Act of 1872 (Rose, 1986). Yet this legislation, it should be noted, still dealt only with children who were looked after by people other than their parents, and in any case it was restricted to babies under the age of one. Nonetheless, it was important (though largely ineffective even within its own restricted terms of reference) in that it signalled a growing concern about cruelty to young children, about the problems of unmarried mothers and about the difficulty of exercising a public supervision of 'children at risk'.

However, during the 1870s and 80s other more general social forces served to keep the issue alive and to give it a wider and greater prominence. Three in particular are noteworthy. First, there was the Revivalist movement which acquired its greatest popularity and influence from about 1860 onwards. The 'rescue' of children became a natural aim of its evangelical zeal and quest for spiritual salvation. It generated an enormous energy which overflowed in many related spheres of social action. Certainly, child rescue activities were closely associated with the temperance and social purity movements (Amulree, 1932). Furthermore, they were given a profoundly important organisational context by the creation of several children's societies; most notably the National Society for the Prevention of Cruelty to Children (Behlmer, 1982), Barnardos (Rose, 1987), the National Children's Home and the Waifs and Strays (Ward, 1990). Some, particularly those set up by the Catholic church, were created partly in response to (and as a defence against) the vigorous campaigning of those with a strong evangelical commitment. Indeed, sectarian rivalries of all kinds imparted a considerable impetus to the child welfare movement.

A second major factor to affect the political importance of child abuse was the rapid development of education from 1870. In particular, once elementary education had become compulsory, children were *assembled* on a daily basis. Their condition was open to scrutiny, especially once a school health service was introduced in the early twentieth century. Those who were not at school could be identified and truancy officers could investigate the reasons in a child's home or detain children at large on the streets. Comparisons could be made, data collected and standards evolved. School-aged children at least became collectively *visible*.

The third social trend that has to be taken into account in explaining the emergence of cruelty to children as an issue in the 1880s is the campaign for the improvement of the social and legal position of women, and especially of mothers with respect to their parental rights. An early success had been achieved in the Bastardy Act of 1874 which had accorded the mothers of illegitimate children full rights with respect to their offspring. By contrast, the mothers of legitimate children only gradually attained parental rights equal to those of their husbands and were not placed on exactly the same footing until 1926. Even so, improvements were won in the intervening years, linked to some extent to the mounting campaign for women's suffrage.

It is against this background that the campaign to protect children from cruelty has to be seen. Spearheaded by the National Society for the Prevention of Cruelty to Children (NSPCC), but supported more broadly as well, it reached its most vigorous and effective level in the middle years of the 1880s. By 1889, after several unsuccessful bills, the Prevention of Cruelty to Children Act was passed which, for the first time, enabled courts to remove children from cruel parents and commit them to the care of a 'fit person'. At first the designated fit persons were largely the voluntary children's societies, but before long the public authorities became the more common choice of the courts.

It is notable that these first moves to create a legal framework for the protection of children concerned cruelty rather than neglect. Child neglect was only added to the principal legislation in 1894 and even then most of the expressed concern continued to be with abuse. However, that abuse did include sexual abuse. Certainly, the 1889 Poor Law (Amendment) Act which enabled boards of guardians to assume parental rights over children in their care in specified circumstances was largely the result of pressure from an alliance of boards concerned about the return of children (mainly girls) to families where they were likely to suffer sexual abuse, most frequently at the hands of their fathers or stepfathers.

This concentration on abuse rather than neglect probably reflected the continuation of the difficulties of actually identifying wilful neglect in the midst of great poverty and stubbornly high rates of infant mortality. In 1890 for example, infant mortality accounted for a quarter of all deaths although the group at risk comprised only 2.5 per cent of the population (Rose, 1986). However, the contrast with the greater likelihood of being able to identify physical abuse should not be exaggerated. That also remained difficult in an era when the corporal punishment of children was not only widespread but officially approved. For instance, the so-called Children's Charter, the Act of 1908, still allowed the courts the option of ordering children to be whipped if found guilty of certain offences (Home Office, 1938).

Nonetheless, as a number of commentators have now pointed out, the emphasis upon the protection of children from abuse rather than neglect does lead to the focus being directed towards men as perpetrators rather than women (Gordon, 1989). The violent behaviour of fathers (particularly drunken fathers), rather than the neglectful care of mothers, was certainly uppermost in the debates of the time.

Complacency: the inter-war years

It is remarkable that after the 1914–18 war the issue of child abuse, and indeed of child protection more generally, virtually disappeared from the public agenda, with the exception of a report from a Home Office committee in 1926 on sexual offences against young people. Certainly there were repeated claims that cruelty was no longer the problem that it had been, and where neglect was discovered it was attributed to the behaviour of a marginalised under-class, where low intelligence, especially of mothers, was regarded as the major cause.

How was it that such a complacent view came to be so widely accepted? There are several reasons which together created the new climate of opinion. There was the reassuring statistical evidence. The number of prosecutions for child cruelty, for example, halved between 1900 and 1921. Likewise, the early twenties saw the first significant reduction in the rate of infant mortality. There was a decline in juvenile delinquency and much less drunkenness, attributed in part to legislation curtailing the opening hours of public houses. All this was encouraging. So too was the firm establishment of compulsory education, with attendance figures reaching very high levels (Home Office, 1923). However, under such 'improving' social conditions, what cases of child abuse there were might have been expected to have stood out more starkly and thereby have attracted more attention. There were at least five reasons why this did not happen.

First, a widespread reliance was placed upon the NSPCC to look after any problems of child protection. With what was now believed to be an efficient and well-established voluntary organisation, what need was there for further action by the state? The whole issue, it was assumed, could safely be left in the Society's hands. The emergence of this view was partly the result of the very success of earlier campaigning by the NSPCC and partly a reflection of the reluctance of government to become involved in a potentially controversial field without the apparent need to do so. Furthermore, the NSPCC was sensitive to any possible encroachment into its sphere of activities by public agencies and was therefore unwilling to admit that matters were anything but under firm control.

Secondly, there was the decline in evangelism and therefore of the idea of the need for the active and missionary-like rescue of endangered children. That decline, together with other social and economic changes, modified the character of the principal children's societies. From being largely crusading, innovative and determined organisations they gradually became bureaucratised. Charismatic leaders were replaced by cautious administrators who were keenly aware of the precarious financial position in which their organisations found themselves. Survival at existing levels of activity was more commonly the aim than the breaking of new ground or the searching out of additional problems.

The third factor conspiring to reduce concern about child protection after the 1914–18 war was the fragmentation and weakening of the women's movement. With its first suffrage victory in 1919 and with equal voting rights being won in 1926, a good deal of the unifying force disappeared from the movement and with it some of the concentrated concern about associated social issues. As Gordon (1989) has pointed out, there is good historical evidence that a heightened political preoccupation with child welfare generally and with child protection in particular tends to coincide with those periods when the women's movement has been strongest, and *vice versa*.

By 1930 a further factor added to the minimisation of concern with issues of child protection; and that was the substantial reductions made in public expenditure (for example, by way of the 1931 National Economy Act) and the consequent contraction of public services of all kinds. This also had the effect of reducing the payment of fees and grants (both nationally and locally) to the voluntary children's organisations, thereby further accentuating their financial problems.

Finally, one ought to return to the fact that the concern which did exist about the protection of children in the inter-war years was largely directed to the question of neglect, and in particular to neglectful mothers. The notion of the 'problem family' took a new and firmer hold, partly encouraged by a Eugenics movement that exercised a powerful influence throughout this period upon ideas about social problems and their solutions (Mazumdar, 1992). For example, in the 1930s proposals for the sterilisation of 'mentally defective' women were seriously debated and recommended by an official committee of inquiry (Brock, 1933). The conviction that a genetically-determined under-class existed was strong. Neglectful mothers were repeatedly described as being of low intellect and in need of firm guidance and education, not least in matters of birth control. Little if anything was said about fathers. As Gordon (1989) points out (but for the USA) it was during these years that the issue of child protection became more clearly and heavily gendered. In the process of focusing on 'problem mothers' however, the scale, nature and complexity of child abuse and neglect was distorted.

The failed campaign: the 1940s to 1960

The end of the war heralded a renewed campaign to bring the issue of child protection back into public prominence. The driving force was the Women's Group on Public Welfare. In 1948 it published a report on *The Neglected Child and His Family*. This was the outcome of the work of a committee of inquiry which the Group had set up, chaired by Eva Hubback. Several things were significant about this well-orchestrated campaign. First, it still concentrated upon child neglect: for example, it was reported that 'all witnesses were agreed that there had been a diminution in recent years of wilful cruelty, and that it forms only a small part of the problem' (p.16). However, the committee did draw attention to cruelty in the form of harsh punishment. Secondly, there was a strong conviction that there remained 'unexplored regions of unalleviated child suffering', revealed in the upheaval of war and, in particular, by the process of evacuation. Thirdly, the campaign called for the establishment of a committee of inquiry, similar to the Curtis committee that had reported on child care in 1946, but with terms of reference that dealt specifically with the need to determine the scale and nature of child suffering and to recommend action to deal with it. Fourthly, there was a clear desire that the state (probably through the agency of the local children's departments that Curtis had recommended) should assume the major responsibility for child protection, and a strong implication that matters should no longer be left to voluntary bodies such as the NSPCC (PRO a).

The pressure which this impressive group of mainly professional women sought to exercise was channelled in three directions. First, there were direct approaches to the Home Secretary (Chuter Ede); secondly, there was organised correspondence in the newspapers, especially *The Times* (1949); and thirdly there were debates in Parliament (Parl. Deb., 1948–49). The latter were secured through the actions of Mrs Ayrton-Gould, a newly-elected MP and former chair of the Labour Party as well as a member of the Women's Group on Public Welfare.

Hopes must have run high that such pressure, together with the election of a reforming Labour Government in 1945, would be successful. In the event, little was achieved and the issue of child protection was once more relegated to a low position on the social welfare agenda.

There were several reasons why an apparently promising campaign should have foundered in this way. First, the government argued that although there was evidence of child suffering there was none to suggest that it had actually increased. In particular, there was no evidence that cruelty had increased. Secondly, the NSPCC, seeing its paramount role being threatened by the tone of the campaign, mounted a lively resistance, particularly in the press (McCann, 1949), maintaining that neither a committee of inquiry nor greater public service involvement were necessary. What is more, the archival evidence makes it clear that the government was unwilling to become engaged in a confrontation with the Society (PRO a). Thirdly, there was a fear of family 'snooping' that was frequently referred to in the parliamentary debates; the state, so the case was put, had no business becoming involved as a family policeman. Fourthly, and perhaps compellingly, the cabinet (and the issue did go to the full cabinet) was fearful that were a committee of inquiry to be set up it would be difficult to contain its scope. Believing that it would mainly be addressing problems of child neglect it foresaw an analysis of the problem that pointed to inadequacies in living conditions, especially with respect to housing. Faced with a monumental housing problem already and great shortages of building materials and building labour, it had no taste for anything that would strengthen the call for action on a front where it had little opportunity to respond (PRO a).

In the event, what happened was that a working party of officials from the ministries most directly concerned was established and asked to report back. They confirmed that there was no evidence of any increase in either child neglect or cruelty, but emphasised that what was needed to improve the existing system of protection was more and better coordination. Their internal report (PRO a) (which was not published) provided the basis for the 1950 joint circular on *Children Neglected or Ill-Treated in their Own Homes* (Home Office *et al.*, 1950). In an appendix to that two-page circular the Government stated its position quite clearly; it had

> 'reached the conclusion that the present need is not for an extension of
> statutory powers, or for enquiry by a Departmental committee, but for
> the fully coordinated use of the local authority and other statutory and
> voluntary services available.'

Local authorities were asked (but not required) to introduce arrangements 'designed to ensure that action is coordinated to make the most effective use of the available resources, statutory and voluntary alike'.

Subsequent inquiries undertaken by the Home Office child care inspectorate showed that the local response was extremely patchy and that most schemes that had been established had achieved little more than the listing of 'known' cases (PRO a). There was a return to complacency and certainly no concern about child abuse. Indeed, the agreed statement to Parliament about the outcome of the working party's deliberations had already said that 'there is comparatively little ill-treatment, that deliberate neglect is found in a small minority of cases only and that neglect – whether deliberate or not – is due to a wide variety of factors . . . ' (PRO a). These sentiments were reflected in the annual reports of local children's committees and in the principal child care publications of the early 1950s. One is hard-pressed to find references to anything but neglect and deprivation: this was as true of the few research reports such as Donnison's (1954) *The Neglected Child and the Social Services*, as it was of more general texts like Ford's (1955) *The Deprived Child and the Community*.

What is intriguing, but unresolvable, is the question of the extent to which these prevailing views reflected the reality. For example, how true was it that these years did not witness any increase in the problems of child abuse or neglect? What was the effect, for instance, of wartime mobilisation upon the levels of violence to children? With most fathers and men of their age out of the home for long periods it is at least conceivable that fewer children were abused, and that with larger wartime family incomes and full employment fewer children were neglected. Have the definitions of abuse and neglect changed in such a way that what was regarded as neglect then is now liable to be classed as abuse?

Prevention embraced: 1960–1972

One group at least was not complacent during the 1950s; and that was the Home Office inspectorate. Although its own enquiries had shown a disappointing response to the 1950 circular, where machinery was working well it was revealing a large number of children 'at risk'. The difficulty was that once such children were identified there were too few staff skilled enough to deal with the problems that came to light. There was also a reluctance on the part of many local authorities to appoint additional child care officers for non-statutory duties.

Instead, the initiative for further action came from the centre. It was, for example, largely pressure from the Home Office children's inspectorate that led to the terms of reference of the Ingleby committee, that was appointed in 1956 to look at juvenile delinquency, being extended to include the consideration of how best children might be prevented from coming into care or appearing before the juvenile courts as offenders (PRO b).

Ingleby eventually reported in 1960, and although there was not a word in its report about child abuse, only about neglect, it did recommend that a statutory duty be placed upon local authorities 'to prevent or forestall the suffering of children in their own homes'. The Home Office invited reactions to the report, but only the London County Council drew attention to the problem of ill-treatment as well as neglect. Both the civil servants and the professionals sounded notes of caution; in particular concerning the likelihood of an adverse public reaction to an enlargement of local authority powers to intervene in family affairs, the lack of trained social workers and the associated lack of experience of working with families in which children were at risk (PRO b).

Despite these apprehensions the recommendation was accepted and incorporated in the Children and Young Persons Act, 1963. Much has been said about the importance of the power which that Act gave to local authorities to spend money on prevention (section 1). Looked at historically, however, that was not its most significant feature. What was of the utmost importance for the subsequent development of the protection system was the radical re-casting of public accountability for the prevention of child suffering that the Act achieved, together with the impetus it provided for the expansion of staffing. In 1963, for example, there were 1,500 child care officers in England and Wales; by 1966 there were 2,400, and 3,000 by 1969. Training was also stepped up. The proportion of qualified field staff rose from 27 per cent in 1964 to 35 per cent three years later (Parker, 1990 b).

Nevertheless, the 'idea' of prevention remained rather generalised and steps to forestall the admission of children to care took various forms and were directed at various groups. It was not until the 1970s that the responsibility of local authorities to engage in prevention was consolidated around the issue of child protection, and an explicit child protection system created.

The rediscovery of abuse: 1973 onwards

The first inquiry into a child death since the Monckton committee's examination of the circumstances surrounding the murder of Dennis O'Neill in a foster home in 1945, was published in the 1970s (Secretary of State, 1974). Maria Colwell had been killed by her father after having been returned home from care. The tragedy attracted enormous attention from the media and represented a landmark in the reappearance of child abuse on the social welfare agenda. Although there had been numerous internal inquiries into the maltreatment of children in residential homes and schools in the years between 1945 and 1973, there had been none concerned with the abuse of a child in its own home.

Yet the Maria Colwell inquiry and the disquiet that it aroused was not the first sign of what has been termed the 'rediscovery of abuse', even though it undoubtedly stimulated a greater measure of popular interest. Renewed concern had begun to mount in the United States as early as 1962 following the first of Kempe's publications (Kempe *et al*, 1962) which suggested that baby battering existed on a much larger scale than had previously been believed. This reawakened concern had found its way across the Atlantic by the mid-1960s, having been transmitted mainly along medical lines of communication. In 1966, for instance, the British Paediatric Association issued its first memorandum of guidance on the identification of the battered baby syndrome. The emphasis upon 'babies' was significant, reflecting as it did the orientation of paediatricians in both the United States and Britain. The risks to older children were hardly discussed at all. Indeed, Baldwin and Oliver's research published in 1975, and quoted two years later by the select committee on violence in the family, concluded that 90 per cent of all 'battered' children were under six months of age.

However, it was not only the strong emphasis that paediatrics generally placed on the younger age group that led to this concentration upon babies. It was also related to the fact that by the 1960s an increasing proportion of births were occurring in hospital. Further, improved methods emerged for the treatment of damaged babies in hospitals (however the damage had occurred) and, in particular, new radiological techniques became available with the aid of which it was easier to determine the nature of injuries.

By the end of the 1960s the renewed interest of the paediatric profession in battered babies had spilled over into wider settings. The Department of Health and Social Security issued its first circular of guidance on the matter in 1970, and in 1974, following the Colwell report, a much more comprehensive circular was prepared that gave detailed guidance to social services departments, the medical profession and others about the management of cases of 'non-accidental injury' as the problem had by then come to be known. Local authorities were asked to establish Area Review Committees (now Area Child Protection Committees), to call case conferences in order to decide what action was to be taken when instances of non-accidental injury came to light and to establish a 'central record of information' (now the register) in order to facilitate good communication between the agencies involved (DHSS, 1974). As in 1950 the way forward was seen mainly in terms of ensuring better collaboration between the services principally concerned, including the police. Unlike the 1950 joint circular, however, the report on Maria Colwell's death provided certain concrete evidence about what was likely to ensure that a well coordinated response was made to protect children at risk.

Thus, by the mid-1970s child abuse had been 'rediscovered', albeit in limited forms. Apart from the specific reasons for this that have already been discussed, there were other broader social trends that encouraged the rediscovery. First, the women's movement had become more active and better organised. Its influence in the field of child and family welfare can be seen clearly in, for example, the setting up of both the select committee on violence in marriage in 1974, and the select committee on violence in the family in 1976. The common cause of battered women and battered children made a renewed public appearance.

Secondly, the rediscovery of abuse was stimulated by the increase in the number of staff in social services departments and by the growing proportion who were qualified. Between 1972 and 1974, after the setting up of the new social services departments, the number of social workers rose by 25 per cent. The proportion who were qualified increased somewhat later, but by 50 per cent between 1974 and 1980 (Parker, 1990 b).

A third and associated factor that increased the likelihood of child abuse coming to more frequent notice during the 1970s was the virtual explosion of referrals of all kinds that occurred once the unified social services departments had replaced the previously separate elements of the local welfare system. We still do not fully understand why that explosion occurred; it seems unlikely that it was simply the result of there now being 'one door upon which to knock'. Whatever the reason, the upheaval and reform of the social welfare services did heighten their visibility and did forestall some of the passing on of referrals between agencies that had gone on before, in the process of which some had disappeared from sight.

A fourth factor that assisted in the re-emergence of the issue of child abuse was the availability of specific statistics, most notably those collected and first published in 1974 by the NSPCC. Though providing far from a complete picture, they did offer a baseline with which each subsequent set of data about child abuse could be compared; and the trend certainly appeared to be upward.

Rowe and Lambert's study *Children Who Wait*, published in 1973, had had a considerable influence in encouraging the re-examination of the need for children to stay in long-term care. By the middle years of the 1970s there was therefore a growing conviction that as well as children being prevented from entering care they should also be returned home as soon as that could safely be done. This constituted a fifth element in the rediscovery of abuse. As more children were placed back at home there was undoubtedly an increased risk that they might come to harm there, especially if the ground for their original admission had been their ill-treatment. For example, in 1960 only 10 per cent of children in care in England and Wales were 'home on trial' but by 1972 that proportion had risen to 30 per cent (Farmer and Parker, 1991). For reasons like these, and because of a growing reluctance to take children into care 'unnecessarily', there may actually have been an upsurge in the number of children abused in their own homes.

The intensification of concern and the sexual dimension

The procedures for registering and making decisions about children 'at risk' which were devised after the death of Maria Colwell provide the framework for those that are used today. The emphasis was, and continues to be, on setting up reliable procedures for identifying those in jeopardy and for securing good professional coordination. Nevertheless, although the principles of these procedures have remained largely unchanged, the issues to which they have been applied have intensified and altered.

They have intensified for several reasons. First, since the publication of the Colwell report in 1974 there has been a remarkable accumulation of other inquiries (both public and semi-public) into the killing, abuse or purported abuse of a child, often one for whom there was already a substantial measure of public responsibility. The three best known reports are those dealing with the deaths of Jasmine Beckford (London Borough of Brent, 1985) and Kimberley Carlile (London Borough of Greenwich, 1987) and that which followed from the unprecedented number of children in Cleveland diagnosed as having been sexually assaulted (Secretary of State, 1988). Although these cases captured an extraordinary amount of public attention, the forty or so others that had preceded them since 1974 had already created the sense of a problem spreading at an alarming rate and of one that sounded a serious warning of the disintegration of certain cherished values, and even of a much wider social malaise. The significance of this steady stream of publicly investigated child tragedies cannot be overestimated. Of course, the press, radio and television played their part in keeping the subject alive; but even the most sensational issues tend to lose their force without further revelations to sustain them.

Concern about the extent of child abuse has also deepened in the last decade because of important changes in the way in which it has been defined. In 1980, for example, the Department of Health encouraged local authorities to include in that definition mental and emotional abuse. Furthermore, it was recommended that registers should be open to children up to the age of 18 and not restricted to the younger ones alone (DHSS, 1980). That echoed what the select committee on violence in the family had said about abuse assuming many forms and affecting children of all ages.

An even more significant shift in the way in which child abuse has been conceived followed from the emergence of sexual abuse as a preoccupying issue in the last few years. The transformation of such abuse into a matter of acute public and political sensitivity dates from the widely reported events that occurred in Cleveland in 1987. It was not simply the fact that so many children in one locality were claimed to have been victims of sexual abuse that caused alarm but also fears that it might accurately reflect the national situation. If it did, then the resource implications for social services departments and for the Department of Health were immense. If, on the other hand, the large number of children considered to have been sexually abused was the result of over-enthusiastic referrals and mis-diagnoses then major questions about the infringement and protection of civil rights had to be confronted.

Whatever the truth of the matter (and it remains elusive) there were formidable consequences. The publicity surrounding the 'affair' alerted professionals and others alike to the possibility that more children were being sexually abused than had been thought. The publicity also exposed in stark relief two long-standing dilemmas in child protection. First, how could the tension between taking action to protect children and respecting their and their parents' rights best be managed (Parker, 1986) and, secondly, how could it be done in the light of so much uncertainty?

The rights and wrongs of intervention in family life acquired a new prominence. The parents of the Cleveland children mounted an active lobby and enlisted support. The inquiry took up their views and criticised the way in which both they and their children had been dealt with by the social services department and by other agencies. In particular, it recommended that parents should be informed and consulted at each stage of investigation, and that children should not undergo repeated interviews and medical examinations, nor be subject to precipitate removal from their families. The concern to avert child tragedies moved to include the concern that the child protection system itself should not compound the abuse that children might already have suffered.

Not only was there renewed uncertainty about the reliability with which doctors (and others) could identify sexual abuse but a renewed uncertainty about its extent as well. Indeed, in its report the Butler-Sloss committee (Secretary of State, 1988) advised 'that great caution should be exercised at the present time in accepting percentages as to the prevalence and incidence of sexual abuse' (p.5). In the absence of firm evidence about the size of the problem there was no yardstick against which to assess claims and counter-claims about its seriousness – a situation in which any extra information is liable to push estimates sharply in one direction or another. In the case of sexual abuse, all the new evidence tended to shift the estimates upwards. Take, for example, the statistics.

Although no national figures for the size and composition of child protection registers were available until 1988 (Department of Health, 1989a), the NSPCC had published details of the registers held by its special units (covering about 10 per cent of the child population) from 1977 onwards (NSPCC, various; Creighton, 1984; Creighton and Noyes, 1989; Creighton, 1992). These showed that as well as an overall increase in the number of registrations (between 1977 and 1985 a growth of 73 per cent) there had been a rapid increase in registrations on the grounds of sexual abuse (from 1 per cent of all registrations in 1977 to 18 per cent in 1985). The DHSS returns that began in 1988 showed further overall increases, of 16 per cent by 1991 for example (Department of Health, 1992), whilst registrations for sexual abuse hovered around 15 per cent of the total (see table 1).

After significant increases each year, however, the number of official registrations has suddenly fallen (by 15 per cent between 1991 and 1992, and by 16 per cent between 1992 and 1993) in part because of the withdrawal of

Table 1 **Children and Young Persons on Child Protection Registers for Years Ending 31 March, England***

	No. on the Registers	Neglect %	Physical Abuse %	Sexual Abuse %	Emotional Abuse %	Grave Concern %	Mixed %
1988	39,200	13	28	15	4	37	3
1989	41,200	13	24	14	5	40	4
1990	43,600	16	27	15	5	41	–
1991	45,300	15	23	13	6	47	–
1992	38,600	20	28	17	7	34	–
1993	32,500	26	37	26	11	8	–

*Mixed categories are incorporated with each relevant category. Some totals therefore exceed 100%.

the category of 'grave concern' that had been used in classifying the registrations until October 1991. Between then and the collection of statistics at the end of March 1992 a good deal of reclassification had doubtless occurred. There were increases in the categories of neglect, physical abuse and sexual abuse. Even so, the dramatic fall in the overall number is not fully explained and warrants investigation.

The abandonment of the somewhat obscure term 'grave concern' shows how easily changes in classification can alter our view of the size and character of the problem. The figures for 1993 during which the category of 'grave concern' was omitted for all new cases registered that year, show that further adjustments have been made to the other categories. There were increases in all categories, but most notably in those of physical and sexual abuse.

Other factors have operated alongside the statistics in shaping and sharpening public awareness of child abuse. For instance, the somewhat greater readiness on the part of those – both adults and children – who have suffered sexual abuse to reveal what happened may well have increased disquiet (Hooper, 1991). Likewise, the increase in the number of accusations of sexual abuse now heard during disputes about custody and access in divorce proceedings also suggests that the size of the problem is underestimated. At the same time, however, some of these accusations are certainly false, being employed as weapons in bitter battles between angry adults (Anthony and Watkeys, 1991).

For various reasons, therefore, concern about child abuse had both intensified and shifted its focus by the second half of the 1980s. This called for new policy and practice initiatives, particularly from the centre. The first of these was the publication by the Department of Health and Social Security in 1988 of guidance about improved arrangements for inter-agency cooperation in protecting children from abuse. Although partly a consolidation of previous guidance, *Working Together* contained considerably more detail about what was to be done, when and by whom. The emphasis, however, remained on the procedures to be adopted rather than on the social work practices that could or should be followed in actually working with the families involved.

The Children Act, 1989 introduced new principles in child care. In particular, local authorities were required to work in partnership with families. They were given a general duty to safeguard and promote the welfare of children in need in their areas and, subject to their age and understanding, children were to be consulted about their wishes and feelings. *Working Together* had to be revised to take account of these and other requirements specified in the Act (Home Office *et al.*, 1991). Even so, the emphasis was still mainly upon the procedures needed to ensure the coordination and collaboration between agencies that had been missing in the Cleveland affair. The 1991 guidelines are detailed, clear and sensitive and, like those of 1988, they have had a considerable impact on local action. Although they do not have the force of law, failure to observe them would call for strong justification. They have become a touchstone for assessing performance in child protection and for apportioning blame when the system breaks down.

Notwithstanding the many undoubted improvements in the child protection system over the last hundred years, we remain in some ignorance and uncertainty about many aspects of child neglect and abuse. Most occurs in the deeply private surroundings of a child's own home, and shame, guilt, fear, powerlessness and confusion conspire to keep it highly secretive. It is not a problem that is readily open to investigation or quantification. As a result, its interpretation is liable to be influenced by unsubstantiated ideas about its causation, about who is responsible and about what public remedies should be invoked. Even a brief acquaintance with the history of child protection helps to put such notions into context and to highlight both the unremarked continuities and the surprising discontinuities that occur.

Although history is a necessary contributor to our understanding it is not sufficient. We also require up-to-date and continuing research in order to monitor what is happening, to test assumptions and to suggest ways forward. We believe that this study, which is part of the Department of Health's programme of studies into child abuse, makes such a contribution.

Chapter 2

Research methods and design

As the previous chapter shows, in the years which followed Maria Colwell's death a spate of inquiries into other child deaths ensured that child abuse remained high on the public agenda (DHSS, 1982; Department of Health, 1991 a). Professional shortcomings were highlighted and child protection procedures successively revised in reponse to these inquiries. During this time, the concept of 'child abuse' underwent considerable 'diagnostic inflation' (Dingwall, 1989), so that the term came to be used for a wide variety of problems which can have an adverse impact on children, whilst it continued to feature prominently in debates about the welfare state and the family.

However, research lagged behind these developments. Whilst there was a wealth of research, particularly in the USA, into the aetiology of child abuse and treatment methods in specialist centres, there was very little research on how child abuse was managed by the statutory agencies, in spite of the fact that it was they who handled the majority of the work. With the exception of the study by Dingwall and his colleagues (1983) into how various agencies detect, investigate and subsequently process cases of possible child abuse, the majority of the information which was used to inform policy was derived from inquiry reports into cases which had gone wrong. Indeed, as we have seen, it was not until 1988 that national statistics on child protection registration were collected (Department of Health, 1989 a). Up until then the only data available had been the figures published by the NSPCC which were based on a 10 per cent sample of the child population of England and Wales (see for example, Creighton, 1992).

In the UK there had been a few accounts and evaluations of the interventions provided by voluntary agencies and in hospital settings in cases of physical and sexual abuse (for example, Baher et al., 1976; Lynch and Roberts, 1982; Dale et al., 1986; Bentovim et al., 1988) and also a few accounts of action research projects (for example, Smith and Rachman, 1984; Browne and Saqi, 1988). In addition, studies carried out by Hallett and Stevenson (1980), Dingwall et al. (1983), Dale et al. (1986) and Corby (1987) all commented critically on standards of assessment at case conferences in the late 1970s and early 1980s. Hallett and Stevenson noted that inter-professional defensiveness and dysfunctional group processes could be obstacles to good early assessment and decision-making. Dingwall and his colleagues concluded that the assessments made at case conferences were likely to result in an underestimation of the degree of risk to the child. Dale and his colleagues gave consideration to the dangers of professionals becom-

ing polarised over case conference decisions and worsening existing difficulties. Corby reported considerable confusion in more marginal cases about
why some children were registered and others were not. More recent research
by Higginson (1992) suggested that conference decision-making was not
based on a careful assessment of risk.

During this time a number of commentators began to identify specific
gaps in the research base. Graham, Dingwall and Wolkind (1985) in a
comprehensive review of child abuse research considered that there was a
pressing need for an examination of the way in which investigations were
perceived, and the kind of behaviour elicited in professionals and lay people.
Gough in his review of child abuse research (Gough *et al*, 1988) commented
on the lack of descriptions of routine child abuse practice and outcome.
Parton (1989) pointed out the need both for knowledge of consumer views
of child protection interventions, and for an evaluation from the perspectives
of social workers and parents of why and how some types of intervention have
beneficial outcomes and others do not. He also emphasised the importance of
evaluating interventions from the point of view of the children themselves.

It was certainly true that whilst a body of literature had developed in the
UK on consumer views of social work and child care (Mayer and Timms,
1970; Sainsbury, 1975; Sainsbury *et al.*, 1982; Fisher *et al.*, 1986) until recently
little had been published on consumer views of child protection. A study by
Brown in 1984 was based on retrospective interviews with 23 parents of
physically abused children, and Corby's study (1987) included interviews
with ten parents whose children had been subject to child protection
intervention. In addition, Gough's research (Gough *et al*, 1989) on physically
abused children under five who were registered in 1982–1983 included
interviews with 29 parents. A subsequent study by Pitcairn and colleagues
(1993) involved interviews with the parents of 43 children who had been
physically abused. Consumer-oriented research has more recently been
directed to the impact on mothers of the discovery that their child has been
sexually abused (Hooper, 1992; Dempster, 1993). Further, there has been
considerable interest in parental participation in child protection conferences
and a number of studies which include parent views have been conducted
with a view to improving practice in this area (for example, McGloin and
Turnbull, 1986; Shemmings and Thoburn, 1990; Burns, 1991; Thoburn,
1992).

This study was intended to fill some of these gaps in our knowledge.
Firstly, it was our intention to examine consumer views of the child
protection process, in particular those of the parents and children as well as
those of social workers. It was therefore decided that no case would be
included in the study unless we could secure permission to interview all the
partipants. This approach has the advantage that, unlike studies of specialist
agency intervention where parents who drop out of treatment are excluded,

parents who refused agency services or who withdrew cooperation were included. Secondly, our aim was to explore the kinds of interventions which are routinely offered to parents and children by social services and other agencies when children are placed on the child protection register. Research and practice developments in child protection, as in other areas of research, have tended to concentrate on the 'entry' processes, such as the identification and investigation of children at risk. Little attention has been paid to the crucial question of what makes subsequent professional action effective (Farmer, 1993 a). Thirdly, our intention was to undertake an examination of decision-making not only at case conferences but also beforehand during the investigation and subsequently during ongoing work. The decisions examined were to include those about whether or not to remove children and when to return them.

Clearly, information was required about an ordinary group of children on the register. Had registration meant that they were protected and how was this achieved? What services had been provided and what seemed to be effective? In undertaking this analysis we also wanted to look not only at professional interventions, but also at key events for the children and parents, to ensure that we gained an understanding of the changes in their lives which had a bearing on outcome.

Now that we have outlined the background to the study we will turn to look in more detail at the design of the study and the methods used. The research aimed to examine a number of specific areas. The first was early decision-making in child protection cases; that is how investigations were conducted and decisions made about the risks to which children were exposed and what actions were taken to protect them. The second was the decision-making processes which took place at initial case conferences and, in particular, the ways in which risk was assessed, decisions about registration made and child protection plans drawn up. The third area of enquiry was the management of registered cases over a 20-month follow-up period, the development of decisions and actions over time and the experiences of the children and parents or other carers who were involved. Our fourth area of endeavour was to describe and evaluate the outcomes both for the parents and for the children whose names had been placed on the child protection register. Finally we wished to see whether it was possible to draw any conclusions about the links between decision-making and intervention in relation to these children and their parents and the outcomes for them 20 months later. In this sense we were interested in considering the continuities and discontinuities which emerged within the operation of the child protection system, especially given its heavy reliance on formalised procedures.

The way in which the outcomes for children involved in the child protection system were conceptualised will be explained in more detail in chapter 17. Suffice it to say at this point that, in considering the links between interventions and outcomes, both 'system' inputs such as the adequacy of the case conference protection plan and 'practice' inputs such as whether the worker had been able to engage the cooperation of family members were considered. In addition, since much that is of vital significance to the welfare of children and their parents inevitably occurs outside the ambit of professional agencies, attention was paid to other key events in the lives of family members, such as changes in family membership or the network of family support.

The main study took place in two local authorities where the use of the child protection register was close to the national average both in terms of the rates of new registrations and the rates of children maintained on the register (Department of Health, 1991 b). Both were shire counties and one had a sizeable urban centre. The arrangements in place for dealing with child protection contrasted in the two authorities. One had appointed specialist child protection coordinators who convened and chaired conferences. The other made use of area managers (who had, of course, line management responsibilities) to chair conferences, whilst meetings were convened by fieldworkers. The burden of work which was handled in the different area offices within each authority varied considerably, as did staff morale and arrangements for staff supervision. Nonetheless, in comparison with many large metropolitan authorities, resources and staffing were at reasonable levels. The practices which we observed avoided the worst examples of over-pressed departments where many child protection cases were unallocated (Department of Health, 1990 a). The patterns which emerged appear therefore to reflect processes beyond those simply attributable to very scarce resources.

Our original plan had been to include a large county authority with a sizeable black population in its urban centre. Unfortunately, the authority concerned delayed its final decision about participation until late in the preparatory stages of the study and then withdrew. Another local authority agreed to take part in the study at short notice. This left us with a dilemma. The two local authorities which had agreed to participate had few black and minority ethnic children in their populations. We could either accept this limitation on our data or attempt, as the study progressed, to address it. Our decision was to take the second course of action. Additional material was collected in a third social services department, a large metropolitan authority, in order to include a group of black and minority ethnic children in the study.

Extending the research in this way proved to be difficult. There were a number of reasons for this. In part it was because ethnic monitoring in the third authority proved to be patchy, and as a result it was difficult to locate cases of black and minority ethnic children on the register for inclusion in the sample. One African-Caribbean and two Asian interviewers assisted us in the fieldwork, but even then suitable matching of Asian parents with an interviewer who spoke the same language was sometimes problematic. A third difficulty was that the parents who were approached were highly mobile and when located were often wary about participating. This was no doubt connected to their general concerns about intervention by white-dominated agencies, with attendant fears about racist treatment and the possibility of unwanted surveillance. It was particularly noticeable that women withdrew under pressure from male family members. As a result, although it was eventually possible to draw a small sample of registered children and to carry out interviews in ten cases, our resources were fully stretched and did not allow for follow-up interviews to be conducted. We are therefore in a position to make some comments on the experiences of black parents but unfortunately we do not have the data which would have enabled us to analyse interventions over time and their relationship to outcomes for this group.

The analysis which follows concentrates on the material from the two principal local authorities in our study. On occasion, additional reference has been made to issues for minority ethnic children and parents, drawing on the material from our third local authority. (For example we comment on the use of interpreters in chapter 7, cultural arguments in risk assessment in chapter 9, and racial matching of social worker and family members in chapter 14.) We realise that our data in this area is very limited; but nevertheless the information culled from our Asian and African-Caribbean interviews may contribute to an ongoing debate about the treatment of black and minority ethnic children in the child protection system. Needless to say, many important questions are beyond the scope of the present study and remain in urgent need of examination.

Study design

At the start of the study, discussions were held with relevant managers, child protection specialist staff, conference chairs and members of the Area Child Protection Committees in each local authority. Practice guidelines and policy directives in relation to child protection were also scrutinised. Professional and parental permission was sought for us to attend initial child protection case conferences. Arrangements were then put in place for us to be notified of initial conferences as they arose. In the authority which used specialist coordinators this worked very well and we were notified of most conferences which were arranged. In the other authority notification was variable with some area offices participating more fully than others.

As a result of this procedure, during 1989 and 1990 the authors attended 120 initial child protection conferences in the two principal participating authorities. At each one we made a full process recording of what was said and by whom throughout the meeting. This was written up afterwards so that a record was kept of key processes and of the themes and issues which arose. We also scrutinised the official case conference minutes for each conference. In addition, details of content and process were entered onto pre-coded schedules on which we recorded 264 items of information about the initial referral, child and family circumstances, the type of abuse or neglect under consideration, the information considered in making an assessment of risk, the contributions of the professionals and parents who attended, and the decisions and plans made. The schedules also recorded a number of researcher judgements about issues such as the influence of different participants on the decisions made, gaps in the information presented, the quality of chairing and incidences of high risk cases which slipped through the net and did not end in registration. The conference data recorded on the schedules were transferred onto computer and analysed using SPSS-X in order to obtain quantitative information about the conduct and process of conferences as well as to examine correlations and to find out which factors were significantly associated, on a chi-square test of significance, with registration. We regarded differences as statistically significant when $P < 0.05$ in a chi-square test.

At the 120 initial conferences which we attended 73 children were registered and were therefore candidates for our follow-up sample. Before looking in more detail at these cases we need to consider whether the children who were registered at the conferences which we attended were representative of the national picture.

The categories of registration in use at that time were physical abuse, sexual abuse, emotional abuse, neglect and grave concern (DHSS, 1988). Using these categories we compared the distribution of cases in our conference sample with the national picture of those registered during the same period. This was difficult to do because of the very variable usage of the category of grave concern in different authorities at that time (see for example, Corby, 1990). Nationally, 40 per cent of registered cases were placed in this category in 1989 (Department of Health, 1990 b) but there were enormous variations in the use of the category, ranging from Barking where it was employed in 81 per cent of registrations to Greenwich, Haringey and Merton where 'grave concern' was not used at all. When we examined the data on all the registered children in our two local authorities at that time, we found that the distribution of registrations in one of them was similar to the national picture. In this authority 47 per cent of all registrations were placed in the category of grave concern as compared with a national average of 40 per cent. In contrast, the usage of this category in the other local authority was considerably lower at 21 per cent. However, our observations of the decisions made at case conferences about which category to use suggested the variable use of categories for similar cases, and we concluded that there was no reason to suppose that registrations in our two local authorities differed significantly from the national picture. The abolition of the category of grave concern (Home Office *et al.*, 1991) will in future make comparisons with national figures much easier.

We then compared the registration categories of the children in our case conference sample with those of all children on the registers in our two local authorities. We found that the case conference sample reflected the distribution of children on the register in the local authority which had provided the largest number of cases. Whilst, as can be seen, the variable use of the grave concern category made national comparisons somewhat difficult, we were nonetheless able to ascertain that the cases registered at the case conferences in our sample were broadly representative of the cases on the register in the largest of our two local authorities. This information is shown in table 2 below:

Table 2 **Categories of Children Registered at Case Conferences Attended Compared with All Children Registered in the Two Study Authorities and in England**

Category of Registration	Initial Case Conferences in Sample	Children on Registers* Year Ending 31.3.89		Children Registered Year Ending 31.3.89 England
		Local Authority		
		A	B	
	%	%	%	%
Physical Abuse	25	29	22	25
Sexual Abuse	25	25	15	17
Emotional Abuse	5	10	2	4
Neglect	8	15	14	11
Grave Concern	25	21	47	40
Other+	12	0	0	3
N = 73	100	100	100	100

* 'On Register' statistics only available
+ 'Other' includes cases of unborn children and others where no decision about the category was made at the initial case conference.

The quantitative survey of case conference decision-making, planning and process formed the first part of our study. The second part was an intensive study of 44 children whose names were placed on the child protection register. This sample was drawn from the 73 newly-registered cases at the conferences which we attended. The cases in this intensive study represented 60 per cent of all the registered cases. (The compliance rate of all parents

Table 3 **Main Concern of Initial Case Conference**
         (Registered cases only)

	Case Conference Sample		Follow-Up Sample	
	No.	%	No.	%
Physical Abuse	22	30	16	36
Sexual Abuse	29	40	15	34
Emotional Abuse	9	12	8	18
Neglect	13	18	5	12
	73	100	44	100

contacted was actually 74 per cent, but as we shall see in a moment, another 14 per cent of cases could not be followed up for other reasons.)

In view of the variations in the use of the category of grave concern and the different cases which may be sheltered under this category, we found it useful to group the cases according to the main focus of concern at the initial case conference although, of course, other concerns had often also arisen. This allowed us to be clear about the nature of abuse or neglect under consideration and to compare the cases in the follow-up sample with the total group of cases which were registered at the conferences we attended. Table 3 shows the resulting distribution of cases in both our case conference and follow-up sample.

It can be seen that there were slightly more cases of physical and emotional abuse in the follow-up sample when compared with the case conference sample, and slightly fewer cases of sexual abuse and neglect. However, the differences are small. Overall the cases in the intensive follow-up group were representative of those in the larger conference sample and of cases registered in our local authorities at that time. (We might note in passing that a comparison of tables 2 and 3 suggests that cases registered as 'grave concern', together with the unclassified cases, had predominantly been concerned with sexual abuse and neglect, while a smaller number dealt with emotional and physical abuse.)

The cases which we did not follow up included 19 families who refused to participate or could not be contacted and 10 who were not followed up for other reasons. These reasons included a family move, the fact that the key worker for the family already had two cases in the study, and on two occasions a request by the social services department that we should not be involved. Since the cases which were included in the intensive study depended on parental consent, we explored further whether there was any bias in the group who agreed to participate in the study. Cases in which parents did not agree to participate were distributed across all types of abuse or neglect, except that there were no refusals in the category of emotional abuse. However, we found that a refusal was especially likely if there were allegations against a male partner who was still living in the household. These accounted for 10 out of 19 refusals (52%), of which four involved allegations of physical abuse, five of sexual abuse, and one of neglect. (In the follow-up sample allegations against a resident adult male had been made in only 25 per cent of the cases.) We also observed that some families who refused to participate were particularly anxious to safeguard their privacy and may have made access difficult for professionals as well as researchers. However, there were other families who agreed to talk to us but strove to keep child protection professionals at bay.

With the exceptions noted above, the children who were included in the follow-up group represented a fairly typical cross-section of children registered by the social services departments in our study. A third were registered because of physical abuse, a third for reasons of sexual abuse, and the remainder were divided between cases of neglect and those deemed to constitute emotional abuse. The characteristics of the children will be examined in more detail later.

The intensive study

Forty-four families with one or more children on the child protection register were included in the intensive follow-up study. In each case we focused in particular on one child in the family whom we term the 'index child', although we also collected data on the child's siblings. The index child chosen was the one who was the major focus of concern at the initial case conference.

Soon after the initial conference the parents, older children and key workers for each family were interviewed and the participants were re-interviewed 20 months later in order to trace developments over time. The research spanned a period of considerable change since the first interviews took place before the implementation of the 1989 Children Act and the follow-up interviews afterwards. In only four cases was it not possible to re-interview parent figures either because they had moved out of the area and could not be contacted or because they declined to participate. This represented a 90 per cent follow-up rate. In one case where a parent declined to be interviewed on the second occasion, she talked at length on the telephone and her daughter was interviewed. In five cases we were unable to interview a social worker at follow-up because the case was by then closed or unallocated, and the social worker whom we had seen at the outset was unavailable. In addition, the parents agreed in all cases that we should receive the minutes of all the review conferences and in all but one instance they gave us permission to see their case files at the end of the study. We also attended a selection of review meetings so that we could observe the way in which these reviews were conducted.

At the outset, 44 mothers were interviewed and also, in a third of cases, a father, stepfather or male partner. Interviews with parent figures were conducted separately in most cases in order to allow for separate points of view to be expressed. All the suspected perpetrators of sexual abuse were male (mostly fathers or stepfathers and a few older boys), whereas the physical injuries had been meted out in similar numbers by father figures in two-parent households and mothers who were living alone. In a few cases there was continuing uncertainty amongst professional agencies about the source of abuse. In cases of neglect and emotional abuse the concern of professional agencies had sometimes focused on one, and sometimes on both parent figures.

The parents interviewed included mother and father figures, abusers and non-abusers. Despite these differences parents had a good many experiences in common. In the following chapters they will therefore be treated as a group, and when important differences emerge, for example between abusing and non-abusing parents, or along gender lines, attention will be drawn to these differences. It should be noted that except in a few of the cases of emotional abuse or neglect, suspicion generally centred on one rather than both parent figures. In the cases of sexual abuse in the sample, no mothers were implicated in the abusive acts and when allegations were made to them by their children they all took active steps which led to the involvement of the authorities.

Interviews with children were restricted to those who were eight or over at the start of the study. Some children preferred not to be interviewed or could not be contacted and in one case a foster carer did not wish the child to be seen. In all, 15 children were interviewed during the course of the research. Particular attention was paid to ensuring that those who talked to us did not feel pressured to do so and that they felt sufficiently in control of the interviews to tell us if they did not want to answer any of our questions, or if they wanted to stop the interview. We practised with children how to refuse to answer our questions using the rehearsal technique developed by Marjorie Smith at the Institute of Child Health.

The interviews with parents, social workers and children were semi-structured and each interview was tape-recorded and transcribed. The advantage of transcribed interviews was that the complete record could be read and re-read by the researchers and others in the process of interpreting the material. In addition, we used a number of measures at each interview, such as those which related to parent health, child behaviour, and the parents' network of support. The measures were used to provide detailed information on the health and well-being of the children and parent figures at the start and at the end of the study, and this evidence was drawn on when the ratings of outcome for parents and children were made. They also served to ensure that key areas of enquiry were covered and in addition they not infrequently led respondents to talk about important issues which might otherwise have been missed.

The measures used with the parent figures were the Malaise inventory and the Rutter 'A' scale (a questionnaire on the child's behaviour). These two instruments were devised for screening psycho-social problems in parents and children (Rutter *et al*, 1970). In addition an amended version of the Arizona Social Support Interview Schedule was used with parents to ascertain the family's social support network and this also identified people who were the sources of unpleasant interactions in their daily lives (Barrera, 1981 and 1985; Gibbons, 1990). The measures used with children were the Child's Depression Inventory (Kovacs and Beck, 1977) and a self-esteem checklist based on domains identified for children (Harter, 1985) and for adolescents (Harter, 1987), which also included the ten items of the Rosenberg Self-esteem Inventory (1965).

Interviews with participants were confidential. Considerable thought was given to what we would do if the interviews or observations uncovered very serious abuse or risk which was not already known to the authorities. We decided that in this situation we would have a duty as citizens which overrode the assurance of confidentiality which we had offered, but that if this occurred we would make every effort to gain the agreement of the participant to share the information with the child protection agencies. In the event, we were not put in this position, but it is clearly an issue of some importance. We did not uncover abuse to children which was not known to the agencies, although one child made veiled hints that he had things to share about which he had been unable to speak. Nonetheless, we did sometimes take a more serious view of the likely harm caused by injuries or sibling abuse to children than that which had been taken by the agencies involved. In the account of the study which follows, the names and some of the details about the participants have been changed in order to preserve confidentiality.

The issue of bias

We wanted to ascertain the experiences and perceptions of respondents who had been involved in child protection registration and its consequences. Our interview format was therefore designed to enable adults and children to identify the issues which they considered to be important. Open-ended questions were used in which respondents were asked to recount their view of events and their attitudes to what had happened. This was one of the ways in which we sought to overcome the problem of negative bias or of the undervaluing of issues important to respondents. Positive bias or the overvaluation of issues of little importance to respondents was given attention by a careful consideration of the kinds and tone of response given to the more specific questions asked and how far the answers matched information given in the rest of the interview.

Issues of reliability were addressed, after careful piloting of the interview schedules, by cross-checking the interview recordings made by the two researchers. Care was given to eliminating leading questions or questions which might have suggested that the interviewer was expecting a particular answer. In addition, similar questions were asked in different ways during the interviews and respondents' accounts were probed more deeply when responses were unclear. In the process of preparation it was considered important to address the question of professional de-socialisation in order to avoid the interviewers being unduly associated with a social work perspective. Checks on the data collected suggested that the quality of data was not significantly different between the two interviewers.

On the question of the validity of the data our concern was to understand people's perceptions. The perceptions of parents, children and social workers about the same situation did, at times, differ widely and it was our task to gain an understanding of these differing perceptions when they arose. At first, we had some concerns that parents might be reluctant to talk about the allegations of abuse or neglect which they were facing. This was rarely the case. What did happen was that parents gave us the 'official' or public account of these events (Cornwell, 1985), one which was often well rehearsed, since by then this account had been given on a number of previous occasions, including in some cases under police questioning. However, in addition to the public account in which parents might deny or minimise responsibility for what had happened, they were at pains to get us to understand the context of events which surrounded an incident of physical abuse or neglect. For example, they were sometimes experiencing enormous difficulty in dealing with their child's behaviour, whilst at other times they wished to stress the normality, as they saw it, of their parenting practices.

Whilst we emphasised that we were independent of social services, for a few parents this was difficult to take on trust, especially at the first interview. We did, however, make a small token payment to parents to thank them for the time they generously gave us. This also appeared to be helpful in differentiating us as researchers from social workers. Most parents and children were willing to talk to us at length and openly about their view of their situation. At the second interview, as trust in us and distance from the events of the investigation and case conference increased, parents sometimes revealed very personal issues which had been troubling them, such as long-standing violence or sexual abuse by a family member.

Social workers were also prepared to talk to us at length about the work in which they were engaged. They were usually willing to talk about the dilemmas and difficulties they faced, although it was noticeable that some workers who lacked adequate supervision were reluctant to criticise their supervisors. Because factors such as training and experience may affect a professional's handling of a case, we sought information on these issues.

Another area of concern was the possibility that the research process itself would affect the conduct of cases. It was occasionally noticeable that a conference chair was very aware of the presence of the researcher and in a few cases this seemed to lead to an especially carefully conducted conference. Similarly, some social workers used the interview with us to give particularly careful thought to the case in question. However, over time and especially over the length of our follow-up period any such effects of the research appeared to diminish as participants became used to the role of the researchers and more pressing events occupied the forefront of their attention (Bottoms and McClintock, 1973; Vernon and Fruin, 1986).

Valid inference

We wanted our analysis to allow us to consider the various forces at play between the main participants. Yet, clearly the same data can be subject to a variety of interpretations. We approached this by involving a specialist in child care in an exercise in which data from a number of interviews were read and discussed. In addition, the two principal researchers met regularly to discuss their interpretation of the data and to cross-check the views which they were forming. Emerging themes were also discussed with colleagues on our advisory committee. A range of people with knowledge and special interests in the area of child care and child protection were involved, including a representative from the Family Rights Group.

Analysis

Throughout the analysis we were concerned to find ways to interpret the data which would not be too slanted in favour of either the professional or the parental point of view. This proved to be a process in which at some points we were clearly more identified with one perspective than the other. To help us gain an understanding of the interaction of the participants we constructed a pro-forma which set out a number of key issues for analysis in which we placed the views of the participants side by side. The formulation of the issues aimed to be broad enough to allow us to consider the different standpoints of different respondents. This approach allowed us to delay a full interpretation of the data until these could be considered in relation to the analysis of the whole interview, areas of convergence and divergence between the participants, and the patterns which emerged. It also gave a context for the interpretation of the ambivalent and contradictory views which may be held by any one person.

Now that the aims and methods used in the study have been outlined, we can turn to look in more detail at the parents, children and social workers who were involved in the intensive follow-up study.

Summary

1. The purpose of the study was to examine the processes of decision-making which led to child protection registration, the subsequent interventions offered, and the outcomes for children and parents 20 months later.

2. The research took place in two local authorities where the rates of new registrations and children maintained on the register were close to the national average. Additional material was collected from a third authority in order to include a group of black and minority ethnic children in the study.

3. One hundred and twenty initial child protection conferences were attended at which 73 children were registered. Our intensive sample of 44 children was drawn from these 73 children and represented 60% of all the registered cases. A third were registered because of physical abuse, a third for reasons of sexual abuse and the remainder for either neglect or 'emotional abuse'.

4. The parent or parents, older children and the key workers for each family were interviewed soon after registration and 20 months later. Interviews were semi-structured and were tape-recorded. Attention was paid to the reduction of both negative and positive bias, and consideration was given to the reliability of the interview data and the reliability of the inferences made. The names and some of the details of the individuals who are described have been changed in order to preserve confidentiality.

Chapter 3

The follow-up sample

The parents in the intensive study

The following table gives a breakdown of the household composition of the families in which the children in the follow-up study were living, both at the time of the abuse or neglect which was the subject of the initial conference and at the time of our first and subsequent interviews with them.

It can be seen that almost two-thirds (64%) of the children had been living in a two-parent or reconstituted family when they were abused or neglected, whilst a third (34%) had been living with a lone mother. By the time of our first interviews, which occurred shortly after registration, the group of children living in a two-parent or reconstituted family had decreased to 36 per cent and 2 per cent of children were living with a lone father. The proportion living with lone mothers was little different at 32 per cent, because although a number of children had been removed from single mothers the exclusion of abusing men from families left a new group of children in lone-mother households. The proportion of children living with foster parents or relatives had increased from 2 per cent to 30 per cent.

Table 4   **Composition of Households (Main Carers Only)**

	At the time of abuse or neglect		At the time of first interview		At the time of follow-up interview	
	No.	%	No.	%	No.	%
Both birth parents	17	39	10	23	9	21
Both birth parents and other relatives	1	2	1	2	–	–
One parent and partner	10	23	5	11	7	16
Mother alone	10	23	9	21	11	25
Mother and other relatives	5	11	5	11	1	2
Father alone	0	0	1	2	1	2
Relatives/friends	1	2	5	11	3	7
Foster parents	0	0	8	19	12	27
	44	100	44	100	44	100

By the time of the follow-up interviews the proportion of children living with two parents or in a reconstituted family had risen slightly again to 37 per cent, whilst lone-mother households had decreased to 27 per cent. The proportion of children living with relatives or foster parents had risen further to 34 per cent.

The main source of income for a third of the families was from paid employment, while two-thirds of the families had to rely on income support or unemployment payments as their principal means of support. There were also a few people who undertook small amounts of work to supplement their benefits. Those in work were mostly in manual occupations, although there were three parents in the study who held professional or managerial posts. Two of these three families were acting *in loco parentis* for the child either as foster parents or custodians. The fact that the majority of families were from the lower socio-economic groups was to be expected as these are the families who form the bulk of the workload of social services departments. However, the situation might have been expected to be somewhat different in relation to cases of alleged sexual abuse since the prevalence of child sexual abuse appears to be unrelated to social class (Finkelhor, 1986). The very small number of middle class families in the follow-up study reflected the fact that relatively few middle-class families had been drawn into the child protection system as judged by the case conferences which we attended. This suggests that the discovery of sexual abuse in middle-class families may in some cases lead to outcomes other than a case conference and registration.

With regard to housing, 28 families lived in houses, 11 occupied flats and one mother had for the past 18 months lived in a bedsit with her child. There was also one family lodging temporarily with friends and two in hostels for the homeless, whilst one mother was living with her children in a women's refuge. Of the 40 families who were not in temporary accommodation only nine were owner-occupiers. These included a few families who were buying their houses from the local council. The majority of families were living in council-rented homes, whilst a few were in privately-rented accommodation.

Twelve of the families considered their accommodation to be totally unsatisfactory. The reasons were varied and included overcrowding, lack of heating, broken plumbing, the lack of play areas, the many stairs to be climbed and collapsed ceilings. Two of these families were facing eviction. Another 15 families found some aspects of their housing unsatisfactory and the reasons included proximity to dangerous main roads, isolation and – for those living with their parents – the desire for their own accommodation.

It is interesting that as many as 82 per cent of the families were known to their respective social services departments prior to the investigation. Indeed in only eight cases had there been no previous social work contact. Out of the 36 families known to social services, in 27 there was active social work involvement immediately prior to the child protection intervention. A quarter of the families had previously had a child on the child protection register. Three sets of parents had had children removed in the past for reasons of abuse or neglect. The great majority of families had therefore had some previous contact with social services departments.

The parents in the study had suffered a range of adverse experiences in childhood. It was known that 11 mothers and one father, or over a quarter of the sample (27%), had been sexually abused as children. In two of these cases mothers still lived in fear of the demands of the abusing relative. This background of abuse was generally known to social services but only three of the parents had received an offer of referral for counselling. There were also three father figures who had a history of having sexually abused one of their siblings. In a further 11 cases a parent had been seriously physically abused as a child. This had sometimes involved quite severe and long-term abuse as one mother described:

> *'My childhood was very rough – very bad. I mean they should have had social workers in those days, because I was battered. I mean that's what you call child abuse, when your mother beats hell out of you for no reason at all . . . I was pushed down the stairs by my own mother . . . My mum did a bit of shit-stirring about me and Dad went berserk and just dropped me from my bedroom window and I broke my legs.'*

Moreover, in 12 cases a parent had spent a large part of their childhood in care or residential special school and another five had experienced extensive separations from their parents as children, either because they had been brought up by a relative or because of frequent moves between parents. In all, two-thirds of the parents (66%) had endured one or more such adverse childhood experiences. Such experiences were distributed amongst the parents of children in each of the registration categories. In addition, family violence either had been, or was currently, a feature of over half of the families. Most involved violence by men to their partners.

Not only this, but the scores for parents on the Malaise inventory were high. The cut-off point which indicates a clinically significant level of psychological distress is seven or more and at the first interview over half of the parents (52%) scored at this level or above. By the end of the study just under half of the parents showed high levels of psycho-social stress, of whom two-thirds had had high scores at the first interview. The remaining third of parents were divided evenly between those who had improved in the interim and those who had deteriorated.

The children in the intensive study

There were 90 children in the 44 families. Over a third of the children in the study were the only child in the family, another third had one sibling, and the remainder had between two and four siblings. These included full, half- and step-siblings. Eighteen of the children in the follow-up sample were boys (41%) and 26 were girls (59%). (Nationally, new registrations in 1990 comprised 48 per cent boys and 52 per cent girls.)

Forty-three per cent of the children in the follow-up sample were under five years old at the time of the initial case conference, 25 per cent were aged between 5 and 10 and 32 per cent were over 10. Whilst the numbers were small, they were in line with national figures on new registrations (Department of Health, 1991 b). Table 5 gives the age breakdown of children in our follow-up sample by the main concern of the initial case conference.

It can be seen that the majority of children in our follow-up sample where concerns centred on physical abuse were under the age of five, whilst for sexual abuse the majority were over ten. Emotional abuse cases were evenly distributed across the age groupings, in contrast to concerns about neglect which were mostly focused on children under five. At the time of registration 32 per cent (14) of children were in care or were accommodated and this compared with a national average of 25 per cent in 1990 (Department of Health, 1991 b).

The children who were subject to registration as a result of sexual abuse had undergone a variety of sexual experiences as table 6 shows.

It is interesting to note that the kinds of sexual abuse in the follow-up study cluster at the serious end and also represent the more severe cases when compared with all the cases considered at the conferences.

Table 5   **Follow-Up Sample**
Main Concern of Conference by Age at Initial Case Conference

	Pysical Abuse	Sexual Abuse	Emotional Abuse	Neglect	Total	
	No.	No.	No.	No.	No.	%
Under 5 years	10	2	3	4	19	43
5–10 years	4	4	2	1	11	25
Over 10 years	2	9	3	–	14	32
	16	15	8	5	44	100

Table 6 **Types of Sexual Abuse***

	No.
Vaginal intercourse	4
Anal intercourse	2
Simulated/attempted intercourse	3
Digital penetration	1
Masturbation of child	1
Sexualised kissing, hugging, fondling	3
Nude bathing with stepfather	1
	15

*When more than one kind of sexual activity was reported the most serious has been recorded here.

Most of the children registered because of physical abuse had suffered bruising rather than fractures, as can be seen in table 7, and they were broadly representative of cases seen at the conferences.

Like the cases in the larger case conference group, the five neglect cases covered a range of situations. Since cases of neglect can cover such a spectrum, those in the follow-up sample will be described in some detail. In one case parents of limited intelligence made no preparations for the birth of their baby, and the mother showed little response to her newborn baby, or ability to care for him. Another mother had neglected her first child who had 'failed to thrive' and physically abused her by biting her. Concerns centred on her newborn baby. A third mother had a two-year-old epileptic daughter who was severely physically disabled and developmentally delayed. The care she offered was basic; the little girl was very under-stimulated, often went hungry and dirty, and witnessed frequent bouts of violence between the mother and her partner.

Table 7 **Types of Physical Abuse**

	No.
Bruising	12
Burns/scalds	2
Fracture to skull	1
Other fractures/broken bones/dislocation	1
	16

In the fourth case, a mother who was in a very violent relationship and suffered from poor health was having difficulty getting close to her preschool child who had become withdrawn. (In these last two cases registration arose not simply because of neglect but because of minor injuries sustained by the child.) In the fifth case there was a series of minor concerns about the lack of supervision of children near a busy road, combined with previous minor incidents of physical abuse. These concerns led to registration when it came to light that the health of one of the children was deteriorating because hospital appointments had not been kept.

As it happened the emotional abuse cases in the sample were an almost complete group of those registered at the case conferences we attended. They were a ragbag of situations which had the common thread that the parents' behaviour was considered to be having an adverse effect on the children. In three cases the child had been brought to conference because of physical abuse. The major focus of concern at the meeting had not been on this incident, however, but on what was seen as one parent's negative relationship with the child which had led to scapegoating. As a result, these cases had been registered under the category of emotional rather than physical abuse. In three cases the central issue was the mother's mental health problems.

In the seventh case a mother who allowed her friends to sniff glue in front of her son was seen as emotionally abusive. Finally, there was one family where there were continuing concerns about all three children who showed disturbed behaviour at school. The behaviour of one of the girls in particular suggested that she was very unhappy. Concern was heightened when the school revealed sexualised behaviour by one of them. These concerns, both long-standing and recent, appeared in the context of parental lack of cooperation and led to registration. In such cases the use of the category of emotional abuse was predicated on an assumption that the children's behaviour was a result of deficient parenting practices.

Source of risk to the child

In the majority of cases it was known, or there were clear suspicions about, who had abused the child or was considered to be neglectful. This person was the father or father figure in 16 cases, the mother in another 16, and both parents in two more. In the remaining cases a variety of others were responsible, that is siblings or cousins (4), an adult step-sibling (1), a grandfather (1) and a male neighbour (1). In the three remaining cases it was not known who had abused the child.

These overall figures conceal important differences between the different categories of abuse and neglect. In cases of *sexual abuse*, the alleged abuser's relationship to the child was the father in five cases, the stepfather in three cases, two grandfathers, one male neighbour, a male cousin and three brothers. All but two of these children were living in two-parent households. Just two children lived with lone mothers: one was a case of sibling sexual abuse and in the other the neighbour was the abuser.

Where the main concern was *physical abuse* the abuser was the father in two cases, the stepfather or mother's partner in three, an adult stepbrother in one, and a lone mother in seven. In three cases it was not known who had abused the child, although suspicion centred on the father in two of these and was later confirmed in one case. It is interesting to note that all the mothers who were said to have physically abused their children were lone carers not currently in a relationship, whilst all the fathers or stepfathers had partners.

It is harder to pin down the supposed source of *neglect* to children, but on the whole it was the mother who was deemed to be responsible for their care and, therefore, for any deficits in that care. This applied in four situations of which only one involved a lone mother. However, in one case both parents were deemed incapable and neglectful.

In the instances of *emotional abuse*, lone mothers were held responsible on four occasions and the mother in a two-parent household in one other. In two cases in which physical abuse was involved in addition to emotional abuse, the father or stepfather in a two-parent household was identified as the abuser. In one situation both parents seemed to be held responsible for their children's disturbed behaviour.

It should be noted that throughout the text the term abuser is used where a person was known or was strongly suspected of having been responsible for abuse or neglect.

Children had been exposed to abuse or neglect for varying periods of time ranging from a month to nine years. Some appeared to have been subject to just one incident of physical or sexual abuse, whilst others were exposed to chronic abuse over many years. It also emerged that in addition to the main incidents of abuse which were being investigated, more than a third of the children (36%) had also been abused by other family members or adults. (The perpetrator was the father in five cases, the stepfather in one, the father of the stepmother in another, the stepmother or mother in two, a male sibling in two, and an unrelated adult in another five.)

The social workers

Our 44 families were allocated to 37 social workers, of whom 28 were women and 9 were men. A quarter of the families were on the caseloads of a male worker. Ten social workers were aged between 20 and 35 at the start of the study, whilst 15 were aged 36 to 45. The remaining 12 were over 46 years of age. All but two workers held an approved social work qualification and in these two instances a qualified worker held the key worker role whilst the unqualified worker did most of the day-to-day work.

The majority of the social workers had worked for many years in social services departments. Seventeen had over ten years' previous experience, seven had been qualified for between five and ten years prior to our study, whilst six had between two and five years' post-qualifying experience. Of the seven workers who had been qualified for less than two years, most had previous relevant work experience which included work in the voluntary and residential sectors.

Teams were organised in different ways but, in most, intake work was handled on a rota basis by members of the team. Most of the social workers were working predominantly in child care or child protection work. Case-loads varied in size and complexity but the majority of social workers handled between 18 and 30 cases, many of which were very demanding. The number of registered cases being carried varied between one and ten. Whilst in just under half of the cases the worker had been involved with the family in the study for less than six months, in the remainder social workers had been dealing with the family for between seven months and nine years. In eight cases social services departments had been involved with families for many years, sometimes from the time of the mother's birth, or from the childhood years of one parent who had experienced care.

Many of the practitioners had attended in-service courses to prepare them for undertaking joint investigations and the responsibilities of the key worker role, and the former in particular were usually highly valued. Inter-agency training was in general seen as useful. Courses on family therapy and counselling were valued and four workers had engaged the local child guidance service in order to develop their skills. Only three considered that their initial social work training had equipped them well for child protection work, however. A considerable number of social workers felt strongly that they required further training in order to carry out the complex and demanding tasks required in child protection practice. In particular, they identified the need for more training in communication skills appropriate for work with young children, in ongoing and long-term work and in the whole area of child sexual abuse:

> 'What I'd like is more, very intense, training at both the practical and academic level in direct communication skills with young children.'

> '. . . there's not much training with families with ongoing, long-term work, like for instance this family. I've been involved with the family for three years – how you distance yourself and then maybe start again . . . giving you confidence in working with the whole family rather than maybe working with the subject in the family who you relate better to, or who is more open to your involvement.'

> *'I still feel very anxious about – not so much the investigation – the area of sexual abuse. I still find it difficult to deal with. Physical abuse is kind of more straight forward somehow, you know what you're dealing with.'*

The main source of support and advice for social workers was their team leader and, in teams with high morale, colleagues were also useful in providing encouragement and advice. Workers in some offices consulted child protection co-ordinators about their cases. The quality of supervision available to workers varied enormously. Just under half the practitioners were very satisfied with the supervision they received (47%), another third were satisfied with some aspects but identified gaps in what was offered to them (32%), whilst a fifth were very dissatisfied (21%).

Dissatisfaction with supervision centred on: the lack of time in which to discuss individual cases; discouragement from discussing the needs and feelings of practitioners and the impact which the work had on them; the lack of experience of some team leaders in child protection work; and the use of supervision simply as a management tool to assess whether more cases could be taken. Those who were dissatisfied with supervision often emphasised that nobody had contributed towards the planning of their cases. They had had to do it alone:

> *'I sort of struggled with that family alone for quite a while.'*

> *'I did feel in those sort of cases that you need to talk about how you feel. And its not even talked about during supervision.'*

> *'It's just up-dating the supervisor. I'd really like supervision where I could look critically at my work and develop my skills.'*

Eighty per cent of the workers considered that managing the family in the study was stressful for them. The particular causes of stress included uncertainty about whether the correct decision had been made, the feeling of unpredictability about what would happen, and the accompanying sense of responsibility for the child's safety:

> *'I think the most stressful thing is having a child in a risky situation and having to accept that that's a risky situation . . . you walk out to your car and you think, "Should I be leaving this child with this family?"'*

> *'It's the worry of the uncertainty of what might happen . . . and feeling responsible for what will happen.'*

A lack of cooperation and openness from the family and the tension between wanting to be helpful and needing to be vigilant also contributed to stress:

'I find it much more [stressful] when there's concern that can't be identified and people aren't forthcoming . . . stress of not knowing.'

'Wanting to be liked. Wanting to be viewed by Mrs Anderson as helpful, and wanting to help her, while being aware that my prime duty is to protect Joanne.'

Several social workers talked of the effect on them when personal feelings were stirred up by cases and they found this especially hard when a 'macho' culture in the office discouraged the expression of feelings or when there was a lack of opportunity to deal with their anxieties by sharing them with colleagues. Some were additionally distressed by the knowledge that their interventions would not be sufficient to provide a bright future for the child and family.

'I deal with a lot of people who've been sexually abused . . . and it certainly gets to me . . . I get incredibly angry and I get very sad. I don't think there's anywhere to off-load really. You just go on to the next client and hope the situation's worse so it blocks out the last one.'

'Pressures build up in a way they needn't otherwise. Things get exaggerated and out of proportion – the anxieties. If they were discussed you'd come to see them as they really were . . . and the other thing is that you lose your confidence totally.'

'I don't care who knows that I am upset, but I do feel that there are people in the Department who judge you if you're upset.'

For some workers the early stages were seen as particulary difficult, when so many vital decisions had to be made, and the anxieties lessened as time passed. But for others stresses remained high as they worried about children left at home in less than ideal circumstances:

'Over the half-term holiday I was very concerned about them . . . I was away from the area and I felt somebody needed to see them during the week that I was away and I had great difficulty getting hold of anybody . . . it was a great worry.'

'There are always certain things seep into you at weekends . . . but I wouldn't say I lie awake at night because there's enough cover and spying neighbours . . . so I feel a bit happier about that.'

The social workers in dealing with these child protection cases had had to endure considerable hostility from family members and sometimes this had boiled over into verbal and physical assault. Two workers were attacked by a parent in the study and this caused them great distress:

'I went home and I just ate and ate and ate all evening. Because I kept questioning – what had I done wrong? Where had I gone wrong? . . . I haven't found anything. I've just tried to cut off from it. Since I've been on this job I've put on weight and I binge more. I don't think there's anything within this office . . . you just try and collar somebody and hope that somebody will listen.'

Having outlined the circumstances of the children, parents and social workers in the study, we can now turn to look at the beginning of the child protection actions which led to the child's name being placed on the register. For most children and families this was the investigation.

Summary

1. At the time of the first interviews shortly after registration, a third of the children were living with lone mothers and a third in two-parent or reconstituted families. The remaining children were living with relatives or foster carers.

2. Over two-thirds of the families relied on state benefits as their principal means of support and as many as 82% were known to social services departments prior to the investigation of abuse or neglect. Two-thirds of the parents had suffered adverse experiences in their childhood such as physical or sexual abuse or extensive separations from significant parent figures. In addition, half of the parents showed high levels of psycho-social stress.

3. Forty-three per cent of the children were under 5 at the time of registration, a quarter were aged 5 to 10, the remaining third were 10 or over. At the time of the conference a third of the children were in care or accommodated. The children were representative of those registered in our two local authorities, although the type of sexual abuse suffered was at the more severe end of the spectrum.

4. The allegations of abuse or neglect concerned the father figure in 16 cases, the mother in 16 and both parents in two more. In three cases it was not known who had abused the child. In the remaining cases a variety of other people were responsible, such as relatives or neighbours.

5. A quarter of the families were on the caseloads of male social workers. Most of the social workers were working predominantly in child care or in some cases child protection work, and in-service training was seen as valuable. Nonetheless, many felt that they required further training to deal

with child protection work. The majority of the workers had experienced considerable stress in managing the cases in our study, and this was increased when the supervision available was poor or support from colleagues was difficult to obtain.

PART II

Early Decision-Making

Chapter 4

The investigation

Our historical analysis shows that during different periods different kinds of harm to children become the focus of public concern. Out of the many and various ills faced by children, some are selected for attention at one time and others at another. This understanding of the selective nature of public and professional concern is equally relevant when we come to examine the contemporary operation of the child protection system.

The children who are eventually placed on the child protection register have been sifted out from a much larger group who were possible candidates for registration. The first step in that process is taken when, from amongst those who are referred on to – or who are known by – social services departments, some children are identified as raising child protection concerns. The work of Dingwall, Eekelaar and Murray (1983) shed light on a number of the subsequent processes of identification, confirmation and disposal which can direct some children further along the path towards registration and others away from formal classification as children at risk of abuse or neglect. Recent research funded by the Department of Health has shown that these filtering processes are operated vigorously. Fewer than a quarter of the cases identified as involving concerns about possible abuse or neglect reached an initial child protection case conference, and only one in seven was placed on the child protection register (Gibbons *et al*, 1993).

The situations of the 44 children in our intensive follow-up sample had all been considered to be of sufficient concern to merit registration. Later we look at how the filtering and selection processes operated at case conferences, but before that we will explore how some children came to the attention of the community agencies, the nature of the investigations which followed, and the way in which the professionals set about determining whether the children were at risk.

Referral

The first step in the process of identifying children as at risk of abuse or neglect is that of referral. When we looked back to see who had first drawn attention to the possibility that the children in our study were at risk, we found that in 45 per cent of the families the children or their mothers or mother substitutes had been instrumental in drawing in other agencies. In relation to a further 14 per cent of the families the first move had been made by a grandmother or other adult women outside the immediate family. Another 25 per cent were referred to social services by other agencies, including schools, community medical officers and GPs, the police, an army welfare officer and a housing officer. In addition, 16 per cent were current cases being held by social services where a build-up of worries had led to a case conference. Thus, professionals identified fewer children as candidates for agency intervention (41%) than did members of the child's family and wider community (59%) (see also Corby, 1987). The large proportion of cases in which action was initiated by children themselves or by their mothers (45%) shows that family members themselves were active in identifying certain situations as presenting unacceptable risks. The distribution of the original source of the referral is shown in table 8.

It is useful to explore the next link in the referral process; that is, to which people or agencies concerns were expressed. In the case of the eight children who disclosed abuse, three did so to their mothers, four to school staff and one to a neighbour. The person to whom the child had confided then contacted the social services department directly or reported the concerns to another agency, such as the police or a health visitor, who subsequently made a referral to social services.

Of the 12 mother figures who suspected abuse or who were concerned about an injury to their child (they included a child's custodian and a foster mother), half contacted social services directly either to report their suspicions or to ask for help. The other mothers took their child to the GP about an injury or they made contact with other professionals such as the police, health visitors, probation officers or in one case the local Citizen's Advice Bureau.

The two grandmothers contacted social services directly, as did two other adults outside the family. One had lodged with the family and witnessed physical abuse to the children, and the other was a mother who reported a conversation overheard by her daughter in which the child had talked at

Table 8 **Initiation of Action which Led to Referral**

	No.	%
Child disclosed	8	18
Child's mother/mother figure reported	12	27
Grandmother reported	2	5
Other adult reported	4	9
Professional reported	11	25
Ongoing social services case	7	16
	44	100

school about her abuse. Another mother who took action for the same reason had contacted the school, whilst one neighbour reported her concerns to the police. It should be noted that the identity of referrers who were not part of the professional network was not usually revealed to the parents concerned. When professionals were the first link in the referral chain they generally contacted social services directly.

The different referral routes along which the various cases travelled had important implications for the development of subsequent events. When family members had themselves sought assistance they were affected by the way in which the referral was handled and particularly by the extent to which the agency's response corresponded with their expectations. When the referral was made by a community agency the impact on family members was influenced by whether they had been informed that this action had been taken. What then did we find out about the expectations of family members who contacted agencies or the extent to which they had been informed when a referral had been made?

All the children who had initiated the referral themselves had made a deliberate move to inform someone about what had happened to them. Most had disclosed sexual abuse, although a small number had told of physical abuse. All had spoken because they wanted the abuse to stop. Some of the sexually abused children had spoken out in order to protect a younger brother or sister whom they thought was next in line to be abused. Moving into their teenage years seemed to make it possible, or more imperative, for some to take action on their own behalf. A specific trigger could determine the timing of the disclosure, such as when a child had viewed a television programme featuring an abused child, or heard a talk or school presentation on the subject, or faced the prospect of re-victimisation when an abusing father who had left the family was planning to return.

Reaching the point of telling was not easy for children, and especially in cases of long-term abuse was itself the outcome of a chain of events which had a long history:

> '*I was leading two different lives. I was leading a life with Dad and a life with everybody . . . I used to think, you know, who would I tell, I can't tell Mum because she was too distant. I thought well who is there, I don't know. I kept thinking what would I say, you know. I tried phoning Childline up twice but it was always the lines were all busy, try again, sort of thing . . . When I was little he said, "Don't tell anybody or your Dad will go away for a long time." And I think that really shut me up since I was about 12, I suppose. When I was going out with Peter . . . I said to him that I have got something that I need to tell someone but I don't know who and I don't know if I can . . . that was a couple of months before. I got to school one day and I was in child care and was really upset, I don't*

know what it was. I felt I have got to tell someone, so I did.'
(Sexually abused girl aged 15).

The allegations of all the children in the study who disclosed sexual abuse
were taken seriously and action was taken to protect them. However, as we
shall see later, they had little idea what 'telling' would set in motion or of the
degree of responsibility which they would feel for the consequences of their
disclosures.

The mothers who had initiated a referral had sometimes done so because
of their increasing concern about the safety of their children. At other times
an incident of unexpected bruising or signs of sexual abuse had led them to
make contact with a professional. They did so for a variety of reasons. When
sexual abuse was suspected the mothers were seeking advice and help in a
crisis as well as protection for the child. Two mothers contacted social services
for help in managing their children whom they were hitting in an effort to
control them. The others who reported injuries to their children were
concerned about the actions of other family members, usually those of their
violent partners. *It is important to note that women did turn to professional agencies
in the hope that they would receive assistance either for themselves or in regulating the
actions of the men with whom they were living.* We shall see later that the responses
from the agencies were sometimes rather different from those which they had
hoped to elicit (see also Gordon, 1989).

The mothers who had contacted social services in order to obtain
assistance in dealing with their children felt unjustly condemned when child
protection procedures were enacted. This disjunction between their expectations of help and the agencies' response could mean that later offers of help
were not accepted. This situation was well illustrated by a young mother who
had requested help from social services during her pregnancy. Her previous
baby had been removed permanently because of an injury she had inflicted.
She was very upset when her self-referral for practical assistance led to
registration. She saw it as counter-productive:

> *'I thought it was so stupid, because things that I would tell them I'm not
> going to tell them now. Because up to the next six months I'm going to be
> absolutely petrified.'*

A similar situation arose when mothers requested help with a teenage child
whom they saw as out of control and instead found that they were held
responsible for having physically abused the child. Clearly, such self-referrals
pose a dilemma for social services as well as risks for the referrers.

Other mothers described how they felt when, after talking openly of their
worries about their children with a professional, a referral was made to social
services without their being informed. The contested issue here was not so

much whether a referral should have been made, but the fact that it had been made behind their backs. This could lead to a parent feeling distrustful of the child protection agencies and could vitiate later intervention. In one case a mother told her health visitor about some marks on her baby. The health visitor referred the mother to social services without telling her. The mother returned home to find the health visitor in her house actually holding the baby, accompanied by a social worker. She was 'just too stunned and too shocked to react'. She feared that the baby would be taken away from her. The effect on her was overwhelming:

> *'I was really too shocked to really respond. And after they left . . . the reality of it sunk in, that I became really really angry, and by the next morning I was furious . . . And it's after the experiences that I've had here, that my trust in the whole system has gone completely. I'd never use it again, never turn to it again. Whereas before I was always quite confident of them.'*

It can be seen that allegations of physical, sexual or emotional abuse, or neglect had arisen in a number of ways. In some cases of sexual abuse the child had purposefully made a disclosure, whilst in others the abuse was uncovered by people outside the family, such as school teachers or neighbours. Thus, sometimes the child had initiated the action and was expecting a response, whilst in others children had no forewarning. The same was true for non-abusing parents. When children found ways to tell their mothers that they were being abused by fathers or stepfathers, the mothers had set off the process of investigation (see also Faller, 1989; Bagley and King, 1990). However, when children shared information about their predicament outside the family – often at school – the allegations were in the professional arena before the mother knew anything about them. Similarly, allegations that a child had suffered a non-accidental injury could be unexpected for parents, as could allegations of emotional abuse or neglect. In other cases, such as when mothers presented their bruised child to a GP, they sometimes harboured suspicions or uncertainties about the injury which made a subsequent child protection referral not entirely unexpected.

It can be seen that at the referral stage both agencies and family members played a part in nominating children who might be considered to be in need of agency protection and that the way in which the referrals were handled had a considerable impact on the parents and children involved.

The agencies involved in the investigation

Once a referral had reached the social services department the next stage in the process involved sifting referrals and selecting those in respect of which child protection action would be taken. At this point decisions were made about which referrals to investigate, who would undertake any investigation and how it would be conducted. These decisions had a profound effect on the way in which risks were construed and the disposals made.

It should be noted that eight families were not subject to an official investigation. Most of these were current cases held by social services departments where mounting concerns about risks to the children, and often also the inability of the departments to effect change, led directly to a child protection case conference. When there was no specific incident of abuse, or when the concerns centred on neglect, no formal investigation was conducted and a particular difficulty was that *at times the full extent of the agency's concerns was not explained to the parents before the conference*. The majority of these cases were classified at case conference as cases of neglect or emotional abuse. A small number concerned physical abuse which was not formally investigated because these were self-referrals by the mothers who had caused the abuse. This left 36 cases which were subject to an official investigation.

At the time of the study, agency procedures in our two local authorities specified that all cases of sexual abuse should be investigated jointly by police and social services. Local authority B also expected joint investigations to be conducted in cases of 'serious physical abuse' and local authority A in 'those cases of physical injury abuse which may have arisen as the result of an assault'. It appears from the data that we collected that workers in our authorities, with few exceptions, were following the procedures.

In 26 cases (59%) it was decided that a joint investigation should be conducted by the police and social services. This included 12 out of the 15 cases of alleged sexual abuse (80%), 10 out of 16 of those of physical abuse (63%) , 1 out of 5 of the neglect cases and 3 of the 8 cases of emotional abuse. Another eight cases (18%) were initially investigated by social workers alone. These comprised one case of a sexually abusive teenage boy, four cases of alleged physical abuse, two of neglect and one of 'emotional abuse'. In one incident of physical injury the social worker was obliged to investigate alone because the police were not willing to provide immediately an officer to undertake the task. In addition, one boy who had been sexually abused by a neighbour was subject to an investigation by the police alone, to the dismay of the social services department.

When family members did not speak fluent English it was important that an interpreter accompanied the investigators. If a trained interpreter was not available then sometimes a black social worker ended up taking on the role, leading to role conflict and the possibility that the social worker would be identified as a police interpreter. This was a situation that social workers were generally keen to avoid, and it was one of a number of problems experienced when interpreters were required. (Others are reported in chapter 7.)

Informing parents about the investigation

When investigations were undertaken, decisions were made about which family members to approach and in what order. In the case of joint investigations these decisions were dictated by police considerations about gathering evidence which could be used in a prosecution. Little attention was given to keeping parents informed about what was happening. For example, there were several occasions when children had not returned from school because, unbeknown to the parents, they were being interviewed at the police station. In such situations one of the parents often went out to search for the lost child. The children themselves were often worried that their parents would be angry that they had not been informed of their where-abouts. One mother whose son had arrived at school with a bruised knee described her reaction to such an omission:

> 'I mean he went to school the next day and never came home. The headmistress did ring and she just said that she had Andrew in the office, and the next thing I knew was that a social worker that I'd never met before, with a police lady, came here and said my son was down the police station . . . I was, well, a bit angry at first that nobody had informed me. I felt that, you know, I'd just been walked all over. Nobody had really bothered to let me know where Andrew was, and he was my responsibility.'

It was usual for parents to remain uninformed until the agencies wished to interview them. However, in one case of sibling sexual abuse where there were no plans to interview the parents, the agencies failed to inform them that their daughter had been interviewed. It was the girl herself, whose arrival from school was delayed by the investigation, who told her parents about the interview. This heightened their anxieties about what had happened and about the agencies' attitude to them. In this case it also served to revive adverse experiences of social services from the recent past:

> 'I've had dealings with social services and they don't consider the parents at all in these things you know.' (mother)

> 'Everybody else knows before the parents get to hear. It's all wrong.' (father)

This evidence shows that at the time of the study, the recommendations of the Cleveland Inquiry that 'parents should be informed and where appropriate consulted at each stage of the investigation' had not always been adopted (Secretary of State, 1988).

In cases of sexual abuse and occasionally physical abuse, when older children were involved, it was usual for children to be interviewed without the non-abusing mothers being informed or involved (see also O'Hagan, 1989). This was the case in three-quarters of the cases of alleged sexual abuse which were subject to joint investigation. Perhaps the investigators hoped to interview the child without any other influence being brought to bear which might affect the evidence. On one occasion it was said that the mother was not invited to her daughter's interview because she had previously dismissed similar allegations. Moreover, the police may have been anxious to apprehend the abuser before he knew about the investigation, and the assumption made was that telling the mother would mean that the male partner would find out. When sibling sexual abuse was investigated the practice was still to exclude the parents from the child interviews and in these cases there could be a non-abusing father as well as mother. Whatever the reason for this practice, it was one which had a negative impact on the non-abusing parents and one which, as we shall see, could influence the way that the case developed. Thus, the conduct of the investigation often marginalised non-abusing parents and replicated their experience of discovering that their child had been abused without their knowledge. At this crucial early stage these experiences made them feel angry and distrustful.

Whilst the exclusion of parents from the early part of the investigation was particularly a feature of cases of sexual abuse it could also occur in other instances when older children were involved. In cases of physical abuse too, young people were interviewed by social workers alone or by a police officer and social worker, often at school, without a parent having been informed.

There will be occasions when it is entirely appropriate to interview children alone in order to make a good assessment of risk, but the importance of informing a parent of what is happening should not be underestimated. It should be borne in mind that there was often one parent who had clearly not abused the child and who could therefore have an important role in supporting and protecting the child in the aftermath of the abuse. When such parents were alienated at this stage the effects could be long-lasting.

The reactions of parents to the allegations

Whilst the investigators had usually deliberated and planned their approach, for many parents, hearing about the investigation came as a complete shock. Even when children or parents had initiated action they had not known what to expect. As one mother said:

> 'The first I knew I had two CID blokes and a policewoman turn up on the door to say that Jane had gone to school at 2 o'clock and said that my husband had been sexually abusing her.'

Another mother who had been informed that her 15-year-old son had sexually abused her 10-year-old daughter said:

> '*The first thing I knew was a policeman on my doorstep at half-past-three on the Thursday afternoon . . . Well, I felt sick! I was very puzzled by the whole thing . . . I was quite dazed.*'

A young divorced mother was subject to a joint investigation after her ex-husband's parents reported her to social services because they found a burn on her three-year-old son. She described the experience:

> '*That was horrible. I felt like I was a child batterer or something . . . They were sitting there saying what they were going to do with my son and that is really frustrating and annoying . . . It is the effect on me. It has just done my head in, all this.*'

The impact of the investigation stage on mothers whose children had alleged sexual abuse was particularly marked, since this was usually the first time that they had heard about the abuse. They experienced shock, bewilderment, anger and the onset of profound feelings of loss. Not only was this experience similar to that of a bereavement but it is one in which there is 'a series of losses extending over time through the life course' and one in which 'a whole world view is threatened' (Hooper, 1992). Mothers who discovered that their child had been sexually abused by their partner faced the pain of the child's suffering, together with the realisation of their partner's breach of trust, and the betrayal of their adult relationship. It necessitated a reinterpretation of the history of the marriage and of their family relationships:

> '*I felt utterly devastated. You go through a whole gambit of emotions before you try to see the future. Things will never ever be completely the same again.*'

> '*I felt stunned more than anything. I think it took about a fortnight before it actually started to sink in . . . I try not to think about it too much, it just goes round and round in your mind and at the end of the day you don't come out with any answers to anything.*'

Some felt guilty that they had not guessed what had been going on or that the child had been unable to confide in them. As one mother said:

> '*It was a shock to me, because Pauline had said things had happened to her since she was five . . . It was ten years of my not knowing that I find very hard to believe. Especially of a man that I'd loved and deep down I still love now. I still find it very hard to think that he would do such things.*'

Determining responsibility and allocating blame

By the time that an investigation had started, the way in which the referral had been handled and the initial approach to parents and children had already had a considerable impact and it was one which would affect future work with the child and family. However, the energy of the investigators was concentrated on the immediate task of determining as far as possible whether the child had been abused, if so who was responsible, and whether the child's situation presented continuing risks.

In all the cases of alleged *sexual abuse* where children had spoken about the abuse the investigators had accepted their account even though, as we shall see, the medical evidence was rarely conclusive. Investigators were usually able to find out the identity of the abuser from the child. However, since all but one of the alleged adult perpetrators denied the abuse there were few convictions as corroborative evidence was rare. The child's protection was usually secured either by the exclusion of the alleged abuser from the household or by the removal of the child.

Cases of sibling sexual abuse were handled slightly differently since the abused children were sometimes assumed to have had more responsibility for their victimisation than were those who were abused by an adult. This was argued more strongly as the victim's age rose. It was sometimes said, for example, that older abused children could have done more to prevent or stop the abuse. In some ways this reflected the views of the parents in these families, whose sympathies were often divided between what was usually their abusing son and victimised daughter. They too were usually slow to condemn outright or put the responsibility entirely onto the abusing child. Arrangements to separate the abused and abusing siblings were handled in a variety of ways. As we shall see later, social services departments or parents often arranged either for the victim or for the abusing child to leave the family.

In cases of alleged *physical abuse* medical evidence was particularly important in order to establish whether an injury was likely to have been inflicted intentionally or accidentally, although of course it was not always possible for doctors to make this judgement. In addition, since some of the children were babies there might be no evidence as to the identity of the abuser. If parents denied responsibility for the injuries, this could make it difficult to decide how much risk there was for the child. Questioning by the police of parent figures or others who might be responsible for the child's injuries was directed at trying to establish who was responsible. In the case of older children, when the identity of the abuser was not in doubt, police used these interviews to stress to parents that their actions were unacceptable and to try to deter them from further abuse.

Establishing responsibility for acts of omission which might constitute *neglect* was handled in a less systematic way. In the case of two-parent households assumptions were often made that the mother rather than the father figure was responsible for the children and therefore for any shortcomings in their care. As we have seen, this has long historical roots and Gordon (1989) has commented on child neglect cases in the 1920s in which 'a mother was considered responsible almost by definition'.

Cases which would later be considered to constitute *'emotional abuse'* fell into three groups. Some, as previously mentioned, involved the investigation of an incident of physical abuse which was reclassified at the conference stage as emotional abuse. A second group of cases involved children whose mothers had mental health problems which affected their parenting capacity, and a third focused on children who were suffering a variety of adverse experiences which were thought to be linked to deficiencies in the parenting they received.

Interviews with children

A crucial part of the early stages of the investigation was the investigative interviews with children. The evidence from them played a key role in the agencies' determination of what had happened. We will look first at the experiences of the children who were interviewed, viewed through their eyes and those of the parents who were present, and then at the experiences of the social workers who helped to conduct the interviews. (Unfortunately our resources did not stretch to discovering the views of the police.) After that we will explore how far the evidence gained from the interviews was used to prosecute the alleged perpetrators.

The interviews with children were conducted either at the child's school or at the police station usually in a specially converted victim support suite. The comments from those non-abusing parents who had been involved soon enough to form a view were generally positive. Social work and police interviewers were seen as good at putting children at their ease, and getting them to talk. The parents often commented positively about the interviewing skills of the policewomen, their directness, and their sensitive yet authoritative manner. The willingness of police officers to take a partisan approach impressed parents, whether the message was that the police were determined to nail the perpetrator in a sexual abuse case, or conversely because sympathy was shown to a middle-class abuser who had admitted his offence and was greatly valued by his family. A number of the non-abusing mothers had subsequently found the policewomen very helpful, since they had maintained contact in order to inform mothers about the progress of a prosecution. In some cases police officers had extended their role further to offer support to mothers or, occasionally, to provide activities for the children.

Comments from the children showed how very painful investigative interviews could be even when, as was usually the case, they were conducted sympathetically. One 15-year-old girl said:

'I was questioned for about two or three hours. It was horrible. They were just asking everything that happened, what he did.'

She was also very worried about what her mother, who was not at the interview, would say. Another 15-year-old girl said:

'I didn't understand why the policewoman was there, and I felt very alone, even though the social worker was very sympathetic and very understanding. I think I was doing a lot of crying at the time.'

Sadly, this girl's mother had been excluded from this part of the investigation even though the girl had initially told her about the abuse and it was the mother who had then reported it.

Younger children sometimes remembered the interviews as less distressing and as providing them with relief. A nine-year-old girl explained:

'I started crying first of all because I was too scared to tell them. And then I told them the whole lot and it was all right.'

A few children had needed more than one interview to be able to start to talk about their abuse, such as this seven-year-old girl:

'Well, the first time it was pretty exhausting. The second time I talked to her it was a lot better.'

The most negative comments made by mothers and children were about interviews in connection with sexual abuse by a sibling. A 15-year-old girl who had been sexually abused by her older brother was the only child who said that she felt that the police had not believed her story. The investigators had accepted that sexual intercourse had taken place with her brother, but there was doubt as to how active a part the girl had taken in the incident. A 12-year-old girl who had been sexually abused by her older brother was subjected to a series of joint interviews. This was in order to elicit the name of another boy with whom it was thought she had had sexual intercourse and whose name she had wished to withhold. She too was not seen as simply the victim in this situation.

Thus, it can be seen that although interviews with children were usually sensitive and geared to the pace of the child, there was a reluctance to accept a situation in which the child withheld the name of an abuser. On the few occasions that this occurred the child was subjected to a series of interviews in an attempt to uncover this information. This runs contrary to the recommendations of the Cleveland Inquiry (Secretaty of State, 1988). The mother of one such girl not unreasonably saw this repeated interviewing as 'very pressurised'.

Things were made more difficult on the few occasions when there were deficiencies in the conduct of the interviews themselves. This was most evident when a specialist police officer was not part of the interviewing team. A case in point was that of Shaun, a teenage boy with learning difficulties, who because he was viewed as an alleged perpetrator was interviewed by a detective rather than a specialist police officer. Unfortunately the detective knew very little about interviewing children and used language that the boy could not understand. Shaun went away feeling that he had been treated badly by the police and the social worker, and it was clear from his account that he regarded 'police and social services' as a single agency. He told us later that he had important things he could not talk to anyone about and that he had not understood what was being asked at the investigation. It later emerged that he was himself a victim of sexual abuse.

Most of the social workers were satisfied by the joint investigation work undertaken with the specially trained police officers (who were all women) and with whom the interviewing of children was conducted. The social workers regarded most of these police officers as skilled and sensitive in the interviews with children. Afterwards, in almost all of the cases, a shared view of events was developed both about the allegation and regarding the action to be taken. Social workers then had the experience of forming a positive alliance with the police officers and felt, as a result, increasingly in control of events. This did much to relieve the anxiety of the investigation. There is reason to suppose that this good collaboration arose partly because of the training undertaken by the specialist police interviewers jointly with their social service counterparts and also because good joint working offered reciprocal advantages for each party.

Working closely with the police, however, was not without some disadvantages. A few social workers voiced concerns about the actions of the detectives (all of whom were men) who were responsible for gathering evidence for prosecution. They were not specialists in child protection and their objectives, as well as the time scale to which they worked, were different from those of the social workers who were charged with the protection of the child. As we have seen, considerations relevant to the collection of evidence for prosecution dictated the order in which family members were interviewed. Social workers could also be instructed by the police not to speak to an alleged abuser until the police had interviewed him. In one case there was a delay of five days before the CID interviewed a father who had whipped his daughter, during which time the social worker was unable to visit the family, thereby leaving the child at risk.

However, the desire of detectives to gather evidence could also affect the interviewing of children more directly. In one case Kate, a teenage girl, was very embarrassed at having to give details of her sexual abuse in front of male detectives who frequently interrupted the interview to apply pressure for her to have a medical in the vain hope that this would produce forensic evidence. She described the experience:

> *'It was really embarrassing at the beginning because you had to describe it, and I didn't like saying it in front of men, and my tutor was there saying, "Just say how you feel, how you would normally say it to friends or something". And I got more upset because it wasn't friends there I was talking to . . . It was a woman constable that I was speaking to, but these two policemen kept coming in asking questions, because they wanted to go and bring him in for questioning.'*

The investigating social worker had also found this experience very difficult:

> *'The pressing need for the CID to obtain evidence quickly to go and arrest the alleged perpetrator . . . put a lot of pressure on the victim . . . In fact, I had to intervene and stop them from doing it and literally put myself between the police and Kate, and tell them to leave her alone. Which didn't make me at all popular.'*

Medical examinations

In most cases of *sexual abuse*, a medical examination of the child was conducted after the interview (10 out of 15 of these cases). For only three children did the medical provide conclusive evidence of sexual intercourse or other corroborative evidence which could be used in a prosecution. When the medical was undertaken by a male doctor girls suffered considerable embarrassment and discomfort and at times, contrary to the recommendations of the Cleveland Report, their permission had not been sought (Secretary of State, 1988). One 15-year-old commented: 'I would have liked to have been asked, yes. But I'm used to it, I'm never asked.'

Arrangements for personnel to conduct the medicals varied. One local authority area office was able to call on the expert services of the local paediatric registrar. There was only one instance where a child suffered repeated medical examinations. This was because the first doctor who conducted the examinations had had insufficient forensic experience to give an informed opinion, so a paediatrician was asked to undertake another examination the following day. It was encouraging to find that the recommendation of the Cleveland Report to avoid second medical examinations had been heeded (Secretary of State, 1988).

In a few instances children were medically examined for other than evidential reasons. On one occasion a medical was undertaken some time after the investigation for therapeutic purposes, in order to reassure a sexually abused girl that she had not been damaged by her father. In another case the girl's long-term foster mother requested a medical because she had reason to fear that the alleged abuser might have transmitted AIDS.

Where *physical abuse* was alleged to have occurred, children were also often medically examined and this happened in 10 out of 16 cases. For three children medical opinion provided conclusive evidence of non-accidental injury where there was no admission from either parent. In another three instances it provided additional weight where there was an admission. In contrast, in the remaining four instances the evidence was inconclusive and was insufficiently strong to provide a definite challenge to the parents' accounts.

When children were examined by hospital doctors the parents had also been questioned by them in order to establish whether their story about the child's injury squared with the medical findings. Parents had sometimes felt that they had been grilled by a hospital doctor who had behaved 'like a copper'. Apart from this there were few adverse comments about the medical examinations of physically injured children, with the exception of one situation involving a physically abused child which was viewed as extremely unsatisfactory by the social worker:

> '*I rang for a medical examination to be carried out by the GP, and he literally whipped in – we were interviewing Tracey at the school – and he literally whipped in in the middle of this interview, dropped her knickers and he was out within, like, a minute. And this was in the middle of a policewoman and myself trying to talk to Tracey. And Tracey has got communication problems and is sometimes a difficult child to get through to.*'

Prosecution of the alleged abusers

After the interviews with the older children had been conducted, the police turned their attention to the suspect and in some cases the suspect's spouse or partner. Interviews with parents or other alleged abusers were held at the local police station. It is perhaps not surprising that parents who were questioned as suspects felt that they were put under pressure by the police (see also, Corby 1987), and this was particularly heavily applied to those with a previous record of offences. Quite often the questioning was prolonged, and in one case a father was kept in custody for 35 hours and questioned twice a day.

Non-abusing mothers who were questioned also found the experience stressful. One stepmother of a sexually abused child was kept at the police station for 10 hours and was asked detailed questions about her sex life. Another non-abusing mother whose husband had hit her teenage son was questioned about her background and this had made her feel that she was thought to be implicated in the abuse:

'I was questioned on my background. I couldn't see what it was relevant. I was right angry because I'd been in care since the age of six . . . when I was eleven I was sexually abused by my father and for some reason or other they won't let me forget it . . . I think people like me, the rumour is that if you're sexually abused yourself you do it to your children . . . "We want to know your background." As soon as he said that, I felt really scared, you know. Why do you want to know my background?'

The police were particularly active in cases of sexual abuse where they interviewed 13 out of the 15 suspected abusers. However, most of these cases were not pursued and only five convictions were obtained, all concerning men, two of which resulted in non-custodial sentences. As we shall see, police action in charging the abuser and the subsequent imposition of bail conditions could play an important role in removing the abuser from the household at the start of the investigation. However, in the long run the situation had to be resolved outside the courtroom because very few convictions were obtained.

Police were also involved in 10 out of the 16 cases of physical abuse. There were only three convictions, two against men and one against a lone mother, and in none was custody used. In a further four cases, police were involved with emotional abuse and neglect where there had also been allegations of physical abuse. None of these led to a prosecution.

In total the police interviewed the suspected abuser in 27 out of the 44 cases in the study (61%). In 18 cases there was no prosecution either because no charge was brought (7), a caution was given (5), or because the Crown Prosecution Service decided that the case was insufficiently strong (6). There was a prosecution in nine cases and the resulting eight guilty findings represented less than a third (30%) of those which started with a police interview (and only 18 per cent of all the cases in the study). Only three custodial sentences were imposed and all were for sexual abuse.

As we have seen, the search for evidence can be a powerful driving force in determining what happens at the investigation stage, and can have adverse effects on what can be done thereafter. In the light of this, the low rate of convictions obtained should give pause for thought. Of course, the introduction of video-recorded interviews with child witnesses in criminal proceedings might produce more convictions by making it easier for children to give evidence in court (Home Office with Department of Health, 1992), although initial figures have not been encouraging. Whether it does or not however, it is likely to reinforce the gathering of evidence as a key factor in shaping the investigation stage.

Scrutiny of non-abusing parents

The investigating professionals did not restrict themselves to interviewing the alleged victims and perpetrators and to assigning responsibility for the commission of abuse or neglect. As we have seen, once non-abusing mothers had been brought into the investigation they also became the subject of scrutiny. Judgements were made about mothers who at that time were often in a state of shock. If they did not react in the way that the investigating team expected, they were sometimes held to be unable to protect their children. When there was an allegation of sexual abuse there was an expectation that the mother should immediately sever her relationship with the alleged abuser in order to ensure the child's safety. In situations where the mother was uncertain about whether she believed her child's allegation of abuse or where she was thought to have retained her attachment to the abuser, the possibility of removing the child was actively considered.

In cases of physical abuse the expectations were less specific as the separation of the child or children and abuser was less often prescribed, but an undue loyalty to the abuser was regarded with suspicion. In one case a mother was kept at the police station for five hours with her two young and fractious children while her husband was questioned about bruises on the baby. He was bailed away from the family. She did not reveal that she knew her husband sometimes hit the children. Instead her reaction was to become upset and aggressive which so disquieted the investigators that the children were summarily removed from her, even though there was no suggestion that she had abused them.

When, as was usually the case, perpetrators of sexual abuse protested their innocence, mothers could be torn between their child and their partner, caught in a situation where believing one meant losing the other. As one mother, whose ex-husband was facing allegations of sexual abuse to her daughter put it:

> 'My ex-husband is maintaining he's done no wrong. But the two girls are both saying, "Yes, these things have happened". So I feel as if I'm in the middle of a see-saw.'

Another mother talked of the conflict of loyalties that arises when the abuser and the victim are siblings:

> 'I was confused, I was split between the two of them. I still am. Very, very split . . . I mean, it is difficult you know, when you are with one of the kids you have got to cut out the other one. And when you are with the other one you have to cut out that one. You can't sort of have all the feelings at the same time.'

Such mothers badly needed help in sorting out their feelings about what had happened. However, an exclusive focus on mothers as secondary perpetrators, rather than as secondary victims, of the abuse of their children often led social workers to judge them as unprotective and to withdraw support. There was a great need for a woman's feelings of shock, self-blame and loss to be understood and for support to be offered to her at this time. This kind of support was rarely forthcoming and this in turn made it more difficult for mothers to provide the understanding and support needed by their abused children. When such assistance was not offered at this critical stage some women remade an alliance with the abuser and excluded the child. Thus, *the conduct of the investigation affected the way in which family members reacted, and to whom they turned for comfort and help and the alliances they formed.* It was in part on the basis of these reactions that decisions were made about removal of the child, prosecution of the abuser and the ability of the mother to keep the children safe from harm.

Summary

1. There were three principal ways in which children at risk of abuse or neglect came to the attention of social services departments. In the majority of cases (59%) the children themselves, their mothers or members of the community initiated action. Another 25% of cases were referred to social services by other agencies. The remaining 16% were current cases held by social services departments.

2. The way in which these referrals about possible abuse or neglect were handled had a considerable impact on parents and children. Two situations had a particularly adverse effect. One was when parents approached social services for assistance and were instead subject to a child protection investigation. The other was when agency workers referred a child to social services without informing the parents, leading to accusations that it was done 'behind their backs'. Both these situations led to a loss of trust in professionals.

3. The search for evidence which could be used in prosecuting the perpetrators of abuse was a powerful driving force in shaping the conduct of investigations. As a result, a number of practices had developed which could have adverse consequences for children and their parents. In the light of the low rate of convictions obtained this should give pause for thought.

4. The interviews of children by social workers and specialist police officers were generally conducted with sensitivity and skill. However, children who withheld the name of an abuser were sometimes subjected to a series

of interviews in an attempt to uncover this information. The least satisfactory interviews were those which concerned cases of sibling or peer sexual abuse.

5. Although medical examinations were frequently undertaken in cases of both sexual and physical abuse, in fewer than half of the cases was conclusive evidence of abuse obtained.

6. Little attention was paid to keeping parents informed about the investigations and in three-quarters of cases of sexual abuse children were interviewed without the non-abusing mothers being informed or involved.

7. The impact of the investigation on mothers whose children had alleged sexual abuse was particularly profound since this was usually the first time that they had heard about the abuse. They experienced shock, bewilderment, anger and the onset of profound feelings of loss. Women who did not immediately reject an abusing partner were often judged to be unable to protect their children. Their need for understanding and assistance in the early stages of child protection intervention was often overlooked. This lack of help in turn made it more difficult for mothers to provide the understanding and support needed by their abused children.

8. During the investigation, ideas about the risks to which children were exposed were formulated, often jointly by social workers and police officers, and attributions of responsibility were made. However, little account was taken of the fact that the conduct of the investigation itself affected the way in which family members reacted and the alliances they formed. Yet it was on the basis of reactions to the investigation that decisions were made about whether children were at risk and how to protect them. Amongst these decisions were those relating to the removal of the child, the prosecution of the alleged abuser, and the ability of the mother to keep the children safe from further harm.

Chapter 5

Early protective action

Actions taken to protect the child at the time of the investigation

Important decisions about how best to protect children were taken at the investigation and immediately after it – especially when it seemed to be necessary to remove the child or to ensure that the alleged abuser left the household. Sometimes police took the initiative, sometimes social services. At other times parents took action to protect their own children.

The investigations themselves generally lasted only a day or two, although this period might be extended because more than one interview was conducted with the child, or because the questioning of the perpetrator became prolonged. In a few cases the process could stretch over several days or even weeks. The actions taken to separate children and suspected abusers were therefore also partly designed to facilitate the process of making enquiries and ensure that children were not put under pressure to retract their statements. The removal of the child or the abuser at this stage could be a crucial intervention which in some cases led to permanent exclusion. Although there were movements in and out of the household throughout the whole of the follow-up period (see chapter 14) the separation of the child and the alleged abuser in the initial stages often appeared to have a considerable effect on the outcome.

In just under half of the cases in the follow-up sample (20), the child remained in the same household as the abuser throughout the investigation and conference period. When separation did occur, suspected abusers and children left home in almost equal proportions. (In 10 cases the alleged abuser was removed, in 11 cases the child was removed, and in another 3 cases both the alleged abuser and the victim left the household.) However, as can be seen from the material in table 9, this pattern varied according to the type of abuse. In situations involving sexual abuse it was rare for no separation to occur, and the alleged abuser was more likely to leave home than the victim. In cases of physical abuse the children and abusers left home in equal proportions; but in over half of the cases the child remained at home with the abusing parent. In cases of neglect and emotional abuse it was usual for the child to remain at home, although a small number of children were removed.

These patterns are complex but important, and it may be useful to explore them a little further.

Table 9 **Action Taken to Protect the Child at the Time of the Investigation or Shortly Afterwards**

	Sexual Abuse	Physical Abuse	Neglect	Emotional Abuse	No.	%
Abuser out of the household	7	3	–	–	10	23
Child leaves the household	4	3	1	3	11	25
Abuser and child leave the household	2	1	–	–	3	7
Child remains in the household with the abuser	2	9	4	5	20	45
	15	16	5	8	44	100

Protective actions in cases of sexual abuse

In the wake of the Cleveland Inquiry (Secretary of State, 1988) there is now a clear expectation that when sexual abuse is suspected the preferred course of action is for the alleged abuser to leave the household, and thus allow the child to remain with the other parent. Schedule 2.5 of the Children Act takes this one step further by empowering local authorities to defray the expenses incurred when an alleged abuser lives away from home pending the outcome of an investigation.

During the investigation or soon after, the removal of the alleged abuser was effected in nine of the fifteen sexual abuse cases, usually by the imposition of bail conditions. In two cases the abuser was charged, convicted and imprisoned as a result of the disclosure and in one case he was already in prison for the offence. However, there were other situations in which the suspected abuser was excluded only temporarily from the household by means of police bail. In some, men were charged but not convicted, and in others they returned home after a period of bail without any charges having being brought. Two mothers took action themselves to exclude the abuser, with help from official agencies and friends. It appeared that the exclusion of the man from the household was often seen as a useful precaution even if it was only temporary and it did provide a useful breathing space in which mothers and children could consider their future without being separated. It did not, as we have seen, lead to a large number of convictions.

In spite of these efforts to exclude alleged abusers it was still considered necessary for six of the sexually abused children to be moved from their families. (In two of these situations both the child and the abuser left home.) Children tended to leave the household when there seemed to be few other options which would offer them protection, either because the abuser was the child's resident sibling or because there was no other parent in the child's household who could take responsibility for the child. In many cases voluntary arrangements were made; for example, some children went to live temporarily with friends or relatives. Nevertheless, most of these placements were a second-best option to the child remaining at home.

In only two instances were the sexual abuser and the child not separated at this point. In one case a young boy was sharing a bedroom with his grandfather who had recently sexually abused a girl outside the home. In the other case a teenage boy who was living permanently with relatives was drawn to the agency's attention after he exposed himself to a neighbour. The family agreed to keep him with them if treatment was offered.

It was interesting to find that in cases of sexual abuse so many children had to leave home at the start of intervention, and that it was often not possible to realise the preferred option of effecting the removal of the person suspected of the abuse. This finding somewhat surprised us and we therefore checked to see if this had also been the case for the larger group of sexually abused children in our case conference sample (52 children). It was. In this larger sample, as many children left home after the abuse came to light as did alleged abusers. It is therefore important to note that when children were brought to case conference for reasons of sexual abuse, in quite a number of cases they had initially left home.

There were particular difficulties in the planning of initial protective action in cases of sibling or peer sexual abuse. In these cases the agencies were uncertain how to treat children who were both abused and abusing. Did they require treatment or punishment? In some cases of sibling abuse the child who was deemed to be responsible was placed away, in others the abused sibling was moved out of the family and in yet others the siblings were separated only very briefly.

Protective actions in cases of physical abuse, neglect and emotional abuse
In the 29 cases of physical abuse, neglect and emotional abuse it was rare for protection to be effected by the abusing parent leaving the household. In only four cases (14%) did this occur, either as the result of the imposition of bail conditions, pressure from the agencies or by means of a prison sentence on unrelated charges. (All were cases of physical abuse.) In another eight cases (28%), however, children were removed; half from lone mothers and half from two-parent families. These were mostly cases of physical injury by a parent even though some were classified as emotional abuse at the case conference. Just one was a case of extremely severe neglect. However, three-fifths of the children continued to live in the same household after registration as before, with the abusing parent present. This, as we have seen, was in sharp contrast to what happened in the case of sexually abused children.

When a male carer was thought to have physically abused a child, the initial protective action was occasionally directed against him (as happened frequently in sexual abuse cases) and attempts were made to exclude him from the household. This could happen by means of attempted prosecution for the offence or by a mixture of police bail and prosecution on other charges since some of the men concerned were awaiting prosecution for other offences, such as burglary.

On the other hand, when a female carer was judged to be responsible for physical abuse, emotional abuse or neglect, the agencies were less likely to try to prosecute the mother and more likely to take action to remove the *child*. The lone mothers who lost children in this way were caught up in situations of extreme stress. The use of accommodation at the time of the investigation was often intended to be temporary and no more than a 'breathing space'. Unfortunately, however, there was a tendency for these 'temporary' separations to become permanent.

Decisions to remove children

The pressure to make safe decisions was illustrated by the fact that, of the 11 children who left the household in the early stages, seven had been removed on an emergency order. In a number of cases such an order was taken when agreement to accommodation might have been forthcoming from parents or when the possibility of placement with relatives had not been explored, even though a relative was offering help.

It became clear that decisions for a child to be looked after were affected by a number of factors which operated in combination. Children about whom there was a high degree of *uncertainty* and where the risks were seen as unpredictable at the investigation stage were likely candidates, unless legal advice made this course difficult to take. It may be that minority ethnic children are particularly vulnerable to separation because of the efforts of families to exclude child protection agencies, and the uncertainty accompanying many of the investigations. This is an issue which requires research. Certainly, commentators have highlighted the overrepresentation of some groups of black and minority ethnic children in care (see for example, Rowe *et al*, 1989; Barn, 1993). One white social worker who lamented what he called his 'lack of communication skills' had been asked to assess a child who was Asian, who had learning difficulties, and who had probably been sexually abused. With commendable honesty this social worker said:

> *'I was left at sea with that. I just didn't know what to do and how to approach him.'*

Because of the crisis nature of the agencies' involvement and the pressures to make 'safe' decisions, children were particularly vulnerable to removal during the investigation if they were *new* cases and therefore relatively unknown. In most cases, of course, the primary reason for the child's removal was the high level of *risk*, rather than the severity of the abuse or neglect which had been suffered. In one such case an emergency order was obtained on a newborn baby in hospital, and a placement was made with foster carers, because of the high risks involved if the child remained with his intellectually limited parents. They had made no preparations for the arrival of the baby, did not cuddle him and seemed unable to learn how to handle him.

In some cases it was not the severity of the injury or even the risk of abuse which led to the child's removal, but rather the mounting concerns about the mother's *mental health*. All were lone mothers. Some came to agency attention as a result of disagreements leading to fights between mother and child, whilst one child had been accommodated at her mother's request when she had to go into psychiatric hospital. Shortly afterwards the child was made a ward of court because of doubts about the mother's ability to care for him. It is interesting that the combination of a mother's psychiatric condition and an incident of risk should be so powerful in propelling children into care. Those incidents which came to agency attention had clearly been taken to signify both the mothers' unpredictability and a deterioration in their mental health. Certainly, further attempts to support them in the task of caring for their children were not made.

Whilst it is clear that there were considerable concerns about the safety and future welfare of all the children who were separated from their parents, there were other children who appeared to be at no less risk and yet who remained with them. For example, whilst two babies were removed because of non-accidental injuries for which neither parent took responsibility, there was a parallel case of an injured baby who was returned to the parents, mainly because of legal advice that there were insufficient grounds for care proceedings. There were also other children who were no less badly injured or who occupied a scapegoated position in the family and who nonetheless remained at home. Some of them, as we shall see, were subsequently removed and some were not.

The effects of joint investigation

There was no doubt that the investigation was a stage during which the stakes for the professionals were high. A child might be at risk and it was the responsibility of the investigators to take action when these risks were severe. The social workers and the police officers involved in the interviewing took their responsibilities seriously and if there was doubt about risk the decisions they made usually erred on the side of caution. However, because investigations were accompanied by professional anxiety it was also possible for those anxieties to escalate.

Although the numbers were too small to draw definite conclusions, we did find that children were more often removed during a joint investigation by police and social services than when the investigation was conducted by a social worker alone. This can be illustrated by the outcomes of the physical abuse investigations. In four cases the child's situation was investigated by a social worker alone and none of the children were removed. All the children remained with their parents or were returned to them from hospital. On the other hand, in seven of the ten cases which were jointly investigated, the child and the alleged abuser were separated.

Of course, it is to be expected that the more serious cases would have been the subject of an investigation in which police were involved, but this was not always the case. Indeed, in two of the four solo investigations the child had suffered physical abuse which was at least as serious as those in the joint investigation group. There was some evidence from the detailed accounts which we were given that at times the joint investigation process itself – during which children were removed from school to be interviewed and parents were subjected to intense questioning by the police – could so heighten the anxieties of the parents that tension and conflict escalated, making the removal of the child more likely.

We should not forget that decisions to separate the child and abuser were made not only by professionals but also by family members. This happened in two cases of sibling sexual abuse where the parents sent their daughters to relatives in order to separate them from the brothers who had abused them. In a third case, a girl who had been sexually molested by her stepfather was placed in a friend's family at her own request.

For minority ethnic parents who had relatives elsewhere in this country or abroad, there was sometimes the option of sending a child to these relatives to escape the unwelcome attention either of an alleged abuser or of social services. One Asian girl was abruptly sent to live with grandparents in India when she started to make known the physical beatings she had been receiving from her father and brothers. Unfortunately, a sympathetic Asian social worker arrived on the scene too late to form an alliance with the mother and prevent the girl's precipitate removal. Sending the girl abroad was construed as a protective act, by a family which felt deeply threatened by the interventions of police and social services.

The loss of control experienced by parents and children

As can be seen, during the investigation the child protection agencies acted decisively to try to determine whether children were at risk and to ensure their immediate safety. Family members were in a position to respond to these interventions, but the balance of power rested firmly with the agencies. This was not a stage at which family members would generally refuse admission to their houses or access to their children, although, as we shall see, this sometimes occurred later.

Indeed, both parents and children spoke of feeling swept along by the investigation without being consulted or, in some cases, without being informed about what would happen next. Even when children had made the first move to talk about their abuse they had no idea what 'telling' would set in motion. The children who had spoken, and some of the mothers, had in varying degrees regarded the information which they had shared as still in the private domain and had not anticipated the rapidity with which it would become 'public'. A sexually abused girl of 15 described her uncertainty and bewilderment as the investigation took place:

> *'I didn't really have time to think about whether to go to the police station or not . . . I didn't really know why I was going there. I didn't know Dad was going to be arrested or anything. I was just sort of taken there. I just don't think I knew anything about what was going to happen. Going down a corridor and not knowing what was going to happen next . . . I was never told what was going to happen.'*

Another mother described her daughter's experience of the investigation after telling her mother about the abuse:

> *'She felt relief at having confided in me, but because it had gone, rollerballed on, she wasn't happy with that at all.'*

This uncertainty and loss of control could serve to magnify the sense of powerlessness which was already a central experience for abused children.

One non-abusing mother spoke for many when she described her experience of the investigation:

> *'Things move so quickly. If you're not really sure of the law, then you're completely whisked along with what happens, without really being explained why things are happening . . . We don't really know what is coming next and at no point does anyone ever sit down and tell you what is going on.'*

Parents were particularly bewildered when they found that the investigation had started as a result of their own actions. One mother had approached her local Citizens' Advice Bureau for advice about her partner's drinking. When she mentioned that he used a stick to discipline her children the matter was reported to social services and a full-scale investigation set in motion:

> *'It was taken out of my hands completely.'*

Her partner, who was arrested by the police, echoed these feelings:

> *'Everything blew up in her face as much as mine and it sort of snowballed from one thing to another.'*

It was interesting to find that this feeling of being out of control was not confined to investigations of intra-familial abuse. In one case, a foster mother had alerted the social services to the likely past abuse of her newly-placed foster daughter. Whilst the investigation was allowed to proceed at the girl's pace, the foster mother's experience was still of a process over which she had little control:

> *'Our whole household, everything, has been totally invaded.'*

The one exception was a sexually abused adolescent who felt that she was consulted on how the investigation was to be handled:

> *'I was consulted on everything and asked my opinions.'*

Not only did parents and children feel that the investigation rolled on like a juggernaut beyond their control, but they themselves were sometimes in a state of extreme anxiety and uncertainty:

> *'I felt like I was a headless chicken running around just panicking all the time.'*

Social workers sometimes shared with parents and children the experience of feeling that they had little control over what happened. As one said:

> *'The process of the investigation takes on a life of its own and you really have to be incredibly strong to alter its course.'*

The circulation of blame

Assigning responsibility for ill-treatment of the children was not the exclusive province of the professionals. Both during the investigation and afterwards, family members were themselves trying to deal with issues of responsibility and blame. Even when children identified the abuser in cases of sexual abuse it was unusual for alleged perpetrators to take responsibility or admit their guilt. Only one did. Some alleged abusers went further than denial, and actively blamed the child for being a liar and making up stories. As one mother said:

> *'Well he's pretty disgusted with it. He can't make out why she started it all . . . He blames her and she blames him. And there's me standing in the middle.'* (Mother of a sexually abused girl aged 16)

Such denial by an alleged abuser could lead children to doubt the evidence of their senses:

> *'For a long while after I'd said things, I went through a time of thinking, "Have I said this?", you know, "Am I just imagining it all?" But then I knew Susan [her sister] was doing it and had it done to her as well.'*
> (Sexually abused girl aged 15)

In a number of cases, in spite of having a clear disclosure from the child, the Crown Prosecution Service decided not to take a case to court because the uncorroborated evidence of a child was considered to be insufficient to win the case. Some alleged abusers took this as evidence that they had been exonerated. In one such case the father responded by broadcasting widely on his CB radio that he was innocent and his son a liar who had fabricated the stories about him.

In cases of physical abuse where children were too young to identify who had maltreated them, the parents generally started out by denying that they were involved. However, when the abuser's identity was known through the child's account or because the act had been witnessed, most tried to absolve themselves of culpability by justifying their actions. The two exceptions were lone mothers who referred themselves to social services, concerned that they were hitting their sons whom they could not control. It is important to note how rarely the parents whose children were on the child protection register for physical abuse had taken responsibility for hitting their children at the outset, and how much more frequent were adverserial situations in which parents defended themselves against accusations of impropriety. This is not entirely surprising in view of the possible consequences of admission.

Similarly, in some cases which were soon to be officially constituted as cases of neglect or emotional abuse by a case conference, *parents completely disagreed that their children's circumstances were harmful to them*. For example, one mother whose 2-year-old child was later registered for 'emotional abuse' because of difficulties in the mother-child relationship explained her view of the matter:

> *'I needed help trying to get people to stand up and listen to me, when it came to my stomach trouble, and yes, I did need help with young Sharon because of her tantrums, because I couldn't control her. Because she was way out . . . [But] I can't see where she's at risk. She's well looked after here. She's happy.'*

Another mother was appalled when her son's distressed behaviour at a time of marital disharmony was regarded as due to emotional abuse:

> *'They would have had a case . . . if he'd been found beaten or ill-treated or neglected. But they haven't, they can't find anything else . . . The only thing they can find is just this . . . He is me. He's my double. If I'm upset, he's upset. It upsets him like mad when he and I don't speak to each other.'*

It was not only the parents who wrestled with issues of responsibility and blame. The children themselves sometimes apportioned blame to their mothers for not having known what was going on:

> *'I sort of resented her because of what was happening and she couldn't see it. And I thought she should protect me and she couldn't.'* (Sexually abused girl aged 16)

In turn, as we have seen, non-abusing mothers often felt guilty that they had not realised that their child was being abused:

> *'I felt as if I'd let her down because I hadn't realised before that there was something wrong.'* (Mother of a sexually abused girl aged 13)

> *'To be honest the last person you think of sexually abusing your daughter is your husband. But even now I still feel really guilty that I didn't notice any of the signs. I didn't put two and two together and make four.'* (Mother of a sexually abused girl aged 8)

They felt diminished or occasionally angry, to discover that their child had not at the time felt able to confide in them about the abuse, whether or not they had done so later. Two mothers actually blamed the child both for not telling sooner and for confiding in someone other than themselves:

> *'I feel angry that she allowed it to continue without telling me and then went and told someone outside the family.'*

Children who had been sexually abused were very prone to feelings of self-blame that the abuse had occurred:

> *'I think I'm to blame because I shouldn't have stayed with him – because my Mum used to go to town when this happened . . . But it was a bit my Mum's fault. No, it wasn't a bit my Mum's fault because I think it was all my fault . . . Some Dad's. But it's really confusing.'* (Sexually abused girl aged 7)

Another girl said:

> *'It depends what kind of mood I'm in. Sometimes I feel guilty, sometimes I don't.'* (Sexually abused girl aged 16)

Children were greatly helped if those close to them tried to counteract their feelings of guilt and to emphasise that it was the perpetrator who was responsible for what had happened. As one mother explained:

> '*I try to reassure her that what had happened wasn't her fault and that I could understand why she didn't say anything.*' (Mother of a 13-year-old sexually abused girl)

When the non-abusing parent was unable to fulfil this role for the child, it was all the more important that a professional did so (see for example, Berliner, 1991 a). We shall explore how far children were provided with such counselling in a later chapter.

The consequences for children of the disclosure or the discovery of abuse

For some children the uncovering of their abuse led to feelings of relief and a lessening of tension. Much depended on the actions of the child protection agencies in the aftermath of the child's statement, in particular whether it was the abuser or the child who left the family, the level of support available from family members or others in the child's network, and for those children who moved, the safety and support offered by the new placement. The *sexually abused* children benefited from the increased protection afforded by separation from the abuser. When they were supported and not blamed by their carers, the relief was especially intense. As one foster mother said of her foster child:

> '*But once that police investigation was out of the way . . . and once Lucy had off-loaded, you could see her starting to relax.*'

Another girl, who went to live with her very supportive separated mother after the discovery that she had been sexually abused by her father, described her feelings thus:

> '*It made me feel a lot better for telling someone, so I could get away from the house . . . exactly as far away from home as possible . . . so I don't have to live with him any more . . . Because I got most of it out of my mind then.*'

The social worker of this girl said:

> '*Literally her eyes are now alive and they actually were quite dead. It's really quite easy to see that she's much happier in so many ways.*'

However, for many children the feelings accompanying disclosure were not limited to relief. *Older children who had taken steps to 'tell' often felt responsible for the consequences of their disclosure*, and the subsequent family break-up or threatened prosecution of the abuser. This could be a heavy burden for them to bear, whether it was the child or the alleged abuser who had left the household. Gail had been sexually abused by her father from her early years but it was not until she was 15 that she finally spoke of it. Her mother felt the loss of her husband keenly when he was sent to prison and placed the blame squarely on her daughter. Gail said:

> *'I never dreamed it would happen like this. I mean never in a million years that Dad would go to prison and things like that . . . I felt very guilty that I split up the family . . . I get very down, I keep thinking why did I say it, you know. I think, well maybe I should have just kept my mouth shut.'*

The children who were most troubled were those who left home as a consequence of disclosing sexual abuse. They had to try to come to terms with the double pain of telling about the abuse and of losing their place in the family in consequence. When the placement proved unsatisfactory their distress was compounded. Margaret, who was 16, left her family after she revealed sexual abuse by her stepfather. Although she had initially asked to go to stay with a friend she had really wanted to be with her family. As a result, she regretted having spoken: 'I wished I'd never said anything'. She also felt responsible for the effect of her disclosure on family members and was anxious to see that her sister Carol was safe:

> *'I think I feel guilty in a way because it's sort of – I don't know – it's hurt my Mum more and Carol and David [sister and brother]. But in a way I don't feel guilty because at least the social services are involved and can keep an eye on Carol.'*

A third teenage girl who had revealed sexual abuse by her brother found that her parents focused their concern on him when, whilst he was remanded to prison, he was beaten up by fellow prisoners. She had moved to friends and was blamed by her parents for her brother's plight and the disruption to the family. She felt keenly the lack of support offered to her by her family:

> *'I hoped that everything would stop. I didn't want to know what happened next . . . I felt, instead of everything getting better, it got worse.'*

However, when children disclosed sexual abuse and the non-abusing mother was able to support them and not blame them for the abuser leaving the family, their feelings of responsibility for the effects on the family were attenuated. Research has shown that children have the best prognosis for recovery when they are believed and supported by a parent (Conte and Schuerman, 1987; Wyatt and Mickey, 1988; Berliner, 1991 b).

When *physical abuse, neglect or emotional abuse* was discovered, the consequences were varied. The care offered to very young children sometimes improved when appropriate support was provided for the parents, whilst others benefited from a move to relatives or to foster carers. However, some children who stayed in their families were blamed by their parents for having revealed them as the source of the injury. Pressure was put on children not to talk about their home lives to professionals or at school, and sometimes parents vented their anger at the children, leading to further scapegoating, blame and sometimes re-abuse.

The formation of alliances

The investigations were experienced by parents and children as very powerful interventions in their lives and, as we have seen, ones over which they had very little control. It was also a time when abusing parents could face prosecution, non-abusing parents feel on trial, and the parenting abilities of both were under close scrutiny. Moreover, the possibility that their children would be removed was an ever-present fear for parents. In this crisis situation, they tried to act in ways which they thought would prevent things getting worse: 'damage limitation' was at the forefront of their thinking. It was at this important stage that a variety of alliances were formed which set the pattern for the subsequent course of events.

The alliances formed depended on the relative strengths of pre-existing relationships both within families and between family members and professionals, as well as on agency interventions during the investigation. In cases of alleged sexual abuse by an adult, most non-abusing mothers sought to ensure that the perpetrator and the abused child were separated. Many mothers aligned themselves with their abused child and ended their relationship with the abuser. However, as we have seen, some mothers continued to care about their partner and experienced a conflict of loyalty between him and their child. At this point the actions of the investigators, including whether prosecution was pursued and bail secured, could be crucial in setting the scene for the exclusion of the alleged abuser and keeping the child in the family.

Clearly the actions of the investigators at this point of crisis could help to strengthen the alliance between the abused children and their mothers or, on the contrary, to weaken it. In most cases this was well managed but when it was not, an important opportunity to influence the outcome for the child in a positive direction had been missed. Margaret's situation illustrated this. She revealed at school that she had been sexually abused by her stepfather and she expressed apprehension about her mother's reaction. She was interviewed by a police officer and social worker and moved to a friend's family without her mother's involvement. This meant that the mother was not given an opportunity to hear her daughter's account of the abuse or to offer her support. She remained unsure exactly what the allegations were and Margaret had no opportunity to discover what her mother's reaction was and to deal with it. In addition, the mother was offered no assistance in sorting out her feelings about her daughter's abuse. This set a pattern for the separation of mother and daughter which the stepfather was able to use to his advantage in discrediting Margaret's disclosure and regaining his place in the family. His return left Margaret's younger sister vulnerable to his sexual advances within the household, whilst Margaret herself was isolated from the family.

When allegations of physical abuse, neglect or emotional abuse were made, couples would generally pull together in the hope of limiting the potentially damaging effects of the investigation on the family. They tried to present a united front to outside agencies. In many cases their accounts of what had happened had had to be given in response to a sudden request for an explanation when an incident or injury had come to the agencies' attention. Denial and silence were relatively effective when there were no witnesses. Going further than this, we know that at least two mothers tried to shield the father figure by taking responsibility for an injury which he had caused.

It was not surprising that in the face of allegations of mistreatment couples often formed a defensive alliance against the outside agencies and that difficulties in the family would not be revealed at this stage. This was one means of retaining a measure of control over a potentially escalating situation. However, it could also mean that *key information about family functioning and the risks to the children, such as marital violence, drug or alcohol addiction, might not be known to the professionals during the investigation and planning stages.* Even when one parent was unhappy about the way her, or occasionally his, partner had treated the child this was often not shared with the investigators for fear that it would worsen the situation. In addition, we found that it was not uncommon for mothers to be subject to physical violence from their partners; but they had rarely volunteered this information to investigators. This became evident later in the study when at the follow-up interviews women started to talk about the violence which they had endured throughout this period. As a result, *although at the case conference stage domestic violence had been known about in 12 of our 44 cases, there were actually at least another 11 such cases in which it had not been revealed.* All but one of these involved violence by men to their partners. This violence had not been known to the investigators or therefore to the subsequent case conference. It was at a later stage that mothers told us about the extent of the violence which they had endured, at which point they had still sometimes kept this information from their social workers. In addition, we found that whilst at the investigation one father's alcohol addiction was recognised as important, the drug addiction of another father figure did not emerge at all at this stage.

Moreover, when the investigation was experienced as invasive and blaming, it increased the likelihood that parents would form an apparent alliance against the perceived threat from outside agencies. In such situations, and especially when they were frightened by the possibility of recrimination or violence, mothers could feel that they had little choice but to ally themselves publicly with their partners. However, although parents often showed a united front to outside agencies, at home things could be less harmonious. Mothers who took most of the responsibility for child care assumed even more after an investigation, frequently giving up work to try to meet what they thought was the agency's view of how they should be more responsibile for their children's safety and welfare. Father figures who were distant from their families became more distant whilst mothers with little self-confidence became even more despondent.

The reaction of siblings to the discovery and investigation of abuse was varied but particularly intense in cases of sexual abuse. The siblings of an abused child might be supportive and grateful if a hated father figure left the family as a consequence. On the other hand, for some siblings the absence of the father figure counted as a considerable loss and they could become hostile to the abused child who was seen as the source of the family's difficulties.

It has already been shown that the way in which the referrals were handled and the extent to which parents were kept informed about what was happening had a major impact on parents and children alike. Sometimes from the parents' point of view their trust in community agencies was broken at this stage, and the chances that a workable relationship could be formed later with the social worker were greatly reduced. In other cases, when the investigation had been experienced as less threatening or traumatic, or the investigator's understanding approach had been appreciated by parents, there was a good possibility that constructive relationships with professionals could later be formed.

At the investigation stage social workers usually moved strongly to ally themselves with sexually abused children and there were also some cases of sexual abuse investigation where workers made good relationships with non-abusing parents (generally mothers) who had acted in accordance with agency expectations to sever contact with the alleged abuser and take steps to provide for the safety of their children. The investigation had still wider effects and could make a considerable impact on relationships within the extended family. In some cases a grandparent became more involved and offered help and support, whilst in others grandparents or members of the extended family backed away leaving a vulnerable parent feeling more isolated.

Since the alliances which were formed at this point had a major impact on the development of events, there is a very strong argument to suggest that *agencies should consider how best to intervene strategically at the investigation stage in order to try to strengthen the longer-term support systems for the child.* It will not always be possible to influence the formation of key alliances, but at least the agencies could consider how to minimise the negative effects of their interventions.

The investigation stage was stressful for social workers, parents and children alike. For social workers the stress was somewhat reduced when and if they were able to form a positive alliance with the police officers with whom they worked. When this happened social workers could start to feel increasingly in control of events and this helped to relieve the anxiety of the investigation. In contrast, the stress for many parents and children continued at high levels and they often felt unable to affect the course of events. During this stage, decisions were taken which would profoundly influence the development of the case. The way the investigation was managed shaped the attitudes of parents and children and the alliances they formed or failed to form. By the end of the investigation, decisions and interventions had crystallised in ways which were likely to determine future child care outcomes.

Summary

1. During the investigation 23% of the children were protected by the alleged abuser leaving the household, 32% of children were removed from home and 45% remained in the family with the abuser present.

2. Action to get an abuser to leave the household was considerably more common in cases of sexual abuse than for the other categories of abuse or neglect. In spite of this, a considerable number of sexually abused children had to leave home at the investigation stage. It was rare for the child and the alleged perpetrator not to be separated in these cases. In contrast, after the investigation three-fifths of the children subject to physical abuse, neglect or emotional abuse continued to live with the parent or parents who were alleged to have abused or neglected them, whilst 28% were removed from their families.

3. Decisions for a child to be looked after outside of the parental home were affected by a number of factors which operated in combination. Children about whom there was a high degree of uncertainty and where the risks

were seen as unpredictable at the investigation stage were likely to be removed, unless legal advice made this course difficult to take. The presence of mental illness in a mother was also viewed as increasing the risks to a child. Because of the crisis nature of the agencies' involvement and the pressures to make 'safe' decisions, children were particularly vulnerable to removal during the investigation if they were new cases and therefore relatively unknown. It follows that similar mistreatment could lead in different cases to different decisions about removal.

4. Although the numbers were too small to draw definite conclusions, we did find that children were more often removed during joint investigations by police and social services than in cases where the investigation was conducted by a social worker alone.

5. Both parents and children felt swept along by the investigation without being consulted or, in some cases, informed about what was happening. It was often a time of crisis for them and many would have welcomed more contact with social workers.

6. The decisions and actions of the investigating professionals had a major impact on the alliances formed within families, which could have enduring consequences for the well-being of the children involved.

7. In the face of allegations of mistreatment, couples often formed a defensive alliance against outside agencies and difficulties in the family such as violence or drug addiction were not revealed. In addition, parents sometimes put pressure on children not to reveal anything about their home life to professionals, especially school staff.

8. Children who had been sexually abused often blamed themselves for the abuse. Those who had disclosed their abuse also felt responsible for the subsequent break-up of the family or threatened prosecution of the abuser. Children who had to leave home after disclosure were especially vulnerable. They had a great need for reassurance that they were not to blame for the abuse or its consequences for themselves and other family members. When the Crown Prosecution Service decided not to proceed with prosecution some alleged perpetrators of sexual abuse felt exonerated and publicly accused the children of having lied.

9. In cases of neglect and emotional abuse, parents often disputed the claims of agency workers that their children's circumstances were unsatisfactory.

10. The impact of the investigation was often to intensify pre-existing arrangements within families. Mothers with little self-confidence became more despondent, mothers who had most of the responsibility for child care took on even more and father figures frequently distanced themselves further from their families.

11. Investigations were stressful for social workers, parents and children alike. The way the investigations were managed shaped the attitudes of parents and children and the alliances which they formed or failed to form. By the end of the investigation decisions and interventions had crystallised which were likely to determine future child care outcomes.

Chapter 6

Conference initiation and process

A short time after the investigation and on average within three weeks of the referral date, a multi-disciplinary case conference was held. At this conference the information collected at the investigation was brought together and shared among representatives of various health and welfare agencies. The family's situation was discussed in detail and a decision about risk was made.

Not every case which had been officially investigated was brought to conference. A recent study has shown that 68 per cent of the cases which are subject to joint investigation are not taken any further (Gibbons *et al*, 1993). On the other hand, a third of the children whose names were on the conference agenda had never experienced joint investigation at all. As previously mentioned, the police had been heavily employed in cases of suspected sexual abuse and physical abuse, but they had seldom been called in to investigate cases of neglect.

Many of the families who were not formally investigated were already 'known to social services', and there were mounting worries about ill-health, accidents, lack of supervision, minor abusive incidents and emotional deprivation. Sometimes a conference was held before the birth of a second or subsequent child, when there had been concerns about the first child, or after a family with registered children had moved into the district. Just occasionally a conference was called without the parents' knowledge, for example if there was a physically violent man in the household or if there were suspicions of severe psychological disturbance such as Munchausen's Syndrome by Proxy. On these occasions the parents were not informed because it was considered too dangerous to alert them.

The initial case conference marked a critical phase in the construction of risk, and it was also concerned with the allocation of services. At the end of the conference some families had children placed on the register and others disappeared from sight; others still were offered social work help, or promised more coordinated services, or referred to treatment agencies such as child and family guidance, or simply marked out for informal surveillance. What happens to unregistered cases is another study – but there is enough information in our conference records to suggest that for these families too there was often some follow-up after the conferences (see chapter 10). A few children from these families were 'conferenced' at a later date, and on the second occasion they were sometimes registered.

Our main task in the research was to study the 44 registered cases which constituted the follow-up sample. But since we also have detailed information about the 120 case conferences which we attended in the first instance, it seems appropriate to draw on this larger group when necessary in order to present a fuller picture. The information which follows is therefore derived from an analysis of the case conference schedules which we completed on 120 initial conferences, together with a study of the official minutes and our own recorded notes and observations. Further qualitative data have been extracted from the interviews with social workers, parents or other carers and children, to which can be added five interviews conducted with conference chairs.

Conference task and functions

The initial case conference was overtly about the management of risk, but it also contributed to the management of professional anxiety. The conference itself could be regarded as a mechanism for defusing anxiety, since it spread the risks and helped to reduce uncertainty. There is an argument for saying that this function needs to be recognised and treated as legitimate.

> 'We believe it to be appropriate to accept this [the sharing and defusing of anxiety] as an explicit purpose, alongside others which are focused on the problems and needs of the family. In work so stressful, we should acknowledge the support functions of the conference for the workers' (Hallett and Stevenson, 1980).

At times this anxiety-reducing function was very apparent to us. The formality of the conference, and the routinisation of the procedures, had the effect of distancing the participants from the emotional impact of some of the distressing information which had emerged during the investigation. It therefore became more manageable.

In the course of one meeting the conference members usually moved through a predictable sequence of tasks, which were roughly as follows.

- Hearing allegations of abuse or neglect
- Receiving information about the allegations
- Sharing background information about the family
- Constructing a chronological picture of events
- Drawing oral portraits of individual family members
- Collecting together concerns
- Assessing risk to the index child and other children in the household
- Deciding whether to register the child or children
- Deciding on a key worker, if necessary
- Forming a child protection plan
- Considering possible legal action (often discussed further in another forum)
- Planning resources

- Allocating roles to various agencies for monitoring and treatment
- Sharing decisions with parents (usually at the end of the meeting)
- Arranging for follow-up and review.

The clear sense of satisfaction when routine tasks were accomplished was expressed by one chairperson as follows.

> *'Even though I can say at the beginning of the conference it's extremely unlikely that we're going to register this one, or that there is a question of risk, I often feel "That's a job well done now".'*

Menzies Lyth (1988) has catalogued the organisational benefits – and the dangers – of defensive psychological detachment in the face of extreme stress. Whilst the Kleinian basis of much of her analysis might not meet with general acceptance, her description of strategies to reduce anxiety in a London hospital can usefully be applied to social services departments. She argues that because decision-making arouses painful conflict, responsibility is avoided by the checking and counter-checking of procedures, by the displacement of responsibility upwards in the form of 'buck-passing' and when things go wrong by the displacement of responsibility downwards in the form of scapegoating. She noticed that when frontline workers were faced with stressful situations, such as nurses looking after dying patients, they dealt with their distress by relying on the ritual performance of tasks and that this pushed out more direct caring.

In child protection work the emphasis on procedures can be seen as a way of managing anxiety about risks to children, as well as anxiety about professional careers in the event of public censure. In the case conferences we attended, the classification of children as needing to be placed on the child protection register because there were current 'unresolved child protection issues' and a need for 'an interagency protection plan' (Home Office *et al.*, 1991) at times acquired a ritual significance. This was shown by the strict adherence to procedures, the refusal to allow procedures to be criticised or challenged (except by identifying gaps which needed to be filled), the occasional emergence of panic among practitioners when procedures appeared to have been breached, and the almost universal tendency to give registration priority over planning. At the close of a conference there was sometimes a feeling amongst professional participants that the 'unresolved child protection issues' had been resolved by the act of registration. At the same time the inter-agency protection plan, however brief and rudimentary, helped to symbolise the fact that the child's future had been made secure.

Many of the key social workers whom we interviewed were only too well aware that:

'a formal procedural framework is essential . . . but this can never be a substitute for individual skill and knowledge. In the final analysis, when the parent and child are talking alone with the worker, no amount of procedural guidance will guarantee that the right things are said and done' (Jones *et al.*, 1987).

However, registration fulfilled a variety of other functions. For many of the social workers interviewed, it was a source of satisfaction that registration might raise the status of the case and *make more resources available*. The conference had an important gate-keeping role; that is, it gave or withheld access to resources such as funding for day care which were in short supply. Registration could therefore be used as a lever to obtain resources, both on an individual level and at the level of setting local government budgets. Since registration automatically involved the agency in a greater output of social work time however, the perceived costs and benefits to the agency, as well as to the individual child or family, were sometimes evenly balanced. These considerations were in the background of many decisions, even though they were seldom made explicit.

In describing the actual process of the initial case conference, it is easy to assume that the decision to register a child was of paramount importance. It *was* of importance, both structurally and procedurally; but most of the social workers whom we interviewed confirmed our observation that the main value of the conference lay in *information-sharing*.

Strictly speaking, information about families was shared by the conference participants in order to arrive at a decision about the level of risk to a child; but when social workers were interviewed about the conferences they had attended, they mentioned a number of additional ways in which information-sharing could be valuable. For example, the conference could be used to alert other agencies to what had been happening in the family:

> *'The first thing, I think, is to make sure that all the agencies are aware of what has gone on, and for them to have all their antennae alerted and terribly sensitive.'*

By collecting together information, it enabled a comprehensive picture of the child's situation to be built up:

> *'I suppose it's information gathering; and that is very important, because I think sometimes everybody thinks they know all there is to know and there's an awful lot more to come to light.'*

Occasionally the conference was said to draw in specific pieces of missing information about the allegations of abuse or neglect:

> *'I knew there was a hearing problem; I had no idea that it was as bad as stated . . . so I was very pleased at him [the doctor] telling me that.'*

> *'What I found was interesting was that although I'd actually had quite a lot of information from the hospital, the police statements are usually a lot more informative, because they've actually got details written down – 'he said, she said' – and observed.'*

There was also information about the general family background:

> *'It was very helpful to have the background information from my colleagues in X [the neighbouring social services department].'*

If the conference was well chaired it enabled a more *integrated* picture of the risks to be formed:

> *'He [the coordinator] was very helpful in bringing it together.'*

At the same time social workers felt that it clarified the number of professionals involved in the case and their respective roles:

> *'It's to identify all the different workers with the family and what their role is.'*

> *'We used the conference for two purposes, one to clarify our own thinking and at the same time to let everybody know what the hell was going on in the family . . . The information was helpful in the fact that I have now found out who the health visitor is, who the doctor is and where she hangs out! And the fact that she does in fact go in there and is quite an active little lady.'*

> *'Everybody knew what everybody's position was. We didn't have doctors thinking, 'Why didn't social services do such and such and such and such?' Because we were actually saying, legally, we couldn't.'*

Sometimes the conference gave scope for the parent's view to be heard, although it was not used a great deal for this purpose. On the contrary, social workers sometimes hoped that parental attendance would add authority to their subsequent interventions by demonstrating to the parent the weight of professional opinion about the risks to the child. (One social worker said of registration: 'It was a decision of the whole conference, which they had to accept.') The meeting was a forum for professional discussion.

> *'I don't think there was anything in my mind I wanted it to achieve . . .*
> *The positives are in getting everyone together at one time in one room and talking.'*

These responses indicate that information was flowing both inwards and outwards from social services, at the initial case conference. When it flowed outwards, it was intended to act as a prophylactic against risk – because all relevant agencies would then 'have their antennae alerted and terribly sensitive' and would refer further concerns back to the responsible social worker. When it flowed inwards, the social services department had more information to use in working with the family, either inside or outside the child protection system. It was not simply information about the case which was helpful, however. There was also information about other agencies – how they worked and who the relevant personnel *were*. The act of liaison which brought a key professional to the conference might have spin-offs in terms of agency working in the future.

Some social workers were prepared to admit that their own work and judgements were under scrutiny, and that they felt on trial at case conferences. In some circumstances they felt that this was justifiable. One social worker said that conference attendance helped to keep her 'on her toes.' A few social workers felt able to use the conference actively to test out their own perceptions of risk, and to correct what they felt to be a lack of objectivity in their own judgements. These responses were characteristic of the more confident social workers, however, since other workers readily admitted that very little new or unexpected information had been presented at a particular meeting, and that very often conclusions had been mapped out in advance. Attendance at conferences was time-consuming for social workers as well as for other professionals, and this was seen as less justifiable when there was a clear-cut outcome which might have obviated the need for debate.

> '*In some ways I do find that the number of case conferences that we hold are a bit time-consuming – time-wasting, dare I say? Because it is fair to say that the conclusion, that the decisions are pretty well known before we actually go in.*'

However, this cost was balanced for professionals by the fact that the initial conference had a clear part to play in *spreading responsibility* for the decisions made. This was a form of insurance for social services and for the other agencies involved. The benefits of sharing responsibility accrued more to social services than to other agencies since the key social worker would carry the main responsibility for safeguarding the child. At the same time it did allow other agencies to off-load their anxieties onto social services. As one senior social worker put it:

> '*They express their own discipline's concerns and it is a protection for themselves . . . They say, "Well, we told somebody. We told the social services." They placate their own consciences, I think.*'

Since the members of social services departments felt 'in the hot seat' as far as child protection decisions were concerned, many of them found inter-agency conferences *protective*. One social worker said that she felt 'somewhat less exposed, having had that backing from different professionals'. For these workers the conference judgement was experienced as a form of endorsement.

The initial conference was, quite rightly, regarded as an important decision-making forum; but it should be remembered that it could make only two decisions – firstly the decision about whether or not a child should be registered, and secondly the decision about who should be the key worker. Everything else which the conference wanted to see achieved was classed as a recommendation. Belief in the powers of the conference, like belief in the validity of professional expertise, may be strengthened by the agencies' need for mutual support. The management of anxiety and the management of risk are linked.

Responsibility and blame in the early stages of the conference process

The conference was sometimes preceded by a lull in the action, as far as family members were concerned; but during the run-up to the conference there were three common developments which increased the parents' feelings of alienation or involvement, and which could increase or decrease the likelihood that the family and the agency would work together well at a later date. The first was *the continuity of 'framing' from earlier events* – that is, the extent to which the official view of the family was consolidated in a conference report.

Development of the official view

In response to the referral, and particularly during the investigation by police and social workers if there was one, recent events in the lives of selected families had been constructed in a way which made a later diagnosis of risk likely or unlikely. Assumptions had been formed about the attitudes of both abusing and non-abusing parents, and these assumptions could turn into self-fulfilling prophecies.

In a previously reported case where a 16-year-old girl had been sexually abused by her stepfather, the social worker who had been present at the investigation said:

> 'I personally was thinking in terms of care on the first day of the investigation, because I immediately had a sense that Mrs Drew was not going to support her children, and that turned out to be correct.'

The family's view of events was often extremely fluid. In the run-up to the conference parents, like the professionals, were trying to reduce uncertainty and anxiety. They were often trying to reconcile one view of events with another, and some parents were trying to devise an account of what happened which made sense to them as well as to everyone else. They had their own 'framing' within which the knowledge of recent events had to be fitted. The abusing and non-abusing parents and the children were trying to *explain* and *understand* what had or might have happened, to apportion blame and usually to present their family circumstances in a positive light. (It was interesting that in the aftermath of investigations there were very few accounts which suggested that there was *no* blame to be apportioned.) At the same time, whilst case conference participants had an interest in sharing information as widely as possible, family members were trying to keep control of the information and to prevent it from spreading in a damaging way beyond the family. This also meant that there were few people with whom family members discussed their concerns and anxieties, and the enforced secrecy could leave them feeling isolated and apprehensive.

Sometimes, during the pre-conference period, both official and non-official accounts of events would become hardened. The official report would be prepared for the conference without alteration; and since family members had formed an impression of what the professional opinions were, their own account of events would be firmed up or elaborated in an attempt to strengthen their defences. If the family closed ranks sufficiently tightly, their anxieties could be translated into blame which fell on the social services.

> '*I do blame social services, to a certain extent.*'

> '*I think we needed help a long time before Sandy got to that stage . . . That's where the social service falls down.*'

> '*Social services has their beak in.*'

Sensitive social workers were aware that the feelings of many family members, including the child, were raw in the aftermath of the investigation; but the family's experience of blame, guilt and anger was not (as so often in the official version) a side issue which needed to be worked with; it was actually part of the story. What needed to happen in the time between investigation and conference, and often did not happen, was that the social worker's understanding should move beyond a simple familiarity with events and circumstances – beyond the collection of 'evidence', in other words – to encompass the feelings experienced by the child and family. When this was done successfully the social worker's report to the conference had a unique contribution to make. More importantly still, it seemed the only way to lessen the feeling of worlds in collision, and to establish some common ground on which subsequent intervention might successfully take place.

The follow-up to protective action

The second determinant of progress during the pre-conference period was the way in which actions taken after the investigation were followed up. At the very least, there was a need for parents and children to be kept closely in touch – otherwise parents felt marginalised, their parental responsibility seemed to be undermined, and they worried that important decisions were being taken at meetings to which they were not invited. Supportive visiting might therefore be essential to the parent's method of managing anxiety. However, at the same time it might be essential to the worker's method of anxiety-management to avoid it. One mother said:

> *'Before the conference I felt a bit as if, you know, you were out of the way and you'd been forgotten about. I mean she was good, she phoned quite a few times; but I think I would have rather seen her and let her explain things more and known more of what was going on – because it seems as if they go to a lot of meetings and things are discussed a lot and you're not involved in it.'*

As at the investigation, it was not unusual for non-abusing mothers to feel that their needs were overlooked. One said that she felt 'totally lost' and another said that she had been 'dropped' after her daughter's disclosures.

> *'There was nothing there. There was no support.'*

> *'I felt very much on the outside. It might have been the next-door neighbour's son for all they care. There's so much going on at the child's end, but you're left out in the cold, aren't you?'*

Sometimes more than a routine 'keeping in touch' was required. Since the investigation had often been experienced as a crisis, there was a need for therapeutic 'crisis intervention'. Generally though, social work intervention of any kind, apart from the immediate protection of the child, was postponed until after the conference so that it might be carried out in accordance with the child protection plan. Consequently *the parents' needs were ignored at a time when they were most acute, and when the situation was fluid and open to change.*

Well-established techniques of crisis intervention require that there is intense input to the family in the early stages of a crisis, and also that the burden of responsibility should be eased when the parent is under severe pressure. If the parents were ignored during the pre-conference period there was clearly no therapeutic input at all; and if the child was removed from the home as a protective measure this was very seldom seen as supportive by parents, who felt that they had been defined as irresponsible and dangerous rather than as people who needed temporary help. The attempt to engage parents at a later date was more successful if the placement of the child had been presented in a positive light, either as a cooling-off period or as a 'breathing space' during which new plans could be considered.

It was of course understandable if the social worker failed to spend much time with the parents, since the period immediately before the conference was usually full of activity and it was often very short. The *Working Together* guidelines stipulate that 'all initial conferences should normally take place within eight working days of referral except where there are particular reasons for delay' (Home Office *et al.*, 1991). Because of the need for extended assessment, this time limit was often exceeded. A somewhat longer time limit would be more realistic.

In some cases frequent visits to the family were necessary to enable the social worker to complete a family assessment, and parents who had felt neglected during the early part of the investigation could suddenly find themselves the focus of attention. Increased visiting was not always welcome, however, if it was simply a reflection of the social worker's desire to gather information for the conference. Where the parent was seeking help and the worker was merely seeking information, they were clearly talking past each other; but the parents who were worst off were those who felt abandoned by the workers and also by significant members of their own family. After the initial experience of loss, when the abuse became known and either the child or the abuser might be removed from the family, there followed in many cases a secondary deprivation when other close family members or friends came to hear of the events and reacted with anger or disapproval. It was easy for social workers to overlook the effects of these multiple experiences of rejection, and to attribute the parent's feelings of blame or guilt to a source known to them.

For example, one social worker said of a woman who had just experienced childbirth and whose child was registered:

> 'She picked up a lot of negative feelings from the hospital staff, which made her feel incredibly guilty.'

But the parent in the same case said:

> 'It's my family, if anyone, that's turned against me – my Mum's side of the family.'

Where a member of the immediate family had reported the abuse to social services, or had given evidence against the parent, the effect on key family members could be divisive. For example, in more than one case where the mother had been in care as a child, the maternal grandmother had given evidence against her daughter when she was questioned by the joint investigation team and thereby hastened the child's progress into care. This 'informing' was not necessarily done out of malice or the reworking of old animosities but out of a genuine desire to see that the child was well looked after, although there could also be undercurrents of self-protection on the part of the grandparent. Nevertheless, the effect on the parent was usually extremely demoralising, and the situation was worsened still further if the worker chose the maternal grandmother as the point of contact with the family because she seemed to be more reliable than the parent.

Sometimes, social workers were very uncertain what to do in the aftermath of the investigation, especially if the abuser had been excluded only temporarily from the household. They waited for the conference judgement in the hope that it would give them a stronger rationale for action. One social worker said that in the period before the conference she discussed a difficult case of sexual abuse with her fellow social workers, her team leader, the area officer and a senior practitioner, in addition to talking to the police and the health visitor. In spite of all the help which was available, however, she was clear that she needed more and better consultancy.

> *'I think with sexual abuse cases, I still feel very much that I'm out on a limb. It's something that I feel that I've got **some** knowledge of – probably more than some social workers have come with – that sort of understanding of the **effects** of sexual abuse; but even so I'm still not sure what is the best line of action, course of action to take where sexual abuse has occurred.'*

It is interesting to note that the mother of the sexually abused girl in this case used exactly the same phrase 'out on a limb' to describe her own feelings during this pre-conference time.

> *'I felt out on a limb, to be honest. Because it all happened on a Friday. And then Saturday morning I rang the police station up and they said he'd been allowed on bail and they explained the conditions of his bail. I didn't have any contact with a social worker over that weekend, and I felt really vulnerable and frightened.'*

The worker's lack of confidence, and the lack of support for the mother, may well be connected. Child sexual abuse created feelings of loneliness and anxiety in worker and parent alike.

The approach to the conference

Another determinant of progress during the pre-conference period was *the way in which the conference was presented to the parent figures*. The social worker usually went to see the family and, unless there were strong reasons against it, invited parents to the conference. The person who received the invitation and responded to it was usually the mother. Thirty-six out of the 120 conferences which we observed were attended by mothers only, 18 by both parents, and six by fathers only.

Since the number of mothers attending conferences on their own exceeds the number of single mothers in the whole study, it is obvious that factors other than family composition were at work. Either social workers invited both parents and only the mother attended, or else social workers chose the mother as someone with whom they wished to work. In both of these situations the result was the same. The mother was singled out as the person who took responsibility for the child.

In cases of sexual abuse the abuser was usually excluded from the conference. In some cases the child had parents who were divorced or separated but who were both still actively involved. In cases such as these it was usual for only the parent who looked after the child to be invited, even though there was no reason for the other to be excluded.

In theory the act of inviting parents to the conference gave them the opportunity to ask questions; but mothers who were still bemused by the investigation asked very little and harboured misunderstandings of what the conference was about. It was not unusual for a mother to fear that care proceedings were on the agenda, even in a case of minor abuse or neglect. One mother whose children were seen by professionals as slightly neglected reacted to the invitation as follows:

> 'I took two or three days to think about it, and I just couldn't go. I'd been so humiliated by all of this that I just don't think I could have sat in a room full of people listening to them put me down . . . I think more than anything I was just frightened that they were going to take the children away from me. That was all that was in my mind.'

Some social workers responded with reassurance, and encouraged the parent to attend. In the above example, the mother's comment about the worker was, 'He said that there was no need to worry like that . . . He's been really good. He's talked to me.' In other cases the social worker offered no encouragement to attend, or invited parents at such a late stage that they had no time to make arrangements for work or transport or child care. Alternatively the parents were notified of the conference by post, and this was seen as one more manifestation of bureaucracy.

> 'I **suppose** I was invited. I've had quite a few things sent from social services.'

In cases such as these there was often a difficult relationship between worker and parents and a tacit belief that the conference would go better if family members were excluded. Some parents were hostile and unwilling to attend, either because they saw it as a pointless exercise or because they had been put off by previous bad experiences of meetings held by social services. Yet paradoxically these were often the people whose views were least well known, and whose presence would have been valuable because they were likely to be hostile to intervention after the conference.

In 20 per cent of the follow-up sample no invitation was issued to family members at all. The reasons given by the social workers for this omission were sometimes intended to protect the conference. They argued, for example, that the parents' behaviour was likely to disrupt the meeting, that their presence might have inhibited the professionals, or that the main purpose of the meeting might have been diverted because of a shift of focus to the parents' needs. In one case the parent was physically unable to attend because she was in hospital. But in the majority of cases where no invitation was issued, the social workers justified this as being in the *parents' interests*. They said that the parents would have found the conference stressful or upsetting, that they would have been intimidated by a room full of strange people, or that they would not have understood what was going on. As can be seen from the responses in chapter 7, these statements reflect quite accurately the experience of many parents who *did* attend – but the social workers were mistaken in thinking that parents and other family members would not have wanted to attend in spite of it.

These findings about parents' desire be involved in conferences are encouraging, and they are supported by research on parental participation such as that carried out by Thoburn and her colleagues (1993). Nevertheless families are not homogeneous, and in child abuse cases the parents cannot be treated as a single entity. Whether or not the mother was responsible for the abuse, she was usually the person who took responsibility for the child and mediated between her husband and the outside world.

Power and influence

Throughout the pre-conference period and in the conference itself, the lead role was taken by social services. Members of the social services department decided whether or not to hold a conference, chaired it, and strongly influenced the registration decision.

The influence of the chairperson was apparent in some cases long before the conference. From the first moment of referral the more proactive chairs busied themselves with contacting other people, both inside and outside the agency. According to their own accounts they were gathering information and checking its accuracy, partly to satisfy themselves that a conference was required, partly to maintain public relations and if necessary to negotiate the attendance of key professionals at the conference, and partly to arm them-selves before a potentially difficult meeting. One chairperson said:

*'I prefer to have quite a bit of discussion before the conference. I prefer to take the phone calls myself and for them not to go through the secretary. And if they **have** gone through the secretary, then they've usually taken down the basic details and I would actually ring back and discuss.'*

The business at all the conferences we attended was conducted in a broadly similar fashion, except that one authority had its conferences chaired by independent coordinators while the other used area managers. The two systems produced very similar registration rates of 61 per cent and 60 per cent respectively; but conferences in the first county tended to be more orderly and to have a clearer agenda. On the other hand, the chairperson was most often mentioned by social workers as being influential in decision-making when he or she was also a line manager, usually the area officer to whom they were accountable. Independent coordinators had considerable power in the meeting and they also had a great range of skills, but since they had no direct responsibility for the work of social workers, it was hardly surprising if they were able to exert less influence over decisions in social work practice.

In addition to administrative skills, the independent coordinators often had considerable expertise, for example in family therapy or child sexual abuse. They performed a support role for social workers, as well as helping to maintain standards, and their contribution was highly valued. Within the agency, however, their decision-making could be dominated by line managers if they did not possess, both as individuals and as a group, considerable negotiating skill. One coordinator complained that although she was heavily involved in child protection work she had no direct influence over the trickiest decision of all – the decision about whether, in a case of abuse or neglect, the child should be removed from the home. In the face of dilemmas such as these, the decision to 'conference' a child may seem relatively unimportant; but registration can be one step on the ladder towards care, as some parents were only too well aware and, as we shall see, the way in which the case was structured and interpreted at the initial case conference could influence events for some time to come.

The conduct of the conference

Our observations support the notion that the conference was mainly advisory rather than executive in its functions (Hallett and Stevenson, 1980). Although members of other agencies could offer advice and opinions, the social services department had ultimate responsibility for any work attempted.

In view of the fact that 'abuse' and 'neglect' are socially constructed concepts, it was interesting to find that there was very little expression of overt disagreement at the 120 conferences we attended (see also Corby, 1987). The meetings did manage to incorporate known mavericks by assigning to them the role of 'devil's advocate'. (The senior clinical medical officer performed this role quite usefully in one authority.) However, in only 10 per cent of the 120 conferences were disagreements aired by professionals about whether abuse or neglect had occurred. Disagreement about future risks to the child was evident in only 17 per cent of cases, and there was similarly little dispute about whether registration was advisable (15%). Interestingly, dissent was expressed slightly more often (in 31% of cases) when the issues were concerned with procedures – for example the way in which professional agencies had been consulted or the investigation had been conducted.

In view of the difficulties surrounding the assessment process and the difficulty of establishing thresholds of acceptable and unacceptable risks, it did seem surprising that the registration decision was made with such a minimum of conflict. What contributed to this situation?

Corby (1987), in his analysis of the child protection system, comments that:

> 'It was rare to observe open conflict at case conferences and most decisions were reached with apparent consensus.'

In explanation he cites the assumption that there is agreement over norms, an assumption which, he says, has a powerful cohesive effect. He also mentions the reluctance of 'outside' agencies to challenge the accepted wisdom of social services, and he lists two other factors which help to concentrate the minds of participants – first of all the risk to professionals from child abuse work, and secondly the time limit on the decision-making process. In general he regarded it as a disadvantage that there was this consensus, since he assumed that individual opinions were not being expressed.

Consensus could conceivably be regarded as an advantage, since it helped the smooth running of the conference; and it could be argued that the lessons of the various *Working Together* documents have been learnt. Regular attendance at conferences certainly contributed to the development of group norms, as we ourselves discovered. (At times we had to detach ourselves fairly firmly from the group in order to make a research judgement.) However, it was a disadvantage if important views were suppressed. In 18 per cent of cases we judged that important contributions regarding the child or the presence of risk were ignored or dismissed, and most of these contributions came from agencies outside social services.

Some pressures towards agreement undoubtedly came from a mixture of professional attitudes and group processes. For example, it was customary to respect the autonomy of the various agencies by not criticising their work or judgements. Partly this stemmed from the fact that every agency had a different experience of the family. Partly it was a question of professional etiquette. Unfortunately it also meant that when cases were 'stuck' because of unsatisfactory interventions in the family, the conference added little towards solving the problems. This was evident on a number of occasions.

The best point at which to influence the proceedings was not of course in the final stages but during the presentation of *information*. At times the accumulation of concerns resembled a game of dominoes, in which each piece matched the one before it and at the same time introduced a new idea. By presenting evidence strongly, either in a positive or in a negative way, a determined agency representative could substantially alter the direction of the discussion.

The person who seemed to us to have most influence in actually shaping the final decision was the chair, in 55 per cent of cases, and the next most influential person was the team leader. It seems likely, therefore, that *a crucial influence in maintaining the no-conflict norm was the lead-role of social services*. However, we must remember that these are not wholly or even mainly process issues. High registration rates were associated with cases of severe abuse and circumstances in which either the child or the abuser had been removed from the household. In many such cases the issues were fairly clear-cut and there would have been general agreement for registration. Corby himself admits that 'in the more problematic grey areas there were more signs of conflict, albeit of a curtailed rather than full-blown form.'

The power of information

The fear of uncertainty, of incomplete information, of not having *control* of information, was present in what many social workers and coordinators said. Our observation of conferences also suggested that when new or unexpected information was introduced in the meeting it was not always welcomed. There was a distinct feeling that it should have been known in advance – that someone should have done more work in order to uncover it. The likely reasons were to do with professional pride (since information-gathering is considered fundamental to a good assessment), with the practicalities of running conferences (since the business must be got through smoothly and in a reasonable time), and with the delicate balance of inter-agency relationships. Any injection of new or unexpected information at the decision-making stage could generate conflict; and if the conflict was severe enough it could not only disrupt the meeting but threaten the foundations of the social network in which inter-agency work was grounded. The utility-value of maintaining this network is considerable and it is important for other cases that it should be maintained (Hallett and Birchall, 1992).

Where extensive liaison work and discussion were carried out before the conference, the meetings did tend to run more smoothly, and professionals who were approached directly by the coordinators were sometimes per-suaded to come to the conference when they might otherwise have stayed away. However, the major disadvantage was that in many cases the parents felt that the result of the conference was a *fait accompli*. As one mother put it :

> *'My feeling was that they'd already decided what they were going to do when we got into that room. And it didn't matter what we said; it would not have altered the decision – which it didn't.'*

Statements such as these support the views of Vernon and Fruin (1986), who maintained that case conferences were not truly decision-making fora but 'instruments which the social worker might use in the implementation of an overall plan or decision that had already been agreed'.

Our interviews certainly suggested that there were strategic reasons for holding conferences, and strategic ways of using conference decisions, especially when the child was likely to enter care. But at the same time the social workers we interviewed had a strong fear of unpredictability, which not only threatened the child by creating an unsafe environment but threatened the professional – in an area in which he or she was extremely vulnerable – by undermining judgements and lowering self-confidence. In the interests of the management of anxiety, as well as the management of risk, this element of unpredictability had to be controlled.

Summary

1. Out of the 120 families whose children were discussed at initial case conferences in the study, approximately two-thirds had just experienced joint investigation by social workers and police. In most of these cases the concerns were about physical or sexual abuse. The other third had not been subjected to joint investigation. They were mainly known to social services, and the concerns were about long-running neglect.

2. The initial case conference served a number of functions, both official and unofficial. Besides making it possible for the child's situation to be examined in an inter-agency context, it acted as a gateway to the official child protection system. It ensured that children who were classified as being 'at risk' would be subject to regular monitoring and review. Some social workers hoped that registration would raise the status of the case and make more resources available. For most workers, however, the main function of the conference was simply information-sharing.

3. Information flowed both inwards to and outwards from social services, at the initial conference. Other agency members contributed material for the assessment, and they also became alerted to concerns about the child. The fact that the case conference made the private situation of the family more public was a source of anxiety for many parents.

4. The reduction of professional anxiety was an important function of the conferences; but it could lead to a preoccupation with procedures and a feeling that going through the formality of registering children would automatically lead to appropriate interventions to reduce risk. In fact the time devoted at the conference to discussion of the child protection plan, which was crucial to risk reduction, was very short.

5. The pre-conference period was a time of uncertainty and apprehension for parents. There was an understandable desire on the part of social workers to wait for the decisions of the conference before any real 'work' was attempted; but the quality of later work could be affected by the input to the family at this time of crisis. Opportunities to establish common ground for later intervention could easily be missed because of the pressures on social workers to obtain a full assessment for the conference.

6. It appeared that the better the support offered to social workers from colleagues and supervisors, the more able they were to offer help to family members. The ways in which parents were informed about and invited to the conferences also influenced their attitudes and the quality of their participation.

7. One important aspect of the conference was that it helped to cement relationships between agencies. Little overt disagreement was expressed about risks or registration, and there was a strong prohibition against any criticism of professional performance. As a result, some important dissenting information was not utilised, and deficiencies in the current handling of ongoing cases were occasionally glossed over.

8. The conference helped to defuse anxiety by spreading responsibility for the decisions made. It provided a form of insurance cover, which many social workers experienced as protective even though they were aware that their own work was under scrutiny. In spite of the strong ethos of collaboration which accompanied inter-agency working, however, the bulk of the power and responsibility for decision-making still rested with social services.

Chapter 7

Problems of participation

"We've lost the paediatrician, unfortunately, but we've gained the parent." This remark was made by a disappointed chairperson at a conference where the paediatrician walked out after being informed that the mother had arrived. The hospital doctor was not prepared to talk in the parent's presence. The incident was unusual; but it illustrates how hard the conference chairs sometimes had to struggle to balance costs and benefits in participation.

The meetings we attended were well organised and they were also strongly grounded in expectations of mutual cooperation. Nevertheless the formal links between agencies were sometimes exceedingly tenuous, and there was occasionally a feeling that any slight wave of conflict might be enough to 'rock the boat'. The increasing participation of parents has to be seen in that context.

The system we witnessed falls somewhere in between the two possibilities outlined by Blom-Cooper in the Carlile Report (London Borough of Greenwich, 1987), although it appears to be nearer to the second than to the first. These possibilities were, firstly, that case conferences would remain the 'crucible of the system' and that everyone involved in the case would be answerable to a single controlling authority. (We found this to be reflected not in the formal structure but in the informal clustering of agencies under the aegis of social services.) The second possibility was for the overall management of the system to be shared, by way of a multi-disciplinary structure which left people accountable within their own hierarchies. This has the advantage of spreading what Blom-Cooper calls 'an awesome responsibility', but it has certain disadvantages which he outlines as follows:

> 'It has the disadvantage of inducing ambiguity in accountability and leaves the door open for confusion, conflict and inter-agency hostility to enter if something goes wrong. It has the disadvantage, given the number of agencies involved, of creating a body with many heads, and would need all agencies to be equal in authority while some, in reality, might reckon that he who shares honey with the bear has the least part of it.'

In an effort to find out what it was like to 'share honey with the bear' we charted the attendance of both agency and family representatives at the 120 conferences which we attended, and we also recorded the degree of influence which they appeared to exercise in the decision-making process.

The professional participants

Clearly no agency could hope to influence the proceedings successfully unless a representative attended the conference. Sometimes a letter or a report was sent, and this was useful; but written material could be regarded as unsatisfactory if it was incapable of being challenged or discussed with the person who wrote it. The way in which risk assessment was constructed in the conference therefore depended heavily on the number of people attending and the agencies from which they came.

Some professionals failed to attend because they had not been invited; but their attendance rate depended only partly on the issuing of invitations. A few key participants, for example probation officers, were regularly invited but rarely came. Others, such as paediatricians, were rarely invited but more likely to come when they *were* invited. Another issue is that people varied in the extent of their influence over the proceedings. Although probation officers failed to attend 81 conferences to which they were invited, their attendance at 11 conferences was associated with a registration rate of 82 per cent. GPs also failed to attend 81 conferences to which they were invited; but their attendance at 30 conferences was associated with a registration rate of 50 per cent. Clearly, either the probation officers brought with them more damaging information than the GPs, or else they were successful in selecting the conferences which really justified their attendance.

The four key agencies which were usually represented at case conferences were health, education, police and social services. One child protection coordinator said that she would refuse to continue with an initial or de-registration conference if fewer than three of these services were represented, or if the representative of a key agency was missing. (For example, there needed to be some representative from the health service if the child was under five.) There was therefore a solid core of regular attenders, to whom others were added if it seemed appropriate to invite them.

Table 10 gives a list of the positions held by the main participants at the 120 case conferences, together with the number and percentage of conferences which these people attended.

Social services

The most frequent attenders at conferences in our study were members of the social services department. Basic grade social workers, who were the people most likely to be appointed as key workers, attended nearly all of the conferences, and since there were often other colleagues who had some involvement with the family at that time or previously, there could be more than one social worker or senior practitioner present.

Table 10   **Attendance at Initial Case Conferences**

Personnel Excluding Chair	Number of conferences attended (N = 120)	Percentage of all conferences attended
Field social workers	113	94
Police officers	100	83
Social work team leaders and supervisors	95	79
Health visitors	71	59
Parents	71	59
Senior health visitors or community nursing managers	52	43
Infant or junior school heads or deputy heads	39	33
Local authority legal officers	33	28
General practitioners	30	25
Secondary school heads or deputy heads	27	23
Community medical officers	27	23
Secondary school teachers	24	20
School nurses	24	20
Infant or junior school teachers	19	16
Paediatricians	15	13
NSPCC officers	14	12
School social workers or educational welfare officers	13	11
Probation officers	11	9
Children	11	9
Residential social workers	9	8
Hospital social workers	9	8
Foster parents	7	6
Hospital doctors apart from paediatricians	7	6
Home helps or family aides	4	3
Representatives of voluntary organisations	4	3
Child guidance social workers	3	3
Home care organisers	3	3
School doctors	2	2
Social services area managers	2	2
School managers	2	2
Child psychiatrists	2	2
Educational psychologists	2	2
Day nursery staff	1	1
Playgroup leaders	1	1
Relief carers	1	1

In 56% of conferences out of the 120 studied, there was one social worker present. In a further 29% of conferences there were two social workers; and in 9% of conferences there were three or more. In addition to this there were team leaders (66% of conferences), senior practitioners or supervisors who were not team leaders (13%), and in two conferences divisional managers or assistant managers attended in a non-chairing role.

The tally of social services personnel was increased still further if we consider other members of the organisation, such as legal officers (28% of conferences) and ancillary staff. Home care organisers appeared relatively rarely (3 times), and so did home helps or family aides (4 times). This finding is surprising in view of the importance given to family support in the recommendations. However, foster parents appeared on seven occasions, (in five of which they came as a couple), and residential staff attended nine conferences, including three where there was a representation of two or more residential workers. Child guidance social workers attended on only three occasions.

As previously mentioned, the person who was most prominent in making decisions about registration was the chair. Apart from the chair, social work team leaders were the people most likely to shape the final decision. They were the most influential participants in 19 conferences (16%) and the second most influential in another 13 (11%). Field social workers appeared to be most influential in only seven conferences, although they were second most influential in twenty-one. The more senior the social work contingent, in general, the higher the associated registration rate.

Health

The health professionals who attended most conferences were the health visitors. Seventy-one conferences (59% of the total) had health visitor representation, and at four conferences there were two or more workers present. Community nursing officers or senior health visitors were present at 52 conferences (43%); but their main aim appeared to be to supervise the health visitors and they sometimes took little part in the discussion. In as many as 22 meetings these senior health workers said nothing at all.

Health visitors attended fewer conferences than police or social workers because their involvement was usually confined to cases in which there were pre-school children. In relation to cases in which they *were* involved, however, their rate of attendance was very high. There were 41 cases in which the index child – the focus of most concern for the conference – was under five years old. In most other cases the main concerns were about school-age children; but the presence of other pre-school children in the family ensured that the health visitor was a regular caller. She was therefore in a good position to contribute information about the *mother*, in addition to assessing any risk to the younger children.

By comparison with the health visitors, GPs attended very few conferences. They were present at 30 out of the 111 to which they were invited, or
25 per cent of the total. Local authority B had a higher proportion of
conferences attended by GPs than local authority A, and the GPs who
attended in local authority B appeared to be more active participants than
their counterparts in the other county. The second authority also had a
greater proportion of conferences attended by paediatricians and by hospital
doctors. On the other hand, local authority A had a higher conference
attendance from school nurses and community medical officers. These
findings suggest that there are local traditions of inter-agency working, and
local patterns of involvement in child protection work, which affect the
liaison between health professionals and social services.

In both counties there was very little involvement of child and adult
psychiatrists, or clinical and educational psychologists, in spite of the fact that
in some cases reports from these professionals might have contributed
substantially to the conference assessment. The reason was probably that they
were not routinely involved with the family. On the other hand, the agencies
which did not send a representative to the conference were not usually
prominent in *treatment*, and if someone from these agencies had been present
at the conference it might have been easier to involve them at a later stage.

Police

Police representatives were always invited to conferences, and they attended
fairly regularly (83% of the total). Seventy-seven conferences in the study
were attended by one police officer, 20 conferences by two officers, and three
conferences by three. The rate of attendance was roughly the same in both
counties.

In spite of the high rate of attendance, it seemed that in many cases the
police presence was a matter of routine and it had no dramatic effect on the
outcome. Since they had been involved in joint investigations, they did at
times present convincing evidence of abuse; but since many of these cases
involved sexual abuse and the abuser was out of the household, the cases did
not always end in registration.

The police presence was associated with the average rate of registration for
all conferences (61%). This was much lower than the corresponding rate for
probation officers, whose attendance was purposeful and selective. In cases
where the police were influential participants the registration rate was
actually below average. On this evidence, the police were not particularly
active in seeking registration – and this accords with our observation that in
many cases they were happy to leave the decision to social services.

Education

The attendance of teaching staff was quite high in relation to the number of school-age children, and it is interesting to note that where clear evidence of abuse was presented by school personnel, there was a registration rate of 84 per cent. This was a highly significant association. As mentioned in our historical chapter, the development of compulsory education and of a school health service ensured that the condition of children was open to scrutiny. School staff in our study were in close touch with some of the children – probably much more so than the members of any other agency – and they also regarded themselves as being *in loco parentis*. In the large sample of case conferences, schools provided the second most common agency to which child protection concerns were reported (after social services departments and before the police). They made a very significant contribution to the construction of risk.

A noticeable feature of many conferences was the size of the schools' contingent – especially if there was more than one school-age child in the family. The representatives came from infant, junior and secondary schools, and they included class teachers, year group tutors, other members of staff with pastoral care, headteachers, and deputy heads. Occasionally there were educational social workers and school doctors or nurses.

The main educational representatives who attended were usually school personnel of senior status, for example heads or deputy heads. Their evidence was always treated with respect, and the registration rate rose in their presence.

Other professional participants

The number of conferences attended by professionals other than members of these four agencies was much smaller, and in general the representatives had less influence. This reflects both the lower number of participants and, in some cases, the level of seniority of staff who attended. The main exception to this was the NSPCC. Representatives from the NSPCC attended 14 conferences, and their presence was associated with a fairly high registration rate of 71 per cent.

Workers from voluntary organisations apart from the NSPCC attended in only four cases. Childminders were never present. One conference was attended by a playgroup leader, and another by a worker from a day nursery. None of these people was particularly influential; but in a few cases foster parents had some influence.

One interesting feature of the case conference data was the association between the number of participants at meetings and the rate of registration. *The higher the number of professionals who attended, the higher the rate of registration, regardless of the composition of the group.* The number of people attending acted as a barometer of professional concern; but when more people were involved in the decision-making process, it is possible that this in itself contributed to a greater likelihood of registration, firstly because it increased the build-up of negative information, secondly because a high attendance generated an atmosphere of heightened concern, and thirdly because responsibility for the decision was shared among a greater number of people. From this point of view the pre-conference telephoning of the coordinator – if it was successful in engaging a greater number of participants – represented a possible escalation of concerns which could have an effect on the outcome.

Parents and other family members

In the case conference study as a whole, parents or other family members were present at 71 out of 120 conferences (59%). As we have already noted, 36 out of 120 conferences (30%) were attended by mothers only. Another 18 conferences (15%) were attended by both parents, and a further four conferences were attended by mothers and stepfathers. Fathers on their own were present at six conferences, and fathers with stepmothers appeared on two occasions. Other combinations of adult family members, including some grandparents, made rare appearances; but the total number of conferences attended by these mixed family groups was only five.

Children were present at 11 conferences. Usually they were young children who could not be left at home. We witnessed very little real participation by children. However, our interviews with older children showed that some wanted to be invited to attend whilst others would not have wanted to go if an invitation had been offered. At 41% of conferences there was no family representative present.

Participation by parents and other family members did appear to be associated with a slightly reduced rate of registration, although the difference was not statistically significant. More importantly, the experience of parents and other family members who attended was clearly of a different order from the experience of other participants. There seemed to be an expectation not that parents would influence the conference judgement *but that they would be influenced by it.*

What we witnessed at conferences could scarcely be described as 'user involvement'. Parental participation was certainly not 'consumerist' (con-cerned with the choice or provision of services) and only occasionally was it 'democratic' (concerned with fairness in decision-making) (see Croft and Beresford, 1992). However, the focus of each conference was naturally on the protection of the child and the *Working Together* guidelines at the time of the study were that parents' views 'should be sought and taken into account, although engaging them in assessment and planning does not mean a total sharing of the agency's responsibility for decision-making.' (Department of Health and Social Security, 1988).

A more complicated picture was obtained when we disaggregated the family. Since most families were represented at the conference by mothers, and in many cases by non-abusing mothers, it appeared that male abusers were underinvolved in the decision-making process. In terms of the accurate diagnosis of risk this could be a considerable disadvantage. An additional problem is that when moves are made towards more contractual working, we need to consider with whom the agreement needs to be made.

The experience of parental participation

Most of the social workers whom we interviewed had positive feelings about the conference. By contrast, many of the parents who attended the initial case conference reported to us that they felt disadvantaged as soon as they entered the room. Usually the other participants were already seated and brief introductions did nothing to make family members feel at ease, since they were clearly in a congregation of powerful strangers.

> 'You walk in and it's formal straight away. I mean, fair enough, everybody introduces themselves; but you just don't listen. I mean I couldn't tell you who was there now.'

> 'I saw all those faces sort of look at me as I walked in the door, and I just got really frightened. I don't even remember half the names of those people, or what authorities they came from.'

Parents were often uncertain why various people had been invited. Sometimes the parents who attended recognised some of the participants; but this was not necessarily helpful if they were unprepared for their presence and suddenly discovered that they knew about the allegations of abuse or neglect. It was particularly damaging if the parent wished to maintain a previous good image or to check the spread of information from the conference. We are reminded of Goffman's (1963) description of the stigmatised person's need to control information which has a bearing on his or her personal identity. The unexpected appearance of a respected GP or local headmaster could seriously upset family members and create fears that the concerns would soon be 'all over the district'.

It was very common for parents to feel threatened by the police presence and to say that they had not been informed about it. Out of the sample who were subsequently interviewed by us, there were 25 lone parents or parenting couples who had attended the conference. Five parents in this group complained that they had not known the police would be there – and one of these parents expressed surprise at finding police and social services 'on the same side'. Two people objected strongly to the presence of the school headmaster, and one man said he was surprised to discover that the army was represented. There were comments about absences as well. For example, one mother said that she wished her doctor and the 'school psychiatrist' had been there, and the implication was that they would have defended her. Regardless of the composition of the group, however, parents often felt that there were simply *too many people*.

> 'We went down there and, you know, didn't just expect all them bodies down there.'

> 'I just thought there was a lot of unnecessary people there that didn't really need to be there.'

Understandably, parents felt that there should be a clear reason for each participant's attendance. If this reason was not immediately obvious, they feared that some people might have come out of idle curiosity.

> 'The police and social worker had to be there; but an awful lot of people were there purely as spectators. They didn't know us.'

The comment, 'They didn't know us' (or its equivalent) was quite often given as a reason why certain participants should have been excluded, and it was usually linked with a lack of understanding of how bureaucratic-administrative processes operate. In many conferences the majority of participants were there representing an agency such as probation, or else supervising the workers who had intimate knowledge of the family. It was not unusual for the parent to accept the presence of the frontline worker (for example the health visitor or the social worker) and to feel threatened by the presence of unknown people who clearly had senior status. As one parent put it, 'I don't see why the head man [meaning the team leader] had to be there'.

In many cases, of course, the supervisors had absorbed the concerns relayed by frontline workers and were sympathetic to the parent. However, the lack of previous contact, and the fact that they did not speak in the parent's presence, contributed to a feeling of social distance which was extremely threatening – especially when combined with a notion that the senior person had indeterminate power. For these reasons, our findings support the *Working Together* guidelines that 'for reasons of both efficiency and confidentiality, the number of people involved in a conference should be limited to those who need to know and to those who have a contribution to make' (Home Office *et al.*, 1991).

The expression of parents' views
In general the range and distribution of attitudes expressed by social workers in interviews seem to support the findings of Thoburn and her colleagues, that most social workers agree strongly with arguments for participation

which are based on beliefs about client rights or improved effectiveness in social work. To a lesser extent they also subscribe to the notion that participation will be therapeutic for the parent (Thoburn *et al.*, 1993). Most social workers saw parental attendance at conferences as part of a general philosophy of participatory practice, even though they admitted that the ideals were sometimes difficult to achieve. (Thoburn and her colleagues found that although 77 per cent of social workers were strongly in favour of the principle of participation, only 31 per cent could strongly agree that they had succeeded in being participatory in practice.)

There were certainly times when the parents' views were well expressed, but since the parents' role in the group was reactive, they often did little except answer specific questions. The bulk of the information supplied to the conference came from professional reports and records. As in other participatory settings, such as the children's hearings in Scotland (Martin *et al.*, 1981), when information was made available to participants before the conference it ensured that conference members were well briefed. The reverse side of this coin was that some participants could have gone to the conference with ready-formed views. We need at least to bear in mind the possibility that some of this accumulated information may be false, that parents who are anxious or intimidated may admit to problems which do not in fact exist, and that even if it is factually sound and reasonably complete, the professional view may not reflect accurately the parent's priorities. As mentioned in the previous chapter, the main function of the conference identified by social workers and conference chairs was the need to bring *information in*. Explanations were needed as well as accounts. This meant that the success or failure of participation, as distinct from a method of persuasion, depended on how far the conference was able to determine the parents' views.

The schedules which we completed after attendance at the 120 initial conferences included our estimate of the parents' contribution to the debate. Out of the 71 conferences where parents attended (usually at the beginning or end of the meeting) there were 44 in which the parents' contribution seemed to enable the conference to learn about their view of the situation. In another 16 cases the parents' contribution was extremely limited; that is, the conference did not find out much about their views. In only 11 cases were parents or carers able not only to express their views but also to participate in an exploration of the relevant issues. They were, for example, involved in discussing the concerns about the child or the conference decisions and recommendations.

This last situation would seem to represent the ideal as far as parental participation in case conferences is concerned. It is worrying to discover that when parents attended conferences it was apparently realised in only 15 per cent of these cases. If we take into account the number of conferences in which there was no family representative present, the ideal was realised in less than 10 per cent of the total. This underlines the difficulties but it gives no cause for optimism.

The effect of partial attendance

Out of the 71 conferences which parents attended, there were 32 in which the parent was allowed in only for the start of the meeting. In 17 conferences the parent was allowed in for a period during the middle of the conference, and in a further 13 cases the parent was allowed in at the end. There were only nine conferences in which parents attended almost throughout – and even in these cases the parents were not allowed to be present during the final decision-making about registration.

At the time of our study the agencies were in the process of introducing and extending the system of parent participation, and it is clear that this had to be done gradually. Nevertheless, *the partial exclusion of parents had damaging effects*. Because they were usually present for only a fraction of the meeting, they very rarely heard the full statement of the agencies' concerns. This meant that their understanding of what was at issue was hampered. They also felt quite strongly that they had a *right* to hear what agencies said about them, to offer alternative explanations and to have their own view heard. When this did not happen, they found themselves burning with suppressed anger and resentment.

> '*I came there, discovered an enormous room full of people I didn't know from Adam, was introduced to them and then asked to clear off into a little room in the middle of nowhere! . . . And I thought, "What is that? What's the point of inviting you to a meeting? What the hell of a waste of time!"* '

Many parents had made an effort to attend at considerable cost to themselves – and this made it particularly galling to be excluded from the main part of the meeting.

> '*I'm self-employed so I don't get paid when I'm not at work . . . I had some trust in the social services department before the conference because we'd been to other meetings. This time police and solicitors were there and I don't know what they said about me and the kids. My trust has finished with them now.*'

The closed door of the conference room was often mentioned in interviews. It indicated that the parent was an outsider, and in some cases it seemed to represent punishment as well. One parent said: "I did feel awful standing outside that door." Another described the waiting period as 'nerve-racking', after she had been kept waiting for three-quarters of an hour, which was by no means unusual. Yet another said that she felt like kicking the door and saying, "Look, I am going to say my say now!" – but she realised that 'you can't do things like that'.

It was interesting that the formality of the atmosphere had a restraining effect. In some cases this atmosphere may be deliberately used to prevent the expression of feelings which would be disruptive in the meeting. As a result of the exclusion, one parent actually found the conference less satisfactory than a court.

> *'I mean you go to court and usually you're there, aren't you? You know what's going on.'*

Members of other agencies, some of whom were well-known to the parent, were of course present during the whole discussion and they were sometimes able to represent the parents' views. Since the parents did not witness this, however, it did nothing to boost their self-esteem.

The need for friends and advocates

When the statements made by parents in the conference were considered, and related to the responses we obtained in interviews, the research shows up a great need for parent support or advocacy. As previously mentioned, most mothers wanted to attend the conference and were glad to be invited; but when they attended they felt intimidated by the large group of professionals.

> *'They're all the same; it's like ganging up on you.'*

> *'Social services had all their defences set up. I hadn't got anyone.'*

The comparison with a court hearing was often made when parents were describing the conference and in some ways it was not inappropriate. The chairperson usually addressed the parent with sympathy, and some parents were grateful for the chance to 'say their piece'; but however carefully the chairperson approached the issues, there was usually a feeling that the parent's account had a lower status than that of the professional participants. The parent was on the defensive, and expected to produce excuses rather than a free-standing account.

> *'Everyone around me seemed to be pointing a finger at me. In parts you could say what you wanted. In other parts people would look down on you. They weren't really taking much notice of what we had to say.'*

In many cases the professional participants were actually sympathetic to parents, and aware of their predicament. We recorded that in a third of the cases where parents attended the conference their presence called forth a positive response from the meeting. In another 28 per cent of cases the response was mixed, and in a quarter of cases it was unclear. There were, though, only 15 per cent of cases in which the response appeared to be negative. In spite of the presence of much goodwill, however, the parents' experiences in the meetings were frequently harrowing.

The interviews indicated that most parents who attended felt exceedingly *lonely*, and since many of the mothers who attended were socially isolated, the experience of attendance must have compounded 'deficits in the social environment' (Murphy and Kupshik, 1992). Although members of social services departments had often involved others like the county solicitor to assist them, parents had rarely been encouraged to bring others as advisers, supporters or advocates. The situation was particularly acute where there were language difficulties.

Problems with interpreters

Parents from minority ethnic groups, as well as social workers and managers, were frank about the difficulties involved in the use of interpreters. The first problem was simply availability. When an emergency child protection investigation was called for, it was not always easy to find an interpreter with the requisite language skills and professional training. Social work managers were heavily dependent on outside agencies (mostly small, independent agencies) for their supply of interpreters, and there was no guarantee that someone provided at short notice would have all the necessary skills including total respect for confidentiality.

The second main difficulty, which was experienced not simply by social workers but by all parties, was that no-one could be quite sure that complex meanings were being accurately and sensitively relayed. In some Asian languages the words necessary for the description of sexual abuse do not exist, or are so rarely used that people would be shocked by their usage, and in many cases a balance had to be maintained between politeness and clarity. The gender and personality of the interpreter could help or hinder. The interpreters who were most valued tended to have worked fairly frequently with social services and had built up a degree of official trust, but it was easy for parents to feel that their own views were not being represented fairly. Many parents in the study as a whole failed to understand what happens when a child's name is placed on the child protection register. For parents from a minority ethnic background it was obviously even more difficult to grasp the meaning of the agency's concerns, or to understand their part in the complex extra-legal process by which registration decisions were made.

It was not usual for parents to employ their own interpreters. On one occasion when a husband wanted to translate for his wife during the investigation his offer was firmly refused. On the other hand, there were occasions when family members with good language skills could act as useful negotiators. One Indian mother claimed that she took over the role of interpreter in the case conference when she realised that her husband, who spoke little English and was accused of physically abusing their children, was becoming more and more upset by the discussion. Her account of this part of the conference debate was as follows:

> *'It was about seeing somebody about the kids' behaviour, because I was saying that my children are really hyperactive . . . They kept on saying we're bringing the children up wrong, you see, and then I had to explain to him in Indian and he understood me more better, because he knew I wasn't trying to harm him. But I think the way she [the interpreter] put it up was wrong.'*

This leads to the third and most commonly expressed difficulty connected with the use of interpreters, which was that a third party could not readily be introduced into the web of relationships without effecting some change. In other words the interpreter was a person, not a neutral being.

Because of the close association between shared language and sympathy, it was understandable if social workers with differing levels of experience sometimes appeared to be uneasy in the presence of workers who had superior knowledge of the parents' language. It was also understandable if parents under threat sought alliance with people who communicated easily with them, and were led to expect that these people would represent their views. One mother recorded her disappointment when a black person at a case conference failed to explain what she meant, when she was trying to tell the social workers about the necessity for treating her child's skin with special cream:

> *'I said, "Tell them what . . . " and he was just sat there like I was embarrassing him about what we have to do . . . But as soon as I started letting off at people he jumped over and come and sat down beside me and told me to calm down. And I wasn't going to calm down.'*

In this case there appeared to be a need for an interpreter, not simply to translate what she was saying but to articulate a point of cultural importance. There was an even greater need for an advocate or friend.

Working with interpreters is a skill which has to be learnt, and clearly there are also particular skills involved in chairing case conferences where the presence of one or more interpreters has a complicating effect on the dynamics. Since true objectivity is impossible, there are always likely to be differing perceptions about who is on whose side.

Sources of parental anxiety

In the case conference schedules we recorded what appeared to be the state of mind of parents during the exchange of information. In 41% of cases they seemed to be extremely anxious, and in 27% of cases they were angry. In four cases their feelings were not clear. In a further 27% of cases they appeared to be reasonably at ease, although some of these parents told us later that they had exhibited more self-control than they had felt.

For one mother whom we interviewed it was the feeling of *exposure*, combined with the diffculty of articulating unpleasant information, which made the conference a distressing experience. In her case it proved a worse experience even than the discovery of the abuse and the investigation.

> *'It is upsetting enough to have to go through it yourself; but to have to go through it with everybody else in one room is entirely different . . . It is more upsetting, really, than going through what you have been through.'*

Knowing the 'rules', being familiar with the language about care or registration, and knowing when or how to speak would have been an advantage. Some middle-class parents – especially in cases of sexual abuse – were extremely articulate; but very few people had the kind of committee experience which would have enabled them to take part on an equal footing. Reference has already been made to the language difficulties of minority ethnic clients. Working-class parents too found themselves up against barriers which were social and cultural, organisational and linguistic.

> *'In that conference room my whole life was talked about by 'experts' and it just annoys me.'*

> *'I didn't understand what they were saying, because they were all talking upper class . . . I mean, as far as I know they could have been talking about putting him in care, for all I know.'*

People felt that what was being judged was their *moral adequacy and fitness as parents* – as indeed it was. It was not uncommon, therefore, for parents to fear that their children might be taken into care if they said the wrong thing, even if care was not actively being considered.

> *'I had to be careful in what actually was being said, because I mean if I'd said the wrong thing, that would have been it.'*

> *'It was constantly going through my head that my kids were going to be taken away from me.'*

> *'I was afraid of losing her altogether. I think that's what I was fighting against.'*

These fears clearly inhibited the expression of parents' views, especially when they were unsure about how a particular piece of information would be received or interpreted. Our interviews show that in many cases the conference was prevented from discovering the parent's true opinions, which were held back either because the parent was afraid of seeming rude and obstreperous (a circumstance which was associated with a somewhat increased likelihood of registration) or because the parent was worried about possible adverse interpretations, especially when the police were present and there was a risk of prosecution. As a result, statements which could have helped the conference members in the construction of risk, or helped the parent by offering a defence, were never aired; and after the conference was over parents continued to cling to arguments which had never been properly discussed or challenged.

Here is one woman's account of what was said by the conference chair, remembered not in tranquility but through a haze of considerable resentment:

> '*I did think the chairwoman, like, was extremely rude. Well, as she said, "There's too much sex in this family, and it's got to stop, and it's got to stop now! Right?" I mean if a parent **knows** what's going on then the parent can stop it; but if a child is outside, out playing . . . .I mean there's no way you're going to know unless somebody **tells** you what's going on! I was too annoyed to even open my mouth much about putting our own point of view . . . She said it was our fault. We should keep an eye on her.'* [Mother of a 12-year-old girl who was sexually abused by her brother]

Skilled chairing was helpful in eliciting the parent's feelings, however, if the chairperson was willing to move forward in small steps and at the client's pace. A parent who was seen as blameless and cooperative and consequently had a reasonably good experience of the conference said:

> '*They asked questions that made it easier for you to say what you wanted. They didn't just sort of sit there and say, "Well, what have you got to say?" They asked questions and helped you to say what you wanted to say.'*

Another factor, of course, was the degree of commitment to participation shown by parents themselves. In spite of strong feelings of loneliness and breach of privacy, and in spite of their fears about making matters worse, some parents made valiant efforts to put their point of view to the conference – and against all odds they succeeded. One mother who was described by her social worker as 'a little bit of a mousey lady' tried in vain to make notes on what she wanted to say before the conference. ('I kept trying to scribble things out, but it just didn't come right.') However, she soon found that 'it was all right once the words started coming'. For some time after the conference it was a source of affinity between her and her social worker, that she had spoken in the meeting and that he was able to say, "Well done!"

Empowerment and disempowerment

Occasionally the conference did manage to offer real support to a parent who needed it, for example if a mother was grieving as a result of her child's disclosure of sexual abuse. Where the mother was not under any suspicion and had indicated a strong desire to protect the child, the professional participants rapidly formed an alliance with her. For example, in a case where a mother had responded to the sexual abuse of her seven-year-old daughter by seeking an injunction against her husband and changing the locks on the door, several conference members complimented her on her actions. Further, since the child was clearly distressed, she was offered continuing help from the social worker and health visitor. The chairperson also made a point of saying that the child was being kept off the register because of the agencies' faith in the mother. In another case where the conference was attended by a child's relative, who had a quasi-custodial role but no responsibility for the abuse, the relative found her attendance at the conference a reasonably satisfactory experience. She found registration protective, since she was not threatened by the conference and felt that the participants were on her side.

> 'It serves simply that if anything else happens, that we've only got one phone call before somebody actually does something. And if something drastic needs doing, then hopefully somebody would do something drastic.'

People suspected of committing abuse or colluding with the abuser did not have such an easy time, and they found conference attendance much more threatening; but they were not always passive or inarticulate. There were times when parents influenced the meeting by presenting their arguments well. For example, on one occasion a young mother gave an unexpectedly spirited defence of her cohabitee and on another occasion a child was kept off the register when an angry father turned up with his solicitor. Men were usually more active in discussion than women. Similar patterns were observed in the Scottish children's hearings.

> 'Fewer fathers than mothers attend hearings, but the level of involvement of those who come is high.' (Martin *et al.*, 1981)

In our study, as in the children's hearings, we found that there was sometimes a tendency for the conference chair to avoid raising contentious issues with the parent and to concentrate instead on subjects which were 'emotionally relatively neutral' (Martin *et al.*, 1981). There were, however, times when the emotions felt by the parent could not be controlled, and he or she stormed out of the meeting. On these occasions it was usual for the chair to make some statement which excused the parent and at the same time mollified the participants, for example: "She can't take the stress." A closer examination of these incidents suggests that they do have some common features, and it is useful to note what they are.

(i) When parents became uncontrollably angry there was often some piece of unpleasant information which was presented as a *shock*. (For example a trusted friend was unexpectedly blamed, or the notion of risk was extended from the index child to other children in the family.)

(ii) When a parent stormed out of the room, there was often more than one family member present. If one family member went out and slammed the door, the other one *stayed*. This meant that the family continued to be represented (at least in part) and none of the conference business was missed.

(iii) Sometimes the chairperson inadvertently embarrassed the family members by placing one of the parents in a situation of 'double bind' – usually by asking for agreement on a contentious issue which was likely to split the family lobby. For example, in a case where a man had physically abused his own children, his wife (who had children from a previous marriage) was asked to agree that her children might be kept safe because she disciplined them herself. She clearly wanted to have this agreement; but at the same time it was tantamount to an admission that her husband was an abuser. She refused to answer and withdrew from the meeting in tears.

Reference has been made to the way in which parents attending conferences could feel stigmatised and disadvantaged; but in situations where the abuse was unproven, blame was sometimes free-floating, and in exceptional circumstances a person suspected of abuse could turn a conference in his favour. Here is the statement of a man accused of sexually abusing his 13-year-old stepdaughter by playing with her in a way which she found distasteful. It is useful to look at the statement which he made at the meeting, to see how the blame is shifted neatly in the direction of the child.

> '*Nothing has been going on with Karen. When she was confronted, she broke down. She said it was a lie. She had some garbled story about a boy. She was angry because I restricted her freedom. She's telling the truth* **now**. *I won't accept blame from the police. If I was charged I'd get a solicitor to defend me.*
>
> *Yes, I was lying on top of her. I was also sitting, standing, pouring water over her [in play] – but the police weren't interested in that . . . Karen was after the attention all the time . . . I try and support her. I see her side of it. I go into*

*school. Karen is taking **advantage**. She keeps asking me not to tell her mother about things at school. Her mother thinks she's rebelled this way rather than in any other.'*

This speech is quite remarkable for the way in which it turns a number of possible negatives into positives. Part of the girl's evidence was that her stepfather was inordinately jealous of her relationship with boys. He turned this into a motive for rebellion. ('I restricted her freedom.') He admitted the offence and at the same time denied its significance – not by attempting to limit the alleged behaviours, but by adding to them in such a way that they were trivialised and the police were made to seem inefficient. He aligned himself with the girl's interests and pointed out how he kept her secrets. (She didn't want her mother to know that she smoked at school, and he is said to have bribed her with cigarettes.) At the same time he aligned himself with the mother, and distanced the mother from her daughter, with the statement, 'Her mother thinks . . . ' (The girl's mother was actually sitting outside the conference room, too scared or embarrassed to come in.)

During the heated debate which followed, the situation became if anything more confused. The teacher who had received the girl's disclosure strongly supported the child. ("She's retracting allegations. He's been getting at her.") The social worker, who felt that some concerns might have been exaggerated but was unsure of her position said: "Investigation has led us further from the truth, not nearer." The senior social worker said: "All *three* people (including the mother) have a strong investment in retraction." Registration was agreed under the category of grave concern. The recommendations were that family work would be offered, with pastoral support to Karen from the school, and that the girl would return home.

This case has been quoted at length because it illustrates a number of the themes which family members and practitioners find themselves struggling with in the conference setting. It involves issues of power, gender, alliances, the construction of events, blame and responsibility, certainty and uncertainty, and consequences of the system. Last but not least, there is the issue of parental participation.

An understanding of dynamics is clearly required by all participants in the initial case conference. They need to be prepared to assist parents who are lacking in confidence, and at the same time to negotiate actively with parents who try to take control after they have committed substantive abuse. If these issues are ignored it is quite possible for parental participation to represent empowerment; but on the evidence of some of our findings, the wrong parent may be empowered.

Summary

1. The key agencies participating in the initial case conference were health, education, police and social services. Social workers attended nearly all conferences and 83% of conferences were attended by police. With the exception of health visitors, the health services were not well represented. This had implications for treatment as well as assessment.

2. The attendance rate did not always reflect the degree of influence exerted by the participants. Although police attended many conferences they were not generally very active in seeking registration. However, where clear evidence of risk was presented by school staff, the associated registration rate was very high (84%).

3. Workers from voluntary organisations, apart from members of the NSPCC, attended very rarely. Only one conference was attended by a playgroup leader, and another by a worker from a day nursery. Child-minders were never present.

4. The person who most often represented the family at the initial conference was the *mother*. 30% of conferences were attended by mothers alone, and only 18% by two parent figures. Children very rarely came. Whether or not the mothers were considered to have maltreated the child, they tended to take responsibility for their families and to mediate between their husbands or partners and the outside world.

5. Although they were keen to participate, parents in general found the experience of attending the conference extremely stressful. They felt blamed and judged as though in a court hearing, and they were haunted by the fear of losing their children. It was only when they were seen as blameless and cooperative that alliances were made between them and the other participants.

6. When parents from minority ethnic groups attended the conference, they had the added disadvantage of language difficulties and lack of knowledge of the proceedings. Interpreters were valuable, but they were not always available, and if their role was unclear they were capable of causing confusion by introducing a third party into the debate.

7. Because the parents' presence in the meeting was usually restricted to the beginning or end of the proceedings, their views were seldom given full expression. They also felt that their views had little impact when professional opinions had been shared in advance. Occasionally, however, some very articulate parents brought forward persuasive arguments in their own defence.

8. In spite of its shortcomings, parental participation was valued by both family members and practitioners. The most commonly voiced criticism was that because parents were excluded for a large part of the meeting, their participation was incomplete.

Chapter 8

Information–sharing

As previously mentioned, the initial case conference was a forum for information-sharing and professional discussion. The topics raised were wide-ranging, but when reduced to its simplest form, the material presented by professional participants at the conference had two main ingredients:

(i)   Information which could be described as 'evidence' of abuse or neglect; and

(ii)   Background information about the child and family.

The chairperson had a crucial role to play in structuring this information and maintaining the balance between contributions. Important clues to the source of risk could be missed if the attention of the conference was focused on other issues. Occasionally it was the *interconnection* between events which was not immediately apparent. For example, the parents in one family were considered neglectful because, according to the health visitor, they did not regularly visit the baby in hospital and because, according to the infant teacher, they frequently failed to pick up young children from school. A comparison of dates showed that on the occasions when they had not picked up the children from school they had been attempting to visit the baby in hospital and *vice versa*.

Many of the problems faced by the chair are of course commonly experienced in meetings of all types. Sometimes voluble people had more than their share of the debate, and potentially helpful contributions – especially from people of low status – were not given the attention they deserved. At other times the discussion became anecdotal and lacking in direction. On the other hand if the discussion was *over*-controlled, there was a risk that some of the participants' views might not be expressed.

It seems appropriate to look at what our research has revealed about the supply of information to the conference, and to see how the various features were combined in the final analysis of risk. The registration decision needs to be considered later in its own right, since it was made for a number of other reasons besides the identification of risk to the child.

Evidence from social services and police

The conference generally began by considering the particular allegations which had provoked the referral. If a joint investigation had been conducted, it was usual for the investigation to be described in detail both by the social worker and by the police representative involved. Sometimes the social worker and the police officer had each dealt with different family members, or had been involved at different stages in the investigation. As a result, complementary rather than joint accounts were offered. Since they were usually reporting on the same events and had had ample opportunity to discuss them, the picture presented by each person was very similar.

The accounts given by social workers and police, together with information from other key participants such as school teachers and health visitors, were highly influential in shaping the assessment of risk. The evidence they gave tended to cover some or all of the following topics:

Child-based evidence

(i)   Direct statements made by the child, suggesting that abuse had taken place.

(ii)   Indirect statements made by the child, perhaps indicative of abuse or neglect (for example strong dislike or fear of a particular person, or expressions of undue sexual awareness).

(iii)   Physical marks noticed during the investigation (e.g. bruising, weals, burns, sores, discharge) and medical opinion if a doctor had been involved.

(iv)   Evidence of neglect or underfeeding (e.g. child hungry, dirty, poorly clothed or unsupervised).

(v)   Evidence of disturbed or distressed behaviour (particularly signs that the child might be 'beyond control').

Parent-based evidence

(i)   Direct statements made by the parent about the abuse (e.g. admissions and denials, threats of abuse, or occasionally fears that it might happen in the future).

(ii)   Indirect statements made by the parent, indicating worrying attitudes (e.g. hostility towards the child, lack of recognition of dangers).

(iii)   Previous history of violence, either in relation to the parent or another adult resident in the household.

(iv)   Evidence of irresponsible behaviour by the parent (e.g. being drunk or high on drugs, or fighting with other adults in the child's presence).

(v)   Lack of cooperation with professional agencies (e.g. open aggression or defensive strategies, attempts at concealment of known facts, or refusal of further involvement).

In general, the amount of child-based and parent-based evidence in the reports to the conference was evenly balanced; but regardless of where the evidence came from, the focus was indisputably on *parental behaviour*. The parent was usually considered responsible for all forms of harm to the children, whether by acts of commission or omission, even if there was no direct responsibility for the injury. For example, in one case where two young children had been sexually abused by a young man who was resident in the household, the parents were blamed for working overtime and leaving the children in his care; and in several cases of physical injury which turned out to be accidental, the charge of abuse was reconstructed as a charge of neglect.

One interesting point to be drawn from the study is the extent to which conference decision-making has changed in the last few years. The predominance of evidence from the joint investigation in the assessment of risk is one of the main features which distinguishes our research findings from those of earlier studies. What Dingwall described as 'clinical evidence' (Dingwall *et al.*, 1983) was under-represented in our study, and where it was present it was often advanced with hesitancy. Dingwall highlighted the need for a combination of clinical and social assessment, but at times in our study the clinical evidence almost seemed to have been replaced by the social (which in effect meant evidence from social workers and police). This is probably a reflection of the high number of sexual abuse cases which were dealt with by joint investigation, where reports of the investigation predominated, and medical evidence was rarely conclusive.

The cooperation of social workers and police and the search for evidence which could be used in court proceedings has brought into prominence the investigative interview. As well as having a profound effect on the parents, this seems to have had a number of observable effects on case conference reasoning. Firstly, there was a tendency for social workers and police in the conferences we attended to concentrate on *recent events*, sometimes to the exclusion of important events from the past. Even previous convictions for violence were not always reported. Secondly, a great deal of reliance was placed on what people *said*, or were reported to have said, rather than on what they were understood to have done or suffered. Thirdly, there was an unexpectedly low emphasis on theoretical linkages, more emphasis being placed on the interpretation of people's statements and the construction of possible logical connections between them.

All of these developments are consistent with a shift towards what Parton (1991) has described as socio-legal discourse, and they have advantages and disadvantages. The focus on recent events, for example, was helpful in making clear the nature of the allegations and the family's response to them; but it is important to note that much of the evidence presented at conferences was concerned with *observed reactions to the investigation itself.* Whether or not the parent's reaction was typical (and our interviews suggest that in some cases it was not), it was *taken to indicate the quality of the parenting normally available to the child.* A parent who was aggressive towards social workers or police, for example, might be reckoned to be potentially aggressive to the child as well. A parent who excluded agencies was considered to have 'something to hide' rather than to be seeking privacy, and a parent who responded to news of the abuse by shocked withdrawal might be labelled 'unable to protect'. In ways such as these, the construction of events recently formed at the investigation was carried into the conference forum; and more distant events of importance, such as the actions of a male abuser in a previous marriage, were sometimes overlooked.

The evidence from social workers and police included reports of observed behaviour, and, as already mentioned, it also concentrated heavily on what parents and children had *said*. Unfortunately, because of the restrictions on parental attendance mentioned in the previous chapter, this information was presented in the form of second-hand reports, usually without the requisite family members being present to challenge them. The reports were also edited and made meaningful by the people who wrote them, according to their own particular ideas of what good child care involved.

Here is a comment made by a male police officer, in a case where a four-month-old baby had been bruised on the cheek. It is worrying that in the polite, inter-disciplinary context of the meeting it was not challenged.

> *'It's possible the husband hit the baby out of frustration. But the child didn't react badly to him. The baby is not afraid of him. It was gurgling in his arms. He seems a good father.'*

In spite of its limitations, the description of the joint investigation, if there was one, provided a peg on which the conference reasoning hung. One point which we found rather remarkable was the degree of agreement between social workers and police. Sometimes the difference in perspective between the two agencies resulted in slightly dissimilar views; but these differences tended to emerge as complementary interpretations rather than as fully fledged disagreements. For example, there were a number of cases of alleged sexual abuse where the child was known to have watched pornographic videos. For the police, this was often something which diminished the evidence because it made it more difficult to establish whether the child had had actual sexual experience. For social workers, on the other hand, the watching of pornographic videos by a young child might be construed as adding to the evidence of abuse, because it indicated that the parent was irresponsible and therefore emotionally, if not sexually, abusive. The division of opinion on this issue did not always take place along institutional lines, however. There were cases where police could be seen to occupy the high moral ground. In terms of the conference outcome these differences were often relatively unimportant, because they tended to affect the likelihood of prosecution rather more than the likelihood of registration.

Apart from occasional differences of interpretation, such as the one mentioned above, the main differences to emerge between social workers and police at the conference were seen as procedural. There seemed to be a definite attempt to keep conflicts at the procedural level, in order to stop them from spreading destructively into areas of agency autonomy or personal relationships. For example, in one case where the social worker's account of the investigation differed strongly and factually from that of the police, the discrepancy was attributed to the fact that the police representative at the conference was not the person who had taken part in the joint investigation. The matter was dealt with on a strictly procedural level, without involving either agency in accusations of inefficiency. The police did sometimes seek the views of conference members on prosecution or cautioning, but in most cases they did not campaign actively for registration. As we have seen, they were happy to present evidence and to leave the final decision about registration to social services. By confining their disagreements to procedural issues, and by supporting the social worker at the conference in return for support offered at the investigation, the police helped to ensure that the joint perception of risk was the one most likely to dominate at the conference.

Evidence from doctors and health visitors

As previously mentioned, health visitors had a high rate of attendance in relation to relevant cases. If the child was of preschool age, or if there was a preschool-age child in the family, the health visitor often visited the household regularly. Because of this, her evidence was treated with respect. It was not always directly concerned with the allegations of abuse or neglect, however. Sometimes it consisted mainly of background information. It was most valuable in cases where the primary or secondary concerns were about alleged *neglect*. In these cases the health visitor was usually able to document the pattern of attendance at health checks, and to make some assessment of the child's development – even if it was simply to say that the child was 'up to his or her milestones'. The health visitors used instruments of measurement such as centile charts, and they often reported problems such as speech defects which might be indicative of understimulation. Many of the problems they reported required specific intervention.

As we have seen, the attendance rate for GPs, in contrast to that of the health visitors, was patchy and regional. Their reports were often very brief and carefully worded, as though they felt the burden of medical confidentiality; and, if they had seen more of the parents than of the children, they sometimes took a parent-sided view. It was not unusual for the GP to defend an alleged abuser. In one case where a man was alleged to have sexually abused his two daughters, the GP (who was male) defended him and was successful in diverting some of the concerns to his wife. This happened in a conference where most of the other participants were women, and it seemed as though the meeting was beginning to divide along gender lines. In other circumstances, however, there were mothers who found that their male GPs were supportive. In a case of physical abuse to a young boy, the GP sent a letter to the conference pointing out that the mother had been suffering from gastroenteritis at the time of the offence and was dehydrated. (She had bruised her son during an argument.) In another case of alleged sexual abuse the GP attended the conference and spoke on the mother's behalf, almost adopting an advocate's role; and in a difficult case involving a handicapped youth the mother said that her doctor was one of the few people who was sympathetic to her.

Where a parent was suspected of being physically or mentally ill, the GP's evidence could be particularly valuable – but the collection and disclosure of information when this had not been discussed in advance could be prejudicial to the doctor-parent relationship, as this quotation from a parent's interview shows:

> '*I went to my doctor for a cervical smear test, a fortnight before this all happened, and he asked me a few things. He seemed quite nice and pleasant and chatty. But then I realised he was asking me about my psychosis . . . It didn't upset me, that conversation. I just said to my friends, "He's marvellous with cervical smears." I didn't think he was asking me awkward questions. Since then I've discovered that I don't **like** all this – but I don't know whether there's any way I can get free from it, apart from just never going to see the doctor again.'*

What this mother did not know was that her GP actually defended her at the conference. Although an approved mental health social worker who visited the household brought back a very negative report of the mother, the GP said that in his opinion she was simply 'an unusual person', perhaps with a minor personality disorder. He did, however, arrange for a visit from a consultant psychiatrist, who might have been of some help if he had been allowed access to the house. (Unfortunately, as a result of the mother's sense of alienation, the door was shut in his face.)

The evidence from hospital doctors in the study was rather sparse – usually because they were rarely consulted. There were of course cases of serious injury to babies or young children which were referred immediately to hospital because the injury needed medical assessment or treatment, and once the child was in hospital, the need for a case conference under child protection procedures might be identified. In one case a small baby was taken to hospital with a fractured skull after she had been dropped on her head by her father. In another case a six-week-old baby was referred to hospital so that an injury could be diagnosed. It emerged that the child had a spiral fracture of the right humerus, resulting from a violent pull or twist to his right arm. In both these cases and in other similar ones the initial conference was held on hospital territory instead of in the social services office, partly to ensure a strong representation of hospital personnel.

Cases such as these, which might be considered classic cases of 'non-accidental injury' of the type brought to prominence by Kempe and his colleagues in the 1960s (Kempe *et al.*, 1962), were surprisingly few in the study. The injuries which children received from their parents, and which counted as evidence of abuse, were usually looked at by the family's GP, or possibly by a hospital doctor, during the investigation. There were worrying indications that some non-accidental injuries known to GPs were not always passed on to social services. For example in one case where a young baby was actually on the register, the baby was admitted by the GP to hospital with a torn frenulum without social services being informed. One child protection coordinator said that she never received a child abuse referral from the child and family guidance clinic, although she knew that local GPs were referring abusing families to the clinic since they were sometimes picked up by social services at a later date. GPs and sometimes paediatric specialists were of course involved in examining abused children at the request of social services; but the doctor who made the diagnosis frequently did not attend the conference, preferring to send a telephoned or written report. As a result, the medical evidence could not be questioned and there was no serious discussion of its implications.

There were cases where the absence of clear medical information made a difference to the conference outcome and possibly also to the child's future. In one case involving a six-year-old boy, for example, the concern was about a fairly minor case of over-chastisement. The mother had slapped the child rather hard, and freely admitted the assault. The GP did not attend the conference, but he sent a rather puzzling note which implied that the boy might be sexually as well as physically abused. This information, which was added to the original concerns, helped to ensure that the child was registered. The previously good relationship between the mother and her social worker deteriorated rapidly and the child ended up in permanent care; yet no allegations of sexual abuse were ever made or proved. (Needless to say there were other concerns about the family, and it is impossible to say that without the GP's action the same course might not have been followed, though the unclear allegations of sexual abuse seem to have contributed substantially to a negative outcome.)

In another case involving suspicions of child sexual abuse, the lack of clear medical evidence at the conference contributed to an *under*-recognition of the dangers. In this case a nine-year-old girl, Tracey, had run away from home and it was thought that she had been emotionally as well as physically abused. The GP was not present at the conference. When he was contacted later he was very concerned about possible sexual abuse, since a medical examination two years previously had shown reddening in the vaginal area indicative of sexual interference which had not been properly followed up by police at the time. This information, since it was post-conference, came too late to stimulate police interest or justify reopening enquiries, and it was not until Tracey was re-abused by her father during the period of registration that the truth about the earlier incident became known.

The under-attendance of medical personnel at conferences, and the lack of clear medical evidence in so many cases, is a matter of concern and we are justified in searching for possible reasons. Time constraints on doctors, the wish not to breach confidentiality, or the wish not to prejudice doctor-patient relationships by becoming involved in family conflict, were clearly present in some cases. In others, medical evidence, although available, could neither confirm nor refute the allegations of abuse. This was especially true of cases of non-penetrative sexual abuse. In others again, there were clearly difficulties in the relationship between medical practitioners and police. There was one paediatrician who complained that he had been completely ignored at the time of the joint investigation, although he was later expected to make a diagnosis which the police might use as a basis for prosecution or cautioning. The reason for the complaint was that the paediatrician found that he could not make an adequate diagnosis without talking to the mother, who could not be reached in the early stages because she was being extensively questioned by police and social services. (We are reminded of the distinction between clinical and social evidence, and the need to combine the two.)

In the above case the paediatrician seemed to be asking for greater involvement, but at the same time he was asking for less responsibility. This is one of the many paradoxes created by the child protection system, and it is difficult to see how it can be resolved. Apart from the need to protect children and also incidentally himself, the doctor had status needs which depended on both involvement and responsibility; and under the present system they could not easily be satisfied.

Another hospital doctor in the study wrote a letter to the conference complaining that he had not been contacted in a case of physical abuse to a two-year-old child. He argued, justifiably, that the child and her younger brother should have been presented at hospital for X-rays. The case was being handled by social workers and police, with the help of a check-up from the local GP, and no-one thought fit to refer the case any further. Once again the complaint was dealt with by a clarification of procedures. The interesting point is that these procedures were discussed extensively at the conference, completely displacing the agenda of risk to the child. It was impossible to tell whose anxiety might be highest – the hospital doctor who had been ignored, the GP who had failed to make the referral, or the members of social services who had taken on themselves the task of protecting the child.

All professionals involved in the child protection system feel vulnerable; but there were signs in the study that hospital paediatricians were sometimes keenly aware, also, of the limitations of their own expertise. If they were invited to case conferences they felt that they were expected to speak *ex cathedra* (unlike other participants who were content to make a partial contribution to the debate) and yet the case might be fraught with uncertainties.

Here are some examples of medically 'grey' cases, which were complicated by professional vacillation and disagreement at the conference. The concerns were about physical abuse in the first case, neglect in the second, and sexual abuse in the third.

(i) One small child had a severe burn on his arm. The paediatrician who examined him could not tell whether the injury had been accidentally caused or not. The mother's explanation, that he had run into the iron when she was holding it, was accepted at first. However, after the case conference the paediatrician changed his mind, since he felt on reflection that the injury was too deep to have been accidental. As a result, the conference was reconvened.

(ii) In another conference there were worries about the possibility of physical neglect to two small girls, one of whom was a baby. Medical checks had tried to establish whether the children were 'failing to thrive'. Even though growth charts were used, the medical practitioners disagreed about their significance, and a firm diagnosis proved impossible. In the case of the baby it was felt that the child was pre-term and therefore of uncertain age (when its life in the womb was considered). In the case of the other little girl, it was felt that she was naturally of small build, and therefore the growth charts had to be seen in this context.

(iii) A small handicapped girl was found to have genital warts, of a type which, in the opinion of the hospital doctor, could only have been sexually transmitted. The mother's former cohabitee was suspected of sexual abuse; but shortly before the conference was held, the doctor read an academic article which indicated that in certain rather rare circumstances the warts could be transmitted by ordinary physical contact. This lent more credibility to the mother's story, since she had always maintained that the infection was transferred by an aunt who had warts on her hands. The matter was never finally cleared up.

There were many other cases where the medical evidence was ambiguous – particularly cases of sexual abuse, including some where attempted intercourse was alleged but the victim was known to be sexually active. In cases of sexual abuse clinical diagnosis was often sought, but it was rarely conclusive. In most conferences, however, medical evidence was of value when it was added to the evidence of other people – that is, it helped the conference members to know that abuse was not ruled out, or on the other hand that the injury was consistent with the explanation offered. In cases of physical punishment the doctor could sometimes say roughly how much *force* was used; and this helped to set the boundary between legitimate punishment and over-chastisement.

In conclusion, the main reasons for the under-provision of medical evidence appear to be: firstly the lack of certainty in medical diagnoses and the risks attached to 'getting it wrong'; secondly the reluctance of some medical practitioners to contribute partial diagnoses instead of embarking on a thorough investigation of their own; and thirdly the wish of some doctors to safeguard relationships with their patients, perhaps protecting them in some cases from the perceived ill-effects of the child protection system.

Fourthly, of course, there was the loneliness of the long-distance paediatricians, who felt excluded from the initial investigative procedures and at the same time responsible for decisions of enormous importance.

Besides the need for medical evidence, there are other reasons for involving doctors, including child psychiatrists, more often in the case conference system. If there are to be improved medical services for the treatment of abused children, it makes sense to seek a greater involvement of medical personnel at the decision-making stage as well.

Evidence from schools

From the above accounts it can be seen that the evidence presented at some of the case conferences we attended would not hold much water in a court of law. But since the meeting was intended to pick up any hint of risk to the child, and since the discussion was at least partly a diagnostic process, the standards of proof were fairly elastic.

The evidence from most agencies generally fell into one of the two categories already mentioned in connection with the contributions of social services and police. It was either parent-based or child-based. Where children were registered, the decision to register was usually preceded by a combination of parent-based and child-based evidence – that is, it included reports of the parent's actions and attitudes on the one hand, and the child's symptoms, injuries or distressed behaviour on the other. The blame usually ended up by falling on the parent; but pride of place was given to evidence which came directly from the child.

The evidence from schools was almost invariably child-based. Neglected and deprived children were identified by their thinness and frailty, their empty lunch boxes and inadequate clothing, their lack of supervision or their tendency to fall asleep in school. In cases of physical abuse, teachers often noticed unusual marks on a child or picked up signs of hidden bruising during P.E. lessons, or felt that the child was unnaturally distressed. Infant and primary school teachers had especially close contact with children and were well placed to pick up concerns. In secondary schools too though, people entrusted with pastoral care were approached by sad children, or had other children brought to them by friends in the peer group who were encouraging them to tell of physical or sexual abuse. When they asked the children for explanations, they were often given the first public account of parental maltreatment.

Here are some examples of abused children whose plight was first made known in the school setting:

> A fourteen-year-old girl had been sexually abused by her father since the age of seven. The offences included kissing, fondling and attempted intercourse. She talked to a friend at school one day after watching a programme on television, and they went together to see their year group tutor.

> A ten-year-old boy came to school with a black eye. When questioned, he admitted that he had been punched in the eye and also in the stomach, after he had been rude to his stepfather's children. The school had previously noticed bruising on the boy's back during a football lesson.

> A five-year-old girl told her teacher that her mother's cohabitee had held a lighted cigarette against her neck. When examined, she was found to have a great many marks and scars of unknown origin.

Because the disclosure or discovery of abuse at school often preceded the formal investigation, the events were recounted in the conference with a particular kind of immediacy. If the teacher or headmaster was committed to registration as well, there was a powerful inducement to register. It was frequently in the interests of both school and social services to have the child on the register, since the staff in both establishments felt a degree of protection for themselves, and the school had an identified social worker who might offer some assistance to the child and family.

Most of the school's evidence was of course acquired from children on their own, or with their peers or with unrelated adults. The opportunity to observe children in these extra-familial settings was seen as unique, in terms of what teachers and headmasters had to offer the conference. (Information from private and voluntary organisations, and also day nurseries and play-groups, was rarely used in a similar way.) In many cases teachers had had the experience of inter-disciplinary training and this led to good cooperation with social services departments in the formal aspects of the case conference system.

> '*Once you've got, say, a school head or a representative of the school that's been on a couple of our courses and they understand the system, then it means the whole school understands that system and it [the allegation] is more inclined to be correctly dealt with.*'
> (Case conference chair)

In spite of the advantages of good agency cooperation and knowledge of individual children, the school's evidence had one main deficit. The teachers and headmasters often had very little knowledge of the parents. This was a considerable handicap, especially where the teachers were white and the children belonged to minority ethnic groups. Members of the school staff occasionally saw parents and children together, for example at parents' days or during medical checks, or when small children were collected from school; but they had little contact with parents who were alienated from the school system or too busy to attend open days. These disaffected or uninvolved groups included many of the parents who were accused of child abuse and neglect. Where a social worker was involved with the family, he or she might well have a different view of the parents, but it was often given little expression in the conference, for fear of upsetting the delicate balance of inter-agency relationships. One social worker who sympathised strongly with the family felt that he had to justify his rather passive acceptance of registration, on the grounds that new evidence had been presented.

> '*Following my involvement, I simply was not observing the things that the school were saying were happening. It was almost as if we were talking about two totally different families . . . However, up until the conference I had not been made fully aware of the extent of Mark's difficulties, so that changed my perception.*'

For teachers and social workers at the initial conference, there was often an exchange of benefits. The teachers looked to social services to negotiate on their behalf with parents who were becoming alienated from the school system. In return for their involvement, social workers felt that they could rely on the school to monitor the child. (This was not always done well; but the belief that it was being done freed the social worker of some anxiety and created space for other tasks.) The teachers also sometimes wanted resources in the form of welfare assistance for children within the school, and they wanted information on the family background of some children who were difficult to control.

Valuable though it was, much of the school's evidence was concerned with children's behaviour in the playground or the classroom – and there was often little recognition of the fact that problems might be caused by defects in the school system rather than parental inadequacy. There was also little recognition of the damage done by bullying, which one mother in the study quite justifiably referred to as a form of abuse.

> *'He's come home from school covered in more bruises than what I've ever known or given him myself. That's from children, as well. Great big lumps and huge bruises, you know, all down his spine. And that is quite upsetting to me, when he comes home at the end of the day like that. I feel it's my duty then to do something about that; but when I do try, I'm just a silly mother.'*

At the initial case conference on the above child, the school headmaster put forward the view that the boy was aggressive towards other children (which may well have been true) and had to be withdrawn from playtimes as a result. He painted a picture of a child who was extremely difficult to control and had a ferocious temper. In retrospect some of these concerns seem to have been exaggerated, since the boy settled well at another school; but they were presented very powerfully in the conference setting, and undoubtedly had an influence on registration.

This raises a question about relevance, which can be applied to almost all of the agencies' contributions. Most of the contributions were not directly concerned with evidence of abuse or neglect, even when evidence is loosely construed. The conference participants were providing background information. This information had a profound significance in terms of the conference outcomes, and we are justified in asking what it comprised.

Background information

After the actual allegations of abuse or neglect, and sometimes mixed in with them, the conference members were given background information about the family. This material, which included verbal portraits of individual family members and accounts of their personal and social characteristics, was usually seen as necessary for a number of reasons. Firstly, it put the allegations in a context in which they might be more easily understood. Secondly, it enabled the conference to scrutinise the parent's personality or life-style in order to make some judgement about the quality of parenting (that is, to make a bridge between child-based and parent-based evidence). Thirdly, it shed some light on the position of other children in the household who might be at risk; and fourthly, it could create a picture of the support systems surrounding the child, so that intervention might be planned and organised.

In our conference study we charted the background issues which were discussed and the frequency with which they were discussed. Table 11 presents some of the results. The percentages are based on adjusted figures, to take account of those cases in which certain topics would clearly be irrelevant;

Table 11   **Information Discussed at Initial Case Conferences**

Information topic	Proportion of conferences at which this topic was discussed
	%
Child's behaviour and development	92
Mother's behaviour and attitudes	86
Father figure's behaviour and attitudes (where applicable)	78
Parenting skills	63
Partner relationship (where applicable)	62
Ability of the mother to protect the child	60
Standard of care of the children	53
Parent/child relationship	42
Availability of support from the extended family	36
Problems during mother's childhood (incl. abuse, neglect, being in care, SSD involvement)	36
Housing situation	33
Financial situation	28
Cleanliness of home	24
Physical health of parent/s	23
Domestic violence	23
Ability of the father figure to protect the child	19
Alcohol problems	18
Availability of social support other than the extended family	18
Mental health of parents	15
Problems during father figure's childhood	14
Drug problems	4

for example questions about the male carer are irrelevant if there is no male carer. The issues were far from being raised consistently or systematically, but the list does give some indication of agencies' priorities and the factors considered relevant in decision-making.

Our observation suggests that in many cases the background information was crucial to the assessment of risk, either because it seemed to confirm an allegation already made or because it provided further evidence of risk in its own right. In addition to this, however, the background material was capable of providing the germ of an explanatory theory. By delving into the family history, and by exploring the network of the child's relationships and the general social context, the conference members could begin to form a notion of the aetiology of the abuse. At the very least, 'contributory factors' could be identified; but *because this information was presented in a disconnected way or linked simply to the diagnosis of risk, its implications for planning often went unrecognised.* Furthermore the parents' absence from this part of the proceedings (see chapter 7) meant that their accounts were not always known. Many important clues to the present situation were therefore missing, if the only information to be shared came from the formal investigation or from the previous records on the family.

It is interesting to consider the conference participants' *selection* of issues for discussion. From the list provided it is possible to single out items of information which might be useful both in risk-identification and in planning, either because they fit together in some form of explanatory theory or because they provide the social worker with a useful 'map'. It is worrying to notice the low percentage of cases in which some of these key issues were discussed. Some possibly significant gaps and anomalies were as follows.

Information about material circumstances

In spite of the proven connection between material deprivation and child maltreatment there was surprisingly little discussion of the families' material welfare. *Financial circumstances* were mentioned in just 34 out of 120 cases (28% of the total) although 41 households were on income support and for another 32 households their means of support was unclear. The situation we recorded is only slightly better than the one described in the study by Gibbons and colleagues (1993), which reported that financial circumstances were minuted as being discussed in 18% of the cases studied. The family's *housing situation*, although slightly more prominent than financial circumstances was mentioned in only 40 cases, or 33% of the total. (The corresponding figure in Gibbons' study is 35%.) This seems a very low rate of representation of the problem, in view of the bad housing situations which were reported to us and which we saw during the course of the interviews.

Apart from the general importance of these issues, of course, there is the question of relevance to the abuse. It might be assumed that material deprivation should be considered more readily in cases of neglect; but the references to housing and financial difficulties were evenly spread, and in many cases of neglect these factors were not discussed at the conference.

The issue of *the cleanliness of parents' homes* was raised across the whole spectrum of categories, although it was most frequently raised in cases of suspected neglect and emotional abuse. The registration rate associated with the 14 parents whose homes were thought to be unclean was 71%, compared with 57% for the 14 thought to have clean homes and 58% for the 89 cases in which this issue was not raised. Like many other items on the list, it was arguably a matter for subjective judgement on the part of the person reporting.

Information about family and community relationships

Although most conferences devoted time to constructing 'pen pictures' of nuclear family members, there was often little consideration of *support from the extended family and other social contacts*. In view of the importance of social isolation as a recognised factor in child abuse, it is surprising that questions about the extended family were raised in only 36% of cases, while other kinds of social support were mentioned in only 18%. (Gibbons also found that social support had a low rating, since it was minuted as a topic which had been discussed in only 26% of the cases studied.) This seemed to indicate that a low priority was given to the question of social support for carers, and that the focus of the child protection system was on the nuclear family rather than on community relationships. Minority ethnic parents could be particularly disadvantaged by an assessment along these lines.

Even within the nuclear family, however, there were anomalies. The *marital or partner relationship between the carers* was mentioned in 62% of the cases where a relationship was known to exist. However, in only 27 cases was *male to female violence* reported between partners; and the associated registration rate was 63% – only marginally higher than average. These results seem to suggest that male to female violence was not regarded as a significant factor affecting risk to children, in spite of the fact that it was present across the full range of households and categories of abuse in the study. (This is a point to which we will return later.)

In general, the conference lacked the information necessary to make a dynamic assessment of relationships, even though individual portraits could be rich in descriptive material. This criticism applies equally to information about adults and about children. The quality of the *parent-child relationship* was clearly considered in only 42% of cases.

In contrast, the *child's behaviour and development* was mentioned very frequently. It was discussed in 92% of conferences, principally because the presence of school staff and health visitors ensured that informed comment was routinely available. (It is worth noting that Gibbons also found the child's health and development high on the list of minuted topics, being discussed in 88% of cases.)

Parenting skills and *standards of care* were questions which were very significantly related to the identification of risk. The question of parenting skills was raised in 76 conferences, and skills were thought to be poor in 52 cases. The standard of care afforded to children was mentioned in 64 conferences and was thought to be poor in 32 of them. Once again, this issue was more frequently discussed than the parent-child relationship. The implication seems to be that good parenting stems from a mixture of moral virtue and expertise.

Information with a positive as opposed to a negative orientation

There appeared to be some pressure on conference members to bring forward negative information, and this fact gives rise to fears that much of the missing information may have been positive. If so, the debate may have suffered for the lack of it. For example, the partner relationship already referred to was thought to be a difficult one in 57 of the 64 cases where it was clearly discussed. Quinton and Rutter (1988) identified positive support from a partner as one of the crucial factors in preventing the inter-generational transmission of parenting problems. In spite of this fact, the partner relationship was mentioned positively in only four cases, out of which three were registered.

Some issues, such as the carer's physical or mental health, were always raised negatively. (That is, it was poor health rather than good health which received comment.) However, particular importance seemed to be attached to the *mental health of the mother*. There were 11 cases where the mental health of the female carer was said to be poor, and 10 of these cases (91%) resulted in registration.

Any evidence of a *problematic family background* on the part of either carer was a source of interest to the conference – but once again most attention was focused on the background of *mothers*, whether or not they were seen as responsible for the abuse. The mother's background was mentioned in all of the 42 cases where she was suspected of the principal abuse and in two other cases where she was not under suspicion. The background of the father, on the other hand, was mentioned in only 14% of cases, although in 51% the father was considered to be the abuser.

Where the parents were known to have been abused as children, the registration rate was not exceptionally high – except in the case of *sexually abused mothers*, where the associated registration rate rose to 77% (13 cases). For these 13 women their experience as sexually abused children appeared to be linked to higher registration rates irrespective of the type of abuse with which the conference was concerned. There was also a 75% registration rate associated with *prior social services involvement*, for the families of both fathers and mothers.

One frequent topic for discussion, and clearly seen as related to the identification of risk, was the *ability of the non-abusing parent to protect the child*. There were 72 cases in which female carers were present in the household and not suspected of the principal abuse. In 46 of these cases (64%) the issue of their ability to protect the child was discussed – and there was a much greater frequency of discussion of the issue in sexual abuse cases than in others. When there was a non-abusing *male* carer, on the other hand, his ability to protect the child was discussed in only six out of 25 cases (24%).

The impact of these discussions on the debate can be seen by the fact that *there was a statistically significant relationship between unfavourable comments made about mothers and the decision to register.* In the 27 cases where comments made about the mother's personality, behaviour and attitudes were unfavourable, the registration rate was 85%. Comments made about fathers also tended to be unfavourable except in cases of emotional abuse; but there was no association between the rate of registration and these unfavourable comments.

One mitigating factor, for both men and women, was a reference to *extenuating circumstances.* The registration rate was 50% where such circumstances were mentioned, compared with a rate of 63% when no such reference was made. The circumstances mentioned were mainly stress factors acting on the carer, such as financial difficulties, poor health, cramped housing conditions, a large number of children or lack of adequate help and support. The child's behaviour was sometimes mentioned as a stress factor, provoking the parent to anger – for example when a small child was excessively demanding, or slept little, or would not stop crying. Stress on the child was occasionally acknowledged as well.

Paradoxically, many of the items mentioned as extenuating circumstances would also count as risk factors if they were presented in a different light. The way in which they were introduced made the abuse or neglect seem less abnormal, and the parent less blameworthy. We are reminded that registration is not simply about risk to children, but about the notion of parental fault. We are also reminded that many so-called risk factors are like coins, whose currency value varies according to the particular conditions of the debate in which they are exchanged.

Is there an information threshold?

It seems reasonable to ask whether there is a 'threshold' of negative information in case conference decision-making which, once it is crossed, results in registration. We can indeed attempt to devise such a threshold from the information presented; but a simple check-list of items is likely to be of limited value, partly because of problems of interpretation and weighting, and partly because the assessment of risk depends on how individual pieces of information are seen to be combined. (We will attempt to examine this in the next chapter.) Furthermore, there is increasing evidence that patterns of registration vary from one area to another (Gibbons *et al*, 1993). At times we were tempted to agree with Corby (1987) that case conferences have 'a logic of their own', and that the system does little more than sort out cases 'in a rough and ready way'.

There was, however, some evidence of consistency in the use of registration once we identified a threshold in terms of the amount of negative information presented and the impact which it had on the participants.

When we counted the items of child-based and parent-based evidence which were brought forward in discussion of individual cases, as outlined at the start of this chapter, and scored these according to their impact in the conference setting (i.e. 1, 2 or 3 depending on whether they were treated as slight, moderate or severe indicators of risk) we found that there was a consistent numerical threshold above which the situation was considered risky and children were usually registered.

This says little except that the degree of risk in conference assessments is best understood in terms of professional concern; but it also indicates firstly that risk is constructed in the conference setting with the agreement of all agencies, secondly that the reports of some participants are particularly powerful in constructing it, and thirdly that it is possible to obtain a consistent reading of conference judgements when they are measured in this way. The category of 'grave concern' is no longer one of the official categories under which children may be registered. However, it seems likely that some aspect of 'grave professional concern' is still the basis of most registrations, whatever the category chosen, and it may well be the common denominator by which all of them are linked.

Summary

1. The presentation of information at the start of the initial case conferences was dominated by material from the joint investigation. The conference members were given detailed accounts of what had happened at this stage, together with descriptions of what various family members had said and how they had reacted to the investigation. Whether or not the parent's reaction was typical, it was taken to indicate the quality of the parenting normally available to the child. This information was treated as 'evidence'.

2. The information relayed from the investigation was both child-based and parent-based, but the focus was indisputably on parental behaviour. As a result, parents tended to be considered responsible for most forms of harm to children even if the harm had not been deliberately caused. If it seemed that an injury to the child had been accidental, the ensuing discussion might still lead to registration under the category of neglect.

3. Clear medical evidence was often missing. Sometimes there was no medical practitioner apart from the health visitor at the conference. At other times clinical evidence was available but it was unreliable or ambiguous. (This applied particularly in cases of child sexual abuse.) Nevertheless the evidence of medical practitioners, when it was present, had a strong role to play in confirming or disconfirming the statements of other people (see also Dingwall, 1983).

4. There were occasional complaints from paediatricians that they had not been consulted in the early stages, or that they had been unable to interview the parents because of the activities of the joint investigating team. It might improve the supply of medical information to the conference if there were clear procedures for the referral of abused children to GPs and hospital doctors when this seems to be required.

5. The wide-ranging 'background material', which included oral portraits of parents and other family members, was an important conference contribution to the construction of risk. It tended to carry the concerns away from the strict details of the allegations into other areas of parenting. Because the parents were usually absent during this part of the meeting, however, the information was incomplete and their views about the topics discussed were not always known.

6. The frequency or infrequency with which certain topics were raised suggests that the parents' *needs* were not always well known. For example, the family's housing situation was mentioned in only 33% of conferences and financial circumstances in 28%. There was little consideration of possible support to the parents from the extended family (mentioned in 36% of cases) or from other social contacts (mentioned in 18% of cases). These gaps made planning difficult, and they also appeared to have a bearing on the outcomes.

7. The child's behaviour and development were referred to very frequently (in 92% of cases); but the parent-child relationship was mentioned in only 42% of cases. This crucial topic was therefore discussed less frequently than the child's behaviour, and less frequently than parenting skills or standards of care.

8. The importance of many of the items introduced was contextual. However, a consistent threshold of risk was found when risk was identified simply in terms of professional concern.

Chapter 9

The assessment of risk

In the conference setting, information was always treated as a source of power. We have outlined in previous chapters how power in the form of information was given and received, shared, withheld or taken.

Because of their vulnerability, and because of the sensitivity of the subject matter, many parents found it difficult to accept the way in which details of their private lives had been made public. With the assessment of risk, the parents found themselves involved in public *shame*. Enforced publicity was accompanied by stigmatisation, both within the professional group and outside it. In spite of, or perhaps because of, feeling blamed, parents who were the subject of assessment often seemed to be trying to assess their own competence in relation to that of other people. Mothers in particular, feeling that their ability to parent was under attack, seemed to be trying to establish their own relative threshold of risk. According to Goffman (1963), such attempts at comparison can be of assistance to the stigmatised individual who

> '. . . can then take up in regard to those who are more evidently stigmatised than himself the attitudes the 'normals' take to him. Thus do the hard of hearing stoutly see themselves as anything but deaf persons, and those with defective vision, anything but blind.'

In a similar way it could help to maintain the self-esteem of stigmatised mothers if they felt that others were performing child care tasks less well than they were, although it also irritated them to feel that social services had singled out the wrong people for scrutiny. One mother whose baby was registered because of injury to a previous child said:

> '*I've been woken up by our next door neighbours . . . Me and Graham [the baby] have both been woken up about three or four times with him whacking his kids first thing in the morning. And really beating them . . . I mean, I've learnt more words off him than I must have in my entire life . . . I hear him actually whacking his kids and them screaming their heads off, and I think, "Well, why am I on it?"* '

Another mother was at pains to point out that although she had hit her child rather hard she had hit him on the bottom instead of cuffing him around the head. She wanted to distinguish what she felt to be legitimate punishment from what she regarded as the actions of a real child abuser.

> '*If I had that sort of attitude in my mind, I wouldn't have pulled his trousers down and smacked his bum, would I?*'

The notion of emotional abuse was particularly difficult for parents to understand and accept, because of the implication that they did not love their children. One couple strongly denied that their son had been emotionally abused, and pointed out in their own defence that they had bought him a pool table. Sometimes the parents clung to the notion that their children had been referred to the conference because of physical injury, when the professionals were actually more worried about the emotional damage which accompanied it. Again, the exclusion of parents from the conference assessment made it possible for them to harbour misunderstandings about both the concerns and the processes of decision-making.

In cases which did not involve physical injury, parents were particularly keen to dissassociate themselves from the stigmatised group of child-batterers with whom they felt that they were being unfairly linked. Their acceptance of the conference assessment often depended on the extent to which it struck home, and they were happier if the blame could be diverted on to other people or impersonal causes. Even where they felt that some aspect of their actions could not be justified, they wanted the positives in their care of the children to be recognised – and they were most deeply hurt when they felt that their experience of parenting had been misunderstood.

If the parents' attitudes were difficult for the conference members to understand and accept, the professional assessment of risk was equally a puzzle to parents. How was the assessment conducted? What methods of reasoning were used?

Methods of assessing risks

We have already referred to the types of evidence and background information presented at initial conferences (chapter 8). Analysis of this evidence tells us much about the agencies' priorities, and it documents the raw material of decision-making; but on its own it tells us little of how the decision about registration or non-registration was reached. To understand that process we have to know something about the way in which various pieces of evidence were combined.

Our observation of conferences and our study of the recorded notes suggest that there were certain standard patterns of reasoning available to conference members, on the basis of their previous experience, and that these patterns were used over and over again in the run-up to the final decision. They are so distinct that they almost form separate models of decision-making, although it goes without saying that they can be combined and frequently were.

There was very little use of theoretical reasoning in the conference assessments. The main ways in which different conferences dealt with the evidence and assessed risk to the child can be classified roughly as follows:

1. Accumulating concerns;
2. Comparing present and previous contexts;
3. Focusing on specific incidents of abuse or neglect.

The central features of these approaches to assessment, and the way in which they tended to influence the later conduct of the cases, can perhaps be illustrated most easily by the construction of a sample case which is capable of being analysed in different ways. Here is a hypothetical case which serves this purpose.

> Mrs X has a young child, John, who is undernourished and badly behaved. One day John is reported to have a bad bruise on his face. He is thought to have been hit by the mother's cohabitee, Mr Y.
>
> In a previous marriage Mrs X had a child who was taken into care as a result of her husband's violence. Her new relationship with Mr Y has been fraught with problems such as debts, homelessness and misuse of alcohol. The situation is worrying, and a child protection case conference is called.

This hypothetical case incorporates many of the actual ingredients of cases in the study. There might of course be definite evidence of abuse, or the cohabitee might admit to having hit the child; but in many similar cases we found the evidence of abuse to be uncertain. If we assume a degree of uncertainty, the assessment of risk is likely to be carried out in one of the three ways already outlined.

1. *Accumulating concerns*

In this approach to decision-making, which is encouraged by the consecutive presentation of information, the conference members virtually pile concerns on top of each other to arrive at an assessment of risk. The incident of bruising, the concerns about underfeeding and bad behaviour, the family's previous history and the material and personal problems of the carers, are all together considered indicative of severe risk to the child. There is no doubt that in this case the child will be registered.

The advantage of this type of assessment is its extreme simplicity. It derives some legitimacy from the notion that there are 'factors' contributing to risk in child abuse cases, and it presupposes that the more factors there are, the greater the degree of risk to the child. The model also has some theoretical validity, inasmuch as many of these factors are indicative of family stress; but it does not allow for the fact that some pieces of information are known to the conference while others of an 'offsetting nature' (such as the extent of family support and social contacts) have simply been left out.

The paucity of background information available to the conference on some subjects, and the negative bias of much of that information, have already been outlined (see chapter 8). These gaps affected the reliability of the cumulative assessment in many cases. Unfortunately, in addition to being ignorant of possible positive as well as negative features, the conference participants were sometimes tempted to ignore any *link* between the factors and to assume, wrongly, that they were all of roughly equal importance. When the diagnosis of risk was made on this basis, the focus of the subsequent intervention was extremely unclear.

One common response of the conference to this lack of clarity was to *operationalise the risk*. When faced with a multitude of worries about health and safety, the conference often felt that the main risk to the child arose from inadequate parenting – but at the same time the concerns had to be made specific. Some conferences, it is true, would not hesitate to register a child like John on grounds of neglect or even emotional abuse (now that the category of 'grave concern' has been abolished); but if the conference was bothered by the diffuse nature of the concerns, it might set the carers a diagnostic task. For example, the parents might be asked to present the child for one or more developmental checks, or to take the child to a paediatrician for assessment. If the parents failed to present the child for assessment, or if the child was presented and there was evidence of developmental delay, then a diagnosis of risk would be made. There are two halves to this form of assessment. The parents' ability to cooperate is on trial, as well as the child's progress.

If the meeting decided on this course of action, there was no obvious reason for registration. Some conferences might register the child to ensure that the assessment would be reviewed. Others might refrain from register-ing, on the grounds that the parents were being given a chance to prove themselves before the hurdle of registration was passed. But if a second case conference was called after this diversionary process, the likelihood was that the child would be registered.

2.   *Comparing present and previous contexts*

Instead of summing concerns or operationalising the risk, the conference members might concentrate on an incident which had caused great anxiety in the past. (In the above example it would be the abuse to Mrs X's previous child which necessitated that child's removal.) The main concern of the conference in this situation would be to investigate whether the same series of events was likely to be repeated. Since the degree of risk to the present child was usually seen as dependent on the similarity of the contexts, the conference members would want to know:

(i)   What were the circumstances which led to the previous abuse?

(ii)   Are the circumstances now similar or dissimilar, and in what respects?

Here is an extract from the minutes, in a case where the assessment of risk was done by the comparison of present and previous contexts. The result is optimistic.

> 'The serious injuries to the previous child, Darren, which led to his adoption, have been discussed and it has been noted that this history presents some potential risks in the current situation. However, there are significant differences in respect of this pregnancy, in that it has been openly acknowledged within the family, and Ms Smith [the mother] appears to have bonded well with Caroline [the new baby].'

In this form of assessment, which was really a kind of pattern-matching, the main focus was on the context of the previous abuse – including socio-economic circumstances, family relationships and emotional support. Since parents were included in the context of the child, the relevant questions were likely to include: 'How similar is the new cohabitee to the previous husband?' and 'How similar is the mother to the person she was?' That is, has she matured, or become more confident, or changed her attitudes?

This form of assessment, in which the conference searched for continuities and discontinuities over time, was more subtle than the simple accumulation of concerns. It was capable of bringing out the link between the factors, for example, the connection between debts, homelessness and alcohol problems, or between alcohol problems and violence. This was a distinct advantage. On the other hand, there was a tendency to assume, perhaps wrongly, that there was a connection between the previous incident and the present one, and this judgement tended to place blame on the mother as the source of continuity between the two. It also suggested that the main aim of intervention would be to prevent the removal of the child, since this was the anticipated bad outcome.

Whether or not there was a discernible 'previous context', of course, the conferences which used this model of assessment were concerned with *plotting future directions*. If the conference wished to take an open-ended view of risk, it might ask, 'In what direction is the situation heading?' or simply, 'Are things getting better or worse?' The case conference report on one mother who was mentally ill and therefore seen as emotionally neglectful listed the following under 'concerns identified':

> 'It appeared that Jane Freeman's mental health was deteriorating. She was not receiving any treatment at the moment even on an outpatient basis, neither was she on any medication. Her behaviour was unpredictable.'

The picture is a downward-sloping graph. In this case the treatment which might have arrested deterioration, and which (just as importantly) might have given the conference faith in the mother's ability to cooperate, was missing. In physical abuse cases it was often considered relevant to ask whether the alleged abuse was a 'one-off' or liable to be repeated and, if repetition was likely, whether there was likely to be an escalation of harm to the child. The direction of change in the ancillary problems had to be charted as well. The conference needed to be told whether the family was resolving its financial problems or falling more deeply into debt, and whether housing and alcohol problems were becoming more acute.

In the above example the baseline for the calculation of risk was probably the condition of the mother prior to her illness. In the case of Mrs X and Mr Y, the baseline for this plotting operation would probably have been the start of the relationship with the new cohabitee; but the conference might choose to plot direction from the earliest known point of involvement, which is more likely to produce a pattern of ups and downs. In the conferences we attended, registration seemed to be less likely if the child's present experience was seen as one point in a cycle, rather than as the start of new forms of adversity. On the other hand, a perceived pattern of cyclical repetition could result in registration when the conference decided that the pattern had gone on long enough – usually because the patience of the various agencies had become exhausted.

In spite of its limitations, this form of reasoning is part and parcel of most decision-making about risk. Agencies cannot avoid the need to make predictions in child protection work; and if these are to be more than inspired guesses, they must involve extrapolations from the pattern of events perceived in the past.

3.   *Focusing on specific incidents of abuse or neglect*
In contrast to the very wide view of risk employed in the previous two models, the conference might feel that the only really important point is that the child has suffered non-accidental injury. If the police representatives have conducted an enquiry which convinces them that Mr Y is guilty (whether or not his guilt can be proved in court) then the conference would probably feel justified in registering John on the grounds that he is at risk of physical abuse. The problem then becomes one of protecting John from the abuser.
Here is an extract from a real assessment report which follows this pattern:

> 'Martha and Jody have given some details of sexual abuse by their father, and their behaviour at school tends to support the view that their statements must be taken seriously.'

The report continues:

> 'The lack of corroborative evidence suggests that charges against Mr J [the children's father] may be dropped. In that event, if he is freed, we may need to take further steps to protect the children if their mother proves unable to do so.'

Police prosecution, if it was possible in the cases we studied, provided a way of removing the abuser from the household, at least for a time. In the absence of the abuser, the risk to be assessed by the conference was lower; but the conference was not necessarily reassured if there was a possibility of his return. If the abuser could not definitely be removed from the household, as in this case, the conference would probably turn to the mother and examine her ability to protect the child. However, protection consisted mainly in keeping the abuser at bay. The mother's standard of care, which was a major issue in conferences which assessed risk by 'accumulating concerns', was seen as less important in this more focused model, because care-giving was connected not with protection but with the child's development.

One social worker whose work was based on this kind of assessment said:

> *'If you didn't know about the sexual abuse you really wouldn't make a fuss about it [the standard of care] because there are so many families for whom it is not quite right . . . They [the children] just need more than they are getting; but if you didn't know about the sexual abuse you wouldn't make a fuss.'*

All methods of assessment incorporate a strong notion of individual responsibility; but this method emphasises it more heavily than most. Who was responsible for the injury and who is now responsible for protecting the child? Even if there was a male abuser, responsibility for the abuse might be seen as shared by the mother (who ought not to have allowed it to happen in the first place), while the responsibility for protecting the child might be hers and hers alone. If the degree of risk to the child was assessed according to the mother's actions and attitudes, it was a small step from this point to deciding that the child was actually at risk *from the mother*, not only because of her low protective ability but because of her poor parenting skills. (Therefore, by a roundabout route, the conference has arrived at accumulating concerns.) The assessment of risk, in a case of this sort, can very easily turn into an assessment of the mother.

In some cases where the assessment of risk became unduly focused on the mother, and planning and intervention followed from the assessment, the actions of social services actually reinforced a situation in which male abusers found it easy to opt out. Worse still, the stresses on the mother might not be recognised, and the social worker might end up by placing the whole duty of protecting the child on a woman who did not have the power to carry it.

Another disadvantage in some cases was that the conference members, by focusing their attention on the responsible adult, failed to distinguish between the experiences of different children in the household. It was not unusual for more than one child to have suffered abuse, and for the youngest (who might well have been responsible for the disclosure) to attract most sympathy, although older children had often suffered more and for longer.

The degree of risk experienced by different siblings, and the extent of their treatment needs, could go unrecognised unless the assessment was sensitive enough to allow this territory to be explored.

Methods which were under-used

There are some ways of thinking about problems, both in social work and in other contexts, which were not very often used in the conference setting. Our impression was that if they had been used, they might have enabled the conference members to arrive at a more realistic and satisfactory judgement in cases which proved problematic, and they might also have opened up the way for future planning. It seems appropriate to note what they are.

(i)   *Analysing the dynamics*
In a few cases the conference members used forms of assessment which were more complex than that attempted during most conferences, and at the same time more dynamic. (The word 'dynamic' is used here in a very wide sense.) The ingredients in these assessments, although not always found together, were as follows.

Firstly, in relation to the evidence of risk and the concerns about the child's protection, risk factors were considered both separately and in the light of the interaction between them. The conference would seek to know, for example, what effect the father's illness or unemployment had on the family. In considering parental behaviour, people would ask not simply what actions or omissions on the parents' part might be causing the child to exhibit disturbed behaviour, but what effect the child's behaviour had on the parents. For example, did it in any way contribute to the likelihood of abuse or neglect?

Secondly, when exploring the background of the family and the personality of the carers, the conference would take into account the relationship between the adult partners, between adults and children, and between siblings or other adults in the household. (This was particularly helpful in cases of sibling abuse, which were not easily dealt with by means of the traditional abuser-victim stereotype.) Another profitable topic for discussion was the interaction between the family and the community, which raised issues of socio-economic status and the presence or absence of social support.

A third aid to forming the child protection plan which our findings suggest would be useful, would be for the conference to chart the family's needs according to the three dimensions which we used in evaluating outcome – that is child protection, child welfare and carers' needs. This form of assessment, if it was sensitively carried out with due regard for the interaction between the dimensions, could help the conference to chart the degree of risk to the child or children and also to pinpoint areas in which intervention might be beneficial. (These are issues which will be explored more fully at a later stage.)

In terms of the supply of information to the conference, as we have seen, the necessary information to provide for a dynamic assessment may not be known – and if it is 'known', in professional terms it may not be recognised by the people who are most involved since they have other frames of reference. For both practical and ethical reasons, assessments which involve discussions of family and community relationships are best conducted with the relevant family members present and contributing. This leads to the final approach to assessment, which was only occasionally represented in the study.

(ii)   *Negotiating risk*
In a conference which placed a high value on parental attendance, the presentation of information would take place in the presence of the parents. This would give Mrs X and Mr Y the opportunity to refute anything which was said about them and also to present their own view of events, which might differ markedly from that of social services. Instead of embarking on a unilateral assessment of risk, the conference would discuss the possible risks to the child with the parents. (Mr Y might be excluded, but only if his behaviour was likely to inhibit or endanger others.)

A child protection conference run totally on these lines would resemble what is now known as a 'case discussion'. It would resemble, for example, a meeting of relevant agencies to discuss diagnosis and future planning where a child is severely handicapped. The child and the child's carers would automatically be involved. There are problems in using this type of conference in a system which (at present) runs on the notion of parental fault, and which relies on the authority of social services to enforce standards of care on what are regarded as recalcitrant parents. Nevertheless, the success of the children's hearings in Scotland suggests that even in a court setting it is possible for the parent's view to be heard and for some negotiation to take place.

Having outlined the methods of assessment which we observed, and having made a quick tally of their advantages and disadvantages, it seems appropriate to look more closely at other aspects of risk assessment, which are crucial to the whole child protection process.

The use and misuse of cultural arguments
The reports of conferences involving minority ethnic families bear witness to the dangers of cultural stereotyping. In the study as a whole we found that many of the families with children on the child protection register were extremely isolated. Black families were no exception to this rule. These findings are consistent with the results of other studies, which show that although many people from ethnic minorities have greater access to care from relatives than their counterparts in the white majority culture, it is not true to say that all minority ethnic families can rely on an extended network of kin

(Boushel and Fisher, forthcoming). This fact is important to note, since arguments based on an oversimplistic notion of 'cultural relativism' can be misleading if the parents in question are separated from, or even scapegoated by, the group to which they are presumed to belong.

The kinship and friendship networks which might have been common in their country of origin, and which did exist in some cases, were missing for many such parents who had been drawn into the child protection system. Housing difficulties were common; and because housing difficulties and social isolation frequently occurred together, it was not unusual for the family to be both overcrowded and lonely at the same time. There were two cases in which social workers were concerned about children being left alone in the house while the mother collected other children from school. One of these concerned a girl who had strange bruises, suggesting either that she had been tied to a chair as a form of restraint or that she had been sexually abused. Since her mother tended to leave her alone or with an adult male babysitter, either explanation was possible.

In spite of the anxieties expressed by Dingwall in his study of child protection (Dingwall *et al.*, 1983), cultural arguments were not much used by conference members as a reason for non-registration. However, since our study focused on children already on the child protection register, we cannot say whether cultural arguments were used to divert black and minority ethnic children at the stages of referral and investigation. (There is a need for further research to explore this issue.) A second point is that even where intervention was indicated, the nature of the child protection plan, and therefore the manner of intervention, was often in doubt. Because they were unaware of how minority ethnic parents defined themselves, there were situations where social workers made erroneous assumptions about cultural *mores* (for example when they claimed too readily that they knew 'how the family lived') and there were also occasions when another professional from the same ethnic group joined the debate on the family's side. For example, a teacher at one case conference argued that in the culture to which she and the family belonged it was perfectly in order for a son to sleep with his father, and that no abuse was implied.

In most cases involving minority ethnic children, risk was assessed by focusing on specific incidents of physical or sexual abuse. The reasons which were offered by alleged perpetrators for discrediting children's own dis-closures of sexual abuse were sometimes given a cultural flavour which added to their credibility; for example one girl was alleged to have made accusations against her father because she disliked the idea of an arranged marriage, and this possibility was carefully considered. Problems of adolescence were also sometimes focused on cultural issues. In one classic case of teenage rebellion, an Asian girl who was said to have been 'led astray' by English and African-Caribbean schoolgirls had apparently been beaten by her father and brothers.

The conference tried to defuse the situation in terms of its cultural implications by using the girl's truancy as a focus for intervention, although when the dimensions of the case were fully recognised at a later date, and a female Asian worker was employed to befriend the girl and her mother, the power relationships began to change.

One blind spot commonly found in assessments was that class and gender were not always seen as linked with culture. Sometimes social workers were sensitive to these issues but did not interpret them in the same way as family members did. For example, whilst assumptions might be made that deprived ethnic families had much in common with white families from lower socio-economic groups, high-ranking Asians resented being treated as working class. There were also hidden status dimensions in the refuge facilities arranged for Asian women and children, which resulted in one needy mother withdrawing from them. In another case, where a zealous social worker convinced an Asian woman that she ought to deal with marital violence by means of an injunction and separation, instead of by conflict resolution, she was blamed for the break-up of this woman's marriage and subsequent social isolation. (The woman had married a relative, and her husband's relatives were also her own.) Once again, this woman was helped by the allocation of an Asian worker; but she drew a nice distinction between ethnicity and professionalism, as two possible facets of a social worker's identity:

> 'She can understand how we live. She knows; but she is more a social worker, even so.'

This simple statement brings forward a real dilemma, in that the priority given to professionalism in child protection work was sometimes in danger of crowding out issues concerned with race and ethnicity. As some of the social work literature has indicated, institutional racism may not be deliberate (CCETSW, 1991). Section 22(5)(c) of the Children Act 1989 has provided a legal basis for anti-racist practice by requiring the local authority to give 'due consideration' to a child's religious persuasion, racial origin and cultural and linguistic background. This requirement is helpful, and acts as a reminder of the importance of cultural factors in decision-making. Nevertheless, giving 'due consideration' is not a particularly restricting exercise (Allen, 1990) and agencies may be able to maintain very different policies on the treatment of minority ethnic children while at the same time proclaiming an adherence to the terms of the legislation.

Our research showed that when black professionals were present in the agency there were lively debates within the teams; but we could not help noticing that when 'joint working' was attempted by black and white staff, the dominant worker was usually white. (Working partnerships referred to in the study included a black social worker with a white manager, or a white social worker with an Asian social work assistant.) One of the tasks of the minority ethnic worker was clearly to alert the agency to factors of cultural importance or to the family's feelings about racism; but when the worker was in a learning role, and invited to accompany the social worker or manager in order to 'gain experience' it would be understandable if pride of place were given to assessments based on white professional skills. Another aspect of the dilemma is that professionalism is heavily dependent on the notion of expertise; but since black workers rightly rejected the notion that ethnicity should be regarded as a specialism, rather than demanding 'a radical rework- ing of the standard and conventional framework of service delivery' (Bhaduri, 1988) there was a risk that cultural factors would be down-graded and treated as peripheral.

In general there was a lack of clarity in assessments of risk where minority ethnic families were involved, and this was related to a confusion of aims and objectives as well as a lack of clear information emerging from the investiga- tions. However, a positive feature of many cultural assessments was that, in the absence of definitive views about parental behaviour, the conference members might concentrate on the degree of visible harm to the child. Another positive feature was that the assessment of risk occasionally led to community action. This happened when the conference had to deal with behaviour which seemed to be abusive but which was clearly sanctioned by the customs of one ethnic group. For example, at one time there were complaints that children were being beaten in the mosque for not under- standing the Koran. It was decided to deal with these complaints by means of intervention at community level. Discussions were held with the leaders of the mosque, and after a short time the punishment was modified.

The absence of theoretical context

One very striking point about the assessment process was its apparent lack of theoretical reasoning. In a case conference which is attended by well- qualified practitioners from different disciplines, why is it that there is so little explicit reference to theories, or to research evidence bearing on the aetiology of child abuse? Would such an assessment not provide an excellent springboard for intervention, in addition to aiding the classification of children at risk?

The absence of formal theoretical reasoning, both in diagnosis and in treatment, has been commented on by other authors. The most readily available explanation is that because of the different disciplines in which conference members are trained, there is no common theoretical framework. Hallett and Birchall (1992), for example, mention the fact that social services depend heavily on the skills and functions of other agencies both in assessment and in treatment:

'Questions, therefore, arise as to the depth and breadth of any consensual knowledge of how child abuse should be handled.'

Corby (1993), too, comments on the diversity and potential incompatibility of theoretical approaches:

'A broad range of theoretical perspectives has been brought to bear on the aetiology of child abuse. They derive from diverse sources, survey the problem at different levels and, as a consequence, do not necessarily complement each other.'

What counts as a theoretical perspective? Reasoning which was overtly based on professional knowledge or expertise was present in most of the conferences we attended, but it was often confined to small-scale, measurable phenomena such as estimates of the child's educational progress or physical health and development. Except where medical evidence was required in cases of non-accidental injury there was very little theorising directly related to the abuse, and particularly to the likely origins of a particular incident of child abuse as opposed to the recording of possible symptoms.

The chairs were the people most likely to introduce theoretical reasoning, since it was they who drew together the concerns and moved the meeting towards the registration decision. Sometimes this input was extremely helpful. One coordinator who had recently attended a course on sexual abuse, for example, was able to identify the behaviour of a parent as being typical 'grooming' of a potential victim for abuse. This suggests that one way of ensuring good decisions at conferences is to improve the theoretical competence of the chairs – not only because the role of the chair is influential but because the chairperson is one conference participant whose attendance can be relied on.

The discussions at the conferences we attended were strongly based in the experience of practitioners. Very occasionally empirically derived principles were referred to, but there was doubt about whether they could be applied in individual cases. (For example, one conference participant said that a sexual abuser of pre-pubertal children might not discriminate between boys and girls; but because the predilections of this particular abuser were not known, the conference was unsure of the risk to any young boys with whom he might have contact.) Besides the reluctance to apply principles in individual cases there was also a reluctance among some conference members to move from data to conclusions – perhaps because any move towards the interpretation of empirical data represents a 'degradation of certainty', and uncertainty is linked with risk.

There are, of course, a number of practical reasons for the avoidance of extensive theoretical discussions. Firstly, there is the time limit. Most conferences did not last longer than an hour. Secondly, as mentioned in chapter 7, there was a shortage of medical personnel at conferences and a virtual absence of psychological reports. It seems likely, however, that psychological reports could not have been furnished in the time available, even if they had been requested and authorised. King and Trowell (1993) have written about the clash of attitudes between court and clinic, and the unreal expectation that anyone can provide an instant assessment of parenting capacity:

> 'Unfortunately there appears to be a belief among some lawyers and judges that for a skilled child psychiatrist this is a simple task – a sort of psychological litmus test. You just look the parents over, ask them a few seaching questions and out comes the answer: 'yes', they do have parental capacity; 'no' they don't.'

Amongst practical considerations which militate against theorising we must include the desire of most conference members to avoid inter-agency conflict. In other words the reduction of individual viewpoints to what Hallett and Birchall call 'consensual knowledge' helps to cement the relationships between agencies and exhibits yet another aspect of the no-conflict norms referred to in chapter 6. Fourthly, however, it may represent a genuine attempt to conceptualise child abuse and neglect as a unitary phenomenon; and this conceptualisation is necessary (it can be argued) because the working of the present system demands that abuse of all kinds is transformed into 'a unitary condition which can be managed by one standardised inter-agency routine' (Hallett and Birchall, 1992).

The methods of assessing risk which we have identified tend to be atheoretical and pragmatic. They confirm that there is good reason for the unease expressed in social work literature about the homogenisation of child abuse theories. On the one hand there are anxieties about the extent to which different forms of abuse are inappropriately lumped together, and on the other hand there are worries that harm to children cannot be controlled and reduced unless there is a clearly identifiable common denominator of risk. Some of these worries seem to stem from the fact that theories used in diagnosis are assumed to be used in *treatment*, and no-one wants the development of 'a unitary notion of a disease syndrome' (Hallett and Birchall, 1992). At the stage of intervention, if not in the initial decision-making stages as well, some differentiation needs to be made between sexual, physical and other forms of abuse and neglect and the varieties of harm which can result from them.

On the evidence of our study, some methods of assessment were more unitary than others; and the interventions also varied in their specificity. Lack of theoretical reasoning did not produce 'realistic' or practicable decisions, however. It was more likely to produce nebulous judgements. Another difficulty was that beliefs which were held on a theoretical level were probably not brought into practice. The same problems have been experienced in other contexts, including the Scottish children's hearings.

'Panel members, like the authors of reports, did not appear to make use of a coherent framework of ideas concerning the causes of delinquency. What is more surprising, they rarely in the course of the hearing applied the theories of delinquency to which we know they adhere' (Martin *et al.*, 1981).

Arguably the decision to be made at the end of the assessment of risk is not primarily a technical decision but a moral one. As Watson (1982) says in connection with the children's hearings, 'the major issues faced and reviewed by a hearing must be resolved by moral judgement, rather than by distinctly professional judgement: moral judgements are not within the scope of professional expertise *as such*'. If the conference decision is actually being fuelled by a moral judgement which remains invisible, it is hardly surprising if the discussion appears to be lacking in theoretical context.

In spite of the popularity and benefits of 'working together', we are justified in asking on what basis the conference members actually make decisions about risk in child abuse cases. The participants may have good experience of working with the family; but the main expertise of the professionals in three of the four key services which are represented at conferences – that is, health, education, social services and police – is not centred on child abuse but on other issues. The recognition of possible child abuse and neglect is only a part (but perhaps an increasingly large part) of their work. Consequently the main incentive to develop specialist expertise in child protection, both in terms of recognising abuse and in terms of providing treatment, rests with the social services personnel who have responsibility for carrying it out.

Perhaps the best way to make sense of the assessment of risk at case conferences is to see it in this context – that is, to see it not primarily as part of socio-medical or even socio-legal discourse (in the sense envisaged by Parton, 1991) but as a bureaucratic-administrative exercise which involves doctors, police and sometimes lawyers in the prioritisation of cases for social work intervention. Theoretical reasoning, when it was present in the conferences we attended, was linked to the type of reasoning which is commonly found in social work practice. For example, theories of psychosocial stress were sufficiently broad-ranging to be used and the notion of risk may have been treated as 'unitary' because it could not be sited in any one discipline.

In terms of the diagnosis of abuse and neglect, and more particularly in terms of the identification of future risk to the child, the chairperson and senior members of the social services department had charge of the decisions in the conferences we attended. The contributions of other agencies were necessary for the reduction of uncertainty; but as we noted in connection with conference function, and again in connection with the role of the participants, the case conference is not primarily a forum for interdisciplinary decision-making. It is a forum in which other agencies provide support (and cover) for the decisions taken by social services.

Features of good and bad assessments

When we review the whole process of information-sharing and assessment, can any firm conclusions be drawn about the worth of the assessments of risk that we witnessed? In relation to later developments, three things stand out as important. First, the best assessments were *based on good information*. This meant not only that all relevant reports were to hand and that there were no significant gaps in the information available to the conference, but that the family members' feelings were accurately represented. The parents' needs, and the child's developmental needs, were known. The chair had also paid some attention to the *balance* of the information, and the way in which different points of view were represented among the participants.

Secondly the best assessments used the expertise of participants as a way of interpreting individual pieces of information, and in the final construction of risk they employed a *variety of methodological approaches*, including plotting future directions and, if necessary, matching present and previous contexts. This enabled the conference to view the situation from a number of perspectives. Some approaches were more suitable than others, depending on the family's background and circumstances, and they also varied in sophistication. In general the more satisfactory assessments were at least partly *dynamic* – that is, they took into account the relationships and interactions between family members, and between family members and official agencies, rather than simply accumulating concerns. Besides being dynamic, they ensured that the meanings of the interactions were to some extent *open to negotiation*. They took into account the expressed views of parents and children, whether these family members were actually present at the conference or not. If parents were present during the assessment of risk, as we have seen, the supply of information was better; and even if parents found the experience upsetting, the possibilities for mutual understanding were increased.

Thirdly, the requirement to negotiate implies that the information should be seen in its *cultural context*. Assessments which involve exploration of the cultural context are of course time-consuming and they need to be done at some leisure; but our research suggests that this is necessary in order to understand the significance of the incident or situation which is the source of concern, and sometimes to initiate community action. Finally, there is a point of paramount general importance: *the assessments which were of most value in the study provided a foundation for planning.* They did not simply result in a judgement that the child was at risk. They led naturally to the formation of a child protection plan.

The provision of a basis for planning, as a function of the assessment, was underrated and at times sadly neglected. In order to fulfil this function, the conference members had to be specific about the dangers. They had to state in some detail the various kinds of harm which were believed to threaten the child and precisely which people constituted the likely source of harm. This entailed making necessary distinctions between the *risk of harm from future abuse* (the source of a need for protection) and the *risk of harm occasioned by past or present abuse* (the source of a need for treatment.) Usually the first of these was admitted and the second was largely ignored.

To provide an ideal basis for intervention, of course, the conference members would have had to go further than the simple assessment of risk. *It is a major disadvantage of the present system that the assessment of risk to the child is not necessarily an assessment of need.* As a result, a further full-scale assessment often had to be done when the conference was over – by which time the child protection plan was supposed to have been formed and the motivation to construct a plan might well have evaporated.

Social workers were probably correct in seeing that the main virtue of the conference as it is presently constituted is not its assessment function but the bringing together (and linking) of disparate pieces of information. The next chapter will look in more detail at the decisions and recommendations which were formed, against the backcloth which the assessment of risk provided.

Summary

1. Under the direction of the conference chair, the assessment of risk tended to follow standard patterns of reasoning. The most commonly used method was to sum all the concerns (i.e. to treat them as being cumulative), or to compare the present with a past situation for the child and to plot directions (to make a judgement about whether the child's situation was getting better or worse). Some conferences focused on specific incidents of abuse or on specific abusers, and others attempted to unravel the family dynamics. The assessment of risk varied in thoroughness and sophistication, depending on which method was chosen.

2. The assessment of risk was hampered by the gaps in information mentioned in previous chapters. Reported observations of the child's behaviour were extremely useful; but the interpretation of this information was in doubt if the quality of the parent-child relationship was unknown. The information also had to be seen in a cultural context.

3. Parents in general found the assessment of risk a very *shaming* exercise. Now that information about their private lives was in the public arena, they found that they had little control over how it was used. They sometimes attempted to reframe the concerns in a slightly less damaging way, and they also sought to maintain their own self-esteem by comparing themselves favourably with 'child-battering' people.

4. The notion of risk at the conference tended to be unitary – that is, the assessment process to some extent dissolved the distinctions between physical and sexual abuse, or between abuse and neglect, and reduced all the concerns to a common denominator of risk. When an explanatory theory was used, it was usually one which was commonly used in social work practice, such as the notion of psychosocial stress; but quite often the conference seemed to be making a moral or 'common sense' judgement, legitimated by the presence of professional expertise.

5. One weakness of all the assessments was that they tended to concentrate on the risk of re-abuse, and to ignore the risk of harm from abuse which had already occurred and which might therefore require treatment. Yet in many cases this danger could be seen to constitute 'significant harm'.

6. Another weakness was that conference members occasionally concentrated on assessing the risks to one particular child in a family although others were also at risk. Where there were siblings of different ages, for example, a young child might be singled out as the main focus of concern although an older child had also been abused.

7. Good assessments were comprehensive and dynamic, were negotiated with family members, and used a variety of approaches; but they were assessments of *risk* rather than of *need*. As a result, too few of the assessments were capable of acting as a basis for future planning.

Chapter 10

Registration

The assessment process engaged in by the conference members resulted in the registration of many children who had on the face of it little in common, except that they were all presumed to be at risk of harm for which their parents could be called to account. Some of these children had almost certainly been abused, either physically or sexually, and some had suffered a variety of depriving circumstances. Others still had not been abused or neglected in any way.

In this chapter we shall look in more detail at who the registered children were, and at what was recommended for them. But first of all we need to take into account the statistical context.

The quantitative framework of registration

Within our case conference sample the proportion of children registered varied according to the main cause of concern. As many as 83 per cent of children in the cases where emotional abuse was identified were registered, whereas the corresponding rate in cases of neglect was only 68 per cent. In cases of alleged physical abuse 60 per cent were registered, and the rate for sexual abuse cases was lower again at 58 per cent.

There was an inverse relationship between the frequency with which certain types of maltreatment were considered at case conference and rates of registration. Sexual abuse cases had a high public profile, and in our study they were often brought to conference in order to ensure that all aspects of the situation were considered and covered. Similarly, Gibbons and her colleagues (1993), in their detailed study of registration patterns, found specific selection processes to be in operation so that some cases – for example cases of neglect – were particularly likely to be screened out at the referral and investigation stage, and in consequence those which reached a case conference were of a particularly serious nature. These selection processes undoubtedly had a bearing on the cases we studied.

A broad study of conference information, from the point of view of both content and process, shows that there are several factors or groups of factors which are highly significant in relation to registration. Some of these are to be expected. For example, a high rate of registration was significantly associated with *the presumed severity of abuse or neglect* – and this of course relates primarily to the information which was brought forward in response to the investigation and its aftermath. High rates of registration were found in association with moderate or severe abuse, the existence of emergency orders, and situations where the child or abuser had recently been removed from the household.

Among the other factors which were significantly related to registration, three groups stand out. They are:

(i)   the existence of secondary concerns about the child;

(ii)   the previous involvement of the family with other agencies; and

(iii)   the combination of female gender and responsibility for the abuse.

There are obviously links between these factors and the methods of assessment which were outlined in the previous chapter. The quantitative material suggests not only that some of these methods of assessment were *regularly* used, but that they were regularly used when the referral characteristics were constructed by the conference in a particular way.

(i)   *Secondary concerns*

In the statistics which we extracted from the case conference schedules 'other major concerns' (that is, concerns additional to the main one provoking the referral) emerged as a factor significantly related to registration. It confirmed our observation that the assessment of risk in many cases tended to be cumulative.

Where there was more than one concern the child was generally registered under only one category. National figures of children on the child protection register show that mixed categories are rarely used. As a result, it is clear that the official system of recording under-represents the number of concerns which conference members have about children, and it does not reflect the way in which concerns are clustered together.

In 49 cases in our case conference study there was no discussion of any major concern apart from the principal source of risk to the child, and the associated registration rate was low at 41 per cent. In 71 cases there was one additional major concern, and the registration rate for these children rose to 75 per cent; but within this group there was a sub-group of 27 cases where there was a *third* major cause for concern, and here the registration rate was highest at 85 per cent.

Is there any discernible pattern in the type of concerns which were grouped together? Almost every possible combination of abuse or neglect was found on at least one occasion; but in the cases presented at conferences there were particularly strong associations between physical or sexual abuse and neglect, and between physical abuse and emotional abuse. Specifically, the results are as shown in table 12.

Table 12 **Combined Concerns about Abuse and Neglect Considered at Initial Conferences**

Main concern	Secondary concerns
Physical abuse	Emotional abuse in a quarter of cases and neglect in a fifth
Sexual abuse	Neglect in a quarter of cases and physical abuse in a sixth
Neglect	Physical abuse in a third of cases and sexual abuse in a sixth

Many of the children in these cases were registered because of 'accumulating concerns'.

(ii)   *Previous involvement with other agencies*

Registration was more likely if certain agencies other than the social services department had formerly been involved with the family, for example probation, child guidance or the NSPCC. Their prior involvement could be taken to mean that problems had existed in the family for some time, or that the family had failed to benefit from previous help, or that there was an 'exhaustion of services' which left few other options untried. However, in some cases the crucial element may simply have been that the involvement of these agencies increased the supply of information about risk to the conference.

Whatever the precise reason for registration, problems which had existed in the past were thought likely to recur – and this lends support to the idea that the conference assessment of risk was not only cumulative but directional. Many children in these cases were registered by comparing present and previous contexts, or simply because the activity of 'plotting future directions' produced a downward-sloping curve.

(iii)   *The combination of female gender and responsibility for the abuse*

When mothers were seen as responsible for abuse or neglect, the child's name was much more likely to be placed on the child protection register than when a father or male partner was responsible. In 78 per cent of the cases in which mothers were held to be responsible, the child was registered. The same happened in only 60 per cent of the cases where a stepfather was thought to have committed abuse, and 55 per cent of the cases in which the putative abuser was a natural father. This applied particularly to cases in which the conference was concerned about specific incidents of abuse or neglect.

This issue of gender in relation to the differential use of registration is additional to the point made elsewhere, that in some cases during the assessment of risk the concerns of the conference became transferred from the original abuse to the standard of the mother's care. In many of those cases the responsibility for the original incident – and the theoretical justification for registration – still rested with a male abuser.

There are two possible reasons for the greater tendency to register children in cases where women were abusers.

(i)   Mothers were more likely to be seen as responsible in cases of neglect and emotional abuse, which in general were associated with higher rates of registration. (As previously mentioned, the rate of registration for neglect was 68 per cent, and for emotional abuse 83 per cent).

(ii)   Physical abuse by a woman was treated much more seriously than physical abuse by a man – especially if the woman was a lone parent. When we considered physical abuse cases on their own, we found that almost all physically abusing mothers were single parents and three-quarters of the children in these cases were registered (77%); but fathers who physically abused were all in two-parent households and fewer than half of the children were registered (48%).

It did appear that social services departments were more willing to intervene in lone-mother households, or perhaps more unwilling to intervene where the man was uncooperative or threatening (Miller and Fisher, 1992.) It may have been assumed that in a two-parent household the mother would protect the child, and therefore registration would be unnecessary. But it is interesting to reflect that the major child abuse tragedies have been injuries to children inflicted by violent men. Of course, it may be that lone parents of either gender will be vulnerable to registration, and that mothers are disproportionately affected because they constitute the majority of lone parents. Nonetheless, it was interesting to note that in two-parent households the question of whether the non-abusing parent could protect the child was one considered far more often in relation to mothers (where it was considered in 60 per cent of the relevant cases), than in relation to father figures (where it was considered in only 19 per cent of the relevant cases; see table 11 in chapter 8).

Certainly we did find that in quite a number of cases mothers who were having difficulty in coping with their children, and who needed practical and emotional help and support, were brought into the system as the result of a bruise or other minor incident. Many children in these families were living in less than adequate circumstances, but this interpretation of everyday difficulties in child care as abnormal placed additional stress on these mothers and meant that they were sometimes wary of practical help which was offered at a later date.

Many parents who needed help because they lived in poor circumstances found the child protection system stigmatising and morally discrediting. Arguably some of these families would have been better helped outside the system, as families with 'children in need'. As we saw in the historical chapter, there is a narrow borderline between deprivation and neglect. Nevertheless there was an understandable desire among conference participants not to pass over any child who was badly treated, for whatever reason.

At this point it might be useful to look at the case histories of some of the children who were registered for the reasons described.

Children who were registered as a result of accumulating concerns

Kevin, aged six, was the subject of a conference and was registered after he came to school with a handmark on his bottom. He had been slapped hard by his mother after he got out of bed and started to unpack the contents of a cupboard in the early hours of the morning. The social worker in charge of the case said:

> *'Mandy slapped Kevin rather hard. In itself, it wasn't serious. But things weren't right. The mother wasn't coping very well. It brought things out that perhaps had been denied before . . . I don't know if there is a risk of sexual abuse, but it follows on from the neglect, because he is left to be at large in the community. I feel he is at risk from anything that is evil that is out there.'*

Kevin was typical of many children who were registered because of accumulating concerns. His mother was a single parent living in poor conditions. She had problems with health, housing, finances, and a series of broken relationships. Kevin's behaviour was very difficult, and social services had been involved for some time. The abuse was simply a 'trigger' which brought the case to conference.

Many concerns in these cases were about neglect. Lucy, aged two, was left for long hours in her cot and was thought to be understimulated. Six-year-old Jerry was said to be underfed since he came to school without packed lunches, and he also lacked supervision when playing or crossing roads. Katrina, aged five, was scruffy, disturbed and uncared-for. Helen (9) was bullied at home and frequently had to play Cinderella, since she was expected to clean the house and look after her younger brothers and sisters.

The 'trigger' in each of these cases was different. In Lucy's case it was a bruise on the cheek. In Jerry's case it was his eyesight, which was deteriorating and urgently needed medical treatment. Katrina complained about abuse by her mother's cohabitee. Helen ran away from home.

Typically, in these cases of accumulating concerns, the social services department had been involved for some time and there was a lot of background information on the family. There were often question marks, however. Sometimes there were worries about unproven abuse, and suspicions of violence between adults in the household. When a new referral was received, the department felt that a conference was justified because something fresh had to be attempted.

Looking forwards If the links between the concerns were clearly perceived by a social worker who not only understood the family dynamics but saw his or her part in those dynamics, registration might be treated as the start of a new episode. Determined preventive action needed to be taken in the form of a new strategy. Sometimes a change of social worker helped. Long-running, endemic problems demanded fresh thinking, good inter-agency working and a range of suitable services.

If concerns remained diffuse and there was no clear focus for the work, the danger was that the situation would continue to stagnate. Some families in the study withdrew behind their own barricades. After the initial shock of registration (which sometimes actually produced an improvement) the family might carry on much as before.

Children who were registered as a result of the comparison of present and previous contexts

This category includes two groups of children. Some, like ten-year-old Andrew who was injured in a fight with his mother, had previously been registered, and during that period of registration help had been offered to the family. (Andrew's mother had received a period of counselling from the NSPCC.) In such cases there had usually been a break in agency involvement and a period of improvement; so risk was associated with a fresh eruption of concerns which it was considered should have been 'cured'.

In the majority of cases in this category, however, the risk to the index child was purely hypothetical. Another child in the family had previously been abused or neglected, or an adult member of the household had committed abuse (physical or sexual) outside the family. The child who was presently the index child had *not* been abused, but was considered to be at risk.

Some of the children registered in these cases were new-born babies. Caroline, for example, was registered at birth because a previous child born four years earlier had suffered a fractured skull. (The previous baby had been removed and placed for adoption.) In another family, a new-born baby called Inga was registered. She already had a two-year-old sister on the register because of minor abuse and 'failure to thrive'; so Inga's name was added to the register as well.

Nine-day-old William was registered and made the subject of an emergency order before he left the hospital. Both his parents had been known in another context and were considered to be quite unable to care for him. Interestingly enough, the previous context for this mother did not involve child care. As a young woman she had become known to social services as someone who had considerable learning difficulties and there were worries about her ability to care for *herself*.

Many of the cases which were assessed in this way involved sexual abuse outside the family, or sexual abuse of a family member other than the index child. In one household the children's father was in prison after an incident of sexual abuse away from home, and in another the mother herself had been abused by a stepfather who was still a member of the household. This mother made the disclosure because she was worried that her four-year-old daughter might be at risk. She saw registration as protective, but her reaction was unusual, since most parents in these cases felt that registration was completely unjustified.

Looking forwards In cases where the child who was the subject of the conference had not been injured, the social worker sometimes responded to the parent's annoyance about being 'labelled' and agreed that registration was unfair. This support could be valuable to a depressed parent. However, if a swift judgement was made that the original abuse was unlikely to be repeated, social work help might be too abruptly curtailed.

In such situations no real assessment could be made of the parent's part in the previous context – and therefore there was no appreciation of its impact on the parent. Although they vigorously denied current risk, some mothers actually harboured feelings of guilt and anxiety about the previous incident. If these feelings were ignored, valuable opportunities for preventive or remedial work were sometimes lost.

In a good follow-up there was careful examination of the previous context and appropriate help was offered; but if it looked as though the chances of success were really very limited and the previous situation was likely to recur, action was taken to protect the child.

Children who were registered as a result of specific incidents of abuse or neglect

In cases where the concern of the conference was focused on a specific incident or disclosure, there were usually fairly clear allegations about abuse or neglect to the index child, and little doubt about what had happened. (Explanations, of course, could be another matter.) The family might be known previously or unknown; but the focus was indisputably on the present concerns, and registration depended on the severity of the abuse or neglect being considered.

In this group there were several incidents involving physical injury by men or women, although that inflicted by men was usually more serious. In physical abuse cases there was generally loss of control on the part of the parent (always worrying for the conference because it suggested unpredictability) and sometimes deliberate over-chastisement. For example, Matthew (10) was beaten with a curtain rod by his father after he had defied him. Frances, aged 11, was grabbed around the throat and pushed up against a cupboard after an argument with her mother. Shane, aged four, was hit by his mother with a wooden spoon; but he was actually registered after he had witnessed his mother defending herself in a fight with her boyfriend. In many of these cases, the physical injuries – even if they were relatively severe – were deemed to be less significant than the emotional trauma which had been caused.

There were also cases of serious sexual abuse in this group. Doreen (16) had been abused by her stepfather over a considerable period, and Elizabeth (15) had been abused by her natural father. Both of these situations came to light for the first time just before the initial conference. Colin (15) was found to have been sexually abusing his sister, and at the initial case conference it became clear that he himself had been the victim of abuse. In these cases the need for protection was acute.

Looking forwards In most of these cases there was little doubt about the need for registration, but the fact that the abuse was clear-cut sometimes obscured the fact that its origins were exceedingly complicated. Agency action in these cases was typically focused on the child's immediate protection. Little might be done to enhance the child's welfare, or to ameliorate the effects of the abuse, and if the child was removed from home family links were not always well maintained.

If the case was handled well, however, intervention was carried out with an eye to the child's future. Action was taken to mitigate the effects of the abuse, in addition to offering protection, and to encourage alliances which might be of help to the child both during and after separation. The wishes of the child and close family members were known and wherever possible respected. If these things were done, there was hope that the damage caused by the abuse could be kept to a minimum and the child's protection secured.

Reasons for non-registration

As we have seen, 39 per cent of the cases considered at initial case conferences did not lead to registration. Even if the risks were slight, the decision not to register the child was usually seen as requiring some justification, and so the reasons for non-registration were usually clearly stated. As a result, they were recorded in our notes and also in the conference minutes.

A study of decision-making in these non-registered cases is potentially rewarding – partly because it adds to our understanding of why some children were registered rather than others, and partly because it helps us to identify any cases that might have slipped through the net. In order to explore these issues we examined the 47 sets of conference notes and minutes for the unregistered cases. This trawl produced evidence of a number of recurring reasons for non-registration, which can be grouped together as indicated in table 13.

This brief analysis complements the material obtained from the case conference schedules and at the same time expands it. The reasons concerned with the actual diagnosis of abuse or neglect were fairly crucial in determining both registration and non-registration; but it was still common not to

Table 13 **Reasons for Non-Registration**

1. *Assessment of abuse or neglect*

   Insufficient evidence of abuse
   Incident considered a 'one-off'
   Situation borderline but stable; no evidence of deterioration.

2. *Family members' response to the investigative interview*

   Abuser responded with openness; produced convincing statement, either accepting
        guilt or exonerating self
   Non-abusing parent responded by showing concern and willingness to protect
   Child was not unduly upset and showed signs of adjustment.

3. *Previous history and reputation*

   Good reports of abuser (e.g. army record)
   Good reports of non-abusing parent (e.g. from health visitor)
   Good reports of child's behaviour (e.g. from school or playgroup).

4. *Likelihood of child's protection*

   Parent would protect
   Child was able to protect self
   Child was already protected by a court order.

5. *Availability of other support/monitoring systems*

   Parent or child would report any new concerns
   Another relative would keep a check on the child's situation
   Professional support/monitoring systems would be in place.

6. *Registration not useful*

   Resources were already in place; registration would add nothing
   Labelling would be damaging for the family
   'Deferred sentence' (i.e. postponement of registration) was thought sufficient to
        produce change.

register children if the evidence of maltreatment was thought to be insufficient, or if there was considered to be little likelihood of a repetition of the
abuse. The list of reasons for non-registration also shows how far conference
members departed from the original allegations when they were considering
registration. They were heavily influenced by factors such as the way in
which people responded to the investigation, and by the past and present
reputation of the carers.

If the accumulation of bad reports and minor worries in some cases led to
registration, it is clear that the reverse could also happen. *Good* reports of
people's behaviour and attitudes militated *against* registration. In some cases
where there was competing information the good items could appear to
cancel out the bad – even if there was little in the way of logical relationship
between them.

Some of the contributions made in support of non-registration can be questioned. The introduction of material such as work records, for example, suggested that the abuser was on trial as a citizen and not simply as a carer of children. Devoted work performance is not necessarily related to success in fatherhood, as one conference recognised when the father (a young soldier devoted to his career) was described as 'army-barmy'. As in a court hearing, however, the physically violent abuser was more likely to be excused if he was 'previously of good character'.

For men in the armed services, but not usually for people in civilian life, work records were readily available to the conference. This situation could lead to discriminatory practice. On the other hand there was often some point in introducing army personnel to the conference, since the army had 'families officers' and other welfare professionals who might offer assistance to the family. Occasionally there were worries that the involvement of senior staff from the parent's work-place might affect future career prospects. (One father whose wife had physically abused their daughter was a senior police officer, and the case was investigated by the local police.) These worries were peculiar to cases involving men, however. It was not usual for a woman's abuse or neglect to be excused on the grounds that she had a good employment record, and registration was never postponed or omitted on the grounds that it might be damaging to her job or career prospects.

The conference participants were sometimes heavily influenced by what the parent looked like. A caring and concerned demeanour, accompanied by some evidence of remorse, was a prophylactic against registration, and in some cases the conference was completely won over by parents who brought with them babies or young children who were well fed, washed and appealing. In one case of this sort, a conference failed to register a toddler whose father had pushed a spoon into the back of his throat while feeding him. During the conference the child was seen to be playing happily.

Where apparently competent parental behaviour was described alongside disturbed behaviour on the part of the child, the conference was caught in a double bind – from which it would sometimes emerge by blaming the child. Evidence of disturbed behaviour on the part of a child was usually treated as an indicator of risk and weighed heavily in favour of registration. (Note the importance of the school's contribution, mentioned in chapter 8.) Evidence of good or normal behaviour was occasionally used in support of a decision *not* to register – but its use was more variable. Sometimes it led the conference to believe that abuse had not occurred. At other times the implication seemed to be that although abuse might have occurred the child was undamaged, and therefore a repetition of the abuse would have no serious consequences.

In many cases the references to children's behaviour – both positive and negative – *failed to make clear the links between this good or bad behaviour and the allegations of abuse*. The behaviour was simply one more weight to be added to the scales. The same problems surround the references to parental behaviour. It was generally considered to be a positive factor if a parent (and particularly a mother) seemed competent, caring and concerned. In terms of the child's total environment this made a lot of sense; but when competing arguments were balanced against one another it could result in some very strange judgements – for example the judgement that a child was less at risk from a violent father if the mother offered good physical care, or that abuse was less likely if the father played frequently with his children.

Dubious judgements

In our attendance at 120 case conferences, we found that our own research judgement occasionally differed from that of the conference members – that is, if we had been part of the decision-making process we would not have supported the decision to register a particular child, or else we would have favoured registration in a situation where it was not used. In order to establish whether there was any pattern in these differences, we recorded the discrepancies.

There were 14 non-registered cases in which, according to our judgement, the child should have been registered; but there were also 13 cases in which registration seemed to have been used unnecessarily or unfairly. The positives and negatives therefore balanced one another. It seems that the present system under-identifies certain types of abuse and over-identifies others. Therefore an important research task was to disentangle the types of situation which, in our estimation, led to dubious judgements.

When we considered the 13 cases in which registration appeared to have been used unnecessarily or unfairly we found, firstly, that there was *no evidence of abuse by the parent to the index child* and secondly that there were *subsidiary allegations of neglect or an inadequate standard of care*. These subsidiary allegations, although minor, gradually usurped the attention of the conference. The children were usually registered because of 'accumulating concerns'; but instead of the suspected abuse acting as a trigger which brought serious cases of neglect to the conference, as happened on other occasions, it appeared that minor concerns about neglect were being inflated to provide a justification for registration, in the hope that the family would be continuously monitored because of fears about unproven abuse.

Our impression was that although there was deprivation in the families the neglect of children in these cases was not a serious issue. The salient feature was that the conference members had not been able to 'let go' of the tremendous anxiety which had been generated by allegations of abuse, and they felt that on one ground or another, the children would have to be registered. From the family's point of view, however, registration was damaging because the parents felt penalised and placed under suspicion, sometimes at a time when they should have been congratulated on taking action to protect their children.

When we turn to the 13 unregistered children who might have benefited from having their names placed on the register, a different picture emerges. These are predominantly cases of *serious physical or sexual abuse where the conference appeared to be confused, misled or intimidated* to the extent that possible dangers were not picked up. In some of these conferences family problems which included domestic violence, alcohol abuse and shoplifting were successfully diverted from the agenda. In one particular case, where there was frequent violence between the parents and physical abuse to an eight-year-old boy, the problems were considered to be so entrenched that registration would effect little change. None of these conferences was strongly chaired, and on one occasion when the chair would have preferred registration she allowed the prevailing mood of the conference to dominate the outcome.

Adolescents were particularly at risk in this unregistered group. There were allegations of sexual abuse which were discounted, although another conference might well have found the evidence convincing. When women and children made statements about male violence in these cases they were accused of lying, their motives were questioned, or potentially offensive behaviour by teenage boys was dismissed as 'horseplay'. Fortunately, however, these cases were in a minority. Generally speaking, children's disclosures were given due attention, and the parents were held responsible. When the local authority was the parent, did the same rules apply?

Registering children who were looked after

There appeared to be no consistent policy or practice at conferences concerning the registration or non-registration of children separated from their parents. When children were thought to be at risk from their parents during care proceedings, the children were sometimes not registered because they were subject to interim care orders – and in these circumstances an 'at risk' judgement might have seemed insulting to the foster parents. In other similar cases, though, children were kept on the register until a full care order was in force. Sometimes the intention was to signal the fact that there might be danger during contact with parents. At other times registration seemed intended to support the department's position by indicating to the court that a multi-disciplinary case conference had considered the children to be at risk.

A particularly acute dilemma arose when a child placed by the local authority was suspected of being abused by a care-giver such as a foster carer. This situation challenged the agencies' assumption that accommodation or care for the child was the highest form of protection available, and understandably there was resistance to the idea of registering children in these circumstances although removal from placement was a likely outcome.

Reference has already been made to the blame which accompanies registration. It is interesting to consider whether children are less likely to be registered in circumstances where the blame would fall on a local authority which has assumed parental responsibility, especially when the chair of the conference is the social services line manager who carries accountability for the decisions made.

The child protection plan

The official guidelines for 'working together' state that before a child is registered the conference must decide that there is, or is a likelihood of, *significant harm leading to the need for a child protection plan* (Home Office *et al.*, 1991). It follows that planning should be an integral part of the proceedings, and the conference agenda included the construction of an inter-agency plan.

At most of the conferences we attended a protection plan was drawn up, at least in outline, but because the conference had spent so long discussing risk or the likelihood of 'significant harm', the planning phase of the conference was very brief and usually confined to the allocation of personnel or services. *The average time spent on the plan was only nine minutes.* The assumption seemed to be that the key worker would draw up a more detailed plan of action and discuss it with the family later. Since the parent was not usually present during the planning process, further negotiation would have been necessary in any case.

This situation left much responsibility in the hands of the social worker, who was usually prepared to carry it; but it weakened accountability to the conference group and created a possible source of discontinuity once the conference was over. It also left inexperienced key workers floundering without sufficient guidance, once the supportive scaffolding of the conference had been taken away. One key worker spoke for many when she said:

> '*I think at the end of the day it's the person working with the family who has to confront all the really difficult issues. So there's a certain amount of help, but ultimately you're more or less on your own.*'

In cases of serious risk, of course, the main part of the protection plan tended to underline the need for care proceedings, although in many such cases the child had already been removed. Sometimes the police wanted to pursue prosecution or cautioning of the abuser, and although the actual decision to prosecute had to be made by the Crown Prosecution Service, the course of police action could be influenced by the views of conference members.

Prosecution was occasionally minuted as a recommendation in the protection plan. There were also recommendations about placement, change of residence or return home for children, and these often consolidated arrangements which had already been made. *Quite often the protection plan simply ratified the decisions which had been made at the time of the investigation.*

In the majority of cases which were dealt with by means of registration, the child had to be protected while remaining at home with the abuser. Placing the child's name on the register seemed designed to act as a warning in many of these cases, in the hope that the parents would mend their ways and that stronger measures would prove unnecessary. In this way registration itself constituted a kind of intervention, and it formed part of an informal 'tariff' of penalties for inadequate child care, the final point of which was the child's removal.

The responses of parents showed that they felt registration to be a penalty, and that they felt on trial whilst it was in place. They had very little sense of a child protection plan, except that in the event of further abuse the department might have plans to remove their children. They realised that accommodation or care was 'the bottom line' even when it was not formally under discussion. Often, however, they had exaggerated notions of the department's powers and intentions. One mother believed that 'anybody could virtually knock on her door by day or by night to see the children', and that they would probably stay on the register till the age of eighteen. Another mother said:

> 'They are using it [registration] so that if another bruise is put on Jan or Nicky they have got the right to take them . . . so we take every bruise to the GP.'

Recommended resources

At the conferences we attended we noted whether the recommendations appeared to be biased towards controlling or assisting the family. In 50 per cent of cases the recommendations were mainly controlling (that is, concerned with monitoring, prosecution, warnings or the threat of care). In 20 per cent of cases the recommendations were mainly concerned with assistance (that is, the provision of support services). In 30 per cent of cases the recommendations were mixed.

Table 14 gives a list of the services mentioned as part of the child protection plan at the 120 initial case conferences, together with the frequency with which they appeared in plans.

It can be seen that 'social work contact' was by far the most common recommendation, since it occurred in 89% of registered cases and 47% of unregistered ones. Health visitor contact was recommended in 23% of registered cases and 26% of those where there was no registration. This was a

Table 14 **Case Conference Recommendations:**
Resources for Support, Treatment and Monitoring

| | Registered Cases (N = 73) | | Non-Registered Cases (N = 47) | |
| | Recommendations | | Recommendations | |
	No.	%	No.	%
Social worker contact	65	89	22	47
Other resources under SSD control	24	33	12	25
Other agency monitoring or assessment	20	27	4	9
Health visitor contact	17	23	12	26
School monitoring	11	15	4	9
Checks by paediatrician	9	12	1	2
School input (welfare assistance)	8	11	2	4
Checks by health visitor	7	10	3	6
Childminding	7	10	2	4
Child guidance	6	8	2	4
Playgroup	5	7	2	4
Checks by GP	4	5	3	6
Family aide	4	5	2	4
Educational psychologist	4	5	–	–
Clinical psychologist	4	5	1	2
Contact with other hospital doctor	3	4	4	9
Child psychiatrist	3	4	–	–
Day fostering	2	3	–	–
Period of respite care	2	3	1	2
Day nursery	1	1	–	–
Contact with paediatrician	1	1	–	–
Parent group	–	–	1	2

N.B. Because resources were often age-related, they were not relevant in all cases.

high rate of visiting in relation to the number of families with children under five.

Monitoring by the school was sometimes explicitly recommended in registered cases where the children were of school age and living at home. This was also suggested in 9% of cases where the children were not registered – probably because a certain amount of risk was suspected and there might be no social worker involved. Inputs by the school apart from monitoring (that is, welfare assistance and pastoral care) were mentioned less frequently, although they often proved valuable at a later stage. In 27% of the registered cases recommendations were made for health checks by paediatricians, health visitors and GPs, but this was the case for only 14% of non-registered children. Nevertheless these recommendations were few in number in both registered and unregistered cases.

It is important to note how rarely specific recommendations for treatment were made. Only six referrals were to be made to child guidance, four to a clinical psychologist and three to a child psychiatrist where children's names were placed on the register, and in cases where there was no registration the referrals were even fewer. The lack of any plan for the treatment of seriously abused children was particularly noticeable. This tallies with our previous findings that medical personnel were often underrepresented at conferences, and that the prevention of harm resulting from the abuse had a much lower priority than the prevention of re-abuse. In addition, the provision for abused children from minority ethnic groups was hampered by serious lack of resources. When specialised ethnic services were required there were delays in assessment and the provision of treatment. There was a lack of suitable residential provision for Asian or African-Caribbean children of either sex, and a shortage of suitable residential workers and foster carers. There was little regular group work for minority ethnic children who had been abused. There were no Asian psychologists, and only one Asian psychiatrist available for referrals.

The category of 'other resources' in table 14 is mainly composed of resources under social services control. For children on the register there were referrals to interest groups and therapeutic groups, which included holiday activities, specialised playschemes, 'intermediate treatment' or adolescent projects, and groups for sexually abused girls. (The latter was recommended on only three occasions.) There were also a few other recommendations for work involving other agencies; for example there was a suggestion that an abuser might receive help from a probation officer on anger control, and that a mother might receive advice on her child's diet from the school nurse. References were occasionally made to plans for joint working, to the arrangement of appointments with a speech therapist, and to input from other professionals such as a paediatric social worker or a community nurse.

In view of the generally held belief that the child protection system gives prioritised access to resources, the number of recommendations for playgroup and childminding seemed surprisingly small (playgroup was recommended in 7% of registered cases, and childminding in 10%), but in a number of cases children already had access to these services. *It was quite common to find that the resources which were recommended were already in place.* On the other hand there were surprisingly few recommendations for support services such as family aides and respite care, and when these resources were subsequently used, they had often been suggested and negotiated by social workers at a later date.

Priorities

The results indicate that once a conference had been held, resources were suggested for both registered and non-registered children, and that the resource provision was parallel; but when children were not registered the provision was at a lower level.

In general the conference recommendations were consistent with a firm and to some extent defensible set of priorities. The first priority was the protection of the child – conceived in a rather restricted way as protection from re-abuse. The second priority was the enhancement of the child's welfare; but emotional and behavioural problems were not necessarily seen as associated with the abuse, even if the abuse had been severe, and consequently they were not seen as requiring special treatment. Thirdly, and to a much lesser extent, the needs of the parents were addressed.

There was little in the regular list of recommendations to benefit parents – with the possible exception of 'social work contact' which was an unknown quantity. If the child was young and dependent the parents might be offered help with basic problems such as social isolation, housing and financial difficulties. However, the information given in chapter 8 shows how infrequently these topics were mentioned at conferences, and if they were not part of the assessment of risk it follows that they would not be part of the protection plan.

Another topic which was conspicuously missing from the conference recommendations was work on the parent-child relationship. Social work literature, and some research literature also, tends to concentrate on the importance of childhood *experiences* and adult *circumstances*; but this denies to adults the opportunity to learn from a structuring of experience. This is a disadvantage which is admitted by Rutter and his colleagues (1983) as follows:

> 'We lack adequate knowledge on the extent and frequency of major improvements in parenting during adult life, and we lack information on the factors needed to bring about such beneficial change, but it is clear that it would be quite wrong to assume that behaviour and personality are fixed once maturity is reached.'

In spite of the care with which decision-making about registration was carried out, it was basically a classificatory exercise. In our exploration of intervention and outcome we shall try to establish whether the registered children were protected from re-abuse as a result of the conference and the actions which followed it. Further, we shall also try to find out whether, in the widest possible sense, the children were protected from 'significant harm'.

Summary

1. The frequency with which children's names were placed on the child protection register varied according to the category of abuse. Cases of

emotional abuse and neglect which were brought to an initial conference were very likely to lead to registration of the child, and cases of physical abuse slightly less so; but in sexual abuse cases the rate was lowest at 58%.

2. Among the items which were significantly related to registration were the assumed severity of abuse or neglect and its accompanying circumstances (for example the incidence of emergency orders, and the movement of abusers and children out of the household). Other highly significant factors were the existence of secondary concerns (for example, evidence of neglect in a household where physical or sexual abuse was suspected), and the previous involvement of the family with other agencies (especially treatment agencies such as child guidance or the NSPCC). These findings support the notion that the assessment of risk was both cumulative and directional.

3. One highly significant factor in relation to registration was the combination of gender and responsibility for the abuse. When mothers were seen as responsible for abuse or neglect, the child's name was much more likely to be placed on the child protection register than when a male carer was seen as responsible.

4. According to the information recorded in the minutes, the decision not to register a child happened for a variety of reasons. These included lack of evidence, an appropriate parental response to the investigation, generally favourable reports of the parents or child and the availability of informal methods of protection. Good items in reports to conferences could sometimes be used to counteract the bad, even if there was no logical connection between them.

5. Some reasons for non-registration were purely pragmatic. Registration was usually omitted or postponed if it was felt that nothing would be achieved by it. Examples included situations where no extra resources were available, where 'labelling' was considered to be excessively damaging for a family or where the equivalent of a 'deferred sentence' (that is, postponement of registration) was considered sufficient to produce change.

6. Unregistered cases where we considered that registration had been necessary were those of serious abuse where the conference was misled or intimidated to the extent that dangers were not picked up.

    Cases in which, in our view, registration had been used unnecessarily were those where there was no evidence of abuse to the child, but minor concerns about neglect had been inflated to provide a justification for registration so that the family would be monitored.

7. There appeared to be no consistent policy or practice determining the registration of children separated from their families. Sometimes children who were subject to interim care orders were registered, either because their situation had not yet been made permanent or because they might be at risk during contact visits. However, there was a tendency for children who were subject to abuse while in substitute care to be kept off the register.

8. Because the conference had spent so long on discussions about risks and the likelihood of significant harm, the planning phase was very brief. The average time spent on forming the child protection plan was only nine minutes. Quite often the protection plan ratified the decisions which had been made at the time of the investigation. It was also common to find that the resources which were recommended were already in place. Specific recommendations for treatment were rarely made.

9. It was encouraging to find that some follow-up was intended for all registered children and for many of those who were *not* registered, although the recommendations varied in specificity and they were mainly concerned with provision of resources. Social work contact was by far the most common recommendation and occurred in 89% of registered cases. The provision of resources under the control of social services was the second most common recommendation (33% of registered cases).

10. There was very little discussion of a child protection plan. Much useful information had been aired; but registration was primarily a classificatory exercise, after which the key worker had to negotiate help for the children who had been identified as at risk.

PART III

Intervention

Chapter 11

Negotiating with parents

The immediate aftermath of the case conference was a crucial stage for intervention. At this time practitioners were negotiating entry to families, attempting to form viable coalitions with family members and setting the pattern for future work. There was a marked tendency for the patterns of interaction established at this time to become entrenched.

During the investigation and initial conference, the situation of the child and parents had been made public and many agencies had been involved. After the conference, the action returned to the more private sphere of the social worker and family members. The responsibility for carrying out the recommendations of the conference was left in the hands of the key worker. The balance of power also shifted at this point. During the early stages of the process power had rested firmly with the official agencies – firstly at the investigation, when the presence of police and the threat of criminal proceedings had overwhelmed parents, and secondly at the case conference where the court-like atmosphere had been intimidating and the nature of the proceedings unknown. Now, however, the social worker was acting alone and on the parents' home ground. Before any plans could be put into action they had to be negotiated with parents and their cooperation (or at least compliance) obtained.

The members of the social services department as a whole – managers as well as workers – had of course derived considerable advantage from inter-agency collaboration in the early stages. By the time that the initial child protection case conference was over, a consensus had emerged amongst the professionals about how the cases in the study should be 'framed' and handled. As we have seen, there was considerable continuity between the view of the family formed by professionals at the investigation and the view developed at the initial case conference. However, this consensus had been possible only because the voices of family members had scarcely been heard in the decision-making process, and if heard they had rarely been influential in determining the outcome. (The one exception was that sexually abused young people were generally listened to carefully when they spoke about their abuse. Their views about where they wanted to live were also often given considerable weight.)

After the conference it was not simply the task of safeguarding the child's protection which fell to key workers. They were also expected to provide the main service for the child and family. In chapter 6 we mentioned that one benefit hoped for by social workers was that new resources to assist the child or parents might be released by registration; but as indicated in the last

Table 15   **Initial Case Conference Plans for the Provision of Resources in Registered Cases**

	%
Social work contact only	30
Some other resources in place, no new resources recommended	27
Provision of new resources under the control of the social services department	20
Provision of new resources by other agencies	13
Provision of new resources by both social services and other agencies	10
N=70*	100

*Information unclear in three cases.

chapter, this often did not happen. Table 15 shows that in more than half the cases (57%) discussed at the initial conference and resulting in registration, no new resources had been recommended as part of the child protection plan as an addition to those which were already in place. When new resources *had* been suggested, they were usually services which lay within the sphere of control of social services (for example, family aides, childminders or playgroups) rather than those within the ambit of other agencies (see also Corby, 1987; Gough *et al.*, 1989).

From this list it is evident that inter-agency working after the conference, at least in terms of the services provided, was fairly limited – and with the notable exception of health visitors few other professionals had been asked to visit the family at home. Social workers had appreciated the advantages of collaboration in the early stages. One social worker said:

> '*Case conferences and meetings are very helpful, and although they produce a certain sort of stress . . . it also reduces stress because it stops me feeling all alone, you know, the sole worker, and the knowledge that I've got everyone with me.*'

However, after the initial conference the former advantages of collaboration sometimes actually became *costs*, since the practitioners had to deal with the negative impact on parents and children of the previous stages of the process. As we have seen, parents who attended part of the conference had often felt marginalised by the professional group. They had rarely been involved in decisions about risk, registration or the protection plan. This was a significant omission since their views were often rather different from those of conference members – and when this was the case, the task of dealing with these discrepancies fell on the social worker alone.

In the aftermath of the initial case conference there were two major hurdles confronting key workers in their efforts to establish the basis of a workable relationship with family members. Firstly, there were *major disagreements* which remained unresolved, that is there were differences of opinion between parents and professionals about the incidents of abuse or neglect, about who was responsible and about whether the children were at risk. Secondly, the working out of procedures had produced *harmful after-effects*. The investigation, case conference and registration had left many parents feeling disaffected and alienated. Since each of these hurdles could have a profound effect on the development of intervention, they will be explored in greater detail.

Agreement and disagreement between parents and professionals about the abuse or neglect

Disagreement between parents and professionals about the findings of abuse or neglect had far-reaching consequences for attempts at social work intervention after the initial case conference. The greater the agreement the greater the likelihood of the social worker forming a working relationship with the parents and child. As can be seen in table 16, disagreement between the professional view formed at the case conference and the views of parents varied along three dimensions: first that of commission (who had perpetrated the abuse or neglect), secondly that of culpability (who was to blame) and thirdly, risk (whether the child was still at risk).

There were just eight cases out of the 44 in our follow-up sample (18%) where there was agreement on all three dimensions of commission, culpability and risk, as can be seen in category one in table 16. Six of these were situations where the mother of a sexually abused child had accepted that the child had been abused and that their partner was to blame, and agreed with social services that the abuser should be out of the household as he presented a

Table 16 **Cases showing Three Dimensions of Agreement or Disagreement between Parents and Professionals about the Abuse or Neglect**

	Commission	Culpability	Risk	%
Category 1	Agreement	Agreement	Agreement	18
Category 2	Agreement	Agreement	**Disagreement**	14
Category 3	Agreement	**Disagreement**	**Disagreement**	34
Category 4	**Disagreement**	**Disagreement**	**Disagreement**	34
				100

risk to the children. In one other case a boy's relatives were clear that he had displayed sexually abusive behaviour and was responsible, and they agreed with social services that only vigilance would enable him to remain in the household with reduced risk to their children. The eighth case was a self-referral for physical abuse by a mother who accepted responsibility for hitting her children and wanted help to change.

In six cases (14%) as shown in the second group, there was agreement between parents and professionals about commission and culpability but disagreement about risk. These were mostly situations where one parent acknowledged that another parent figure or family member had sexually or physically abused their child. However, they disagreed with professionals about the future risk because they believed that the child would be safe with the abuser either because the latter had 'learned his lesson' or because of the protection which they themselves could offer.

In a third and larger category of 15 cases (34%) shown in category three, there was disagreement on two out of the three dimensions: parents and professionals agreed about commission but disagreed about both culpability and risk. These were situations where parents accepted that they themselves or another family member had been the agents of the incidents causing concern. Nonetheless, they advanced a variety of reasons to absolve themselves of culpability and to claim that the child would not be at risk in the future. These were mostly cases of physical abuse, with a smaller number of cases of neglect or 'emotional abuse' by parents. They also included three cases of sibling sexual abuse where parents minimised the harm the abuse had caused. The justifications the parents put forward for their actions included non-intentionality (a bruise or burn had happened accidentally); provocation (the child's behaviour was so difficult that he or she had provoked a beating); atypicality (the incident was a one-off outburst of temper which was out of character); normalisation (hitting the child was normal chastisement); and minimisation (a son's sexual abuse of his sister had done her little harm). In all the cases in this group the justifications advanced for the incidents of concern were accompanied by a view (not shared by social workers) that the children would not be at risk in the future.

In the last group of 15 families (34%) shown in category four there was disagreement on all three dimensions. These were mostly cases of physical or emotional abuse, or neglect. Where a child had sustained an injury the parents had said it was not caused by them; they had no idea how it had happened or someone outside the family must be responsible. In the other cases, parents defended the way they were bringing up their children, and hotly disputed the view of the case conference that they were neglectful or emotionally abusive parents. Since commission was denied, it follows that parents did not see themselves as responsible for the child's situation and denied that the child was at risk.

In less than a fifth of the cases, then, was there agreement between the social worker and parent on all three dimensions. Where agreement prevailed there were relatively few problems for social workers in establishing a workable relationship with parents, and in most of these cases the practitioner was involved with a non-abusing mother. Importantly, in the remaining 82 per cent of cases there was disagreement between the parties about risk, and often also about culpability and commission.

The effect of disagreement on social work intervention

In the early stages of work with families, these disagreements affected social work intervention in a number of ways. First, in some cases parents fundamentally questioned the legitimacy of child protection intervention. This was especially true for cases in which a number of general concerns about a child had been constituted by a conference as amounting to neglect or emotional abuse. Sometimes case conference members or social workers had not conveyed their concerns clearly to parents, who did not understand the reasons for registration. At other times parents disputed this interpretation of their parenting.

Secondly, at the stage of the investigation and case conference, assumptions were made by professionals about possible areas of disagreement with parents about risk and culpability and these assumptions had then shaped the ways in which agencies had dealt with families. For example, at the investigation stage a mother who was thought likely to side with the abuser rather than the child might not have been informed about the investigation or involved in discussions about placement. Moreover, parents who were known to be critical of social services or who disagreed with professional views had sometimes not been invited to case conferences. On one such occasion the parents were kept waiting throughout the conference and not invited in. For these and other families the experience of official scrutiny and its outcome had sometimes been so alienating that the investigating social workers had very little chance of establishing trust, no matter how well-intentioned they were towards family members. This was never the case when there was agreement about risk.

Thirdly, planning how best to intervene – short of removing the child – was a daunting task for social workers faced with disputed information about risk and responsibility for the abuse, and accountable to managers under a tight procedural system. Abusing and non-abusing parents in contention with professionals could easily feel themselves the cause of frustration, uncertainty and in some cases disapproval. Not surprisingly, parents in conflict with the social services tended to share as little information as possible with the worker. Indeed, the effects spiralled, since the more control or censure that family members felt, the more likely they were to deny responsibility.

Sometimes parents looked for other alliances, for example with the alleged abuser, with a trusted friend or, occasionally, with another professional.

It is important to recognise that issues of censure were not restricted to parents considered to be abusing or neglectful. As already mentioned, there was a kind of contagion effect whereby imputations of blame spread quickly to encompass non-abusing parents (mainly mothers) who did not act to protect the child in the ways social services departments or others expected of them, and to parents who remained emotionally attached to their abusing partners. These issues, individually and together, affected the ease with which a workable coalition could be formed between the parent and social worker, and between the social worker and child.

The after-effects of the earlier stages of the child protection process

After the initial conferences were over, disagreements about risk were not the only hurdles facing the social workers who were shouldering the responsibility for safeguarding children. At this stage parents were frequently feeling alienated and hostile for different but not unrelated reasons. In particular, the early interventions at the investigation and conference stages had had a negative impact on parents in over two-thirds of the cases in the study (70%).

The reasons for parents' disaffection have been set out in chapters 4, 5 and 7 which dealt with the investigation and case conference processes. Some parents were very angry at being accused of abusing or neglecting their children. As we have seen, this was particularly likely to happen when a series of concerns about child behaviour had been reconstituted as emotional abuse or neglect (and therefore by implication substandard parenting); when the index child had not been injured; or when registration resulted from questionable injuries which in retrospect may well have been the source of wrongful accusations. Sometimes, as we saw in chapter 4 on the investigation, this was combined with grievances about the way in which the referral had been made:

> *'Definitely, I felt stitched up . . . because I ain't done nothing to hurt my own son . . . They just made me feel as if I was a child batterer to be quite honest . . . And if they were actually here that day they would see that that was a pure accident . . . To be quite honest I can't stand none of them and they are all interfering busybodies. They think they are experts and they are not. I feel they can't understand how I feel . . . I can't wait until they are out of my life . . . I can't stand social workers.'*

> *'What they've done, I feel, is very detrimental to my character: it's going to be there with me for ever – for the rest of my life . . . I felt that they were being dishonest. She [the health visitor] betrayed the trust that I put in her*

in discussing things . . . My trust in the whole system has gone completely . . . I refused to have the health visitor in my home.'

Other parents deeply disliked what they saw as the disapproval of professionals and the degree of interference with their private and personal relationships:

'They saw me as a colluder because I want to stay with my husband. The chair said I'd done nothing to stop it and it went on for nine years [her daughter's sexual abuse]. That was an absolutely appalling thing to say.'

'Well, she doesn't like the way I run my life, or I run my home . . . She had the cheek to turn round and tell me that I should never discuss anything or talk about anything in front of my son . . . I felt like a criminal and I felt as if we were entirely – we were wrong in the way we'd brought Matt up.'

We need to remember that almost all of the parents and most of the children experienced the investigation and conference as processes over which they had had no influence, and some of their anger can therefore be traced to this feeling of *exclusion*.

'I've had absolutely no say over what's been decided.'

'It was taken out of my hands completely.'

*'Because with social services as they are now – not involving the parents – there's nowhere for the parents to go to talk over with somebody, you know. So you're shut out, and you don't know what's being discussed or anything . . . And I feel that social services, they should come in and they should talk to the parents. I mean, really **talk** – not, you know what I mean, not keep things back, really talk to them . . . They've got their own opinion and that's all. They're not interested in the parents.'*
(Mother of a 12-year-old girl who had been sexually abused by her older brother)

One mother commented wistfully:

'It would have been nice to have been asked what we could have done with.'

How far can these reactions be traced to parents' experience of the investigation and case conference, and how much to the individual social worker's actions, attitudes and intentions? Obviously these various strands are connected. In the stressful circumstances of the investigation and preparation for the case conference, the professionals had often placed more emphasis on gathering information which would assist in the assessment of risk than on understanding the views of parents about the kind of help they needed. It is understandable that help, at that stage, had been accorded a lower priority than risk assessment; but since help was likely to be needed to ensure that the child would be safe in the future, an important opportunity was being missed.

Whilst parents wanted to be more fully consulted, their apprehension about child protection interventions led them in turn to ration the information which they shared with the social workers. Problems which parents thought would be discrediting were not aired in the early stages – especially, as we have seen, those concerning domestic violence and alcohol or drug abuse. One mother said:

> 'They writes everything down in their little books . . . You have to be careful about what you say . . . I mean, you can tell them a **certain** amount, but like if you told them the whole of it, it might go further than what you expect, which since this all blew up . . . I'm a bit wary of doing at the moment.'

Almost half (45%) of the parents in the follow-up study actively disliked and distrusted their social worker as a consequence of their experience of the investigation, and a quarter had requested a change of worker. In only one case was this request accepted. An impasse between the social worker and parents was taken to confirm the parents' intransigence. For these families *the way the investigation and conference were handled, together with the fact of registration, was sometimes so alienating that the investigating social worker had almost no chance of establishing trust.*

It was in the context of these disagreements between parents and professionals and the after-effects of the early stages of the child protection process that social workers set about planning how to work with the child and family. It is to these issues that we will now turn.

Social work plans

The outline child protection plan and its associated recommendations, which were drawn up at the case conference, set a framework within which the key social workers could construct their own detailed plans. In this process they were helped in varying degrees by team leaders and sometimes by more senior managers. As we have already noted, the contribution of other agencies after the initial conference was reduced, and decision-making from this point onwards was even more firmly under social services control.

One of the main constraints on the social worker at the start of the intervention was of course the situation of the child and family as regards household composition. It will be recalled from chapter 5 that during the investigation or in the immediate aftermath of the initial conference, almost a third of the children in the study were no longer living with their families.

Forty-five per cent were living with the abusing parent or relative and 23 per cent had remained with the non-abusing parent after the abuser had left the household.

When we asked social workers how they planned to work with the child and family, they very rarely had recourse to any documented plans. In general, however, they knew what their objectives were, and they were prepared to state what actions might be taken in pursuit of them. Their sense of accountability to the conference varied. There were slight differences in their approach to planning, depending on whether the chairperson was a social services line manager, in which case the conference could easily be seen as having a supervisory role with the expectation that the recommendations would be translated into action. Conferences chaired by independent coordinators tended to be somewhat 'judicial' in their approach (for example, they spent more time weighing the evidence), and the corollary to that was that the key social worker often assumed more discretion when it came to the implementation of the conference plan. On the other hand these differences were slight when compared with the adequacy or inadequacy of the child protection plan, which varied from one conference to another. (See chapter 15 for more information on this subject.)

Most social workers who were on the point of engaging with families had more than one aim in view. In general all their objectives were congruent and intended to be worked on simultaneously; but some practitioners indicated that their second and third aims were more in the nature of contingency plans. For example, the first aim might be to retain the family intact with the help of domiciliary services and a small amount of respite care; but if the worker found that this was not consistent with the child's safety the second aim might be to seek a care order, and the third to find a placement which would enable the child's welfare to be enhanced.

This 'branching' programme of objectives lends some substance to the anxieties of parents, who constantly feared that their child might be in danger of removal. It is also interesting that sequential planning applied principally to the movement from 'preventive work' to removal. There were fewer plans which were designed to work in the other direction – that is, which took into account the child's possible return to the family and which constructed strategies by which it might be achieved. The only aim which appeared regularly in connection with the home situation when children were being looked after was *assessment*; that is, to establish whether or not the risks still existed. However, the situation was slightly different where the child was placed with another family member. In these cases the social worker was more prepared to recognise that frequent contact was on the agenda.

Naturally enough, the majority of the social workers' aims were concerned with the protection of the child. Out of 94 aims for which we have full details, 40 were concerned with the child's protection, 28 with the promotion of the child's welfare and 16 with meeting the needs of parents. Another 10 aims were concerned with what might be described as 'family welfare' – for example keeping the family together or improving levels of communication in the household. All of these aims were linked in some way to the protection issues.

One of the most prominent findings concerned the *person* who was nominated most frequently as the main target for intervention. In the social workers' statement of aims there were 24 separate references to work with mothers, 15 to work with children and five to work with both parents. There are only two references to work with fathers – one where the social worker wanted to improve the child's access to a divorced father, and another where the social worker hoped to get an abusing father admitted to a group run by the probation service. In view of the fact that the sample includes seven cases of physical abuse where the father figure was the alleged abuser, and that in six cases this was given some recognition in the child protection plan, there seems already to have been a shift in direction brought about by the social worker's choice of focus.

The second point of interest is the *nature* of the work which was envisaged. Here are a few of the stated aims, which convey the flavour of the social workers' intentions:

- To assess the mother's parenting ability
- To get the mother to consider the effect of her behaviour on the child.
- To help, advise and instruct the mother on how to look after her son
- To persuade the mother to give up shop-lifting
- To emphasise the consequences of solvent abuse
- To get the mother's cooperation for psychiatric help
- To encourage the mother to protect her children.

In many of these cases gains were made; but when outcome was considered at a later date, none of the cases for which these aims were given had an entirely satisfactory outcome. Some cases which had a better outcome (including successful child protection, enhancement of the child's welfare and the meeting of the parents' needs) included the following statements of social work aims in the early stages:

- Building up a relationship with the mother so that she can talk about her problems
- Help for the mother, leading to the rehabilitation of the child
- To get the parents to understand the aim of the work with the child, and later to work on their responsibility to protect her.

The method by which improvement in the mother's care or a change of attitude was to be achieved was primarily discursive, that is the social worker planned to visit regularly and discuss the issues. By contrast, the intervention planned for children consisted mainly of the provision of resources. Apart from placements these included priority day care (playgroups and child-minders), holiday activities, school trips or out-of-school activities, and occasionally referral to a child guidance worker or clinical psychologist for help regarding the impact of the abuse. According to some of the stated objectives counselling was to be offered to children, but this was usually in the context of 'helping the child to come to terms with events'. Sometimes the social worker hoped to increase the child's capacity for self-protection. However, it was more usual for the social worker to aim to protect the child at home by means of monitoring and by giving advice or encouragement to the mother.

A major obstacle to the implementation of social work plans was that parents' needs were generally defined by professionals, and narrowly so, in relation to the protection of the child. The parents' own views of their needs and priorities in relation to the welfare of their children were given little attention. What then did we discover about parents' understanding of the plans which had been made for working with them and with their children?

Parents' understanding of social work plans

In the immediate aftermath of the initial case conference, parents were waiting to discover what having their child's name placed on the child protection register would actually mean. They feared that it meant that they would have to allow professionals almost limitless access to their houses, their children and the intimacies of their private lives. For many of them it marked the beginning of a phase in which they expected frequent contact with professionals. On the other hand, for the key workers who were appointed to supervise the children the case conference marked the end of a period of intense and often stressful activity. As we have seen, their attention was sometimes diverted by pressing matters such as the management of children's placements. As a result there was sometimes a lull in social work activity at this point, which surprised, alarmed or angered parents and did nothing to help their understanding of plans.

Shortly after the initial case conference, when parents were asked by us about the plans for intervention made by the worker, they usually reacted blankly and said that plans had not been discussed with them. They placed their own meanings on events, reacting to what the worker and other professionals did and inferring from this what was in store or what might be expected of them:

> 'She gives me the impression that I've got to do what they want, or they seem to get it in for you and sort of make it harder than it is.'

> 'Well I mean they're checking up on us and I've got to go and see the health visitor once a week, and she strips him down – takes his clothes off to weigh him and everything.'

Interestingly, uncertainties about the plans and views of social workers were not restricted to parents who were under suspicion. Carers about whom there was no suspicion also expressed similar doubts. One example was a relative looking after an abused teenage boy. She was bewildered by the lack of direct feedback on how best to deal with him:

> 'I mean if they think that he's better off going to foster parents or to a special school or whatever, then I'd rather they said so, rather than let us think, "Oh, he's better off here. We're doing the right thing by keeping him here" . . . I mean they know what I think about this, but **I don't know what they think, because nobody's ever told me.**' (Our emphasis)

How true was it that parents were being kept in the dark? Was it simply that they did not understand or forgot what the social worker had said? In view of the intense disagreements amongst the parties, it would be surprising if the plans for intervention were entirely welcome.

When we asked social workers to state their aims, we also asked whether these aims had been discussed with family members, and whether they were accepted and shared by them. To discover how far social workers considered that their plans were feasibile, we also asked to what extent they were hopeful that their aims might be achieved. Practitioners' responses are shown in table 17 below:

Table 17 **Social Work Aims**

Overall Objective	No. of aims relevant to this objective	Discussed with family	Accepted by family members	Social worker hopeful of achievement
Child's protection	40	32	20	27
Child's welfare and development	28	20	17	18
Parents' needs	16	14	12	10
Family welfare	10	7	8	9
Total	94	73	57	64

The responses show that social workers had reported with commendable honesty that 22 per cent of their aims had not been discussed with the parents and children involved, and when discussed, almost 40 per cent of these aims had not been accepted or were not shared by family members. At the same time, we were struck by the fact that social workers were not hopeful of the achievement of a third of their aims. This situation is understandable when we consider the reactions of family members to child protection interventions.

Active resistance to social work intervention

As we have seen, in some cases the chances of laying a solid foundation for intervention had been severely restricted by what had happened in the early stages, and parents actively resisted the interventions of the worker. This active resistance to intervention took a number of forms. After the conference, two sets of parents would not allow the worker into the house. In another case the social worker attempted a visit accompanied by the conference chair, who wished to underline the risks to the child; but although the parents could be heard moving around inside the house, the door was not opened. It was also not unusual for social workers to arrange to visit at an agreed time only to find that the family had gone out, and written requests for parents to come to the office were often ignored.

However, a more usual response was for parents to offer minimal compliance. One mother who strongly resented registration allowed the worker in to see the child, but refused to engage with the agency in any other way. In two cases where family members felt that they had not been involved or consulted, and that they were the subject of deep disapproval, a situation of mutual distrust was set up, as a result of which the family members sabotaged and subverted sessions with the worker. An adolescent described the way her family did this:

> 'They said every fortnight we'd get together – one week here and then after two weeks we'd go over to social and have a meeting, and they put all these one to five questions, "What shall we do next?" and all this. And as soon as they were out of the room to talk against each other I put "Six: What to do with social workers?" My brother had a few ideas! And my Dad and Mum. Shoot them . . . They talk about what they want to talk about. They don't ask if we wanted to talk about anything else. They didn't ask that. They just got on with what they wanted to talk about and that was it.'

A social worker who had been on the receiving end of the resistance of another family said:

> 'The mother could be very obstructive. And so could John, because John would then – because he was taking his mother's attitude about not needing us and why are we involved. So he used to be quite rude to me at times, but in a very polite way, if you see what I mean . . . I always got offered a cup of tea. So there was that part to it, you know – go through the polite motions and things. They tolerated me, you know, really. And one time John had put a whoopee cushion under the seat that I was going to sit on – great fun, Ha! Ha! And things like that, when I was trying to keep my credibility in all this . . . Because it would have been easy for it all to have broken down . . . I did find it quite harrowing at times.'

There were also forms of minimal compliance which could be described as 'playing the game'. Sometimes the game was one in which the social worker took part, either knowingly or otherwise, so that the overt demands of the child protection system were met. Two mothers described it as follows:

> '[The social worker says] "How's baby? Isn't she lovely? How's baby? Have you got any problems? Can we help you in any way?" And I just say: "Yes thank you". "No, thank you." in the right places. "Oh well, then if there's nothing more, I'll be off then". And that's it . . . There's been too much damage done to give me any confidence in them.'

> 'You have to play the game, see? You have to make them think that they're in charge, and then they're all right.'

At other times 'playing the game' involved more of a dramatic performance on the part of the child's carer, who knew what his or her role was supposed to entail:

> 'People's going to put on an act when people come aren't they? I mean I could be now – if you weren't here – I could be hitting her. When Sue [the social worker] come it was exactly the same. I mean Gerry [the cohabitee] wouldn't play with her until Sue come, and then it was all play, play, play, and her thinking that he was so good and everything. But as soon as she went it was back to normal again.'

When parents were obstructive or refused to engage with the worker except at the most superficial level, practitioners faced an enormously difficult task in deciding what to do – and they also had to cope with being the target of parents' not inconsiderable anger. Not surprisingly, these were some of the most stressful cases for the workers.

On one occasion a mother's anger at the way she had been treated was expressed directly in a physical assault on the worker:

> 'She wouldn't go so I pushed her and I said to her supervisor, "I don't know who you are, or whatever you are, I want you to get her out my house before I flatten her." And I meant – I was going to hit her, and I wouldn't have give a shit – I wouldn't give a damn if I got done for it. Because I felt that I was set up on that day anyway.'

One worker who was excluded after the case conference by a family with whom she had worked for some time previously, said:

> 'The case conference was worrying, and the family rejecting me afterwards. Those four weeks of no contact were quite hard. I felt out of control. I was relieved when mother came to the office about Helen.'

Although such families were seen as difficult and resistant, the parents and children were reacting to what they saw as a major threat to them and at times they had grounds for this reaction. In some cases parents had probably been wrongly accused of abuse. In others the early agency interventions had been experienced as heavy-handed, whilst in yet others there had been a series of escalating misunderstandings fuelled by very different perceptions of abuse and risk between parents and professionals. Account needs to be taken of the fact that parents in this situation were often engaged not just in fighting against the professionals but in fighting *for* what they saw as the good of the family.

There were, however, a few cases in which apparent resistance to social workers' intervention was not driven by strong feelings of resentment, but arose from apathy or indifference. Long-term clients of social services sometimes did not react negatively to registration, since they saw it simply as a further aspect of an involvement with which they were familiar. Indeed, it often made little difference to them. This reaction was evident when the relationship with the worker was regarded as relatively benign, and when the early stages had not been particularly traumatic. Sometimes, for example, there had been no formal investigation. However, this situation was far from being beneficial because there was a tendency for things to continue as before and there was little leverage for change. As one mother put it:

> *'Well, Lucy was on the list down in Green County as well, when me and my husband used to fight a lot . . . It's not hurting being on there again. It doesn't really bother me that it's on there.'*

The social worker on this case commented:

> *'There are basic problems in getting any sort of work off the ground. I don't feel confident that Rose [the mother] sees any point to the contact. Doesn't have any expectations of advantage to her or to Lucy from the contact. She knows all about limits, and we can't do anything. She says, "Sod it. What are you going to do about it?" And you can't do anything.'*

There were also negotiations *within families* about how outside agencies would be managed, as very often mothers felt that they had been held responsible for their children's welfare and wished to ensure that no new bruises were found on the children, even though they might have no control over violent partners. One strategy adopted by mothers was to take the child to the doctor about any bruise sustained. This acted as an insurance policy but was also sometimes intended to act as a deterrent to abusing partners. We found that a typical pattern was one where the mother tried to work with the agencies, especially if she was being offered emotional support or material help, whilst her partner avoided seeing the worker or resisted any interventions which were offered. As we have seen, children were also often instructed not to talk at school or to social workers about what was happening in the family. Sometimes abusers had tried to drive this message home by abusing the child again after the original allegation had come to light, to punish them for telling the authorities what had happened.

In ways such as these, the attempts at official intervention were resisted and subverted. In some cases the intervention itself was used by family members, either to reinforce a pattern of family functioning or conversely, to change it in order to try to protect the child.

The importance of the social worker's approach

Whilst, as we have seen, some family members took active steps to protect themselves from the interventions of the professionals, nonetheless in most cases there was some room for manoeuvre. After the conference, social workers, parents and children were engaged in both covert and open negotiations about the form that future interactions would take. Much depended on the approach adopted by the social worker at this stage.

Three interconnected issues emerged as important components of effective practice in laying the foundations for subsequent work. The first was whether the worker was able to convey *an attitude of respect and liking for the parents*. When parents experienced the worker as respectful and accepting of them, even though they saw registration as stigmatising, they were sometimes prepared to work towards a situation in which de-registration would be possible:

> *'It's like he* [the husband] *said, "What's the point in shutting these kind of people out, because we'll only make things worse for ourselves." So we're happy to talk to him* [the social worker]. *You know obviously if he can help us then we'll try and help him in any way. There's no point in shutting the door on these people, because they can turn round and . . . go to a court or something and they'd get their own way anyway to enter our home, so we don't look at things like that. No, these people are welcome to come into the home.'*

> *'I mean I don't mind Sally* [the social worker] *coming round at all. We get on really well with her, don't we? She's all right she is . . . We have got the blame for something that we didn't know anything about and that we haven't done. But I'm just glad we're on the list because it might just open their eyes and prove to them that we haven't done anything, you know.'*

The second way in which social workers could prepare the ground for later work was in *recognising and understanding the points of view of family members*, especially when they had suffered difficult experiences in the early stages of intervention. The approach of social workers to alienated parents was varied. We found that half of the social workers were acutely aware of parents' feelings about the early stages of intervention and tried hard to build up trust:

> *'They do accept the need for registration, but I think they have a lot of feelings about it that we're not hearing.'*

> *'She was very, very upset indeed and very concerned – broke down in tears . . . She was obviously very sort of hurt and embarrassed by the fact that it [registration] happened.'*

However, *half of the workers underestimated the impact of registration* and the burden it placed on parents. One worker, talking of registration said:

> *'I don't think it bothered her, to be honest.'*

Yet, this mother felt acutely discredited:

> *'It's like an infringement of our lives, you know. And I feel I'm just made out to be a really awful mother. And the more that it's put down, the more harder life becomes . . . it's more that I've got to cope with.'*

Since registration was experienced by the majority of parents as morally discrediting, it was important that subsequent intervention, if it was to succeed, assisted in restoring parents' self-esteem and sense of moral worth (see also Farmer and Parker, 1991). The workers who appreciated the hurt and humiliation experienced by parents were in a better position to show understanding and provide such help.

Careful negotiation with family members after the conference about the work to be done, combined with an acknowledgement of their feelings, provided important preparation for the work itself. For example, in one case a social worker was successful in gaining acceptance to do individual work with a girl about sibling sexual abuse, although the parents had been angry at their treatment during the investigation and were very wary at the prospect of social services re-entering their lives. She described the hurdle of approaching the family as follows:

> *'There was social work involvement previously and they had a lot of feelings about that, so I had to really negotiate my way in really on a different footing, and with the agreement of the family.'*

She also described the process of gaining acceptance, which involved spending time with the family, acknowledging the pain the parents still felt about their previous contact with social services and finding a plan of work which at least one of the parents saw as useful:

'There was a lot of anger . . . I had a meeting with them about what I wanted to do, what I intended to do and just setting out the rules and the reasons for that . . . The first few visits . . . the family needed to go over why I was visiting, and there was a bit of the anger from the past and anti-social work feeling. So really how I achieved it was a lot of discussion really with them, answering their questions as honestly as I could . . . explaining the purpose of why I wanted to see Julie, and basically it was around self-protection and assertiveness really – saying "No". I say that because the mother in fact latched on to that . . . Yes, she needs to say "No".'

The third key element in the initial approach to family members was that of *finding enough common ground with family members to fashion a plan.* Since the plan had to be shared it had to be a plan which addressed the child's and the parents' needs, as well as simply dealing with the protection issues; but as we have seen, parents often had different views from the professionals about the main sources of concern. For example, in a number of cases which were registered as physical abuse to teenagers, parents considered the central issue to be their difficulty in controlling the child and they saw the abuse as a by-product. Finding ways to assist parents with the difficult or disturbed behaviour of their children was an important component of ensuring that children's needs for protection were addressed (see also Fisher *et al.*, 1986).

In addition, whether single or in couples, parents faced a range of adverse circumstances such as poor housing, debts and social isolation, and offers of practical help with these immediate and pressing issues were greatly appreciated as well as bearing directly on the ability of parents to cope with their children. Such help could even offset the disadvantages of the child protection system. As one mother put it:

'She comes round every Tuesday. That's how tight they are on my back . . . She stays about ten minutes you know, and gives me the rights and wrongs – what I should do and what I shouldn't do . . . But she's helping me out quite good Mrs Lyman is. You know, she's helped me sort all my bills and everything out . . . Mrs Lyman is fine.'

However, in practice, when the focus was on 'protection' the structural disadvantages faced by family members in relation to such issues as their housing and financial situations were often very low on the social worker's agenda (Boushel and Lebacq, 1992), and this corresponds with the low rate of discussion of these issues at the conference (see chapter 8). Several parents complained that they had received no help with housing problems, for example (see also London Borough of Lambeth, 1987; Farmer and Parker, 1991). The social workers in these cases often felt that they lacked influence over such resources, and the difficulties presented by organisational and administrative barriers should not be underestimated. Nevertheless, in a few cases where determined action was taken by a social worker or probation officer, the family – or just the abuser – was rehoused. Thus, it is clear that attention to the broader issues of the needs of parents and children was important in establishing workable relationships with family members. However, as we shall see later, inattention to these needs would also hamper the ability of workers to provide protection for the children.

Having looked at the negotiations which took place between social workers and family members after the initial case conference about how intervention would proceed, we will turn in the next chapter to consider the ways in which professionals conducted their work and the services which were provided for the children and family members.

Summary

1. In the majority of cases (57%) no new resources had been released as the result of registration, and apart from contact with health visitors, very few services were provided by members of the inter-agency network.

2. After the initial case conference the key social worker had the main task of negotiating entry to households and implementing the child protection plan. This task was hampered in the majority of cases by deep and sometimes enduring disagreements between parents and professionals – disagreements which were concerned with commission (who was responsible for the abuse or neglect), culpability (who was to blame) and risk (whether there was any continuing danger to the child).

3. As a result of these disagreements some parents fundamentally questioned the legitimacy of social work intervention. They were assisted by apparent shifts in the balance of power, as the social worker was now working on the parents' home ground.

4. As well as coping with the alienating effects of disagreements, the key social worker had to try to counteract the negative effects of the investigation and initial case conference. In 70% of the cases parents had felt blamed, marginalised and in some cases excluded. These experiences were not conducive to the build-up of trust.

5. The protection plan outlined at the conference set a very broad framework within which social workers constructed plans which set out their own aims. Out of the 94 social work aims reported to us, 40 were connected with the child's protection, 28 with the promotion of the child's development and 16 with meeting the needs of parents. Another 10 were concerned more broadly with the welfare of the family.

6. Parents had very little understanding of the social workers' plans, most of which involved work with the mother.

7. Some families actively resisted intervention – for example, by locking the social worker out or by maintaining an attitude of minimal compliance. However, long-term clients of social services sometimes reacted to registration with apathy or indifference. This reaction was particularly common when the relationship with the worker was regarded as relatively benign, and when the early stages of child protection intervention had not been particularly traumatic.

8. Strategic thinking was not unique to agency members. There were negotiations within families about how the outside agencies should be managed. Family members also used the child protection system to regulate each other. For example, mothers would take any bruise on the child to the doctor, both as an insurance policy and in the hope that this would act as a deterrent to abusing partners.

9. The workers who were most successful in engaging parents conveyed an attitude of respect and liking, combined with a recognition of the parents' point of view. By incorporating family members' objectives, they also managed to find enough common ground on which to fashion a plan.

Chapter 12

Intervening in cases of child sexual abuse

There were 15 children who were registered under the category of sexual abuse and of these 12 were alleged to have suffered sexual abuse themselves. Among these 12, two children had entered the child protection system not primarily because of their own abuse but because they themselves had shown sexually abusing behaviour. The other three children in the sexual abuse group were the focus of concern because of their contact with a known abuser and the risk that they would become victims if no action were taken to protect them. Eleven were girls and four were boys. Of course children who had been sexually abused had often suffered a range of other adversities so that, for example, a third had also been subject to neglect or physical abuse. In spite of this degree of overlap with children registered under other categories, there were distinctive ways in which these children were dealt with, and these will now be discussed. It is important to bear in mind that there were other features of care management which they shared with children registered under other categories and these will also be noted.

As in rest of the text we have used the term abuser in this chapter where a person was known or was strongly suspected of having been responsible for abuse.

The subsequent movements of children and abusers

As we saw, one of the early and key decisions which had to be made in dealing with children at risk of abuse was whether it was necessary to separate them, either by arranging for the abuser to leave the child's household or by removing the child. It will be recalled from chapter 5 that, at the time of the investigation, in seven cases of sexual abuse the alleged abuser had left the household, in four the child was moved, in two both the child and the alleged abuser left home, whilst two children remained in the same household as the person suspected of abuse..

What then were the developments which occurred in the course of our 20-month follow-up period? Of the nine suspected abusers who left the child's household four stayed away, either because they were serving a prison sentence or because the mother made it clear that the relationship had ended. One alleged abuser remained a regular visitor to his family, another returned when no charges were brought against him and as a result his stepdaughter had to remain out of her family until he later left of his own accord. Two adolescent boys who had abused their sisters later returned home because in one case no prosecution was brought and in the other no suitable placement could be found.

There was just one instance of a sexually abusing *parent* (a father) who experienced a planned return to his family and it is interesting to note that he was the only middle-class abuser in the study. He agreed to attend a series of groups for perpetrators run by the probation service both before and after his brief prison sentence, and he then returned to the family under specified conditions and with the consent of the daughter he had abused.

Of the six children who left home when their abuse came to light, two were still away 20 months later while the other four had returned to live either with the non-abusing parent or with a parent who had already been separated from the family at the time of the investigation. How was restoration achieved for the four children in question? Two had been involved in sexual abuse with a sibling. One returned home from relatives at her parents' behest after a very brief period away. The older brother who had abused her still lived in the family, but the worker set up an intensive programme of work to assist the girl to protect herself, that is to learn that she could make decisions about the kind of intimate contact that she had with others and could refuse unwanted advances. In a second case of sibling sexual abuse the abused teenage girl, Mary, was also sent to relatives by her parents, but she remained out of the home for almost a year. The responsible social worker took a very different view of the risks to the girl if she rejoined her family even though Mary was older and had suffered less severe abuse. In the end she returned of her own accord against the wishes of the worker. The variation in practice appeared to be related to the different attitudes adopted and plans made at the outset by each practitioner. Neither child was on a care order.

The third child negotiated re-entry to the family for herself. She stayed in a schoolfriend's family for nine months until she was able to go home safely because her abusing stepfather had left the family. The fourth child was removed from her abusing father and later rejoined her separated mother. It is interesting to see that in a number of these cases the child's return was brought about by the efforts of the child and non-abusing parent rather than by the design of the social worker (see also Thoburn, 1980; Vernon and Fruin, 1986; Farmer and Parker, 1991; Bullock *et al.*, 1993). It should also be noted that the lack of counselling and advice to mothers – or to both parents in cases of sibling sexual abuse (see also Gomes-Schwartz *et al.*, 1990) – appeared to play a part in extending some of these separations (Farmer, 1993 a).

As we have seen, two of the children who had initially been separated, did not return to live with a parent. The only sexually abused child who was on a care order was in foster care when he revealed abuse in his family of origin. He remained in that placement. The other child was accommodated in a residential school throughout the follow-up period to afford protection from a paedophile neighbour.

The high levels of distress suffered by the children who were obliged to leave home have already been mentioned. These children had endured a *double loss*. Not only had they been abused but disclosure had also meant the loss of their family. It was noticeable that *the key issue affecting their welfare became whether they could return to the family*. For these young people the experience of abuse and of being rejected by their families became closely interwoven. Some felt that placement away from home was a punishment for telling about the abuse, and others that they had not been believed or had been held to blame for what had happened. For all of them it was hard to feel that telling had been the right thing to do when it had had such dire consequences.

The distress experienced by the children who were excluded from the family after disclosing abuse was evident from the suicide attempts made by two of them and the high scores on the depression inventory for all of them (see also Gomes-Schwartz *et al.*, 1990). The depression scores reduced dramatically for those who later returned home. One 16-year-old girl described some of her feelings at leaving her family thus:

> *'Because I've always thought that if you've got children or something, you should stick by them and believe what they tell you or whatever – even if it means sort of leaving your husband . . . And she [the mother] always said she felt the same way as well, but then when it come to it, she didn't . . . We did arrange for me to go home, and then my mum come into court on the day crying, saying that she didn't know what she wanted. So they put me into care for another month. And then we went round to see my mum and she said that he'd come back and promised to love her and give up his girlfriend and she didn't know what to do.'*

This girl, not surprisingly, harboured regrets about having disclosed the abuse:

> *Interviewer:* 'What did you feel after you'd told?'
> 'Wished I'd never said anything.'

These findings would suggest that those children who are moved out of their families as the result of an allegation of sexual abuse are a very vulnerable group. They require particular attention if the effect of revealing the abuse is not to be compounded by the impact of rejection by family members.

Monitoring

Once decisions had been taken about the living arrangements of the sexually abused children, the responsible social workers had to decide how best to ensure that the children were safe from further abuse. Where the alleged perpetrator had left the household, these decisions turned on the practitioners' views about whether the non-abusing mother was able to protect the child from the alleged abuser. If a mother had demonstrated her determination to sever all connection with him and to keep her children safe, then the case was often quickly closed. When workers entertained uncertainties about the mother's capacity to look after her childrens' interests and exclude her partner, social work contact continued so that an assessment could be made about her intentions and actions.

For those children who were looked after it was generally thought that their safety had been temporarily secured, especially as it was usually assumed that the alleged abuser would have no further contact with them. Contact between alleged perpetrators and their victims had often explictly been ruled out as a condition of bail, and even when criminal proceedings against the abuser did not ensue, registration was often used in order try to prevent the resumption of contact.

When children had not been separated from the family members who had abused them the monitoring of the child's safety was conducted in a variety of ways. Workers who were doing regular work with an abused child were in a position to monitor the child's safety themselves. However, when they were not, they relied on other family members to let them know if things were amiss. In these situations practitioners would ask the most reliable informant to let them know if there were any worries, typically the mother, but in one case the grandmother and in another the sister. In one such case, Shelley aged 16 who had disclosed abuse by her stepfather was out of the family, living with friends. She was worried about her younger sister Katy who had also been abused and was still living with the stepfather. Whilst she was anxious to assist the worker in trying to ensure her sister's safety she felt, not unreasonably, that the worker should have taken more responsibility for this task:

> 'Well, sometimes if we're talking about Katy or something, and if I think she might be in trouble or something, she'll sit there and she'll go, "Mm, yes, well what do you think we can do about that?" And I sort of think, "Well, you should be telling me what you are going to do about it, not asking me what I want you to do about it." '

Interestingly, as can be seen from this example, the children whose safety proved particularly difficult to secure were often the *siblings* of the child whose abuse was the centre of professional attention. Some had also been abused but less seriously; others appeared to have escaped victimisation up to that point.

Although only a few of the perpetrators had been put on probation or imprisoned, when probation officers were involved they could play a useful part in keeping other agencies fully informed about the offender's movements and about parole plans. In one case where an abuser returned to his family, the probation officer worked closely with the social worker in setting house rules for the man's return which would enhance the girl's safety and in getting the family's agreement to apply them. However, in another case the probation officer was instrumental in reintroducing a man with a background of sexual abuse into a family from which the social worker had hoped to exclude him. Indeed, some of the situations which proved especially difficult to monitor were those where women took new partners with a history of sexual offences into the family, and where the social services department was unsure of what action, if any, to take.

The other situation in which monitoring could prove problematic was when sexually abused children were reunited with a family member who had abused them. Sometimes, as we saw, this occurred as the result of the initiative of the child and family members after the social worker's attempts to arrange a suitable placement for the child had failed. In some such cases the worker had lost the initiative and there was a consequent reduction in social work involvement at the very time when the child was returning home (see also Farmer and Parker, 1991). In one situation of this sort, an adolescent boy who had very poor impulse control returned home to live with the sister he had abused with very little social work involvement or monitoring.

Of course, in cases of sexual abuse the task of ensuring that the child did not suffer re-abuse was wider than that of regulating contact between the alleged abusers and their victims. Some, but by no means all, of the abused children displayed indiscriminate sexualised behaviour which made them vulnerable to re-abuse. Others were at risk from the attentions of predatory adults of their acquaintance or from the arrival in their households of new male partners who had a history of sexual offences.

Thus, the overall picture was one in which initial protection was usually ensured by separating the child and the alleged abuser. However, for a variety of reasons over which social services departments had varying degrees of control, some children continued to be at risk either from the original abuser or from others. Whilst a great deal of effort was put into arranging for the childrens' protection at the start of registration, as time went on the original arrangements sometimes broke down, family members moved in and out of households and local authority workers had reduced leverage with which to supervise the safety of the children (see also Farmer and Parker, 1991).

Direct services for children

There is a fairly wide professional consensus that all sexually abused children require an assessment of their need for treatment and that many would benefit from a period of individual counselling or group work after disclosure in order to counteract their feelings of guilt and to aid their recovery (see for example, Faller, 1989; American Academy of Pediatrics, 1991). Other studies have suggested that, nonetheless, sexually abused children often do not receive service or treatment (see for example, Frothingham, 1993). In a study of children who were referred for reasons of sexual abuse, many of whom were not placed on the register, Sharland and colleagues (1993) found that only 29 per cent received any therapeutic intervention. In our study of registered children the proportion who received treatment was considerably higher (58%). A 'programme' of individual work was offered to seven of the 12 abused children, one of whom was also an abuser. (Three of these seven children were living away from home.) The one-to-one work was provided by child guidance social workers, a psychologist, an art therapist or by fieldworkers.

The help was very brief for two of these seven children. In one case the sessions ended at the child's request, but service was discontinued for the other because of the dissolution of the child guidance service in that local authority. The other children enjoyed more prolonged contact lasting between four months and a year. All the children for whom the counselling lasted for some time spoke in interview of its value. One who was aged 17 by the time of the follow-up, described the contribution that her child guidance worker had made:

> *'She made it okay to talk about it* [the abuse], *and made me think about what had actually happened and how I felt about it, and why I felt that. So I suppose that's why I really miss her . . . I think people that go through, like, telling someone, they should be offered the chance of child guidance. And **if at the time they don't want it, they should be offered it again a few months later** . . . To me it was so important. I mean **at the time I didn't want it**.'* (Our emphasis)

Another child who was 10 had felt a pressing need to talk to her social worker about her abuse and suffered great distress when she felt this was not possible. At the time, Jane and her brother and sister were being taken out for meals and outings by the worker:

> *'As soon as she started spoiling us and everything I couldn't really talk to her, because she's like spoiling us and then I thought, "If I do talking to her [sic] about it, it will spoil all the other fun and everything" . . . When you desperately, desperately want to talk to her you can't. And then your heart goes – say it sinks, so you can't talk to her because she's enjoying herself.'*

Fortunately this practitioner later recognised Jane's need and offered her individual life story work, which she valued.

Another service which is often considered helpful to children who have been sexually abused is attendance at a group specially designed for them. It was somewhat surprising to find that only one of the sexually abused children actually attended such a group, although two others did not do so either because the child did not wish to attend at the time or because no group could be found in the area. The possibility of group attendance had been suggested as part of social work plans considerably more often than it had been possible to put into practice. The one girl who did attend a girls' group found it 'ever so good. It really helped a lot.' She went to the group after having a considerable number of individual sessions, and it was our strong impression that these had served as vital preparation for the group.

Two girls took part in art therapy groups. For one of them it appeared to have offered little of lasting benefit in relation to the abuse, since she still suffered recurrent nightmares in which her father came to shoot her for telling about the abuse and she showed other signs of continuing disturbance. The other child, who was 11 at the time of the follow-up, had been puzzled about the intention of the group. She told us that she would have liked to have known its real purpose at the outset as she might then have talked to the art therapist about what had happened. Her mother had assured her that it had nothing to do with the abuse. Happily, she received additional individual work.

The children who received little direct service

We also investigated the situations of the five sexually abused children who received no individual or group work despite their considerable needs. Three were placed away but two were living at home. We found that the initial choices about the focus of the work with the children were crucial in determining which services were offered. Once a course of work had been chosen and mapped out, a change of direction became unlikely. In some cases the worker's attention was taken up with finding or maintaining a suitable placement out of the home. These efforts took two children to establishments where, unfortunately, individual work on their abuse was not offered. Indeed, the placements had adverse effects on both children since they were bullied and teased about the abuse by other children in the placement and both became suicidal. In the other cases where children did not receive individual help a variety of other issues, such as arranging for the exclusion of the abuser or the protection of one of the child's siblings, became the focus of the worker's attention and the need for work with the child got lost.

Alison's situation illustrates the way in which early choices about intervention become set and do not change. At the age of 15 she disclosed that her father had sexually abused her over a number of years. The social worker devoted her attention first to obtaining a supervision order and then, after finding Alison difficult to engage, she concentrated her attention on her more extrovert younger sister to try to ensure her future safety. Since it was considered that the mother could protect the children, visits to the family were quickly reduced, although the children remained on the register for 11 months. Subsequent events proved that insufficient help had been offered, as the mother felt unsupported and Alison became suicidal. At follow-up Alison continued to have concerns about being 'dirty' and different from her friends and was afraid that there was something wrong with her. At that point her GP was planning to refer her to a sex therapist. It was interesting to find that although Alison's depression and suicidal thoughts were reported to review conferences, the reviews and associated procedures had not succeeded in remedying the lack of direct help being offered to her, even though the idea that she should be referred to a child psychiatrist was twice raised. (The impact of reviews will be described in more detail in chapter 15.) The fact that no such referral was made appeared to be linked to the low priority of the case once it was considered that the children were in no immediate danger and to the worker's focus on the sister.

It is important to note that six of the seven children who received some direct work relating to their abuse all showed improvements in their development at follow-up. (The seventh child who had attended only an art therapy group did not.) By contrast, in all the cases where sexually abused children were not offered individual direct work or group work, there were significant deficits in their development at the time of follow-up. Since numbers are small, such a finding should be treated with caution. Nonetheless, the difference was striking.

There were three families in which the children had not been abused but were sexually at risk because they had been living with an identified abuser. In all of these cases, the abuser left the household, and social work involvement was continued thereafter in relation to a variety of other family difficulties. Nonetheless, they remained classified as 'sexual abuse' on the register.

Services for non-abusing parents and carers

If the interventions offered to sexually abused children were far from comprehensive those made available to the parents were even less so. The priority for workers was to ensure the child's safety. The needs of the non-abusing mothers both for counselling about the impact of their child's abuse on them, and for advice about dealing with their victimised child, went largely unmet. In addition, some would have welcomed assistance in sorting out their conflicting loyalties to those who were close to them.

The mothers who demonstrated an ability to protect their children found that intervention quickly terminated:

> *'Well, I think to start with they were concerned about Hannah's welfare and safety, but it just seemed as if once they realised that she wasn't in any real danger, then they didn't want to know. They just left you to get on with it.'*

On the other hand, those mothers who were thought to harbour a continuing allegiance to the abuser or whose parenting skills were seen as deficient, were viewed as partially culpable and found themselves subject to *regulatory* visits, even when the abuser was securely off the scene. One mother in this situation, described how she saw her social worker:

> *'I dislike the woman intensely. She is not the sort of person that I would ever feel that I wanted to confide in anyway, and the children feel the same . . . They see her as an inquisitor. They don't see her as someone who's come to help us. [She is] someone who is very much dealing with 'a family where* **this** *sort of thing has happened' . . . where maybe I'm a colluder.'*

Only one mother was given the opportunity to attend a group for mothers of sexually abused children, although several spoke of their desire to meet other mothers who had been through the same experience. This mother was enthusiastic about the group and what she had gained from it and she and some other mothers had started up a self-help group of their own:

> *'Initially it was initiated by a ten week course from social services and the NSPCC to help mothers of children that had been abused. After the ten week course, there was six of us that decided that as we'd all formed such a good group between us and we'd all helped each other during various stages of the abuse, that we were going to form our own self-help group . . . There's plenty of help there for the children, and there's ironically, plenty of help for the abuser, but nothing for the mother that's left to cope with all the problems.'*

The group was appreciated not only for the opportunity to share experiences about their child's abuse and its impact, but also to share ideas about how to handle the resulting difficulties of their children:

> *'I mean I was going through an awful lot of problems with Mandy. So I brought them up at the meetings and two or three of the mums had already gone through the same stages that I was going through. And they just said to me, 'Well, when mine were going through that stage I done this and I done that', and it was really good.'*

It was sad to find that with the exception of this mother, none of the other non-abusing parents received any counselling or other intervention about the impact which their child's abuse had had on *them*. Yet, as we have seen, the discovery that a child in their care had been abused and violated by their partner had a traumatic effect, and necessitated a re-evaluation of the past, of the mother's parenting capacity, and of her relationship with the child. It was worrying to find that at follow-up 20 months later some mothers were still expressing deep feelings of anger and pain at their child's abuse which they had been unable to resolve.

It should also be noted that in four instances it was known that the mother of a sexually abused child had herself been abused sexually in childhood. In only one of these was a referral made for counselling about her own abuse, although the discovery of the child's victimisation could stir up painful memories from the past. This was in the context of very scarce resources for adult survivors.

Our study revealed therefore that in cases of sexual abuse, social work attention was primarily directed at ensuring that the children were safe from re-abuse. Other needs which arose in the family were often not seen as a priority, partly because they were not seen as bearing on the question of the child's safety and partly because of the limited availability of services.

Assistance to parents in managing their children's behaviour

If the personal needs of non-abusing parents were not prioritised, it might be supposed that help would have been directed towards the management of their sexually abused children since many displayed disturbed behaviour. However, such help was rarely forthcoming when children were living at home (see also Farmer & Parker, 1991). The exception was one mother who was advised on the use of a star chart to modify her child's behaviour. In a small number of cases children were placed outside the family because of their behavioural difficulties. This lack of management advice left most mothers in the position of having to fashion their own ways of dealing with such problems as depression, suicidal thinking, self-blame, eating disorders, stealing, sexualised behaviour, and indiscriminate approaches to strangers. In addition, little assistance appeared to be offered to them about the ways in which they could help in their children's recovery, for example, whether it was advisable to talk about the abuse. There were a number of possible reasons why such help was not provided. One was the constraint on social workers' time and the encouragement to close such cases. Another was that many social workers simply did not know how best to advise parents in this difficult area.

Nonetheless, it was interesting to find that support and advice about child management was sometimes provided to new care-givers such as foster carers when social services departments had placed children with them. This occurred when the children challenged the resources of the new care-givers and specialist advice was needed to support the placements.

Services to perpetrators

Only one of the adult sexual abusers received any treatment. As we have seen, this involved attendance at a series of groups for perpetrators run by the probation service both before and after a period in prison, and in this case the abuser was able to return home. Treatment for adult perpetrators was seen as the responsibility of the probation service, but since few abusers were on probation or parole and the motivation of reunification rarely existed, treatment was a rarity.

Sibling sexual abuse

Where sexual abuse between brothers and sisters had occurred, the ways in which it was handled varied markedly. Sometimes the focus of intervention was on the abuser and at other times on the victim. It was rarely directed at both. When the focus of the work was on the perpetrating sibling, the abused sibling received no help at all. As we have seen, there were also major variations in whether the abuser and victim were separated and if so which child left the family. These different management decisions were not directly related to the apparent level of risk in the situation. The help given to the young perpetrators varied widely. In one case the abusing child remained at home and received individual treatment from child guidance, although the provision of this service was delayed by a year because of the clinic's preference for family therapy. In another, the boy was placed in a psychiatric unit, which failed to offer appropriate treatment.

Overall, it can be seen that the pattern of intervention with sexually abused children on the register and with their families showed that agencies were effective in ensuring that early action was taken to protect them. The provision of direct help to children about the abuse which they had suffered was variable and was severely limited by the dearth of specialist services, such as child guidance, child psychiatric and psychological services. The multi-disciplinary approach of such services and their separation from the statutory agencies was viewed positively by children and mothers. In spite of the pressures of their caseloads, some fieldworkers continued to provide skilled direct work with children and this was greatly appreciated. However, when the children's safety was assured because non-abusing mothers had demon-strated their ability to protect their children, social services intervention terminated rapidly. It was worrying to find that the impact of the abuse and of its discovery often lasted long for both children and their mothers, and that without continued assistance their situation often worsened.

In the next chapter we will look at the services which were offered to children when physical abuse, neglect or emotional abuse had been identified.

Summary

1. In cases where children were registered on the grounds of sexual abuse it was generally assumed at the outset that children could only be made safe if the alleged abuser and the child were separated, and this occurred in 87% of cases (13 of 15). Reunification of children with adult abusers was rarely contemplated although it did occur when the abusers were siblings. This contrasted with practice in relation to children subject to other forms of abuse or neglect where children were more likely at the start of intervention to stay with the abusing parent.

2. During the investigation or soon after in just under half of the cases the alleged abuser left the household, whilst in the remainder either the child moved out or both the child and the abuser left home. In just two instances, at the outset, an abuser and child were not separated.

3. Most of the adult perpetrators who left the child's household stayed away because the non-abusing mother ended the relationship. However, for those mothers who in this and other ways showed that they could protect their children, social work intervention quickly terminated. The consequences of the abuse and of its discovery were often long-lasting for both the children and their mothers and their difficulties could deepen without continued assistance.

4. Of the sexually abused children who left home when their abuse was discovered, two were no longer living with family members at the end of the follow-up period, whilst the remainder had returned to the non-abusing parent. Most of these returns were brought about through the efforts of the child and the non-abusing parent either because a child's placement in care had proved unsatisfactory or because the abusing parent had left the household.

5. High levels of distress were evident among the older children who were placed away from home as the result of disclosing sexual abuse. They often felt that placement was a punishment for speaking about the abuse. As time went on the key issue affecting their welfare became whether they could return to their family.

6. Half the sexually abused children were provided with individual counselling about the abuse and its impact on them. This was highly valued by the children concerned and all showed progress in their adjustment by follow-up. Only one child attended a group for sexually abused children, although another two attended art therapy groups.

   The children who received no direct help in relation to the abuse all showed significant deficits in their adjustment at follow-up. In addition, some had been placed away from their families and endured teasing and bullying about the abuse in the placement.

7. Little counselling was offered to non-abusing mothers either about the impact on them of the discovery of the abuse or in relation to supporting and managing their children, many of whom displayed disturbed and difficult behaviour. Only one mother attended a group for mothers of sexually abused children, although several expressed the wish to meet other mothers who had been through the same experience.

8. For some parents the discovery of their child's abuse revived memories of sexual abuse in their own childhood. Referrals for parents to receive counselling about their own abuse were rarely made.

9. Only one adult perpetrator received any treatment. He attended a series of groups for abusers run by the probation service and subsequently returned to his family with the consent of his sexually abused daughter.

10. The management of sibling sexual abuse varied markedly. Sometimes the focus of intervention was on the abuser and at other times it was on the victim. Very different approaches were adopted by different workers in relation to whether the abuser and victim had to be separated.

Chapter 13

Intervening in cases of physical abuse, neglect and emotional abuse

The interventions offered to children and other family members where physical abuse, neglect or emotional abuse had occurred took a distinctly different form from those provided for sexually abused children. At the outset, the majority of children were not separated from the parent or parents who had abused or neglected them. This put a premium on effective monitoring. Difficult judgements had to be made later about whether the children who remained at home were safe and whether those who had been removed could be returned. In addition, when important information about risk issues in the family were concealed from frontline workers, these judgements were especially hard to make. Since reliable means for predicting future risks were not available (Dingwall, 1989; Parton, 1989) social workers had to contrive to minimise risks without having a well-founded knowledge base on which to draw regarding how to protect children from parents who had already shown a capacity to harm them (Melton and Flood, 1994). Thus, their main task was the management of uncertainty.

Twenty-nine out of the 44 children in the intensive study were the subject of concerns relating to physical abuse, neglect or emotional abuse. Of these, 16 had entered the system for reasons of physical abuse. Another five children were placed on the register because of neglect. Finally, eight children had been registered because they were considered to have been emotionally abused and this included three children who had also been physically abused or assaulted. Just over half of the whole group were girls (52%) and just under half boys.

The subsequent movements of children and abusers

As we saw in chapter 5 in cases of physical abuse, neglect and emotional abuse, after registration, three-fifths of the children continued to live in the same household as the parent considered responsible for their abuse or neglect. It will be recalled that 28 per cent of the children were removed during the investigation or soon after, and that in only four cases had the abusing male parent left the household.

As time went on, however, a number of changes took place to these arrangements. Three of the four abusers who had left the child's household at the outset later returned. One violent and unstable man rejoined his wife at the end of his prison sentence for burglary. The children were away in respite care at the time but the reunification of the family was being actively considered. Another young man rejoined his cohabitee and her children after a brief period away on bail. A third abuser who returned did so after the local authority's application for an interim care order was rejected. He gave every appearance of cooperating with the social worker. However, he had not admitted to his alcohol problem and later re-abused his baby son. The fourth man did not return to the stepchildren he had beaten.

Of the eight children who were removed at the start of the child protection interventions, five were still away at the end of our study. In over half the cases the context for the decision for permanent separation of these children was the mental illness of mothers, most of whom were single and had been known to social services departments for some time. The deterioration of the children's circumstances signalled by the abuse combined with the unpredictability of the mother's behaviour seemed to be decisive in the move for permanent separation. In the other cases, parenting standards were considered to be sufficiently aberrant and threatening to the children's well-being to justify the step of permanent removal. By the time of our follow-up interviews, moves towards securing a permanent future for these five children were well advanced, either by means of adoption or an application for a residence order for the child to live with a relative.

Although it is interesting that only three of the eight children who had been removed during the investigation returned home, the number is too small to permit firm conclusions. Nonetheless, it does suggest that where these categories of children are removed there is a considerable depth of concern and that they will only be returned thereafter in rather special circumstances. Indeed, that was the case in our three examples. They went home fairly rapidly, after periods of between one week and three months away. A bruised baby was returned to her mother after the father left the household. A second baby who had been seriously bruised was returned because of the responsible worker's commitment to reunification. (She knew the mother well and believed, in spite of medical evidence to the contrary, that the bruising had been caused accidentally. Dissenting professionals were absent from the review conference at which the decision for the child's return was discussed.) The other return took place in quite different circumstances. A teenage boy who had been hit by his rejecting stepfather was suddenly taken home from accommodation by his mother, although the worker had been planning a long-term alternative. The first child mentioned was re-abused when the father returned to the family, whilst the other two were, in our view, living in less than satisfactory conditions at follow-up 20 months later.

Although at the outset 18 children had remained in the household with the abusing parent, as time went on a third of them (7) were removed when the agencies became alarmed at the risks to which they continued to be exposed. Four of the children were removed after a reoccurrence of the abuse or neglect which had been the original cause of concern. Another two children, although originally subject to physical abuse, were subsequently removed for other reasons: sexual abuse in one case and abandonment in the other. One other child was accommodated because of his family's severe housing difficulties. All of the seven children who were removed from home were still away at the end of our follow-up, although return was under consideration for two of them. However, it should be noted that there were two other cases where the removal of the child was only averted by the admission of the whole family to a residential family centre.

The movements of the children who had been subject to physical abuse, neglect or emotional abuse were very different from those experienced by the sexually abused children. In cases of sexual abuse, the exclusion of the perpetrator from the household allowed almost half of the children to stay with the non-abusing mother, and of the remainder who moved out of the family for their protection most were later able to return. However, although most children subject to physical abuse, neglect or emotional abuse remained with their parents at the start of intervention, as time went on a number of them were removed to protect them. In addition, the majority of those removed at the beginning did not return home. By the end of the study two-fifths of these children (41%) were being looked after, another two-fifths (41%) were living in the same household as the parent who had abused or neglected them, and the remaining fifth (18%) were able to live at home because the abuser had left the household. Over half of the children (52%) had been separated for all or part of the follow-up period.

Children who remained at home and were at risk

During the course of the follow-up period there was a group of children who remained at considerable risk. In spite of this there were factors which prevented them entering care. The most salient factor was that they all involved cases with which the social workers were engaged before regis-tration and that no new assessment of the children and families had taken place at the initial conference or at the reviews thereafter. In these instances the approach to the family was more one of general support than of vigilance about child protection issues. Moreover, the workers had come to have a high threshold of tolerance for the standards of the parents and held low expectations of what could be done to effect change; for example, because the parents were from the travelling community or because they had learning difficulties. It was by no means clear why in these families the children could continue to be physically abused or neglected (or both) without this triggering the use of accommodation or care, although it was sometimes connected with a lack of concrete evidence. However, when a social worker had come to regard a high level of risk – or even actual abuse – as acceptable within a family, he or she could forestall or divert resort to removal. As we will see in chapter 15, since it was the social worker who framed the case for the review, other conference members could rather readily be persuaded to this point of view.

For the children who remained at home and where risks coninued to be evident, there were two 'models' of social work involvement. In one, as just described, there was a minimisation of concerns in which the worker's stance was firmly one of maintaining the family intact. In the other, the social workers harboured serious concerns about the children's safety with their families. In these cases renewed harm was taken to confirm the gravity of the risks to the child and the willingness of workers to tolerate the situation diminished. This was always accompanied by a worsening relationship between the parent and the worker. In these situations children were increasingly marked out as candidates for removal and a new incident, however small, could then trigger the child's removal (see Fisher *et al.*, 1986).

Monitoring

Clearly, we would expect a close watch to be kept on abused and neglected children on the register. We found that the monitoring arrangements which were in place for children under five relied principally on health visitors. The most stringent arrangements were made for babies, both because they were seen as particularly vulnerable and because it was possible to incorporate monitoring arrangements into routine health checks. In five cases, the case conference recommendations specified that a child should be weighed regularly by the health visitor either at the clinic or at home. Three of them were to be weighed undressed so that any injuries would be revealed. One other mother who refused to see the health visitor because of her anger at the way in which the referral had been made took her baby to the GP for regular checks.

The arrangements for monitoring were noticeably less rigorous for preschool children over two. Some were seen regularly by professionals, for example at a specialist hospital unit or at a family centre. Sometimes, the social worker assumed the primary responsibility for keeping an eye on the child during visits. However, not all children under five were supervised closely, and in two cases the only monitoring that was carried out was done by the social worker in the course of rather infrequent visits.

The schools played a prominent role in monitoring the well-being of children at risk who were of school age. In some cases arrangements were made that the school would report any injury or concern to social services, but in others it was assumed by workers that the school would fulfil this role even when it had not been formalised. The success of this *laissez-faire* monitoring then depended on the school's interest in the child or the zeal with which particular schools followed up any concerns which came to their attention. In one case of neglect the social worker took on an overtly monitoring role, laying down minimum expectations to the mother about providing school lunches, having the children escorted on their way to school, and attendance at a medical specialist, and then checking that these expectations were met. However, it was rare for social workers to assume such a direct policing and monitoring role not least because they were so reliant on the good will of the families to maintain access to their homes and to vital information. They generally preferred to exercise their monitoring role discreetly or to rely on others (see also Corby, 1987).

It was noticeable that with the school-age children monitoring arrangements had often not been placed on a firm basis. When asked about this, social workers not infreqently said that the school or other agencies were aware of the concerns about the child as a result of registration and that they expected that anything worrying would be referred to them. This optimistic assumption was held even by workers who were aware that these key agencies had not referred problems to them in the past. When asked about monitoring, and specifically about whether a particular agency had undertaken to do it, one social worker said:

> 'Do you know we haven't actually discussed this. I don't see enough of the children. I think Brenda [the mother] would tell me if she'd hit them and marked them. Boswell House [an activity centre] would keep an eye open because they were very concerned about it, and again the child guidance worker would come back to me if there were marks on the kids. The school are also aware, because they came to the child protection conference they know the children are on the child protection register. I'm also assuming that they, if they saw bruises, would come back, because it's their responsibility as well as ours to report.'

This same worker, earlier in the interview had said:

> 'I do get pretty angry in some conferences where the health visitor will come in and say, "Oh, this, this and this has been happening", or the school was saying, "We're very concerned about him" – and not one of them has bothered to phone me and tell me. I think it's a bit much to expect the social worker to do everything – to do some work with the family and also to keep constantly phoning round all the other agencies to see how things are going with them. I think it should be on them to contact me if they have concerns.'

In contrast, a few social workers made regular contact with other agencies to elicit information about the child, and this activity tended to increase as reviews approached and the key worker was expected to prepare a full account of the child's progress. However, it should be noted that such liaison could be very time-consuming.

There were five children out of the 12 abused and neglected children aged five or over for whom no satisfactory monitoring arrangements had been made. In two of these cases the social worker visited infrequently or not all, and in two no formal monitoring had been set up. In a fifth unsatisfactory case, although the worker was aware of continuing physical abuse to the children he accepted the low family standards and did not initiate action to protect the children.

Although social workers rarely saw themselves as the first line of defence in providing monitoring, there was considerable variation as to whether they used their visits directly to elicit information about the child's well-being. A typical comment from one who did not was:

> '*I rely on the school to report, you know, obviously, if there's any bruises or concerns or Amy has said anything . . . I don't plan to see them [the children] alone.*'

In contrast, another worker described her practice in this way:

> '*I'll actually go down on the floor and I'll talk to him [the baby] and play with him and give him things and just see what he's doing and how he responds . . . and I watch how they respond to him and how he responds to them, how he responds to anybody else around . . . If I went on a visit and found him very, sort of whiny, not very happy, perhaps not very responsive, I'd want to know why. And I would actually ask why.*'

Another worker made similar comments and added that she would ask about any suspicious marks:

> '*I always look for anything visible and the way that Denise is behaving and mother's attitude to her. I don't say, "Let's have a look at this week's bruises", but I would ask, "What has she done to her eye?"* '

It is clear that the reliability of monitoring arrangements varied considerably and that in some cases there was continuing opportunity for role ambiguity. The situation would be improved if formal arrangements for monitoring and liaison were made and agreed between social services and other agencies. This could be done at child protection conferences.

Direct services for children

What then were the kinds of intervention which were offered to the children in cases of physical or emotional abuse or neglect? For nine of the 17 children under five direct input was provided in the form of mother and toddler groups, playgroups, childminding sessions, day nurseries, speech therapy, and medical attention to correct specific conditions, as well as attendance at specialist units for disabled children. In two other cases the social worker provided direct work with the child. In one case this was play therapy with a disturbed four-year-old, and in the other the social worker, together with a family aide, provided play sessions for the mother and her three-year-old daughter which helped to repair their ailing relationship and provide stimulation for the girl. It was also clear that the provision of full-time substitute care had supplied some children with the nurturing and stimulation that had been lacking in their family of origin.

A variety of services was supplied to school-age children. Schools played an important role for five of the 12 children of school age, either by providing special welfare assistants, teachers for travelling children, special school placements, or by the particular care and help offered by involved heads and class teachers. Out-of-school and holiday activity sessions were also valued by two children. In addition, foster placements or brief respite care offered five children a break from their families and some positive experiences of family life. For a few children the health services provided useful intervention. This included, in one case, crucial attention from an eye specialist, and in another, psychiatric inpatient care for a teenage boy who was encopretic, with attendant counselling for his parents and follow-up help and support from a community psychiatric nurse.

Whilst, on the whole, children appeared to benefit from the services which they received and made some emotional or behavioural gains (Gough, 1993), a few did not. This was especially likely when subsequent events showed that the original physical abuse or neglect which had led to registration had continued unabated.

The focus of intervention

Since so many of the children continued to live with a parent who had abused them, the task confronting social workers charged with the responsibility for ensuring that the child was not exposed to further abuse or neglect was clearly very difficult.

The first question to ask is whether the focus of intervention was on the abusing or the non-abusing parent. Whereas all the abusers in cases of sexual abuse were male (mostly fathers or stepfathers and a few older boys), the physical injuries had been meted out in similar number by father figures and by mothers. In a few cases there had been continuing uncertainty amongst professional agencies about who had abused the child. All of the abusing father figures had been living in two-parent households and all of the mothers had been living alone. In cases of neglect and emotional abuse the concerns of professional agencies had sometimes focused on the mother, and sometimes on both parent figures, and only in one case on a father figure alone. As we have seen, neglect in particular was generally taken to denote deficiencies in the care offered by mothers since they were assumed to be responsible for the children's well-being.

Little differentiation was made, either at case conferences or subsequently, in relation to the different circumstances in which physical abuse could take place. The situation of lone parents, usually lone mothers, who undertook the main care of the children and who through lack of social support, impoverished circumstances and diminished personal resources were unable to cope with a child, appeared dissimilar to that of father figures who were not undertaking the main care of the children and for whom physical violence was more likely to be an established response to frustration or a way of establishing dominance (Straus, 1979; Bowker *et al.*, 1988; Parton, 1990; Hearn, 1990).

However, not only was this differentiation rarely made but one of the striking findings of our study was that the centre of attention in cases of physical and emotional abuse particularly, was frequently not the abusing father figures but the mothers. Thus, in two parent families, *the focus usually moved away from an abusing father figure onto the mother. In all cases, once attention focused on mothers, the issues around which the work revolved were not the abuse itself but more general concerns about child care. In some cases this had the effect of obscuring the risks to the child.* Before exploring the way in which intervention moved away from father figures we need to look at the associated issue of domestic violence.

The missing link with domestic violence

A second and very important issue to emerge from the study was that the *shift of focus from men to women often also allowed men's violence to their wives or partners to disappear from sight*. (In a similar way, at the national level, although violence in marriage was the subject of a parliamentary select committee in 1975, it has until recently achieved little visibility at government level apart from a few legislative changes which occurred as a result of private members' bills. There are welcome signs that this may be beginning to change with the Home Office circular in 1990 on policing domestic violence and the recent establishment of an inter-departmental committee on domestic violence.) In our study we found that the men who physically abused their children were frequently also violent to their wives; yet it was rare for incidents of domestic violence to be accorded much significance in the management of cases. The importance of domestic violence as an issue in many of these cases became more prominent as the study progressed.

Whereas in cases of sexual abuse some form of family violence had been evident at the time of the abuse in two-fifths of the cases, it was rarely a key factor in subsequent case management principally because of the exclusion of many of the abusers. However, amongst the 29 cases of physical abuse, neglect and emotional abuse, there were 17 instances (59%) in which there was also other current violence in the family apart from the child abuse which had brought the case to conference. This was usually a man's violence to a woman, except that in two cases parents were violent to each other, in one case the woman was violent to the man, and in another there was violence amongst the older children and between them and their mother. In some instances the violence was not a relevant factor for most of the intervention, because of the separation of the child and the parent. Nonetheless, in a third of all the cases in this group (10) domestic violence featured significantly but was not dealt with either in relation to the power imbalance within the family, the risks to the mother and children, or in relation to its relevance to whether the mother was able to protect the children.

It was as if these two manifestations of violent behaviour, domestic violence and abuse to children, were regarded as quite unrelated despite the increasing research evidence which demonstrates the connection between them. A study by Bowker and colleagues (1988), for example, found that men who beat their wives also physically abused children in 70 per cent of the cases where children were present in the home. Other studies reviewed by Hughes and colleagues (1989) found similar levels of association. (See also Goddard and Hiller, 1993; Stanley and Goddard, 1993; Browne, 1993). The importance of the link between domestic violence and child abuse was explicitly brought out in the report on Sukina Hammond's death by the Bridge Child Care Consultancy (1991) and has also featured in other inquiries into child deaths.

Only occasionally was the fact that the child was *witnessing* violence to the mother noted as unsatisfactory and in only two instances was there concern about the resulting effects on the child (Jaffe *et al.*, 1990). In addition, alcohol and drug abuse were noted as occurring in over a quarter of the cases in this group (8), although interventions to address these problems were rare.

Domestic violence was also a feature of the cases involving minority ethnic children. In seven out of ten of these cases in the sub-group, the allegations were of physical abuse to a child, and frequently there was abuse from the husband to the wife as well. Damaged pride and low socio-economic circumstances had a part to play, as well as ill-health in the male carer. In one case where a man had attacked his daughter with a stick, his wife said that he had started drinking heavily over the last few months because his previously successful business was in difficulty and his colleagues were making fun of him. In another case which involved physical abuse and alcoholism the father was unemployed and suffered badly with asthma. Although both of these parents believed in corporal punishment, the incidents of abuse were not expressions of cultural norms in the strict sense. They seemed to be abuses of male power which stemmed from frustration, illness and deprivation.

The deflection of attention away from the men who were abusers

How was it that the centre of professional attention was so often on the mother rather than the abusing father figure? How had this occurred? A fairly typical pattern in cases of physical abuse by a father figure was for social workers to offer emotional support to the mother, sometimes coupled with material help and occasional services to the children, such as activity groups. In some cases this deflection was assisted by father figures who made sure that they were out during social work visits or who refused to engage in discussions with the worker about the child. In addition, since these father figures were known to be violent men, they could be intimidating to professionals.

In other cases, the worker tried to deal with the abuser and the risks he posed to the child by attempts to remove him from the household. In one case of physical abuse to a five-year-old girl, the worker tried at the start to put pressure on the mother to exclude her violent and abusing partner. However, since persuasion was unsuccessful and there were no grounds for prosecution, the worker then focused her attention *faute de mieux* on the mother and general child care issues. This mother did not tell the worker about her cohabitee's continuing violence but the children's behaviour throughout the period was strongly suggestive of sexual and physical abuse.

In another case where the father had physically abused his nine-year-old daughter, Beverley, it was partly the male social worker's strong identification with the father which influenced his perspective. The worker joined the father in viewing the girl as difficult and disobedient and he offered general support to the parents by means of financial and material help, whilst relying on the mother to 'protect' the child. Work was not directed at the father's abuse (interpreted as discipline, albeit excessive), nor on child management issues. The worker knew about the father's violence to his wife and that the children witnessed these scenes and were distressed by them. He also took no action when the father later assaulted his son. No protective action was taken until Beverley finally disclosed sexual abuse by her father. She took this step in order to protect her mother from further violence after her mother's arm had been broken by her husband.

However, the processes by which attention was deflected from the abuser could be more complex. In one case a small baby was bruised by his father who, during questioning by the police, admitted that he had caused the injury. The initial case conference, whilst acknowledging the father's abuse, concentrated on the mother's so-called 'failure to protect'. This happened because the mother had denied knowing about the bruise on her baby and had clearly been anxious during the investigation not to say anything which might incriminate her husband. There appeared also to be a view, not spelled out as such, that she was irresponsible to leave the children in her husband's care whilst she went out to work. Although the husband initially left the family, he subsequently returned, but by this time he was denying both the abuse and his drink problem. In the face of this denial, the worker chose initially to make an exploration of the father's childhood separations the focus of her work. This seemed to represent a 'safe' area for both the worker and the parents. In this case the father was closely involved in the work, but it did not address the risks that were posed by the father's drink problem and his ready resort to violence. Six months after this case was de-registered the father re-abused his baby son and on that occasion his wife reported the injury to the authorities.

The absence of a clear focus on abusing behaviour needs to be noted because, as we have seen, when the locus of risk was unclear, surveillance could be ineffective. This has also been a theme in a number of inquiries into child deaths such as those concerned with Jasmine Beckford and Tyra Henry (London Borough of Brent, 1985; London Borough of Lambeth, 1987). However, the absence of work directed at the abusing behaviour was understandable since appropriate skills are not well developed nor are they generally in the repertoire of methods used by social workers (Adams, 1988; Hague and Malos, 1993). Moreover, although the possibility of work on anger control was mentioned in relation to two men, little progress was made since both were very reluctant to accept any treatment.

The interventions with parents

In general, social workers relied on separation to effect actual protection. Some children, as we have seen, were separated at the start of child protection intervention, whilst others were removed later as concerns about the child mounted and abuse or neglect continued. When children were at home the work of fieldworkers was largely concerned with monitoring, whether carried out assiduously or delegated to others, and also with the supply of limited resources, such as funding for day care or activity groups for children. Advocacy was sometimes undertaken with housing departments, but there was considerable variation as to whether such tasks were seen as a valid part of child protection work. Some social workers provided emotional support to mothers whilst others, instead, attempted to apply pressure for better standards of child care. *Pressure alone in the absence of practical assistance or emotional support was noticeably unsuccessful,* and if standards did not improve the children in these families tended to enter the care system.

The views of the mothers showed that what mattered to them was whether they felt that the worker understood them and was prepared to address the issues which they identified as important in their lives and those of their children. They wanted sympathy and compassion. Practical help was also greatly valued:

> *'She's marvellous, and if she weren't I'd be lost for most of the time I'm here, because she's a marvellous person. And she doesn't care if you're upset and you cry in front of her.. She lets you cry. She's that sort of person; and I feel comfortable with her.'*

> *'She doesn't seem to want to sit down and really listen. She just asks me how the children are and just asks me how me days were at home, and that's it really.'*

At the case conference stage, as we have seen, there was an absence of analysis of the likely causes of the abuse or neglect to the child and subsequent interventions were also often not aimed specifically at reducing risk (Department of Health, 1988 a). Of course, good risk assessments were not easy to make, but it did lead to situations in which 'supportive social work' might be offered which contributed little to addressing the underlying problems in the family or to reducing risk. In most of these cases, alchohol or drug problems or continuing violence by the father figure to the mother had either not been seen as significant by the worker or were being concealed. As a result, violence which either directly or indirectly posed a risk to the children was ignored.

In a small number of cases social workers undertook direct work aimed at improving the relationship between the mother and child. In one case of emotional abuse and another of neglect these were notably successful and mothers gained in confidence and derived more pleasure from their interactions with their children. Work aimed at change was also conducted where children had been removed but active intervention was taking place with the goal of restoration. In a similar way a variety of difficulties were addressed when whole families had been placed in a residential setting. In one example this provided an opportunity to assist a mother to break her addiction to valium.

Some areas of family life such as the marital relationship were closed to workers because the parents did not wish them to be examined. In addition, a considerable number of parents were living with extremely difficult or disturbed children, but help with these children was often not forthcoming because few resources were available. Some attended day care or special schools and respite care was occasionally provided, but specialist treatment was rarely available. Advice about how to deal with children was not usually included in social work activity.

Occasionally, a long process of assessment of family functioning and parent-child relationships was put in train. This could last weeks or even months and often guidance was sought from the 'orange book' (Department of Health, 1988 b). Unfortunately, these 'assessments' were frequently expected to perform other functions, such as delaying or justifying difficult decisions, and they often therefore became a substitute for action or for more direct assistance and made little contribution to subsequent work (see also Gibbons *et al.*, 1993).

The efforts of social workers were also supplemented in some instances by assistance from other agencies. This included financial counselling for learning-disabled parents by a community psychiatric nurse; treatment for psychiatric conditions by GPs, psychiatrists and mental health workers; and counselling from probation officers and army welfare officers. Sometimes it was the GP or a family aide who was able to gain a mother's trust when others had failed to do so, and on occasion professionals such as a health visitor or probation officer provided help which was not forthcoming from social services because the parents were so disaffected by registration that they had shut out the social worker.

As we have seen, the initial reaction of the majority of mothers to the decision to register their child was a negative one. However, such a reaction might be seen as acceptable, or even necessary, if one function which registration is intended to fulfil is that of deterrence. Of course, it is not possible to say definitely whether registration had acted as a deterrent as no further abuse might have occurred without it. Nonetheless, other evidence suggested that, in at least five families out of the 29 where concerns centred on physical abuse, neglect or emotional abuse, registration did appear to exert some leverage on the mother to offer a better standard of care to her children. These were all cases where social workers had established relationships which the mothers viewed as positive.

However, *registration appeared to be experienced as an additional pressure or burden for at least ten mothers. In all of these situations they felt blamed when the decision to register was made, even, it is important to note, when it was the father figure who had abused the child.* Mothers generally felt that any shortfall in the care of their children was ultimately their responsibility, even in areas over which they had no control. They sometimes gave up their part-time work either to safeguard their child or to demonstrate to the local authority that they were being 'good mothers'. Father figures, on the other hand, sometimes reacted by opting out of the disciplining role completely after registration, and this put further pressure on their wives or female partners.

At the same time registration was in many cases used by the local authority either to apply pressure to get parents to cooperate with their interventions, such as in getting a mother to take her child to a mother and toddler group, or to pave the way for more coercive interventions, principally removal into care.

In general, practitioners favoured an approach which aimed to offer general support or the alleviation of stress to one which was aimed directly at the parent-child or parent-parent difficulties which led to registration. In particular, the evidence suggests that the general orientation of social workers was not to work on modifying abusing behaviour but rather to endeavour to improve the circumstances of certain family members. This, though falling short of a direct attack on the problem was more successful than attempts simply to apply pressure to secure change.

Situations where parents denied culpability

There was a small group of cases of physical abuse, neglect and emotional abuse which presented special dilemmas to social workers. They were the ones where neither partner had admitted responsibility for abusing the child. When a single mother denied such responsibility at least there was no other person in the household who might take the blame, but without an admission the worker could feel uncertain about how to proceed. In one of these cases the mother resolved the dilemma by keeping the worker at arm's length and instead the child was seen regularly by the GP. In another, the worker reacted by accepting the mother's explanation that a burn to her toddler was accidental and retained only a low level of involvement.

Denial in the context of a two-parent family was also problematic as it made it even more difficult to know where work should be directed. In the absence of a history of how the abuse had occurred, specific stressors could not be identified. It also meant that once there were known to be 'secrets' within the family, workers had to manage high levels of uncertainty and this naturally heightened their anxieties. One approach to cases of non-admission in two-parent families was to set up a lengthy assessment period in the hope that more information would be obtained about the child's likely safety. Another was to insist on regular checks for bruises.

In cases of emotional abuse or neglect it was not uncommon for parents' norms about reasonable standards of child care to be in conflict with those of professionals. As we shall see in the next chapter, such disagreements had a major impact on the developments which took place in the 20 months during which we followed up the children and their families.

Summary

1.   During the investigation 28% of the children who were later registered for physical abuse, neglect or emotional abuse had been removed. Another 14% of children were able to remain at home because the abuser left the household at this point. At the time of registration three-fifths of the children continued to live in the same household as the abusing parent.

2. The majority of the children who were removed at the investigation stage remained away. By follow-up, moves towards securing a permanent future for most of them were well advanced, often by means of adoption. Only a few were restored to the parental home.

3. In addition, a third of the children who had initially remained with an abusing parent were subsequently removed as a result of renewed physical abuse or neglect.

4. By the end of the follow-up period two-fifths of the children (41%) were in care or accommodation, another two-fifths (41%) were living in the same household as the parent who had abused or neglected them, and the remaining fifth (18%) were able to live at home because the abuser had left. In all, over half (52%) of the children in this group were separated from their families for all or part of the follow-up period.

5. Some children who were exposed to continuing risks did not enter care. Most of these were cases which had been open to social workers before registration and the social workers involved had developed high thresholds of tolerance for low parenting standards. In addition, there was usually a lack of concrete evidence of abuse.

6. The most effective monitoring arrangements were those made for children under the age of two and these relied on the routine checks carried out by heath visitors.

    For children over the age of five the school played a prominent role in monitoring their well-being. Key workers assumed, not always correctly, that as a result of the initial child protection case conference school staff would report any concerns to them. In a minority of cases the key workers themselves took on an overtly monitoring role.

7. A variety of direct services were provided for children under the age of five, including day-care provision, speech therapy and medical services. In two cases the key worker provided very valuable direct work to the child or the child and mother together. Some of the deprived children who entered care were provided with valuable compensatory experiences.

    School-age children received help from a variety of sources, including extra assistance at school, holiday activity sessions, respite care placements and from the hospital and psychiatric services.

8. Although physical injuries to children were inflicted in equal numbers by father figures and lone mothers, the focus of work in both kinds of case was almost exclusively on mothers and revolved around offering emotional support, sometimes coupled with material help and occasional services for the children.

9.   This shift of focus onto mothers, even when the father figure had abused the child, allowed men's violence to their wives to disappear from sight, even though in 59% of cases there was current violence in the family which was usually directed by male partners to mothers. Other research evidence has shown the connection between men's violence to their wives and to their children. The fact that many of the children witnessed frequent violence to their mothers was given little attention.

10. Practitioners favoured approaches which offered general support or the alleviation of stress to mothers, to one which was aimed directly at difficulties in the parent–child relationship. Work which was confined simply to applying pressure on mothers for change was particularly unsuccessful.

11. The absence of analysis at the investigation and case conference of the likely causes of abuse or neglect to the child meant that risk areas were often not addressed. In particular alcohol problems or domestic violence, which had sometimes been concealed from the workers, often continued unabated.

12. Social workers were faced with particular difficulties when neither parent had admitted responsibility for causing an injury to a child, or when in cases of emotional abuse or neglect parents' norms about reasonable standards of child care were in conflict with those of professionals.

Chapter 14

Developments over time

In the preceding chapters we examined the situation in which social workers found themselves after the initial case conference, and the range of interventions that were offered both to children and their parents. We now turn our attention to the ways in which the families' situations changed and developed over time.

The effect of disagreement between parents and professionals about risks to the child

It will be recalled from chapter 11 that by the stage of registration there were varying degrees of disagreement between parents and professionals, firstly about the commission of abuse or neglect, secondly about culpability for the incident and thirdly about the current risks for the child. The cases fell into four groups, ranging from those of maximum disagreement which presented the most serious challenge to social workers to those where there was full agreement.

When we compared the levels of disagreement between parents and professionals at the start of intervention with those that we discovered at follow-up 20 months later, we found that in many cases there had not been a substantial change in the views of the main parties. Moreover, the extent of disagreement had had a major impact on the intervention. The children who went into the care system were almost all from the families where there had been most disagreement with the professionals, that is, they were from categories three (disagreement about culpability and risk) and four (disagreement about commission, culpability and risk) shown in table 16 in chapter 11. It is clear then that such disagreements were associated with an increased chance of care being invoked. In some cases of disagreement the children had been removed at the outset of the investigation; but in others the continuing divergence of views between parent figures and professionals led to increasing concern about the child's safety. When professionals considered that these children continued to be exposed to risks, the likelihood that they would be taken into care rose sharply.

However, there was a crucial mediating factor which affected whether, in situations of disagreement, children would be subject to compulsory removal. This was whether a workable coalition was established between the social worker and at least one parent figure, in which the parent was considered to be cooperative. When this occurred, even when disagreement about risks endured, children were much less likely to be removed. This accords with the findings of Dingwall and colleagues (1983), who comment on the connection between non-cooperation and the use of coercion.

There were a few instances in which the views about abuse or risk expressed at follow-up by parents were somewhat different from those which they had entertained at the start of the study. This occurred most often when mothers, after separating from violent or abusive partners, later admitted to the dangers which these adults had presented to their children. It also happened when parents recognised the improvements that had occurred, sometimes as a result of intensive help from a social worker, and thus implicitly acknowledged the deficits in their previous standards of care. Occasionally social workers also revised their views of risk downwards as they got to know families better.

Not only did the likelihood of the child being removed increase when there was disagreement, but there was also an increased likelihood of re-abuse. The majority of the children who were abused or neglected during the follow-up period were in categories three and four, where there was the most disagreement. However, it should be noted that one feature of category one, where there was least disagreement, was that many of the abusers were out of the household, and so the risks were lower.

Continuities and discontinuities in the parents' responses during the early and subsequent stages of intervention

It will also be recalled from chapter 11 that the early stages of child protection intervention had had a negative impact on 70 per cent of the parent figures in the study and that, in consequence, many felt belligerent or diminished. It was obviously important to explore how far these feelings were sustained throughout the follow-up period or how far later events led parents to feel differently.

In three-fifths (58%) of the families for whom the early stages of child protection had had a negative impact there was a marked improvement by the end of the follow-up period. In about half of these cases the improvement was due to the worker's patient attempts to build up relationships and to provide help which was acceptable to the parents. In the majority this was made possible by a change of worker. The successful new workers were not associated in the parents' minds with the earlier painful events, and were accepted as long as they adopted a non-blaming attitude, showed respect for the parents and – with suitable directness and honesty – were prepared to work hard on issues which the parents identified as important.

A case in point was that of a father who had been opposed to the social worker's plan to offer his abused daughter sessions on self-protection, but who came to approve of the plan:

> 'She was very open with us – told us exactly what she was doing, what she wasn't doing. What she tried to explain is she's coming to try and talk to her [the daughter] as an outsider, to talk some sense into her, which I think did work. She was so friendly at the same time.'

Another mother told us:

> 'I had it hard for six months with Gail [the first social worker]. And then Marion took over, and my life just got easier every day. I couldn't believe it.'

At the start of intervention one mother was faced with a worker who disapproved of her, thought that she should leave her husband and offered no practical help with the family's escalating housing and debt problems. By the time that a new worker took over the case the family was homeless; but she offered the children temporary respite care, threw her weight behind the family's housing application, and managed to form an alliance with both the mother and her violent husband. Often the parents contrasted their first social worker with whom things had gone badly with a second worker who had adopted a different approach which made them feel valued. As one mother said, 'With the new worker my word seems to count'.

In a few cases, the tension between workers and parents lessened when there were changes in household membership, such as when an abuser left. In two instances an impasse between the parents and workers was overcome when the family moved into a residential family centre. Other parents developed a more positive attitude to intervention as a result of the help that they received from other agencies, particularly the probation and health services, or from friends and relatives.

Whilst for these families the negative impact of the early stages gave way to more positive feelings, in the other two-fifths of families the initial negative impact was still strongly felt by parents 20 months later. In half of these cases children had been removed permanently from their parents' care. Some of these parents had to deal with the loss alone since, as we have seen, social work service tended to be withdrawn from parents once the children were bound for long-term care. Others had been more fortunate and had had some support from their extended family, from a new partnership, or from psychiatric services.

In the remainder of families the child had not been removed but the parent or parents remained in dispute with the agencies as to whether their child was at risk. As one mother said:

> 'To me Richard went through hell. So did my husband and I with both those case conferences . . . They were like hanging committees . . . and it was all for nothing in my opinion.'

Some of these parents felt that the interventions offered had been misplaced or even harmful. They included situations in which non-abusing mothers had felt blamed and put down by workers, or where children had been moved to very unsatisfactory child care placements. It was notable that in hardly any of these cases had there been a change of worker, so there had been no opportunity for a fresh start.

For those parents who had entered the child protection system without negative consequences, relationships with workers rarely became conflictual. Yet this did not always mean that all was going well. In some cases appropriate assistance was offered and accepted and this led in due course to de-registration. In others, the intervention was seen by parents as too brief, or as ineffective, although relationships between the parents and worker still remained cordial.

These findings suggest that when events during the early stages of child protection intervention have left parents feeling alienated from the protective agencies, there may be in many but not all cases, an opportunity to salvage the situation. However, this is only likely to occur if the agencies find a way to go back and understand the source of the disaffection of family members and an alternative approach which will be more productive is found. Certainly there is evidence from the study that in such situations a change of worker after the investigative stage could be helpful.

There were 20 cases where parents had wanted a change of social worker. Principally as a result of administrative reorganisation, there was a change of worker for eight of these families, and relationships improved significantly for the majority of them (6). For the other 12, where early difficulties between the parents and the social worker had been apparent and the worker remained unchanged, these difficulties persisted throughout the period of the follow-up, and in most cases placed severe limitations on what the social worker could achieve.

Alliances between family members and professionals

It became plain that an issue of major importance was which family members were engaged by professionals. This was no simple matter. Clearly, social workers needed to build alliances with key family members in order to increase children's protection. However, this was difficult when the needs of a parent and child appeared to be in conflict, or when the extent of important family problems such as domestic violence and alcoholism were either unknown or were denied.

It was noteworthy that different patterns of alliance emerged in different family situations. In families with children under 10 the interventions of practitioners were mostly aimed at the parent or parents, with occasional work on the parent-child relationship. Where older children were involved there was a tendency for the worker to form an alliance *either* with the parent *or* with the child, but not with both. With adolescents it was common for the worker to build up a relationship with the young person rather than the parents. This situation could arise because of the worker's disapproval of the parent's standard of care, or of a mother's continuing loyalty to an abuser. Occasionally it appeared to be because workers had more confidence in working with adolescents than with adults. Parents were quick to note this approach:

> *'Sometimes I just sit and talk to her and you can sort of tell she's – well, you know more or less she's on Jackie's side straight away. It's all a bit one-sided . . . They seem always to consider what Jackie wants to do, where she wants to go, but what **we** want out of it, they don't seem to understand any of that . . . She can't understand why I can't stand there straight away and say I believe Jackie, and sort of more or less disown my husband.'*

> *'I tend to think that she's more interested in the older, the teenage type. She doesn't give me the type of impression that she's for a family, you know.'*

Whilst older children were initially grateful for the understanding and support that they received from the social worker, the absence of positive feelings about parents was quickly apparent to them. Unless permanent separation from the parents was envisaged, this lack was often a barrier to successful work with young people; and when parents responded by being negative about the worker, children either adopted these attitudes themselves or found themselves in a conflict of loyalty between the social worker and the parents. For one 13-year-old boy a relationship with the social worker would have been impossible:

> *'Mum actually hates her. She was trying to come and take me away and everything. She was trying to make my mum and dad admit that they was abusing me and everything.'*

Another 10-year-old girl, who for the first time had a social worker who was actively trying to help her, derived little benefit from the experience because she was so upset at the way the worker treated her mother:

> *'She had a go at my mum and I was very mad about that. The other day when she came, I had a good mind to have a go at her. She can be really nosey sometimes.'*

In cases of sexual abuse it was especially common for workers to ally with the abused child and to offer little support for the non-abusing parent. Yet research has shown that women who do not immediately reject an abusing partner may eventually be able to sort out their painful and conflicting feelings with appropriate help and assume responsibility for protecting their children (Macleod and Saraga, 1988; Faller, 1989; Gomes-Schwartz *et al.*, 1990). This study confirms those findings. The lack of help for non-abusing mothers made it more difficult for them to offer their children support and assistance towards their recovery. When children had been removed from home this could lead to delay before return occurred, either because of the time it took to rebuild relationships without outside help, or because the worker was actively preventing a desired return. These children would have been greatly helped if the social worker had supported the non-abusing parent and worked towards strengthening the alliance between the parent and child.

A much rarer scenario occurred with teenage children when the worker focused attention on the parent figures and neglected the child. In these situations, sexually abused children received no direct work on the impact of the abuse. Very occasionally workers identified strongly with the parents of physically abused children, mistaking abuse for legitimate control. When this happened they failed to gain an understanding of the children's situation and it was possible for continuing physical abuse to be ignored.

In cases of sexual abuse by siblings, social workers faced a yet more complex situation in which as well as the parents there was a child victim and a child abuser. In these cases the social worker tended to build an alliance with either the child who was the victim or the one who was the abuser, but not with both. The parents were often given little attention so that their distress about the abuse went largely unacknowledged. This was partly because they were often seen as in some way to blame, either because the abuse was thought to reflect unhealthy patterns of family functioning or because it was taken to suggest a lack of proper parental management. As a result, workers failed to recognise and mobilise any resources within the family that might have been enlisted to prevent further abuse. Moreover, the parents' concerns about the importance of repairing the relationship between the siblings usually went unheeded.

Clearly there are dilemmas in making alliances with both parents and children when their interests are thought to differ. Yet in most cases where these issues arose, the future of the children was likely to lie with their families. Irreconcilable differences were usually dealt with by long-term care – and even in those cases the contact with their former home remained important to the child.

It appeared then that in many cases the social workers' actions were child-centred rather than parent-centred – partly because of a concentration on the child's interests but also because time was limited and the importance of the parent to the child was not always fully recognised. At times workers identified with the child and this accentuated their disapproval of the parents. *The children who derived most benefit from social work intervention were those where social workers (or sometimes other professionals) had succeeded in engaging **both** the children **and** significant parent figures.*

The matching of social worker and carer in minority ethnic cases

Engaging significant family members was not an easy task, and it was still more complex when the work was with black and minority ethnic families. In the sub-study, racial matching of social worker and parent or carer was achieved in seven of the ten situations examined, in the sense that non-white workers were paired with non-white family members, but full ethnic matching – which would have taken into account shared cultural traditions – appeared to exist in only five cases. In four cases there was a complete match across the dimensions of race, gender and ethnic group.

Although they were so few, the proportion of matched cases in this sample was actually surprisingly high in view of the fact that there was no systematic policy of racial or ethnic matching within the agency. The reasons for this were partly ideological and partly pragmatic. Firstly, the social services department dealt with a range of ethnic groups whose composition could not entirely be reflected in the composition of the teams. Secondly, there were other grounds for selection besides ethnicity – particularly gender, age, experience and professional skills. Thirdly, there was a genuine wish to preserve equal opportunities for black social workers, by refusing to relegate them entirely to specialist ethnic roles.

Some problems were caused by the speed with which the child protection system had to operate. Social workers who took part in the joint investigations and became key workers were often allocated rapidly, without much opportunity for detailed consideration of the fit between the practitioner and family members. One team manager pointed out that although the suitability of the worker was considered, accurate matching in the initial stages was virtually impossible – not simply because of the limited availability of staff but because the dynamics and preferences of the family were largely unknown. This meant that any perceived imbalance would have to be corrected at a later stage.

The responses of parents suggested that they had clear views about the appropriateness of certain choices; but their preferences were not always known to the agency or reflected in the agency's priorities. We found two instances where the allocation of a minority ethnic worker gave the illusion that a match had been made – but since the worker and parents came from completely different cultures, there was no real empathy. In one of these cases the family seemed happy to accept a female social worker who was Asian but from a different ethnic group, and felt that this was marginally preferable to having a white worker. In the other case, however, a black male worker from a different ethnic group was regarded by family members as presumptuous in assuming that he 'knew how the family lived'. The details of the situation suggest that he failed to invervene on behalf of a woman and children who were actually in need of help. By defining the family's pattern of behaviour as 'cultural' he also inadvertently strengthened the role of the domineering husband.

Gender was a very important factor in matching, and in many cases it appeared to be as important or even more important than race – although it had to be seen in a racial context in order to be understood. It was especially an issue for Asian women who wanted to be seen by a female worker, and it is clear that the combination of race and gender matching could be a powerful force for change.

In spite of the importance of ethnic matching there were a few parents who actually preferred a social worker from a different culture. One mother who was of mixed African-Caribbean and white European parentage did not welcome a black social worker because she saw herself as living a 'white life-style' (by which she may have meant a middle-class life-style), and she saw the selection of a black social worker as discriminatory. The position she adopted could be described as 'assimilationist' (Ely and Denney, 1987).

> *'I don't think I should have the choice. I think I should have been given any social worker that was available. No, I wouldn't choose a white one rather than a black one because I have no qualms about colour at all. But I don't want to be sent black policemen every time I rob a bank, or black social workers every time Cindy [the child] gets a bruise.'*

Conversely, one white woman who was the mother of a child of mixed parentage was pleased to have the help of a black male social worker who she felt would be 'better for the kids'.

> *'Their Dad's black – so that if there was any problem I could never turn round and say he's being racist or prejudiced . . . He's not going to look at them as being different, or anything like that.'*

This woman favoured a policy of integration based loosely on a philosophy of cultural pluralism. Besides providing a defence against allegations of prejudice, she hoped that her black male social worker would be able to forge links with her ex-husband's family and strengthen the children's sense of identity. By treating her as a friend and making her feel valued, he also helped to ease the sense of loss caused by her husband's absence.

This example serves to remind us that social work is both personal and political, and that family members as well as social workers have political views. These views are not necessarily immutable and in some cases much can be gained by discussing them. At the very least, they need to be recognised.

Changes in household composition

The engagement of significant parent figures was also affected by the fact that over the 20 months of the study family membership often altered. At the time of the investigation or immediately after the conference ten male abusers, most of whom were fathers, stepfathers or live-in partners, left the child's household or were excluded from it. In addition, as time went on another seven father figures left the household, usually because of a breakdown in their relationship with a partner which was sometimes accompanied by violence. *It was only after such separation that some mothers were able to reveal the extent of the violence which they had suffered.* In some cases they revealed this in interview with us, but withheld the information from their social worker. In addition one father was killed in a road traffic accident. In total therefore 18 out of 28 father figures left their families during the study and all but three failed to return.

In addition new adults joined some of the households. In six of the families the mother formed a new partnership after her relationship with the abuser had ended. There were also 14 lone mothers at the start of the study, of whom seven made a new partnership during the course of the follow-up period. Three other mothers left home for a short time and then returned. This meant that in only a third of the families (36%) had the situation of the parents remained unchanged throughout the study. When we add to these changes the movements of children which have already been described, the composition of only six families remained the same from beginning to end (14%). It can therefore be seen that the families in the study were subject to a great deal of change and disruption.

The interventions which were viewed as most important by the parents

We now turn to look at what the parents themselves regarded as the main influences on them during the course of the follow-up period. In some of these the professionals had played a major part but in others they had not.

By the time of our follow-up a third of the parents in the study considered either that the intervention of social services had had a negative impact on them or that it had led to no improvement:

> *'It's just as hard now as it was eighteen months ago. She's still got to come to terms herself with what's happened. She's still very frightened that Daddy's going to come back.'* (Mother of an eight-year-old sexually abused girl.)

In contrast, almost a quarter of parents saw social services help as having contributed to positive changes in their lives. In all these cases the workers had succeeded in forming an alliance with the parents and had been able to work towards change. A variety of interventions were offered, including preparation for returning children from substitute care, direct work with sexually abused children, counselling for the parents of a victimised child, and sympathetic support for neglected children and their mothers. Sometimes the work of social services had been supplemented by help from other people such as a health visitor, grandparent or friend.

In another 13 per cent of situations other agencies were named as offering the most significant help. Examples included a police prosecution which led to a custodial sentence for an abuser, thereby freeing his adult daughter, whom he had abused, and her child to lead their lives in less fear. Considerable appreciation was also expressed for the treatment provided for adolescents by a psychiatric unit and a child guidance clinic, and for the assistance with budgeting provided by a community nurse. Help with housing was greatly valued, partly because of improved living standards and partly because it enabled families to move away from the unwanted repercussions of involvement in the child protection system, including the disapproval of neighbours. As many as 39 per cent of the families moved house during the study period. In one case a local vicar paid off a family's rent arrears and enabled them to move after a particularly violent incident which was known in the neighbourhood. A new council house enabled people to leave unpleasant memories behind them – and of course the provision of alternative accommodation for an abuser could be critical in reducing the risk to a child. In another case a resident grandfather was rehoused with the help of his probation officer after an incident of sexual abuse.

Of course professional help was not always so important. For almost a quarter of parents the most significant help which they received had apparently been from their relatives and friends, whilst another 10 per cent of parents had themselves taken action to improve their circumstances. Amongst the first group, grandparents were the most frequently mentioned source of support and some, as we have seen, had been drawn into a helping role because of the crisis caused by registration. Sisters, aunts and ex-partners were also mentioned as helpful. Some mothers had been greatly assisted by close friends or by the parents of their closest friends who gave both emotional and practical support.

The parents or carers who had made changes for themselves spoke of finding acccommodation, moving from one town to another, sorting out benefit entitlement, finding a new partner, and changing their lifestyle in order to provide more protection for their children. One was a foster carer dealing with a disturbed sexually abused nine–year–old girl who said: 'I feel that anything that's happened to Natalie therapeutically or otherwise has come from us.' She felt unsupported in coping with Natalie's difficulties and had read extensively in order to be able to offer her the help she needed.

Parents often cited more than one source of influence on them during this period, so that the interventions of social services, other agencies, relatives and friends had often combined to augment or offset each other. The two examples which follow illustrate the way in which a poor start to intervention, when followed by a benign cycle of interactions, could result in improvements for the child and family. In each case there was a combination of help from social services, family members and friends.

Seven-year-old Jerry was registered because of a medical condition which was not receiving specialist attention. All three children in the household were seen as neglected and underfed. The father took little interest in the family, and the social worker was firm about the fact that child care standards had to improve.

After registration the burden on Jerry's mother increased, because she gave up her job to look after the children and this worsened the family's financial problems. She became very stressed. She left home for a week without saying where she was going.

For a while, it looked as though the couple's marriage might break up; but a personal friend helped them to talk over their difficulties. Meanwhile the maternal grandmother, shocked by registration, offered her daughter more assistance. The social worker helped by regular visiting, by providing transport to hospital and holiday activities for the children, and by boosting the mother's confidence. By the end of the follow-up period there was less conflict in the family and the standard of child care had improved.

The development of events in another family illustrates how agencies can exert a positive influence even when relationships have become hostile, if a change of worker is offered.

An inexperienced social worker was concerned to find that Susie, a young mother, was unwell and having difficulty coping with her two-year-old daughter. There was also a bruise on the child. The bruise was discussed not with the mother but with a senior colleague, who activated child protection procedures and arranged for a doctor's appointment. This left the mother feeling alarmed and angry. She had suffered a loveless and abusive childhood, was living with a violent partner, and she had been distressed about her lack of relationship with the child.

The situation worsened at a loosely chaired conference for which the mother had not been prepared, and at which she felt on trial. Her request for a change of worker was refused. The case conference left her feeling discredited, and she did not feel able to risk getting close to her daughter in case social services removed the child.

There was a definite possibility that the child in this family would enter the care system. However, two subsequent events had a major impact. Firstly, the original worker left and a new one was allocated. Secondly, Susie's partner moved out. The new worker discovered that offers of childminding had not been taken up because Susie was afraid of violence from her ex-partner if she went out; so a family aide was introduced for play sessions. The worker adopted a consistent, encouraging and non-blaming attitude and gradually rebuilt Susie's shattered trust. Susie also gained from renewing contact with an older woman friend whom she regarded as a mother figure. A downward spiral was gradually replaced by an upward one.

Registration, as we have seen, could have the effect of causing existing patterns of family relationships or problems to be further entrenched. However, the subsequent development of events could be influenced by a variety of agents in the direction either of further harm or benefit to the child and family.

It was noticeable that when parents reported that social services input had been negative or neutral, they very rarely had any effective source of alternative help. In contrast, *when the efforts of social services to help had been successful, these efforts had often been augmented by the assistance of other agencies, relatives, friends or partners.* Sometimes it was such benign help behind the scenes which, when added to agency interventions, had tipped the scales in the direction of change.

The interventions which were viewed as most important by the children

To fill out the picture of developments and how they were perceived we asked older children what had been helpful to them during this period. Just under half the children were positive about the help which they had received from the social worker or from another professional.

Individual work about their sexual abuse (or sexually abusing behaviour) was highly valued by a number of children. Furthermore, all these children had had significant support as well from their parents or relatives (or in one case from a boyfriend) during this period. This reflects the pattern mentioned above.

However, individual work was not always welcomed, especially if it was made to wait until after the completion of care or criminal proceedings. One sexually abused girl in this situation said:

> 'I did go to see a child psychologist for a couple of months, but it got – I don't know – I didn't like talking about it. I just wanted to shut it out at that time.'

This girl got more help from her social worker, whom she found to be 'really, really nice'. She also went to stay with her best friend's family after she had revealed the abuse, and received a considerable amount of support from her friend's mother.

Three children mentioned that they liked the activity groups which had been arranged by the worker, although in a number of cases transport arrangements had proved unreliable. One teenage boy had appreciated his time in a foster home and wished he had been able to stay there. After he returned home, to his disappointment the social worker did not visit.

However, a subsequent stay in an adolescent psychiatric inpatient unit had been beneficial and he saw the follow-up provided by a psychiatric nurse as very helpful.

On the other hand, just over half of the children saw their contact with social workers or other professionals as negative or ineffective. For some this was because the workers were disapproving towards their parents, and this was not offset by the fact that they had sided unequivocally with the child. For others it was because they disliked the social worker's attitude to them. This generally meant that the worker had been unable to relate to children on their level. Young people commented that workers talked down to them, insulted their intelligence, or were inattentive whilst with them:

> 'I reckon she's hard of hearing – she keeps asking me, "What?" . . . If she asks me a question and I answer it, if she don't like it, she'll say, "What?" or just completely ignore it.'

Children who had bad experiences in placements complained of bullying and sexual harassment by other children. Sometimes these experiences had soured their view of social workers, although this was not always the case. Continuity of relationships could be important and the loss of a valued worker a source of regret. One sexually abused child had suffered from several changes of worker. The second one was a man, and since this girl had been abused by her father, she not unreasonably felt unable to talk to him. At follow-up she had made little progress in recovering from the abuse.

The children who regretted having spoken about the abuse were those whose circumstances had significantly worsened as a result, for example because they had been separated from their families or had had unsatisfactory placements. None of the children retracted their statements about abuse, although a few physically abused children were punished by abusing father figures for speaking. There were, however, considerable risks of depression or even suicide unless children were given help in coming to terms with the abuse and with the consequences of it becoming public. These findings serve as a reminder of the importance of seeking both to understand the child's feelings and to ascertain their wishes and their view of their situation.

Children wanted comfort, but like their parents they also wanted to understand. They needed help in coming to an understanding of their experiences which would form the basis for their recovery. Lesley, the sexually abused girl whose mother was unsure whom to believe, and who went to live with friends during the pre-conference period, said that her main memory was of 'crying all the time'. She received some comfort from the daughter of the house and also from this girl's mother, who understood her attachment to her mother and was instrumental in changing her view of events.

> '*At first I was crying a lot and hating my mum and that. But Janet [her friend's mother] sort of sat me down and said that it really weren't my mum's fault – that she couldn't understand it had happened. It was just a mental block that she'd put towards herself because she didn't want to believe it. So I suppose that helped a bit.*'

This piece of amateur psychology from a personal friend helped Lesley to come to terms with her mother's lack of support, and to construct an account which was less hurtful. Another boy of low intelligence who had been looked after because he was both sexually abused and abusing clearly did not understand the course of events, and failed to appreciate why he was in residential care. After the investigation he assumed that he was being punished for 'getting in trouble with the police' or because he 'didn't get on with me mum or me dad'. Sadly, the importance of helping this boy, and others like him, to understand what had happened, and why, was not recognised.

By the end of the study, a number of children were still living in unsatisfactory circumstances or were struggling with unresolved issues about their abuse and its consequences, which were affecting their personal adjustment and future life chances through their impact on peer relationships, school attendance and further training.

Now that we have examined the views of the parents and children about the interventions which were provided for them, and some of the developments which took place over the 20-month follow-up period, we will turn to look at the role of child protection reviews and the influence which they exerted over what happened.

Summary

1. The children in the families where there were high and enduring levels of disagreement between their parents and the professionals involved about who was responsible for the abuse and whether the children remained at risk, were those most likely to be re-abused or neglected and to enter the care system. If at least one parent was seen as cooperative, even when divergences of view persisted, children were very much less likely to be removed compulsorily .

2. For three-fifths of the parents who had felt alienated and marginalised after the investigation and case conference, these feelings were later attenuated. In half of these cases this was because of the worker's efforts to rebuild relationships and in most this was made possible by a change of social worker. However, for the other two-fifths of parents the initial negative

impact was still strongly felt 20 months later. In hardly any of these cases had there been a change of worker. These findings suggest that when events during the early stages of child protection intervention have left parents feeling alienated from the protective agencies, there may in many, but not all, cases be a chance to salvage the situation if the source of disaffection of family members is understood and an alternative approach is found which will be more productive.

3. With older children social workers often sought to make an alliance with the child but not with the parents, of whom they sometimes disapproved. Children were aware of this absence of positive feelings about their parents and it was often a barrier to successful work with them. Children derived most benefit from social work help when practitioners had been able to engage both the children and significant parent figures.

4. Minority ethnic parents had clear views about the choice of social worker for their family. Most parents wanted a worker from the same ethnic group, but gender was also very important to them. It was especially an issue for Asian women who wanted to be seen by a female worker, and the combination of race and gender matching could be a powerful force for change.

5. During the course of the study, eighteen father figures left the families of the children under discussion and 13 mothers made a new partnership. Another three partnerships broke up and were reconstituted. In all, in only a third of the families in the study did the situation of the parents remained unchanged throughout the period. When we add to these changes the movements of children which have already been described, only six families were unaffected (14%). It can therefore be seen that the families in the study were subject to a great deal of change and disruption.

6. The principal sources of intervention which parents mentioned as bringing about positive change were assistance from social services (22%), other agencies (13%), and relatives and friends (22%), whilst 10% cited improvements which were due to their own efforts. In contrast, a third of parents considered that the intervention of social services had had a negative impact on them or had led to no improvement.

7. When parents reported that social services input had been successful, these efforts had often been augmented by the assistance of other agencies, relatives or friends. In spite of a poor start to intervention a subsequent benign cycle of interactions could lead to major improvements. It was noticeable that those parents who had found social services intervention to be negative or to have had little effect, had very rarely had any alternative source of help.

8. Half the children were positive about the help which they had received from social workers or other professionals. Individual work in understanding and coming to terms with the effects of the abuse or other specific difficulties was particularly appreciated. The children who had not gained from their contact with social workers or other professionals had felt that they had been patronised or talked down to or had disliked the workers' attitudes to their parents. The children who regretted having spoken about their abuse were those whose circumstances had significantly worsened as a result, for example because they had been separated from their families or had been bullied whilst in substitute care.

Chapter 15

The impact of the initial child protection plan and subsequent reviews

Given the risks inherent in child protection work it is important that progress is regularly reviewed, that reassessments are made and that if necessary, steps are taken to deal with unsatisfactory situations. The main procedure by which this is achieved is the child protection review conference. The functions of reviews are spelled out in *Working Together Under the Children Act 1989* (Home Office *et al.*, 1991). It is expected that during such meetings the arrangements for the protection of the child will be reviewed. This involves an examination of the current level of risk in order to ensure that the child continues to be adequately protected, a consideration of the effectiveness of inter-agency coordination, revision of the child protection plan and deliberations about whether registration should be continued or ended.

The regularity with which review conferences were held varied between our two authorities. In the one in which specialist coordinators acted as chairs the review dates were fixed at initial conferences and then at subsequent reviews. When risks were considered to be high, the first review was sometimes held within a few weeks of the first conference and often within three months. In the other authority, arrangements for setting dates and inviting agency staff to reviews were left to the key worker, but since this was a considerable administrative task it was not surprising to find that more than six months would often elapse before the first review was held. Most children were subject to more than one review before de-registration took place and since registration could continue for quite long periods it was not unusual for there to be a record of three or more reviews on each child, whilst two children had been subject to as many as eight reviews by the end of the study.

The review meetings were chaired in the same way as the initial conferences, that is either by independent coordinators or area managers. The person taking the chair was usually, but not always, the same as at the initial conference. The number of professionals attending reviews was variable. When concerns continued to be high the number of professionals attending could be similar to that at the initial meetings, but in general fewer were present. Parents, on the other hand, were more likely to be invited and to attend. Health visitors and school staff were frequent attenders and police officers also joined the early reviews.

The gathering of a group of professionals at regular intervals is a costly exercise and it was therefore important to explore what part these meetings played in the development of the cases. Our evidence suggests that in certain situations the initial conference could play a key role in influencing the course of events but that, on the other hand, rather less influence was generally exerted by subsequent review conferences. We will now examine these issues more closely.

The initial child protection plan and subsequent protection

There was enormous variation in the quality of the plans for the child's protection which were drawn up at initial conferences. Some amounted to a concerted plan to try to ensure the child's future safety. Others were little more than a general statement that some service would be provided. In some cases the frequency with which professionals, such as the social worker and health visitor, should visit was tightly specified and considerable thought given to options for treatment for the child. In others the interventions to be provided were left to the discretion of the key worker and other agencies.

When we examined the initial protection plans made in relation to the children in the study we judged that in *just over a third of them, there were deficiencies in the plan because it left important areas of the child's protection unaddressed*. Shortcomings were particularly evident in relation to arrangements for monitoring the child, to the interventions to be provided for the child and other family members, and to contingency plans if the suggested line of action did not eventuate. An example of a protection plan which we judged to be adequate was that made for three-year-old Lorna, who had been registered for 'emotional abuse' principally because of concerns about the poor relationship between her and her mother and because of the mother's physical abuse of a previous child. The recommendations which covered the arrangements for visiting by the social worker and health visitor, as well as the specification of direct services to Lorna and her mother, were as follows:

1. The social worker was to visit fortnightly.
2. The health visitor was to visit monthly.
3. There was to be direct work with the mother about the issues which caused her stress. This was to be carried out either by the social worker or by a therapist.
4. Lorna was to continue to attend playgroup three times a week; two sessions were to be paid for by social services.
5. Relief care for Lorna was to be considered in the holidays.
6. The mother was to continue on antidepressants and to consult her GP.

In contrast, the plan for Josie, a 12-year-old girl who had suffered long-term sexual abuse from her brother Shane, failed to consider how she might be protected or what kind of help or treatment she might need. The suggestion of consultation with the legal section was somewhat symbolic since neither a care nor supervision order were under serious consideration. There was no mention of help or treatment for her. The recommendations were as follows:

1. The police were to submit the case to the Crown Prosecution Service but with the likelihood that Shane would be cautioned.
2. The social services department was to consult the legal section about legal action to protect Josie.
3. The parents were to be advised that the children had not been protected and that they would need to cooperate.
4. There was to be support for Shane.

It was interesting to find that there was a relationship between the adequacy of the initial protection plan and how well the child was protected thereafter. In 82 per cent of cases where we had judged that an adequate initial plan had been made, the child had been protected, that is to say they had not been re-abused or grossly neglected. On the other hand, when the initial plan had been deficient, in half the cases the child had not been protected during the follow-up period.

However, part of the reason for this connection was that a higher proportion of the children in the group whose plans we had judged to be adequate were looked after and their protection out of the family had been easier to secure. We therefore looked in more detail at only those children in each group who remained for at least part of the follow-up period with one or both of their original parent figures. It emerged that the continuities between the adequacy of the initial conference plans and the outcome in relation to the child's protection for those children who stayed at home were mediated by a crucial intervening variable. This was whether the case was or was not a new one to the key social worker as opposed to the social services department.

The majority of the cases where children remained at home and adequate initial plans had led to subsequent protection were new to the key social worker. This meant that at the initial conference, members had felt able to fashion a detailed plan without treading on professional toes, and that afterwards the worker had been able to approach the family without preconceptions. In several of these cases there was a clear line between the plan formed by the original conference, to which the worker closely adhered, and the child's protection. For example, one social worker visited weekly because this had been laid down at the conference and it was a prescription from which she considered that she could not depart. Workers who were appointed newly to cases at the stage at which they were identified as involving child protection issues were more likely to take the line that: 'It was my job to carry out the wishes of the conference', than were social workers who were already involved and had a pre-existing view of the work needed by the family.

One illustration of this was where a small baby suffered an injury to her leg and both parents denied having caused it. The recommendations set down that the social worker was to visit weekly, which she duly did, in spite of difficulties in working with the parents:

> *'I think the bit that surprised me was the weekly visiting. I mean, initially I thought, "Oh, gawd", you know, "Weekly visiting. How am I going to fit that lot in?" . . . With this family, I suppose to some extent it has kept me on my toes – I haven't been able to be complacent. Because, actually visiting the family, there's been very little to work on, and it would have been very easy to just give up and say, "Oh, the baby's okay. The baby's going up to clinic. [The health visitor] will let me know if there's any problems. I'll just keep in touch." So to some extent because the conference had said, yes, weekly visiting, I keep going and I keep in there. So I think without that I think I might have taken the easy way out and maybe not gone in so often.'*

The baby was also weighed, undressed, weekly at the clinic so that any new injury could be picked up. The child was not re-abused. In another case the recommendations dwelt in detail on how aspects of neglect such as missed meals, late bedtimes and safety issues should be tackled. Monitoring arrangements were also specified. It would be a bold worker who did not comply. In practice the social worker tackled the issues head on with the parents. Although this initially put the mother under increased pressure, standards did improve because the worker was seen as friendly and helpful and because relatives stepped in to help. Clearly, there was a direct connection in these cases between the initial plan and the subsequent protective interventions.

In contrast, in the majority of situations in which children had not been removed but where protection plans were deficient, the cases had been known to social workers before the initial child protection conference. One characteristic of these cases was the conjunction of a social worker who lacked a clear purpose in his or her work, and a conference 'plan' which also lacked direction. There was a tendency either to leave the details of intervention open for the social worker to decide or for the recommendations of the conference simply to list what was already on offer to the child and family without any reconsideration of their needs. In addition, issues about the monitoring of the child were frequently omitted. Of course, we should not forget that some of these families had longstanding or multiple difficulties which were hard to change. In some, social workers had hoped that registration would give added authority to their efforts to work with the family. In others, they had considered registration to be unnecessary. It is worth noting that *the plans generated by child protection case conferences in relation to these cases which were already 'stuck' were rarely able to offer assistance in solving problems.* This was partly because of the general absence of an understanding of why the abuse or neglect might have occurred in the first place, and partly because of a reluctance to criticise the actions of individual professionals.

An example of a case in which an inadequate protection plan was connected with a subsequent lack of protection was that of a family where there were high levels of violence between a mother and her children. Although social services were already working with the family, little help was being provided because the social worker rarely visited and transport arrangements to activity groups for the children had lapsed. The child protection plan was simply a restatement of the services previously provided, although a review of the history showed that they had been ineffective. Moreover, no attention was paid to the fact that the practitioner was overworked and unlikely to offer an improved service. He had received no supervision for over a year and felt lost as to what to do about this family, as he said:

> *'I've had several cases I've felt particularly inept at working with. I don't know whether it's been about me – it's an area of work I don't find easy – I just haven't got the kind of temperament for, but I've had a couple of families where I've been working for a year and got nowhere. I've lost track of where I'm going and I've really dreaded having to go to see them.'*

The *feasibility* of implementing the conference recommendations was not considered. The worker made even fewer visits than before and the mother's needs for personal support and intervention about her depression and isolation went unmet. After de-registration high levels of violence continued culminating in injuries to two of the children. In this case there was clearly a link between the deficiencies in the original social work and in the conference plan, and the lack of subsequent protection.

It might well be thought that it had been not so much the allocation of a new key worker which had affected protection, but rather that such allocation would be a feature of cases which were new to the social services departments. It would be reasonable to expect that cases long known to local authorities would be particularly difficult to manage. It was therefore interesting to find that the allocation of a new key worker at the time of the conference was related to the child's protection, whether or not the social services department was already involved with the family. Table 18 which follows shows that *where social services had been involved at the time of the referral and a new key worker then took over, all the children were protected. In contrast, in ongoing cases in which the previous social worker continued their involvement only half the children were protected.*

Table 18   **The Relationship between Previous Social Services Involvement, the Allocation of a New Key Worker and the Subsequent Protection of the Children**

| | Child Protected | | Child Not Protected | | All |
	No.	%	No.	%	No.
SSD involved at time of referral and new key worker	9	100	–	–	9
SSD not involved at time of referral and new key worker	13	76	4	24	17
SSD involved at time of referral and previous social worker continues	9	50	9	50	18
	31		13		44

The initial child protection plan and subsequent intervention

The plans made at initial conferences not only affected the child's protection but also had some impact on the subsequent interventions, both because conference members occasionally furnished useful ideas about possible help for children and their parents, but more particularly because the existence of a specific recommendation from an initial conference increased the likelihood that other agencies would regard the provision of such a service as a priority. As a result, the recommendations made at the initial conference stage for specific interventions did raise the chance that they would later be realised. For example, when direct help was provided for sexually abused children it had featured in the initial conference recommendations in half of the cases. On the other hand, amongst the group of sexually abused children who received no direct help there was only one initial plan in which such help had been suggested.

This evidence suggests that the plans made at initial conferences set a framework for subsequent practice in relation to both protection issues and to subsequent interventions. *This framework was particularly likely to have a continuing positive influence when the key worker was new to the case at the time of the initial conference and when the recommendations were specific, feasible and tailored to the protection and treatment issues of the particular child and family.*

Initial conferences could also have an enduring effect on the way in which the risks to the child were construed. As we shall see, it was rare for a review to question a dominant view once it had gained general acceptance. This can be illustrated by contrasting the different reactions to suspicions of sexual abuse which were evident at the review stage in two different cases. David was a 12-year-old who had been drawn into the child protection system as a result of a suicidal gesture at school. As her rather lengthy psychiatric history emerged from the records at the initial conference, the mother began to be seen as in some way suspect. There was an escalation of concern at the conference which was out of proportion to the risks involved. The mother was viewed as being to blame for David's difficulties and her anger and extreme distress at the child protection interventions intensified a view of her as a 'difficult woman'. When, at the second review, the school reported that David had handed sexualised drawings to his teacher the concern escalated further with the possibility being raised that his mother had abused him. It was recommended that another investigation should take place. Fortunately, before this could happen it was discovered that several boys had handed in such drawings and the matter was dropped.

This reaction was in contrast to the way in which information about an allegation of sexual abuse to Jenny, aged ten, was dealt with at review. She had been registered because of her disturbed behaviour and because of long-standing suspicions of sexual abuse implicitly thought to be perpetrated by her father. At the fourth review it was reported that she had disclosed sexual abuse by her older brother whilst they were in foster care together. The investigation which followed was inconclusive. Unusually, especially for a girl about whom there was so much concern about sexual abuse, no action was taken and Jenny and her brother remained together without any intervention to keep her safe. The members of the review allowed this information to pass without comment, simply accepting the key worker's minimisation of the significance of the girl's disclosure.

It is likely that a number of issues played a part in the different responses to the possibility of sexual abuse in the case of these two children. These certainly include both the minimisation of abuse by a peer and of such abuse occurring in the apparent safety of a care placement. Nonetheless, the escalation in the case of David did seem to relate to a process in which the suspicions of the initial conference were apparently being confirmed, whereas inattention to Jenny's alleged abuse occurred because it failed to fit the preconceptions formed at the first conference. The phemomenon by which new information is selected and interpreted as confirmation of a previous hypothesis has been noted by other commentators (for example Moore, 1985; Sheldon, 1987). *It is important to be aware, especially at reviews, that the ideas about risk which are formed at initial conferences can have an enduring influence.*

The impact of reviews

At review conferences the key worker would provide an up-to-date picture of the child and family and of the work provided. There were also usually contributions from school staff and health visitors. These reviews did provide an opportunity for the risks to the child to be reconsidered and on a number of occasions the chair, or more rarely another professional, pointed out areas of risk which needed to be reviewed. These tended to be situations where it was clear that an overly benign view of events had been taken by professionals, such as when a worker was disputing a medical opinion that a child's injury had been deliberately inflicted or a practitioner had too readily believed that a violent cohabitee had left the family. Occasionally, certain review members were so uneasy about the risks which had been taken that they registered a dissenting view, although as with initial conferences this was usually restricted to dissent about the enactment of procedures. In one such case, a sexually abusive boy had returned home without any safeguards having been put in place for his abused sister. A recommendation was made at the following review that the children were not to be left alone together; if they were, care proceedings would be considered. The police officer and community nurse manager who were present expressed the view that the boy should not have been allowed home before a review had been held.

The protection plan made at the initial conference or a review meeting did form the basis for monitoring the performance of professionals, since their implementation could be checked at the next meeting. This form of 'quality control' was operated more vigorously by some chairs than others. In one authority a system was later introduced where each review began by checking whether the recommendations of the previous meeting had or had not been implemented.

Of course, there were a number of reasons why recommendations made at the initial conference or at reviews were sometimes not put into practice. One was where the child's and family's situation changed from one time to the next, so that the original plan was no longer appropriate. Another was where the recommended resources were not, in practice, available. A third and related reason was that the original recommendations were simply not feasible, an issue which was given surprisingly little consideration at initial and review meetings. It was not uncommon for a meeting to hear that a particular intervention was not working, frequently because it was unacceptable to family members. All too often, however, it was simply recommended again. This was particularly evident in relation to family therapy, a form of intervention which appeared to hold considerably more appeal for professionals than for family members, who often had good reasons for their refusal to participate, such as a previous experience of this method which had left them disillusioned.

A fourth reason for recommendations not being implemented was because the social worker or another professional saw them as inappropriate, and in effect sabotaged them. Finally, some recommendations were not implemented because doing so was not seen as a priority by the professionals concerned. Whilst few practitioners would ignore suggestions which directly concerned the child's immediate protection, other recommendations might be taken to have less force, and there were limits on the powers of reviews to insist on their implementation. Where recommendations were made but not acted on it was also common to find that little help was being provided for any family member. It was therefore part of a larger pattern of work which lacked direction and purpose. For example, in one case developmental checks on a three-year-old were recommended at the initial conference and again unsuccessfully at the following two reviews. In another, counselling for a sexual offender and for the mother and children was recommended but not provided. There was also a case in which much-needed treatment for a sexually abused girl was recommended at two reviews but not provided. The limited authority of the review forum was demonstrated by the situation in which the appointment of a key worker 'as soon as possible' was the recommendation at four reviews. No-one was appointed until the sixth review.

Whilst the question of the implementation of recommendations was at least on the agenda of review meetings, *they were much less effective in identifying gaps in provision*. If a professional raised an issue, such as a missed health check or speech therapy appointment, this generally led to a recommendation that it should be 'followed up'. But it was rarer for recommendations to be made about issues which had not already been raised by one of the workers involved. This was no doubt partly to avoid cross-professional criticism. For example, in one case where the traumatic impact on the mother of her son's sexual abuse had continued unabated, four reviews were held before direct help for her was recommended. In another family, although it was suggested that grief counselling should be provided for the children after the father was killed in an accident, no recommendations were made that the mother should receive similar help. This was partly because, as a result of perceived deficiencies in her mothering skills, she was seen as requiring control rather than help. There were also some types of service which rarely featured at either initial or review conferences. One of these was help for non-abusing parents and relatives in cases of sexual abuse.

The research in the third local authority suggests that there were even more deficits in the provision of services when the family belonged to a minority ethnic group, and that these deficits were not always picked up at initial conferences and reviews. Dominelli (1989) has outlined the dangers that black clients will fall victim to the twin discriminatory processes of exclusion and inclusion; in other words, they may be unduly excluded from services providing valuable resources and at the same time included in measures to effect control. Unfortunately this appeared to be happening in some of the cases we studied.

The social services department cannot, of course, be blamed for deficits in the routine services of other agencies, although the deficits experienced by minority ethnic groups were often greater than might be tolerated in white, middle-class communities. In one case, for example, a child with special educational needs had been out of school since he and his African-Caribbean mother moved to the city almost a year earlier. They had been told to expect that the city would have more facilities than the town they had left; but the suggestion that they should move may have been a form of ghettoisation, because the reverse turned out to be the case.

> *'He's supposed to be starting to Juniors, by law. My boy hasn't got a school! It will be a year in October. If I kept him away from school I would be in jail, so where does it tally?'*

In this case the child was waiting for assessment by the educational psychologist. The fact that he had not been attending school overburdened his mother, who also had a younger child, and this situation appeared to contribute substantially to the risk of abuse. Yet in spite of the fact that the child was listed on the child protection register, his educational need did not seem to have been picked up and dealt with during a series of reviews.

Clearly, review conferences showed the characteristics of any meetings where the quality of discussion depends on the extent of preparation undertaken by the participants and on the quality of the chairing. However, the attendance of parents and children offered an additional opportunity for them to voice needs which might otherwise have been forgotten or to question the appropriateness of what was being done or recommended. Although parents took part in review meetings more often than they had at initial conferences, children rarely did so. Parents usually found the reviews less intimidating than the initial conferences because they were smaller gatherings and because, by then, they had become more conversant with the way the meetings were run. Nonetheless, it was difficult for them to say what they needed since this generally involved some criticism of the professionals present. Even when they did succeed in speaking out they were not always successful in getting their requests met.

In fact, there were only a few reviews at which parents did voice their criticisms. In one, a mother pointed out the lack of support which she and her husband had received from a social worker who had stopped visiting. It was interesting to find that this was then reframed by review members as a 'successful' intervention and a continuing low level of social work was written into the recommendations. The minutes of the review ran as follows:

> '. . . it seems that there has been an improvement in the last six weeks when Mr Wingman [social worker] has not been involved. Indeed, there were always more problems both in [another local authority] and in [this authority] when social services were involved and there is a

history of authority figures not getting on well with the parents so it
was decided to see what would happen if there was no input.'

At another review a 16-year-old girl, with the full support of her mother,
asked for a change of social worker. The response was to arrange a meeting to
'find a way forward'. The meeting, however, did not agree to the girl's
request. There was just one case where a child's guardian, who was articulate
and middle class, successfully applied pressure on the agencies for the child in
her care to receive individual treatment. She did this by describing in detail
the difficulties she was facing in dealing with the boy's abusive behaviour.
Although the request was acceded to, the guardian's concerns were reconstructed as a negative attitude to the boy. The review minutes record that:

> 'The conference was concerned to hear of the negative attitude to
> Gavin which the family appeared to hold and hoped that this would
> feature in any future work.'

It can be seen that review conferences tended to function reactively and
that since social workers provided much of the key information they also
provided the context in which it was viewed. Sometimes this was the frame
set at the initial case conference but at other times and, especially in cases
which had been on the key worker's caseload before the initial conference, it
was not.

Whilst the reviews fulfilled a number of functions in terms of reviewing
risks and plans for the child, *once a pattern of case management had been established
it was usually endorsed at subsequent reviews, even when it was deficient.* For
example, the protection plan at the initial conference recognised the fact that
the father figure had been physically abusive in six out of seven relevant cases.
However, it was interesting to find that the later shifts away from dealing with
the implications of this recognition, which were noted in chapter 13, were
not challenged at the subsequent reviews even when there was evidence of
continuing risks to the children.

A more detailed example may help to show the way in which review
conferences tended to reflect rather than reappraise interventions. Three
children were at risk from the mother's partner who had a history of violence
and sexual abuse. The initial conference made no specific recommendations
for action, and the worker could not secure agreement for the man to move
out. Meanwhile, the probation officer, who had a narrow view of his role,
helped to re-establish the abuser in the family. The reviews showed that once
this course of action had received endorsement from the agencies which were
involved, the focus of attention moved away from the dangers this man
presented to the children (which had at least been spelled out at the initial
conference) and came to rest on supporting the family. Indeed, by the third
review it was recommended that, 'Mr Freeman should be encouraged to

build a relationship with the children', a situation in which the risks to them would most certainly be increased. The children in this family continued to show disturbance and behaviour suggestive of sexual abuse until the man left the household of his own accord.

There were a number of other cases in which, because the original plan omitted to mention how monitoring or appropriate interventions with the parents or child might be achieved, the focus quickly moved away from the abuser onto the difficulties of the children. These were then viewed as separate from the issues of abuse. Again, the reviews simply reflected but did not challenge these shifts of focus, leaving the children vulnerable to further damage.

However, there were a few occasions when review chairs actively sought to bring about a reconsideration of the management of the case. These attempts met with little success when the chairs were not line managers since their authority was limited and most of the key decisions about entry to care and day-to-day case management took place in the context of discussions with team leaders or in quite separate care planning meetings.

Dianne's situation illustrates the way in which the best endeavours of the chairpersons could be frustrated. Dianne was nine when she was placed on the register after running away from home because of the beatings she had endured from her father. There were also concerns about possible sexual abuse. She made it clear that she wanted to be accommodated. The social worker who was already involved with the family was sympathetic to the father and saw Dianne as disobedient. The conference chair was unhappy at the lack of action in the wake of Dianne's distress and fashioned a plan for a further investigative interview to take place with her, in the hope that this would lead to a reassessment of the need for action. However, no recommendations were made at the conference about monitoring Dianne or intervention with her parents. There were therefore no such recommendations that could be checked at the next review. The social worker resented what she saw as interference from the chair and continued with her approach of supporting the parents. At subsequent reviews – there were five before any action was taken – continuing concerns about the children were discussed. These included severe violence to the mother witnessed by the children as well as assaults on them. However, the recommendations which were then made concentrated on possible services for the children, such as childminding and respite care, rather than on any interventions with the parents. No action was taken until 17 months after registration when Dianne disclosed that she had been sexually abused by her father. It was only at this point that she was removed. Again, an initial conference plan which did not specify an approach to the family that was tailored to the nature of the risks, allowed the worker not to address them. The reviews did nothing to put this right. At the same time it must be acknowledged that such cases do present formidable problems to professionals who are balancing the risks to children who remain with their parents against the risks to them if they are removed, particularly where evidence in support of care proceedings is thought to be deficient.

However, and by contrast, it was of considerable interest to discover the clear connections between the initial conference plans and children's subsequent protection in cases new to the key worker when recommendations were carefully made and tightly specified. The importance of the initial conference in setting an agenda for future action becomes even more significant given the way in which, once a pattern of case management has been established, review conferences have only a limited impact on altering its course. There is, of course, one major exception: one of the key functions of review conferences is to decide whether or not to remove a child's name from the child protection register. It is to these decisions that we now turn.

Summary

1. Over a third of the protection plans made at initial child protection case conferences failed to address important areas relating to the child's future protection.

2. There was a close relationship between the adequacy of the initial child protection plan and the child's subsequent protection. In 82% of the cases where an adequate protection plan was made at the outset the child's safety was achieved. However, where the initial plan was deficient, in 50% of cases the child was subsequently re-abused or neglected.

3. Our evidence suggests that the plans made at the initial conference set an outline agenda for subsequent practice both in relation to the protection of the child and to the interventions which followed. This agenda was particularly likely to have a continuing influence when the case was new to the social worker (although not necessarily to the social services department) at the time of the initial conference and when the recommendations were both specific and tailored to the protection and treatment of the child and family.

4. Child protection review meetings provided an opportunity for 'quality control' to take place, that is for monitoring how effectively the protection plan had been implemented. This was done with varying levels of rigour at different reviews.

5. There were a number of reasons why the recommendations made at conferences or reviews might not be put into practice. One was that in some cases a child's or family's situation changed so much that the original plan was no longer appropriate. Another was the lack of availability of recommended resources. A third reason was that the recommendations

were not always feasible, sometimes because they were unacceptable to family members. A fourth reason was that in certain cases the social worker either saw the recommendations as inappropriate or made their implementation a low priority.

6. The reviews also had an important role to play in ensuring that areas of risk to the child had not been overlooked. However, although the chairs sometimes alerted the keyworker to such risks, in practice the power of review chairs or other professionals to bring about a reappraisal of the management of cases where the child appeared to be inadequately protected was limited. This was because many important decisions about the child, including decisions about accommodation or care and about restoration were taken within a different part of the social services structure. This was especially true when reviews were chaired by specialist child protection coordinators.

7. Key workers provided much of the crucial information which was made available to review meetings and so implicitly provided the 'frame' in which it was viewed. Once a pattern of case management had been established it was usually endorsed at subsequent reviews even when it was deficient. Overall, review meetings functioned reactively and major gaps in provisions were frequently not identified.

Chapter 16

De-registration

By the time of the follow-up interviews with parents, some 20 months after the start of the study, 80 per cent of the children had had their names removed from the child protection register, leaving 20 per cent still registered.

Those who had been de-registered had remained listed for periods ranging from one to 19 months. Nine children had been registered for less than six months, 12 for between 6 and 11 months, and 14 children for periods of between 12 and 19 months.

With the help of the data that we collected from reviews and interviews with social workers, it was possible to categorise cases according to the major reason for de-registration. The results are shown in table 19 below.

Table 19 **The Principal Reasons for De-Registration**

	No.	%
Improvement in the child's circumstances	12	34
Child looked after or living with relatives	10	29
Changed perception of risk	6	17
Registration considered to be counter-productive	4	11
Abuser out of the household	2	6
Child reached the age of 18	1	3
	35	100

This table of course underrepresents the number of situations in which the abuser had left the household. In some cases where this happened early on, the child's name was nevertheless kept on the register until the situation seemed relatively stable – or at least until the mother showed that she was willing and able to protect the child. The child was de-registered several months later because of a general 'improvement in circumstances' although one of the key factors was probably the absence of the abuser.

Improvement in the child's circumstances

For children in a third of the families de-registration came about because there was considered to be a definite improvement in their circumstances. For some of these children social work input had been effective; but there were also cases where the child's environment was better because of a move of house, medical treatment, or increased support from the wider family. At the point of de-registration the child's situation was generally more stable than it had been previously, and in cases of physical or sexual abuse there had been no obvious recurrence of the concerns which had caused the child to be registered in the first place.

The review conference at which a child was de-registered was in some ways a mirror image of the initial conference. Even if the focus of attention had 'wandered' during the course of reviews, the summing-up process involved in de-registration forced agency members to return to the original concerns and to reconsider the risks which had been seen to exist in the first instance. De-registration did not necessarily follow, of course, since new sources of anxiety might have been uncovered during the period of intervention. (For example, two children who were originally registered because of physical abuse were transferred to the category of neglect and remained registered.) Nevertheless, an improvement in the family's circumstances was generally seen as relative to the situation which had existed at the time of registration.

In cases where the initial conference had assessed risk by treating concerns about the child as cumulative (see chapters 9 and 10) de-registration usually took place because each of these sources of anxiety had been addressed and dealt with – albeit in a piecemeal fashion. In one such case the children's health problems had been treated, the standard of care and supervision had improved, and all the recommendations from the initial conference and reviews appeared to have been carried out. If the child was living at home, the cooperation of key family members with social services and other agencies was usually a necessary forerunner to de-registration. Social workers too were often aware of the importance of offering a reward for improvements made. At one final review conference there was some professional resistance to de-registration when it became known that the mother was pregnant; but the social worker argued strongly that the child should be de-registered, since the mother was in a new relationship and she did not want to start her new family under a cloud.

In deciding whether the degree of 'improvement' justified de-registration, the chair and conference members usually took into account three sets of factors. First they sought evidence from schools, social workers and health visitors that the risks to the index child no longer existed or had considerably *diminished*. (This was a similar process to the information-sharing which had led to registration at the initial conference.) Secondly, they wanted to be reassured that the child's current situation was stable and relatively *predictable*. (The existence of some minor risks could be tolerated as long as they were capable of being foreseen.) Thirdly, the conference members looked at *the professional inputs which had been provided*. De-registration was usually taken to signify not only that the family was considered to be 'safe', but that the professional agencies had done something to bring this situation about (see also Giller *et al.*, 1992).

How good were the assessments which led to de-registration? In spite of the care with which they were often done, there were few indicators of 'improvement' which could be considered entirely reliable. Much stress was placed on reports by school teachers that the child's behaviour in school had improved, or that the child seemed happier and healthier than before. As at the initial conference, the evidence of school staff was regarded as particularly important because of their close contact with children out of the family. As at the initial conference, too, the health visitor was expected to provide information about the progress of children under five. However, because of the lead role of social services throughout the registration period, and the importance of the key worker in providing information for reviews, the decision about de-registration usually followed the wishes of key workers and their supervisors.

In these circumstances it was easy for quite small movements to be exaggerated. In cases where the problems were thought to be cyclical, for example, it was not unusual for the child to be de-registered during an 'up-swing' in which some genuine improvement could be claimed, although there was no guarantee of lasting benefits. It was also common for advances in *ostensible cooperation* to be seen as representing improvement, even though the family's compliance was no more than superficial. In one or two cases there were continuing concerns about 'something going on under the surface', and some of these suspicions were later found to be justified.

Nevertheless, the reports from social workers and parents suggested that in many cases real improvements had been achieved. Some of the inputs which contributed to progress, and which were valued by children and parents, have been described in chapters 12 and 13. They included counselling, material help and psychiatric treatment; but in many cases of specific abuse, and also in cases where children had been registered because of the comparison of present and previous contexts (for example if another child in the household had been injured previously) the absence of non-accidental injury during the period of registration contributed greatly to a view that the situation had changed for the better.

Children looked after or living with relatives

Children were often de-registered when they were looked after or were living with relatives since this was seen as an arrangement which could be relied on. However, there were occasions when looked-after children were kept on the register until some specific objectives, such as a permanent placement or regular arrangements for contact, were settled. In all there were ten children (29%) who were de-registered because they had been removed – in some cases permanently – from the household in which the abuse occurred.

The fact that children had been removed did not of course mean that they were protected from all dangers, or that their welfare had necessarily been enhanced. (These issues will be explored more fully in chapters 18 and 19.) The most that could be said was that children were protected from a repetition of the original abuse or neglect, and that accommodation offered a fresh start. Nevertheless, important decisions had to be made for these children in the wake of registration, and de-registration was sometimes embarked on with confidence simply because the child's situation would continue to be monitored in a different system of reviews.

When children had been removed from their families they were subject to different risks from those living at home. Their progress depended on additional factors such as choice of placement, maintenance of family contact, and arrangements for return. For children in minority ethnic groups, the situation was particularly hazardous. There were occasional conflicts between the professional staff involved in child protection work and the adoption and fostering officers. As a result, one child who had been removed from a minority ethnic family on the grounds of abuse was almost returned to his parents after a very short time, because of cultural arguments in favour of his continued residence in the household. At the same time the absence of suitable carers added substantially to the risks attached to keeping children in accommodation for extended periods. Because of the lack of minority ethnic workers in residential homes, there were concerns that black children and children of mixed race who were accommodated by the local authority for their own protection would develop a confused sense of identity – yet the child's situation was often complex and the worker's concept of identity 'nebulous' (Owusu-Bempah, 1994). Here is one social worker's description of two siblings who were of mixed white and Asian origin, both of whom had been in a residential home for some time:

> *'Pramilla associates with African-Caribbean culture very much, because her mother's boyfriend at the moment is African-Caribbean and she has a little boy from this relationship . . . Pramilla speaks patois and kisses her teeth a lot and likes a lot of African-Caribbean culture. Suresh [her brother] doesn't really pick up on that at all. Suresh is aware that his father is of mixed parentage, and he's aware that he is of mixed parentage . . . He said to me before now when we've talked about fostering that he would like to live with a white couple, which I feel will cause him problems in the future.'*

In the above case the boy had his wish and a white couple was found to foster him; but before arrangements could be completed the couple moved to a country district with an all-white population, and because of this the agency decided that the boy should remain in residential care. Sadly, both children remained registered, because although they were being looked after, there were problems in their relationship with family and community and their situation was not considered stable. They were, however, in a minority, since living away from home was generally equated with protection and it was seen as a good antecedent to de-registration.

Changed perception of risk

By contrast with cases in which there was evidence of positive improvement, there were others (one in six) where de-registration seemed to have been brought about by a change in the official perception of the risks to the child. This was usually due to the increased knowledge gained about the family during the period of registration. In such cases, although there was no obvious progress, de-registration occurred because there was no evidence of further harm and the key social worker felt that there was therefore less need for involvement.

In many of these cases the original injury remained unexplained; but the situation was reinterpreted as harmless as long as there had been no re-injury or suggestion of other risks. Confirmation of the absence of serious risk to the child had usually been gained from regular monitoring, for example by a social worker, GP or health visitor.

De-registration in these cases did not necessarily mean that official involvement ceased. In two cases it was proposed that the health visitor and the social worker should both continue to visit the family. In a third case where continued help might have been offered, the family 'vanished' following de-registration – and the alarm shown by the social worker when she discovered this, was indicative of the anxiety which lingered on in cases of injuries which were probably, but not certainly, accidental.

In other cases where de-registration appeared to be brought about by a changed perception on the part of the social worker or monitoring agencies, the source of the injury was known and to some extent explained, but there had been some initial uncertainty about the mothers' ability to protect their children or to cater for their needs. Sometimes the main purpose of registration was actually to provide a framework for assessment. When the social worker got to know the mother better, areas of competence were uncovered and some problems were discounted; but the interesting point is that social workers were not always aware that their perceptions had changed. It was only when some of them were reminded at our second interview of their previous statements, that they remembered how negative their earlier impressions had been. As a result, they sometimes misinterpreted their change of perception in the light of increased information as a real change in family circumstances.

Registration seen as counterproductive or ineffective

In 11 per cent of cases the child was de-registered because there was considered to be a danger that continued registration would prove counter-productive or ineffective. The main fear was that the family would withdraw their cooperation if registration was maintained. For example, in one case where a 16-year-old girl was requesting de-registration, the family strongly supported her. A convicted abuser was returning to the family after his prison sentence but the parents pointed out that since they had complied with social work plans for some time, de-registration was not only appropriate but deserved. They said that they would not cooperate with the agency any longer if this fact was not acknowledged. This use of de-registration as a 'reward' for cooperation is similar to that of restoring children home as a reward for improvements made (Farmer and Parker, 1991). At a certain point in both of these processes the momentum for exit from the system is hard to resist.

Sometimes anxieties about the ineffectiveness of registration were linked with more positive reasons for de-registration. For example, in one case where a girl was living safely with her aunt she saw continued registration as a punishment for having disclosed sexual abuse. There was therefore an incentive to de-register quickly. In another case a father requested de-registration after there had been an improvement in his son's adjustment at school, because he preferred to have the continued intervention of the army welfare services. This request was granted.

In the second two of these three examples, the use of de-registration was plainly warranted, and yet it created a certain amount of anxiety for social services. The main reason for this seemed to be that in these cases de-registration was initiated by family members (see also Farmer and Parker, 1991). We are reminded that at the initial case conference, in spite of the emphasis on participation, parents had been excluded from the actual debate about whether or not the child should be registered. During the period of intervention, if things went well, the social worker and parents might agree that de-registration was a target to be aimed at; but it was always made clear that the decision could only be made by professionals at a review conference.

There is a fine balance of power in child protection work, and occasionally registration was used as a weapon by one family member against another. In addition to providing ammunition for marital disputes, for example in divorce cases, it could be used by children against their parents. There was one case in the study where adolescent children refused to be controlled by their mother, arguing that she was not allowed to hit them because they were on the register. Since this worsened conflicts in the family, registration was seen as counterproductive and the children's names were removed.

In some cases where registration was resented by adolescents the period of surveillance ended automatically when they reached the age of 18. This point of departure was probably regarded as a welcome release, not simply by the young people and their parents but sometimes by the key workers as well.

Subsequent adverse events

Not surprisingly, many families experienced continuing difficulties after de-registration. Two children were re-abused after their names had been removed from the register. In the first case, where the child was re-abused by her father, the mother contacted the police and he was charged with actual bodily harm; but with the father out of the household, the mother was offered help from social services and the child was not re-registered. In the other case there was re-abuse by the mother. She had been distressed when de-registration led to the cessation of social work visits. Twelve months after de-registration she assaulted her son and he was placed in foster care. Social work contact was resumed but the boy was not re-registered.

There was also considerable deterioration in a further three cases after they had closed. In the first of these, social work visits had again ceased on de-registration; but the mother became dependent on alcohol and rejected her children. Social work visits were re-started and the child who was the subject of our study received art therapy from child guidance. In another family where social work visits had ceased on de-registration, the teenage girl subsequently ran away from home but returned quickly. Although the mother contacted the social services her call was not followed up. At the time of our second interview her relationship with her daughter, who was truanting and sniffing solvents, was poor. A third child was found to be in a situation of continuing risk following de-registration when her mother – who had been warned of the dangers of having a partner with a history of sexual abuse – formed a relationship with a man who had a similar background to her previous partner and who was also physically violent. At the end of our study a conference was about to be held to discuss this, but it was thought unlikely that re-registration would follow.

There seemed to be a great reluctance to readmit children to the register if fresh concerns came to light immediately after the period of registration was over. There was a strong feeling that another period of registration would not achieve anything, since everything possible under the child protection procedures had already been done. (Again, this mirrors the reluctance to remove for the second time children who have been restored home to their families after a period away on a care order (Farmer and Parker, 1991).) Renewal of registration was therefore avoided on the grounds that it would be counterproductive or ineffective, and cases of re-abuse which did not justify care proceedings were dealt with by means of covert monitoring, offers of social work help on a voluntary basis, or help from other sources.

The parents' awareness of de-registration

In our follow-up interviews with parents we asked if they knew whether or not their children had been de-registered. Four-fifths of the parents were aware that de-registration had occurred or that registration was continuing. The rest were uncertain.

Six replies (14%) indicated that the parent had no idea whether the child had been de-registered or not. This lack of awareness was often combined with a total lack of understanding of what registration meant.

> *'I don't know what the child protection register is, and I think it's a real*
> *trouble that she's on one, because it makes me out to be a child batterer or*
> *something . . . I didn't even know she was on it, to be honest . . . It*
> *bothers me enormously. Why should she be on there?'*

> *'I think it's off now, yes. It might be back on now because they've got them*
> *in there [accommodation], but I don't know.'*

The mother of one child in foster care thought that her daughter was still registered, although she had been de-registered a year earlier, and the parents of other children were confused about whether care orders and supervision orders meant the same as registration. It is worrying that some parents saw registration as having the same force as a legal order.

When more than one child in the family had been registered there was even more room for confusion about whether or not registration had continued, and if so, which child was affected. The mother who gave the following reply was referring to her son Matthew who was *still registered* at the time of the follow-up interview.

> *'I don't think Matthew is, no. Well, Matthew's nearly 17 so I suppose he*
> *wouldn't be, would he?'*

She did, however, know that her younger daughter was still registered, and she seemed to feel that age was the main criterion according to which decisions about de-registration were made.

Did parents' explanations for de-registration match the official ones?

Where de-registration had taken place and parents were clearly aware of it (21 cases), 14 replies indicated that their understanding of why it had happened matched the official account. However, in seven instances the parents gave different reasons for de-registration. One mother said she knew of no reason why her child's name should have been removed from the register, and she and her husband could only think it was because their abusing son was not being prosecuted.

> *'We was quite shocked, actually, when they did take her off. . . I reckon because Gary got away with it . . . They reviewed it [registration] and they just decided that they wouldn't renew it − and they'd just drop it.'*

The father of a child who had been removed to foster care, with plans for adoption, believed that his driving ban had led to de-registration. He thought that social services had felt threatened by the possibility that he would drive to the foster home and snatch back his child. One mother whose young daughter had been de-registered because of improvements said that she could think of no reasons at all for de-registration. Another whose child's name had been removed from the register after the abuser left the household said that she had been told the reasons but could not remember them.

In the nine cases where children were still registered, parents were asked if they knew what would be needed to have their child's name removed. One mother believed that there was a minimum period during which a child's name must remain on the register:

> *'Apparently if a child's on the list they're on there for about a minimum of two years.'*

Similarly, another mother said:

> *'We've got that new law in now. If they've been on the register for over two years they can come off in February, because she comes off when she's four-and-a-half.'*

Few parents saw that their own actions would contribute to de-registration, although they did recognise that registration was a period during which they would be on trial. One mother said that she had to prove that she could care for her child:

> *'Prove that I'm capable of looking after her properly. Make sure she had her breakfast and she's clean and tidy − washed . . . just generally care for her.'*

It was understandable if parents felt that they had no control over the timing of de-registration because it often took place at the end of a period of official involvement, for example at the end of a course of treatment or when the social worker was leaving. The improvements which had taken place might well have been greatest in the initial stages; but the fact that they were gathered together and emphasized at the point of de-registration contributed to the feeling of ritual for both social workers and parents. De-registration was a 'rite of passage'. For this reason it was often beneficial for parents to attend the final review, even if they had attended none of those in between.

The parents' feelings about de-registration

The parents' feelings on learning that their child's name was to be removed from the child protection register were varied. Those who had felt stigmatised by registration were obviously relieved, and many welcomed the privacy that would follow. Others regretted that they would lose their social worker and the support that they had been receiving.

Two mothers told us that de-registration was welcomed because it freed them from the fear of being wrongly accused of abuse should their child suffer an accidental injury. In one of these cases the mother had worried about possible repercussions from any discovery of marks on her child, even though the original registration had been for sexual abuse by her husband.

Another mother whose partner had physically abused her child was relieved at de-registration because it removed her sense of responsibility for the offence. She said that registration 'made me feel as though *I'd* done it'. This was in contrast to the views of another mother who said of registration: 'That really doesn't affect me anyway; it's him [ex-husband] who's got to carry it, not me'.

The importance of privacy was stressed by one parent who said after de-registration: 'They're not poking their noses in now'. Sometimes, however, there were even greater benefits. One mother welcomed de-registration because the social worker's visits had apparently caused violent rows between her and her partner:

> *'If she didn't come up I didn't hear nothing or he wouldn't have to hit me for her coming up. I thought [on learning of de-registration], "Thank God for that. I won't have to be hit any more".'*

It was interesting to note that parents had different views on telling their children about being on the register. One mother whose children had been kept fully informed saw de-registration as of great benefit to them. She said that they were, 'Pleased, ever so happy. They were free. They could get on with their lives.' Another mother said that de-registration would make no difference to her children because:

> *'I didn't discuss it [registration] with them . . . it sounds a frightening thing to say to a child – you're on the at risk register. It puts the idea in their minds that they are at risk and it makes them more worried.'*

The mother whose children had used registration as a weapon against her thought that the situation could only improve once they were de-registered because 'they [the children] didn't have anything over me.' Another parent whose child was still registered felt that the continuance of registration disrupted the household. She said: 'It makes an awful lot of difference because it feels they've [social services] got power over you. It puts a strain on the family.' Some families, however, found that registration had not altered their lives:

> 'We didn't feel any different whether they were on the register or not, our lives still carried on . . . It didn't physically change our lives whatsoever.'

There was a belief, expressed in two families, that the removal of a child's name from the register did not signal the end of their involvement with social services. One mother was 'over the moon' when her son was de-registered but added that she was 'still a bit wary . . . There's always a possibility or even a risk that he can go back on it if they want to put him back on it.' Another mother who held a similar view said of de-registration: 'In a way, the child is never forgotten.'

Most parents welcomed de-registration because it freed them from the stigma of child-battering; but occasionally a mother did not welcome it because she feared the loss of social work visits. The following comment was made by a mother who did not view registration in a particularly negative way:

> 'It didn't bother me either way, whether they kept her name on it or took it off. I was just more concerned with getting some help and getting things sorted out.'

The following mother, whose child was still registered, had not found that registration brought any benefits:

> 'I can't see that there's been a damned bit of difference through him being on the register. I don't really know how the register works because it's never been explained to me properly. In fact I had more help with Ben **before** he was on the register . . . It's a complete and utter waste of time as far as I'm concerned . . . It hasn't hindered us, but there again it hasn't helped us.'

There were different views about the effect that de-registration might have on the chances of parents being accepted as foster carers or childminders in the future. One mother saw de-registration as wiping the slate clean:

> 'That's it now, they can't come back at me at all. If I went fostering they wouldn't mention the fact that she was on the register because that's past.'

In contrast, one couple felt that because they had had a child on the child protection register they would be prevented from ever becoming childminders or foster parents. This was the impression they had received from social services.

'According to what they say, even with the children off the register we don't stand a chance. If somebody was ill they wouldn't let us look after any children.'

Finally, it is worth mentioning again that some families felt that they or their children had suffered through other people's knowledge of their registration. One mother said that although she was not bothered who knew about registration, she was concerned when other children shouted abuse about her son and daughter.

'It was quite slanderous really. I said, "If you say anything like that again I shall go to the police". It was to do with Jill and Peter and it was not nice.'

The parents in another case had asked police to intervene because of gossip following registration. When the police would not act, their solicitor suggested that they threaten the offending neighbours with a solicitor's letter and subsequent court action. This stopped the gossip.

One mother said that she did not mind who knew of her child's registration because:

'A lot of my friends know what I'm up against with Maxine [the child] and they know the problems I'm getting with her.'

This situation was, however, unusual. Most parents were greatly relieved when their child was de-registered because of the strain of keeping the knowledge of registration from 'outsiders'. These outsiders could include neighbours, colleagues at work, employers, members of the extended family, and even comparative strangers such as the receptionist in the doctor's surgery. One mother had been acutely afraid that she might lose her professional job if her child's registration became known to her employer.

After the initial case conference when the concerns had been made public, the parents could never be sure who knew about the allegations and who did not know. De-registration did not necessarily prevent the continued spread of gossip which could be extremely damaging; but at least it furnished parents with some evidence that the monitoring agencies were satisfied that the child's future was reasonably secure, and that this distressing episode in the life of the family had been officially closed.

Whilst de-registration marked the end of the official involvement of the child protection agencies, we followed up all the families in the study for a period of 20 months. In the following chapter we look at the developments and outcomes for children and families by the end of this period.

Summary

1. By the end of the study 80% of the children had been de-registered. Nine children were removed from the register after less than six months, 12 after between six and eleven months and the remaining 14 after periods of between one year and 19 months.

2. For a third of the children (34%) de-registration came about because of improvement in the child's circumstances, often as a result of professional intervention. In another 29% of cases it was the child's entry to care or a move to relatives which led to de-registration.

3. In 17% of cases children's names were removed from the register because of a change in the official perception of risk. In most of these cases there was no real improvement, but neither was there any recurrence of abuse or neglect to the child. In 11% of cases de-registration occurred because continued registration was considered to be counterproductive or ineffective.

4. Very few children were de-registered simply as a result of the abuser's absence from the household, although it was often a strong contributory factor. De-registration could also happen automatically when the child reached the age of 18.

5. There was a deterioration in the situation of five children (11%) after de-registration had taken place. In two of these cases children were re-abused.

6. In a fifth of the cases parents were unclear whether their children's names had been removed from the register or not. A number of parents harboured misapprehensions about why their children had been de-registered or what would need to happen for de-registration to take place.

7. When parents learned that their child's name was to be removed from the register, their reactions varied. Those who had felt stigmatised by registration were relieved and felt cleared of blame. There was also relief for those parents who had been concerned about the spread of gossip in the community, and who looked forward to greater privacy. Others regretted the loss of valued social work support.

8. A few parents feared that the fact that their children had been on the register would count against them – especially if they wanted to apply to act as childminders or foster carers in the future.

PART IV

Outcome

Chapter 17

The dimensions of outcome

The whole question of how to define 'outcome' in child care or child protection cases is one which until recently has been eschewed, in view of its complexity and the difficulty of establishing causal connections in the absence of controlled experimental situations. True 'outcomes' could only be considered if data were available on the developmental status of children before both the abuse and child protection intervention and if these were then compared with similar data at a defined end point. Even then it would be difficult to disentangle the effects of abuse from the effects of interventions or other events.

Of course, in the real world children who will be subject to abuse cannot be identified before the abuse occurs – although useful comparative data can be obtained from very large longitudinal birth cohort studies. Our approach has been to study a group of children publicly identified as at risk, many of whom have already been abused or suffered less than adequate parenting. In addressing outcomes we are attempting to describe the 'states of affairs' of these children 20 months after the start of child protection interventions. In this respect, our research study has something in common with outcome studies for children in care (Parker *et al.*, 1991) although both the composition of the sample and the reasons for official involvement are different.

Since our main purpose in undertaking the research was to further our understanding of the working of the child protection system, we decided to address outcomes in terms of the overall aims of the child protection system itself. Our view of these aims was based on Department of Health publications, in particular *Working Together* (1988), *Working Together Under the Children Act 1989* (1991), and *Protecting Children* (1988). Our thinking was also influenced by the Department of Health's draft report *Child Protection: A Guide to Self-Monitoring and Inspection* and the *Report of Inspection of Child Abuse Services in Cumbria Social Services Department*, produced by the Social Services Inspectorate (1989).

These documents suggest that the fundamental aim of child protection procedures is to *protect children from harm*. A second aim suggested in *Protecting Children* and reiterated in other reports is the *promotion of children's physical, emotional and intellectual development* which we have termed their *welfare*. A third aim is that of *meeting the needs of other family members*, especially the parents or other carers. These three aims are connected and they represent widening definitions of protection from harm. They may also be conceived as being arranged in a hierarchy of importance, the most important being the first.

Dividing the outcomes into these three dimensions reminds us that non-recurrence of abuse is a necessary but not a sufficient measure of outcome, since even though children are not subjected to renewed assault, they may not be receiving a satisfactory standard of care (Lynch and Roberts, 1982; Calam and Franchi, 1987; Farmer and Parker, 1991). If the input of social services and other agencies is to be regarded as satisfactory, progress on more than one dimension is required.

Use of the dimensions

In evaluating outcomes, our first task was to decide *whether children had been protected*. The 'researcher judgements' we made were based on a consideration of each child's protection over the whole length of the follow-up period, since once a child had been registered as being at risk it seemed reasonable to assume that the involved agencies would try to make that child's safety a priority. If the child was not safe in spite of these efforts, then arguably the system had failed the child.

By the time of our follow-up interviews the majority of the children had been de-registered in the belief that they were no longer at risk. It seemed important to have a follow-up period which, because it often extended beyond de-registration, would allow that assumption to be tested. At the same time a fairly strict test was applied, inasmuch as we sought to know whether the child had been protected from physical and sexual abuse and also from neglect (in terms of gross lack of supervision or physical care) during the whole of the follow-up period. Lack of protection was evidenced by re-abuse or neglect or living with perpetrators without safeguards.

The second dimension of outcome was *whether the child's welfare had been effectively enhanced*. This was taken to include issues relating to the physical, emotional and intellectual needs of the child. Since children's progress can fluctuate, it was decided to look at this question primarily in relation to the situation at follow-up. The presence of significant and enduring problems in any of these areas was taken to signify that the child's welfare had not been effectively enhanced. Whilst welfare is a fairly general concept and embraces a range of needs, the way in which we used it will become evident from the more detailed explanation of this dimension.

Similarly, progress on the third outcome dimension of *whether the needs of the main caring parent or parent substitute had been met* was determined primarily in relation to the situation at the point of follow-up. Most attention was paid to the parent who took primary responsibility for looking after the child (usually, but not always, the mother). Again, the presence of significant deficits for the main carer was taken to mean that the needs of that person had not been met – as long as they could reasonably be expected to have been addressed during the period of intervention.

The judgements about progress on the second and third outcome dimensions, like those about protection, took into account the actions or interventions of any agents. The outcomes were therefore seen as related to the inputs and actions of family members and the participants themselves as well as those of professionals.

The research evidence

The judgements which informed the ratings made on each of the three dimensions drew on a variety of sources of evidence. First, information was obtained from the follow-up interviews with parents, children and social workers. This was compared with material from the first interviews. During the final interview participants were asked to describe their current situation and the main events which had occurred in the intervening period, and to identify the most significant influences. It was only after interviewees (that is the parents, other carers and children) had selected the events and issues which *they* saw as important that specific questions were asked about agency interventions and their effects. In this way a composite picture of the outcomes for the child and other family members, and of important influences on them, was built up from the accounts of the key participants. These were further supplemented by a scrutiny of the relevant case files.

To help with the formation of judgements about whether a child's welfare had been enhanced, questions were asked about this at the first and follow-up interviews and the views of informants were solicited about what, if anything, had aided the child's progress. In addition, when the child was aged between five and fifteen, parents completed the Rutter Scale A questionnaire about their child's behaviour at both points. When children were interviewed they were asked about their progress and well-being and what, if anything, had made a contribution. In addition, at each interview the children completed the Child's Depression Inventory (Kovacs and Beck, 1977) and a modified version of the Susan Harter self-esteem scale. The scores obtained using these measures fed into our judgements about children's progress.

At both first and second interviews, parents and social workers were asked to complete a short questionnaire about their perception of the main problems in the family to which the child belonged. Comparison of the responses was illuminating. Parents also completed the Malaise Inventory and the Arizona Social Support Interview Schedule at the first and follow-up interviews so that information could be obtained about their mental health and social support networks. The scores obtained provided evidence of parents' social vulnerability and health needs, and contributed to our judgements about how far the needs of the primary carer had been met.

It was on the basis of this range of information that judgements were made by the researchers about the 'outcome' for each case. These judgements were cross-rated blind by each researcher and it was reassuring to find that there was a high degree of consensus in the majority of the cases.

The first dimension: protection from harm

Given that registration was intended to ensure that children were protected, how complete was the protection offered? By follow-up, a quarter of the children (11) had been re-abused or neglected. Of these, five children had experienced physical abuse, four sexual abuse, one neglect, and one a combination of physical abuse and neglect. Two other children had been living with known perpetrators of sexual abuse without any safeguards, and so it was considered that they too had not been protected. *In all, 30 per cent of the sample (13 children) had not been protected by the work carried out during registration.*

Out of the five instances of physical abuse, the original abusing parent had abused the child in four cases. The injuries involved a torn frenulum to a baby in one case, facial bruising to a baby in another, repeated 'accidental' injuries to a two-year-old in a third, and a black eye to a 13-year-old in the fourth. The fifth child suffered a black eye inflicted by his sister, the original abuse having been a harsh beating by his father.

Protection from sexual abuse was, as might be expected, more complete. None of the children, as far as we know, suffered a recurrence of sexual abuse by the original abuser. Four children had been sexually abused by the time of the follow-up, but only one at the hands of a parent. This was a father who had originally come to the attention of child protection agencies for reasons of his physical abuse. The other two girls had been sexually abused by their brothers and the fourth was an abused boy who had been subjected to sexual bullying in a residential unit. The two occurrences of continuing or renewed neglect involved a profound lack of physical care combined with bruising to a three-year-old child, and lack of supervision for a five-year-old as a result of her mother's drug addiction.

In half of these cases, once the re-abuse or neglect was identified, social services took immediate action to protect the children from further harm, either by removing them or by procuring the expulsion of the abuser. In one case the mother herself removed her son from an abusive placement.

However, for the remaining half of the group of children who were abused and neglected during the 20 months of the follow-up, protective action was either delayed or did not occur at all. It took five months to remove one child who was neglected and physically abused, because of excessively cautious legal advice from the local authority about the evidence which was needed before care proceedings could be initiated. The neglect of another child continued unabated until eventually the mother developed a new relationship and standards of care improved. A third child lived with a Schedule One offender for well over a year until the man was rehoused.

Finally, in four cases no protective action was taken. We found the common thread in these cases was that after the initial conference they had been framed by social workers and other agencies as ones where the children were not really at risk, either because the original injuries were now seen as accidental or because the abusers were no longer thought to present a serious danger to the children. In this situation, the signs of possible maltreatment were played down in the absence of unequivocal evidence.

How was protection achieved?

Whilst 30 per cent of the children suffered further abuse or neglect, the remaining *70 per cent (31) had been protected*. For 14 protection had been effected either by placement away from home or by the removal of the abuser for the entire follow-up period. Thus of the 31 children who had been effectively protected, this protection had been achieved by total separation of the child and the abuser in 14 cases (45%). Another nine children (29%) had been separated from the abuser or placed in supervised accommodation for part of the time.

It is interesting to find that only eight out of the 31 children who were protected had remained safe while living with the abusing parent for the entire follow-up period. How had their protection been achieved? Two of these were cases of neglect, in which the care of the children had significantly improved as a result of the support and help offered by the social worker or by friends and relatives or both, and two were cases of 'emotional abuse' in which family circumstances improved sufficiently for the children to be no longer at risk. Three were cases of physical abuse, one of which had probably been wrongly diagnosed, whilst in the other two careful monitoring took place in the context of a strong and helpful relationship between the social worker and the parents. In addition, there was the case of a teenage boy who had initially displayed sexually abusing behaviour but who, as a result of careful management by his carers and appropriate treatment at child guidance, was able to stay in his family.

Looked at another way, since 14 of the children in the whole sample were separated from the abuser for the entire follow-up period, the remaining 30 children spent at least part of this time with an abusing adult (or an abusing child). Of these 30 children, as has been noted, 13 (43%) had not been safe. This might be seen as a rather disappointing result from a system specifically designed to ensure children's safety. It does, however, demonstrate some of the difficulties of protecting children who continue to live at home with an abusing parent.

The second dimension: enhancement of the children's welfare

Having looked at how well the children in the study were protected, we can now turn to examine the second dimension. How successfully was the children's welfare enhanced? *In 68 per cent of the cases (30) the child had clearly made gains by the end of the follow-up period.* Sometimes these gains were not large; but they were very apparent when considered in relation to the starting points of the children concerned.

How was progress achieved?

Our results indicate that when children's welfare was enhanced it sometimes occurred almost as an accidental spin-off from child protection interventions. Some improvements occurred because the child was allowed to develop normally once the threat of physical or sexual abuse had been removed. Other benefits can be traced to the fact that allegations of abuse or neglect had brought the family's problems to the notice of official agencies. For example, when defects in children's health were mentioned at case conferences, action was usually taken to remedy them. The key worker's search for resources to relieve stress in the family also brought the children into contact with holiday activities or friendship groups, as a result of which children's social relationships improved.

In spite of the rather piecemeal approach to developmental needs, there were a number of ways in which children's welfare was satisfactorily promoted during the period of the study. As with protection, one of the key variables was whether or not the child was living with the abuser. The type of provision also varied depending on whether the child was at home or looked after.

1. Change of residence.

Just over half of the 30 children (16) who made progress had moved to a more beneficial family environment . There were clear signs that entry to care or a move to a relative or a separated parent with whom they had not been living before the conference, had been beneficial. In general they had been living in abusive, unpredictable or emotionally depriving environments and very often they made significant developmental and weight gains after the transfer.

Of course movement did not necessarily entail separation from parents. Some children benefited from a move to another house, and two of the children gained when the whole family was placed in a residential family centre, where the children were able to attend an on-site nursery and receive attention from speech therapy and medical services. In total, the welfare of 16 children was promoted either by placement in substitute care or by a change of residence.

2. *Agency interventions.*

Just under half of the children (14) who made progress did so whilst living at home. The gains of nine children appeared to be linked to interventions provided by social workers or arranged by them. Of these, four had the benefit of skilled direct work by the key worker, and three benefited from direct provision such as a place at a playgroup. Two children who made major gains in their emotional adjustment had received therapeutic help from child guidance workers.

3. *Help from family members and friends.*

Some children who were living at home gained in confidence through settling into a new school and making friends, or through contact with helpful adults or relatives. Often the publicity about registration was disadvantageous; but when the news fell on sympathetic ears, more help might be given to the parents (for example by grandparents) and standards of child care improved. A few children also enjoyed close and nurturing relationships with one or both of their carers, and these relationships continued after registration as before.

Where were the deficits?

Having looked at the variety of ways in which children's welfare was effectively promoted during the follow-up period, we will now turn to scrutinise those less fortunate children, 14 in all, who continued to show significant deficits. Eight of them were at home throughout the follow-up period, five spent part of the period of registration away from home, and only one child was away from home for the whole period.

What distinguished the service received by these children?

1. *Unsatisfactory placements.*

For two sexually abused boys who were aged over ten the placement away from home was itself unsatisfactory and probably harmful. One boy complained of bullying at his residential school and being mocked about the abuse he had endured. He became increasingly depressed and suicidal. No adequate educational assessment had been undertaken and the school was unaware of the exact nature of his severe learning difficulties. A sexually abused and abusing teenage boy who was placed in an adolescent psychiatric unit was also bullied and sexually harrassed. The placement represented to him, as he put it, 'the worst days of my life'. In neither case, as might be expected, was the children's welfare enhanced.

2. *Cases which were closed or accorded low priority.*

A few cases had been given low priority and the social worker had quickly withdrawn, leaving important areas of difficulty untouched. *As soon as the protection issues no longer dominated the agenda, it was easy for children's other needs to be ignored.* For example, if the abuser had left the household and the mother was thought capable of protecting the child, social work services were often withdrawn or maintained only at a low level. This often left children's welfare needs unmet.

3. *Lack of recognition of important areas of need.*

Eight cases remained open for some time, but they were characterised by a lack of recognition of important areas of need. In some cases it was children's disturbed behaviour which was not addressed. A range of cases fell into this group. Sometimes a social worker offered emotional support to a mother; but no action was taken to help the mother with child management problems or to offer direct services to the child. At other times high levels of child disturbance and unhappiness at home were not seen as unusual, and the child's need for assessment or treatment was not identified, often because the family was well known to social services. However, sometimes a different situation occurred. Services were provided for children, but they did not gain because there was no satisfactory input to meet the needs of the primary carer on whom they depended. Consequently the children's progress was impeded.

The findings regarding the degree to which the children's welfare was promoted show the crucial importance of those services which were provided and arranged by social workers and which directly addressed children's needs (Gough, 1993). Children suffered when no adequate assessment was made, or when insufficient attention was paid to understanding the dynamics of their situation, so that action could be directed at the parts of the system which prevented them from making progress.

The third dimension: meeting the needs of parents

When we turned to the last of our three outcome dimensions we found that *in only 30 per cent of cases (13) had the needs of the main parent or carer been met,* an issue which was clearly accorded much lower priority than those directly concerned with the registered children.

The parents in our study had a range of needs, some of which were related to the abuse. First there were physical and material needs related to low income and inadequate housing. Secondly, there were emotional needs stemming from poor relationships in the home or community, and tenuous support networks. Thirdly, there were health needs, particularly the mental health needs of mothers prone to anxiety and depression. Fourthly, there were needs to be met that were specifically to do with child care, such as the inability to understand and control the child's behaviour whilst expressing affection and warmth.

All of these needs predated the child protection referral, and in most cases they predated the abuse. In addition, there were others that were associated with the abuse itself and the involvement of official agencies. For example, there was a need for counselling and support in the aftermath of the discovery of abuse, and assistance in coming to terms with the scrutiny of child protection agencies.

How were the parents' needs met?

In general the material needs of the carers – such as the need for better housing or financial help – were seen as outside the province of the social worker, even though their effects in terms of stress were recognised. However, in some cases rehousing was secured when social workers gave their backing to a request for a transfer or move. Occasionally, eviction notices and demands for fuel payments were staved off, if they came at a time when the family was experiencing severe difficulties. Although the advantages gained were sometimes only temporary, the relationship with the worker often improved, and parents became more receptive to intervention when they felt that the social worker was sympathetic enough to take their part.

The lack of family support or social isolation was not always known, since it had not always been discussed at the conference, as we saw in chapter 8. Even if it had been discussed it was often treated only as a matter for 'counselling', although in some cases the social worker was already in touch with other relatives and could work in a way which took their contribution into account, for example where grandparents took an active interest in the family and were willing to share formally or informally in child care arrangements. Again, social isolation could be lessened if the mother was referred to a group within the community, provided that suitable resources existed and that she was helped to overcome social and psychological barriers in order to make use of it.

Problems relating to the parents' physical health and their day-to-day child care were more often addressed with the help of the medical services. Health visitors were very active in visiting families with children under five, and many parents found them an invaluable source of friendship and advice. Parents' problems with adolescent children were only occasionally tackled by sympathetic social workers who were willing to work with the parents as well as offering help directly to the child. The child protection system relied heavily on input from the school to children in this age group. The lack of contact between school and home left parents out on a limb, unless the social worker was very active in making the links, and it was only in unusual cases (for example where there was a teacher appointed to deal with travelling children) that the school appeared to be involved in anything resembling a domiciliary service.

The main interventions from social services which contributed to the meeting of parents' needs were as follows.

1. *The maintenance of links with looked-after children.*

When children had been permanently removed from their parents, the needs of the parents often went unmet; but the situation was different when the key social worker made a point of maintaining contact. Where placements had been made with relatives rather than foster parents, it was often easier for the parent to retain regular contact with the child, to their mutual benefit.

2. *Practical help and work on parent-child relationships.*

As previously mentioned, some parents had been assisted with a range of practical difficulties. In addition, parents particularly benefited from well planned and purposeful social work which was directed towards helping them in their relationship with their children. Most of the work with parents was intended to improve standards of parenting, although one couple who had learning disabilities were offered services (such as a day care club) in their own right.

3. *Use of the mental health services.*

In some cases where mothers were seriously disturbed or mentally ill, they were offered substantial help from the psychiatric services and community mental health teams. Mothers who were resistant to receiving such help, although they clearly required it, benefited from the involvement of a mental health social worker who was not too closely identified with a hospital setting. This person could be a valuable 'friend' for a distressed mother – particularly someone who was suffering from the loss of her partner or child.

4. *Mitigation of the ill-effects of registration.*

Most parents felt blamed and stigmatised by registration. The quality of their child care, in consequence, was sometimes impaired by feelings of inadequacy and low self-esteem. Skilled social workers managed to recognise and repair this loss.

Where were the deficits?

In addition to looking at successful interventions, we need to examine the situation in the remaining 31 cases where less satisfactory arrangements were made to meet the needs of parents.

1. *There was little service to parents where children had been removed.*

In many cases where children had been permanently removed, the parents subsequently received little help from the social worker. As a result, they had difficulty in coping both with practical problems and with their feelings of grief. In view of the emphasis in the Children Act on the maintenance of contact between children and parents, and the emphasis on preparation for restoration wherever possible, we would have expected to see more evidence of help in this area; but in several cases the period leading up to the child's removal was one in which the relationship between the parent and social worker was very strained.

2. *Cases which were closed or accorded low priority.*

Again there were some cases which were closed rapidly or accorded a low priority because it was felt that the child was no longer at risk, either because the abuser had left the household or because the original risk to the child was thought on closer inspection not to be very great. This left a range of parental needs unmet.

3. *A narrow focus on the child's protection.*

In other cases, parents' needs were neglected when the work focused narrowly on the child's protection and attention to the parents' requirements was not seen as relevant to the achievement of that goal. *A narrow concentration on the child's protection, if it excluded parents' needs, limited the extent to which the child's welfare could be enhanced, since these issues were bound together.* Children who had to leave their families after disclosing sexual abuse were a case in point. Counselling and help was rarely offered to the non-abusing mothers. If the mothers had been offered help during this crisis period and the alliance between the mother and child had been strengthened, some children might well have returned home sooner, and the debilitating period of uncertainty about whether or not they had been believed by their mothers could have been shortened.

4. *The lack of recognition of important areas of parental need.*

As in the case of children, important areas of parental need could simply go unrecognised. This was often the case when the key issue was the man's violence to the woman, and when alcohol or drug problems were involved. Some mothers had not revealed to the agencies the full extent of the violence which they endured and which they told us about. Other parents were under considerable stress because treatment for disturbed children in their care was either not forthcoming or was unduly delayed.

5. *The failure to engage with disaffected parents.*

A fifth reason for parents' needs not being met was that they had been alienated by their previous experience of social services – that is by events at the time of the investigation, by their current worker, or by a combination of these – and consequently the worker was unable to reach them. There were some parents who would not allow the social worker who had been involved in the investigation to visit them, so that surveillance had to be delegated to other agencies, and there were others who presented a front of minimal compliance. In a few particularly worrying cases, the worker's concern for the child, coupled with a lack of success in bringing about change, led to an attitude of deep disapproval of the parent. It was only when these feelings altered (sometimes by a change of worker) that progress could be made.

In conclusion it can be seen that the majority of the children in the study were protected after they had been registered (70%), and that the welfare of most of the children was enhanced (68%). In far fewer cases, only 30 per cent, were the needs of the main carers met. In some cases, typically those where the children were permanently removed, the needs of the child could be partially catered for in the absence of attention to those of the parents and other family members. However, in others, despite the assertions made in *A Child in Trust* (London Borough of Brent, 1985) the needs of the child could not be met in isolation from those of the parents. They were integrally connected. This is an issue to which we will turn in the next chapter.

Summary

1.   The outcomes for the children were assessed on three dimensions which related to the aims of the child protection system as outlined in Department of Health publications. The dimensions were first whether the children had been protected from harm, second whether their welfare had been enhanced and third whether the needs of the children's primary parent or carer had been met.

2.   By the end of the study 70% of the children had been protected, and the welfare of 68% had been enhanced. In far fewer cases, only 30%, had the needs of the primary parent or carer been met.

3.   The majority of the children who had been *protected* had been separated from the abuser for all or part of the follow-up period. Of the remainder who remained safe while living with the abusing parent, protection was achieved in a variety of ways. In most of these cases, relationships with social workers were seen by parents as helpful, and in addition the risks to the child were openly addressed. These professional interventions were often complemented by help from the parents' wider network.

4.   Despite registration, 30% of the children had not been protected. Five children suffered physical abuse, four sexual abuse, one serious neglect and one was physically abused and neglected. Two other children continued to live with known perpetrators without any safeguards. After an incident of re-abuse or serious neglect came to light, in almost half of the cases protective action was taken immediately either by the

removal of the child or the expulsion of the abuser. For the remainder of the children their protection was only secured after considerable delay, or else their maltreatment was not seen by social services as warranting further action.

5. Just over half of the children whose *welfare was enhanced* moved to a different placement either in care or to other family members. The remainder benefited from skilled direct work from social workers and child guidance workers, and from services such as day care, after-school activity groups and welfare assistance at school. A few made more indirect gains as they matured and developed confidence through settling into school and enjoying the support of friends.

6. There were a number of reasons why deficits in the welfare of children were evident. Some experienced unsatisfactory placements in care and others received no direct service because concerns about their safety quickly diminished after registration. Once protection issues no longer dominated the agenda, children's other needs were often not seen as requiring service in their own right. Sometimes the help offered to the children was inconsistent, disrupted or not based on a clear assessment of the needs of the child and parents.

7. The situations in which *the needs of the primary carer were met* were characterised by planned and purposeful social work in which practitioners strove to understand and address a range of parental needs in the context of improving the child's welfare. In some cases practical difficulties or the need for social support were addressed. In others the main work was directed at bringing about improvements in the parent's relationship with the child. Occasionally the child was being looked after but the parents were able to maintain regular contact whilst also receiving services in their own right – including in some cases much needed mental health services.

8. It was common for the needs of the main carer to be given little priority in child protection work. This occurred in a range of situations. One was when the child had been permanently removed and there was little emphasis on contact. Another was after the rapid closure of cases in which the child's protection was thought to be assured. A narrow focus on the child's protection sometimes precluded any attention being paid to the needs of the parents.

9. Parental needs also went unmet when important areas of difficulty were unrecognised, such as family violence or drug and alcohol abuse; or when treatment was not forthcoming for disturbed children whose behaviour caused undue stress on family members; or simply when parents had been too alienated by the early stages of child protection interventions to be reached by professional agencies.

10.   Unfortunately the needs of parents and their children cannot be totally separated, and neglect of parents' needs often had an adverse effect on the child's progress. Sometimes the child's protection was also affected.

Chapter 18

How the outcome dimensions combined

In the last chapter we looked at the action of social services and other professionals in relation to our three main outcome dimensions – the child's protection, enhancement of the child's welfare and the meeting of the needs of the primary carer. Of course, we have to bear in mind that the cases in the study varied in relation to the severity of the abuse which the children had suffered, their levels of need and the risks to which they were exposed at the time of the initial case conference. These factors had a bearing on the outcome in addition to the inputs from professional and non-professional sources.

In order to obtain a clearer view of the overall outcomes experienced by the children in the study it is necessary to examine the ways in which the outcome dimensions combined. When the three dimensions were considered together, we found that they produced six identifiable categories of

Table 20 **Combined Outcome Dimensions**

CATEGORY 1 (10 cases – 23%)	
Child protected	YES
Child's welfare enhanced	YES
Needs of primary carer met	YES
CATEGORY 2 (12 cases – 27%)	
Child protected	YES
Child's welfare enhanced	YES
Needs of primary carer met	NO
CATEGORY 3 (9 cases – 21%)	
Child protected	YES
Child's welfare enhanced	NO
Needs of primary carer met	NO
CATEGORY 4 (3 cases – 7%)	
Child protected	NO
Child's welfare enhanced	YES
Needs of primary carer met	YES
CATEGORY 5 (5 cases – 11%)	
Child protected	NO
Child's welfare enhanced	YES
Needs of primary carer met	NO
CATEGORY 6 (5 cases – 11 %)	
Child protected	NO
Child's welfare enhanced	NO
Needs of primary carer met	NO

outcome. (Two other combinations would have been possible; but there were no cases which fitted them.) The six categories and the number of cases which fell into each are shown in table 20.

As well as studying the effect of the combined outcomes in the sample cases, we wanted to be able to identify the principal interventions which might have led to them – and we also wanted to be able to distinguish the results of social work activity from those states of affairs which had probably arisen by 'chance', or which had arisen mainly as a result of the action of family members and friends. We found that there were five variations in the relationship between intervention and outcome as shown in table 21. Professional intervention refers to inputs provided by social services or other agencies.

Table 21   **Relationship between Intervention and Outcome**

		No.	%
(i)	Professional intervention had a *positive* effect on the outcome	15	34
(ii)	Both professional intervention and the assistance of others had a *positive* effect on outcome	11	25
(iii)	Professional intervention had *little* effect on outcome	12	27
(iv)	Professionals had *little* effect, but the assistance of others had a *positive* effect	3	7
(v)	Professional intervention had a *negative* effect	3	7

When we related this classification to our six outcome categories, we were able to identify those families which had benefited most from agency input.

Finally, we looked back at the decisions taken in the early stages of each case to see whether there were any features of the content or process which appeared to have had a bearing on the outcome. This analysis helped us to build up a picture, first, of the way in which certain combinations of interventions had interacted to produce particular composite outcomes, and second, of the progress of cases over time.

The combined outcome categories

The six categories of outcome which we identified are described below, together with a brief description of the cases which were included in each. In this analysis we have concentrated on the salient features, which varied from one group to the next. We have been helped by being able to draw on the rich variety of issues which, throughout the rest of the study, have emerged as important. These issues include the interventions of social workers and other professionals, but also the contributions of family members and friends, the circumstances of the children and their families, the nature of the abuse, and certain aspects of the decision–making process.

CATEGORY 1   (23% of cases)

Child protected	YES
Child's welfare enhanced	YES
Needs of primary carer met	YES

In this first and most successful group of outcomes there were positive results on all three dimensions. Most were cases of physical abuse or neglect and almost half of the children in this group spent some or all of the period away from home. They were therefore protected wholly or partly by being separated from the abuser. The children who remained at home, or who spent part of the time at home, were protected mainly by the actions of family members combined with social work help, which included effective monitoring, offers of support, counselling to increase the children's own ability to protect themselves, or advice to the parents on making preparations for their children's return.

How did the 'protection' which was provided affect the child's welfare and the meeting of the parents' needs? This question has to be addressed firstly in the context of the separation of the child and the abuser. When the children in this category were away from home the placements were happy, having often been selected or approved by the child. Family links were well maintained. As a result, the children developed as normally as possible and the parents' needs were also taken into account, because they continued to see their children even though they were unable to offer them full-time care.

The children who left home and who qualified for inclusion in this best outcome group were predominantly young adolescents or pre-adolescents. Some of them had gone to stay with a relative, either temporarily or permanently. Others had left one separated parent and gone to live with the other. For example Sophie, a nine-year-old girl who had been sexually abused by her father went to live with her separated mother, and Jonathan, a seven-year-old boy who was beaten by his mother's cohabitee went to live with his father. Joanne who was eleven and who had been abused by her mentally ill mother was made a ward of court, and taken to live with her favourite aunt. Ten-year-old Andrew was placed with his grandmother under a care order; and twelve-year-old Colleen, a girl who had been sexually abused by her brother, moved back home of her own accord after a short time spent with her older sister.

All of these changes took place with the agreement of the children or were actually initiated by them. Because the children were living with another family member the situation was more 'normal' than if they had had to be placed with strangers, and it was easier for the children to explain the situation to friends. When Andrew was interviewed, for example, he made a clear distinction between the experience of living with his grandmother (which he liked) and the experience of being 'in care' (which he disliked). Yet to the social worker these experiences were less clearly differentiated.

A major contribution to this category was therefore judicious decision-making about the removal of children, together with a happy choice of placement. The ability to describe care as 'living with a relative' reduced the sense of stigma. At the same time the fact that children were still in touch with their parents lessened their sense of bereavement; and when there was still a sense of loss on the parents' part (as happened fairly frequently, especially if there had been a court hearing) the maintenance of family contacts for the child in care ensured that their needs were given at least some attention. For example, Joanne's mother was rehoused with the help of the community mental health team, and Andrew's mother received a special programme of counselling and support. In Jonathan's case the mother's needs were met primarily by the transfer of responsibility, because she clearly needed (and wanted) to be without the day-to-day care of her son.

Not all of the children in this first category were removed, of course. In cases where children had remained at home for all or most of the period, their protection and progress were facilitated by attentive social work. What patterns could be observed in these arrangements? Once again the age of the children appeared to be important. Whilst in this outcome group the children who left home were all aged between seven and thirteen, the children who remained at home were all below the age of seven. This probably reflects the greater provision of services to families with young children. Whether or not the child was removed, however, the social worker was regarded by the mother or by both parent figures as being sympathetic – and sometimes the worker had even succeeded in reversing the trend towards alienation and hostility caused by previous interventions, including the effects of the investigation, conference and registration. *The alliance between the social worker and the parents, which occurred when the parents' needs were recognised and at least partially met, was an important factor in securing the protection of the child.*

Scrutinising the cases in this category enabled us to see the relationship between meeting the needs of the primary carer and progress on the other dimensions. There were of course cases where the simple provision of a service, such as transport for parents to visit a child in hospital, was enough to benefit the child. In other cases, however, there were less obvious benefits. When the parent's own needs were satisfied, the child in care was happier and felt less guilt about any disclosure. This 'freed' the child to make progress if opportunities for development were offered (and usually for members of this group they were offered by the social worker or by the people who had taken on parental responsibilities). This contribution to the development of the child in substitute care was of course additional to the benefits that were derived from direct contact with the birth parent – benefits such as improved self-esteem and a sense of continuity.

While these results are encouraging, it should be noted that some cases in this group showed more improvement than others. Obviously the starting points were different, and there were differences in the *extent* of improvement. There were also accidental positive spin-offs from social work intervention and from the contributions made by other people. These could make a considerable impact. Jonathan's successful placement with his father, from whom he had been separated, was not the result of a social work plan; his father simply stepped in to fill an obvious need once the boy had been registered. In one case of neglect, the maternal grandmother increased help to her daughter when registration made her realise that she was having difficulty in coping. In many of these cases registration was intended to act as a warning to the parents; but what actually happened was that the shock of registration acted as a catalyst which *called forth increased resources within the extended family*. In other words the professional judgement that the child needed protection was reinterpreted by family members as a need for support to the mother. As a result of this unofficial intervention, which happened in response to the official one, the child was protected and the child's welfare was enhanced. This suggests that much might be gained in some cases by involving members of the extended family from the beginning (Marsh and Allen, 1993).

It is no surprise to discover that, when the relationship between intervention and outcome was examined, most cases in this group fitted the second of our descriptions of intervention; that is, *both professional intervention and the assistance of others had a positive effect on the outcome*. This meshing together of agency and family action appeared to be crucial. In other categories of outcome we shall see what happened when it did not occur.

A sample case from Category 1

Jane was a baby who was admitted to hospital with a fracture. The parents could give no explanation for the injury, but the child was not removed – principally because of advice from the legal department that there were no grounds for a care order.

Registration drew the maternal grandparents into a more active helping role with the young parents. The social worker was also well-liked and seen as helpful. No further injuries or causes for concern were evident during the follow-up period. Since Jane appeared to enjoy a close and improving relationship with both parents, her name was removed from the register after 10 months. The mother, in particular, had benefited from the help given by the child's grandparents and from a social worker who understood her needs.

CATEGORY 2   (27% of cases)

Child protected	YES
Child's welfare enhanced	YES
Needs of primary carer met	NO

In the second group of outcomes there were cases of physical abuse, neglect and emotional abuse, together with a few cases of sexual abuse. In this group, which was the largest in the sample, over half of the children were looked after away from home at some stage during the study. The other children spent most of the time at home with the alleged abuser present.

When this outcome group is compared with the previous one, there are several striking differences. First, the children who lived away from home were almost all fairly young and were placed with unrelated care-givers. By contrast, all those who were living at home were young adolescents. This, it will be recalled, is the reverse of what was found in Category 1. Secondly, in this group there was not such a good relationship between the parents and the social worker. Good family or social support for the parents was also absent, either because the professionals had not succeeded in mobilising it, because it had not materialised spontaneously, or because it had never existed in the first place.

Thirdly, when the children from this group were looked after, the links with their previous carers were not well maintained. Sometimes the severance of links was a matter of deliberate policy. For example, three young children were removed from their birth parents and placed for adoption. At the time of the follow-up study the condition of these children had improved; they had been protected and their development had benefited. However, the condition of the birth parents had deteriorated, to the extent that they were living in extremely distressing circumstances. One mother lived alone, in a chronic state of grief for her missing children, and it was obvious on our second visit that her mental health had deteriorated. Another couple had given up attempting to care for their flat (which had originally been one of the tasks set by social services) and we found them both lying on a mattress surrounded by rubbish. The man was angry. The woman was depressed. They both said that they would like to move to another area and have another baby.

The picture presented by the families in our second category suggested strongly that the agency had been right to remove the children. On the other hand there was an element of self-fulfilling prophecy which could not be ignored. Arguably also, these parents had needs which should have been met in their own right. The claim usually made by social workers that they were rejecting help was no doubt true. Nonetheless, they all had a great longing for information about their children – even anonymised information which would have reduced some of their anxieties. However, social work services to the parents had usually terminated after the children were removed.

The parents of the other children, some of whom were placed away and others not, were somewhat more fortunate; but there were still tensions which existed because the parents did not like the worker, or because they did not like what was being offered. In some cases regular help to the parents had been discontinued. A poor relationship with the key social worker and a lack of services for the parents seemed to be connected. There were problems of poverty, homelessness, mental ill health and social isolation which were not being addressed because there was an insurmountable barrier between the parents and social services. At some stage in these cases the social worker seemed to have given up trying to help the parents, and had concentrated instead on the protection and welfare of the child.

In view of the generally bad relationship between parents and social services in these cases, we are justified in asking how it was possible for children to live at home and be protected – and even to show signs of progress. In order to unravel this conundrum we had to look at a number of different factors. First, protection was secured for those children who remained at home by improvements in the family's circumstances, brought about by help from outside agencies (such as child guidance or army welfare services) or by the efforts of the parents themselves. Secondly, most of the children benefited from *direct services* such as the provision of day care. Thirdly, in most cases where children from this second category lived at home with the 'abuser' (usually in these instances a woman) the categories of registration used at the case conference were emotional abuse and neglect rather than physical or sexual abuse and the risks were not considered to be unduly severe. Fourthly, a feeling of resentment against social services sometimes helped to make the family feel more united, or at least to strengthen the mother-child relationship in a way which produced some improvement. Finally, some of the gains for the child could be attributed simply to maturation over time.

Sometimes, of course, the difficult relationship with social services was mirrored by bad relationships with other agencies, who were equally likely to be excluded. Children were quick to pick up the antipathy of their parents to outside agencies. Geoff, for example, was seen by a clinical psychologist but he did not talk much in these sessions because, taking his cue from his mother, he felt that the agencies were aiming to remove him. On the other hand, some children whose parents had been alienated from social services intervention, were helped by other professionals. Certainly, two sexually abused children from different families benefited from individual therapeutic sessions at the child and family guidance clinic. Several children in the study were helped by pastoral care at school, or by a one-to-one relationship with a school welfare assistant. The alienated parents were often more difficult to help; but three mothers in this group spoke of receiving good advice from their probation officers, one derived some comfort from the army welfare service and another had a supportive alliance with her GP. One couple who were particularly isolated were admitted with their children to a residential family centre, where the children made considerable progress as a result of the services provided although the parents still felt that their own needs were untouched. When the relationship between intervention and outcome was considered, we found that most of the cases in this group were ones in which *professional intervention had had a positive effect on the outcome for the child*, but other family members were not fully engaged.

A sample case from Category 2

At the age of 16, Becky disclosed to her school tutor that she had been sexually abused by her step-father since she was nine. This abuse had progressed to full inter- course in her teenage years. Her step-father went to prison, which ensured her protection, and her adjustment was considerably helped by individual counselling by her social worker and attendance at a group for sexually abused girls.

However, her mother was profoundly alienated from the worker, who had warned the family that it was highly unlikely that the step-father could ever return – although this was what her mother very much wanted. The girl was helped by therapy. For her, the agency input was successful. But the mother kept the social worker at arm's length, because she had not been fully involved in decision-making and her own goals had not been incorporated in the targets set. Because she had a poor relationship with the worker and little friendship elsewhere, her own need for support and consolation remained unmet.

CATEGORY 3   (21% of cases)

Child protected	YES
Child's welfare enhanced	NO
Needs of primary carer met	NO

The third category of outcome was heavily dominated by cases of child sexual abuse. Registration was usually a response to the disclosure or discovery of abuse, or else it had happened because of concerns about a previous child in the family. Apart from the preponderance of sexual abuse cases, the other outstanding feature of this outcome group was that professional intervention had had little effect on the outcome. In most of these cases we recorded that *social services intervention had had little effect, or that the positive features of the outcome had been brought about by other means, chiefly by the action of family members and friends*. In one case the official intervention actually had a negative effect, as a result of a highly unsatisfactory placement.

What this pattern signified in most cases was that the focus of the agency's work was squarely on protection, and other issues were neglected. Very often the alleged abuser was out of the household so the child was safe from further abuse, and the mother was being relied on to protect the child.

The broad reasons for the deficits in children's development have already been set out in chapter 17. For instance, the needs of children and non-abusing mothers were given a low priority, and even if the original priority had been high the social worker withdrew too quickly and cases were closed, leaving important areas of need untouched. As previously mentioned, when protection issues no longer dominated the agenda it was easy for the children's other needs to be overlooked. At the same time some social workers did attempt to form helpful alliances with family members but were rebuffed – either because they were seen by the parents as being too closely identified with the child's interests or because the child rejected them. Children did not always accept that abuse had occurred, or that intervention was necessary. In some of these cases children sided with their parents, and shut out the social worker.

In six cases in this category children would undoubtedly have benefited from therapeutic work to help them overcome the effects of the abuse. Even when they were technically 'protected' and their names had been removed from the register, some children showed worrying signs of disturbance on tests of depression and self-esteem. The age-span was wide. There were four children over the age of 13 and the sexual abuse victims ranged in age from 4 to 15. Two physical abuse cases involved babies. None of the children were living permanently away from home.

The lack of therapeutic input for abused adolescents in this category suggests that they were assumed to be less susceptible to damage than younger children; yet for these young people the abuse had often gone on longer. There was also a need for general work on the children's relationships with their parents and for attention to be paid to school attendance and educational and career opportunities. Research studies of the consequences of child abuse (for example, Lynch and Roberts, 1982; Calam and Franchi, 1987) have emphasized the dangers that children will underachieve at achool, leading to reduced options in terms of employment and social contact, and also that some will rush too quickly into partnerships and have problems in forming long-term relationships. Some of these difficulties had already been experienced by children in this outcome group. When indications of future problems were ignored, because of a narrow focus on protection from re-abuse, it was clear that the *long-term* protection of the child from 'significant harm' could not be assured.

Short-term protection issues were more firmly on the social worker's agenda than the longer-term ones and – as can be seen from the results – short-term protection for the children in this category was achieved. However, the brusque handling of the cases often created difficulties for parents and their children.

The needs of non-abusing mothers for asssistance in dealing with the aftermath of the discovery of the abuse were not addressed. A number of the mothers were still traumatised by the revelation of their child's abuse 20 months later. In many cases this had adversely affected their child's progress, either through a troubled or over-protective mother–child relationship or through the direct transmission of their fears and anxieties to their children. This illustrates the interrelationship of the outcome dimensions. *For many children who remained at home there were severe limits on how far it was possible to enhance their welfare if the needs of the parent on whom they depended were not addressed.*

In addition, mothers who had themselves been abused, sexually and in other ways, found that distressing memories were awakened by the investigation. One mother in this group was pleased when her child's name was removed from the register, because it signified what she referred to as the start of a 'new life'. She had no wish to prolong surveillance under the child protection system; but she continued to worry, she told us, about the effects of her *own* abuse and eventually sought help from the health visitor, who referred her to a clinical psychologist.

To uncover the deficits in these cases we have to go back beyond the stage of intervention. At the time of the joint investigation a pattern had been formed, according to which the protection of the child was conceived simply in terms of the separation of the child and the alleged abuser. At the initial case conference the recommendations about separation that followed had in most cases been ratified. On the other hand, recommendations for treatment or other help for abused children and their mothers had been sadly lacking, and there had been little discussion of a child protection plan. The discovery of the child's abuse had revealed needs which the child protection system had been unable or unwilling to meet.

A sample case from Category 3

Sharon was 14 when she told her mother in a letter that her father had been making sexual advances to her – a situation which she had found very disturbing. Strengthened by the fact of registration the mother got her husband to leave, which protected Sharon from further incidents. However, because the mother was considered able to protect her daughter, social services intervention was brief. After a few sessions focusing principally on the marriage the case was closed. Sharon was offered no individual help and eventually sought counselling herself at school.

By the end of the follow-up period the relationship between Sharon and her mother was very difficult. It had been worsened by the mother's attempts to restrict her daughter's freedom, because she had developed a general fear of her daughter being abused. These difficulties had been evident when social services were involved but they had not been addressed. Sharon had been protected, but neither her needs nor those of her mother had been subject to effective intervention.

CATEGORY 4   (7% of cases)

Child protected	NO
Child's welfare enhanced	YES
Needs of primary carer met	YES

This small group of cases is unusual inasmuch as the families received good input from social services and progress was made on a number of fronts; but at the same time the protection of the child was not effected for some time. The risks identified at the initial conference had centred on neglect and at first, despite registration, further neglect occurred. However, as time went on, parenting standards improved as a result of active social work and cooperation from the parents, combined with assistance from other family members such as grandparents or new partners. In all the cases in this group *both professional intervention and the assistance of others had had a positive effect on the outcome.*

Sometimes no actual abuse had occurred (to the best of our knowledge) but the child was still at risk. We have already referred to a case where a small boy shared a room with a relative who had been found guilty of sexually abusing a teenage girl. The social worker was heavily involved in helping the parents, who had long-standing problems connected with poor health, learning difficulties and poverty, but because the protection of the child was not given much priority it was quite some time before the relative was found alternative accommodation. Another child who had been registered because of emotional abuse was exposed to danger by being left alone more than once while her mother was high on glue. Nevertheless, the child made progress and there were gains in the mother's maturity over the period of the study, partly as a result of good social work support and partly because of the help which the mother received from other sources such as probation. For all these children a range of direct services had proved helpful.

None of these families had been subject to police investigation. The cases had all been open to social services before the initial child protection conference. These cases remind us that the risks which are attendant on maintaining the family intact must always be balanced against the costs of removing a child – and also that in most families there is a variety of problems with which social workers are supposed to deal. In the face of multiple problems it was not always easy to determine the chief source of risk to the child, and it was hardly surprising if social workers occasionally set priorities which other people might have wanted to challenge. Nonetheless, the outcomes for these children suggest that the decisions which had been made were ones where the benefits for children had outweighed the risks.

A sample case from Category 4

Nine-year-old Adrian was registered because of previous concerns about the way his mother neglected the children. She frequently went out drinking and gambling. In the wake of a family crisis, during the period of registration, the children were again neglected and left without supervision.

Principally as a result of the mother's neglect, the children were removed from her and placed in a foster home. In foster care Adrian made considerable gains. He put on weight, his concentration improved and he gained socially from attending clubs. His mother was helped by a worker at the local women's refuge, by her own parents, and by another woman with whom she formed a partnership. In the beginning she had been extremely negative about the social worker; but when a new worker took over she began to work with her towards the children's return. After a very slow start to intervention, which was accompanied in the initial stages by continuing risks, the situation started to improve.

CATEGORY 5   (11% of cases)

Child protected	NO
Child's welfare enhanced	YES
Needs of primary carer met	NO

The cases in this category demonstrate what happened when the agency concentrated on service inputs, in the absence of a good relationship with the parents. Neither the child's protection nor the parents' needs had been catered for. Nevertheless this outcome group included cases which are notoriously difficult for social workers to deal with, and intervention was never a simple matter.

After registration the children in this category were all living at home with the alleged abuser present. However, by the end of the study three of the five had been removed. They were all under the age of ten, and in four cases under the age of six. The principal reason for registration was physical abuse but in all of them there was a number of other worries, including neglect and violence. (Most of the children were registered because of 'accumulating concerns'.) In spite of regular monitoring and apparent compliance with the requirements of social services there was a high degree of family secrecy, and the agencies had constant worries about the possible concealment of abuse. These concerns were justified, since our interviews uncovered many incidents of domestic violence in the families, and some of the incidents had been covered up. All the children suffered further ill-treatment, sometimes of a serious nature.

However, concerns about the child's protection ensured that the family was visited and sometimes anxiously monitored – and because of such anxieties some basic services were provided for the children. As a result, the children's welfare was enhanced even when their protection was not secured.

Young children in this group were given services such as developmental checks and speech therapy. They were also given ready access to playgroups, childminding, relief care or holiday activities. The motivation behind the provision of these services was often partly to create opportunities for monitoring the child outside the home. The resulting improvement in children's development was often marginal but credit must be given for the fact that it was achieved at all.

In all of these cases the work was directed at the mother, but in the background there was severe and prolonged domestic violence from the men in the families towards the mothers. Since in all the families it was the father figure who presented the risks to the children, the impact of the work with mothers was limited. Two of the mothers attempted suicide during the course of the study, one of them on two occasions.

In three cases there was a male social worker who had little sympathy with the mother and blamed her for most of the family's problems. Clearly this was not helpful; but in one case when the male social worker left and was replaced by a woman the situation did not improve, since the woman was seen as too child-centred in her attitudes and was therefore unpopular with *both* parents. Meanwhile the abusing husband withdrew even further beyond the agency's reach.

The social workers in these cases often disregarded violence between adults, treating it as being beyond their control. Nevertheless, children in these cases were emotionally distressed by watching violence between their parents, and they also risked being subject to violence themselves, either deliberately as a result of the male carer's aggression, or accidentally because they were sandwiched between warring adults. Some children actively wanted to protect their mothers from physical violence, and this kind of responsibility was assumed willingly by a girl who could be classified as a 'parental child'.

The parents in these cases were struggling with a multitude of problems such as ill-health, poverty, unemployment, inadequate housing and social isolation. Clearly these problems were connected and compounded; but when the needs of the mother were explored in our interviews, the need which often came uppermost was for help and understanding (and sometimes for protection) because of her emotional dependence on a violent man. However, little help was provided for these and other problems because there was a poor relationship between the social worker and the parents.

The plans made at the initial case conference had usually been focused on providing resources, in the hope that if social services managed to remain involved, monitoring of the children would be achieved.

A sample case from Category 5

Petra was a three-year-old partially disabled girl who was placed on the register after sustaining minor injuries. Because of her disabilities she already received intensive help from health and social services, and occasional respite care. The main concerns centred on the very poor level of physical care which she received, the long periods of neglect during which she was underfed or cot-bound, the large number of injuries she suffered and the high degree of violence which she witnessed between her mother and her partner.

For five months at the start of the registration period Petra suffered further neglect and injuries. After careful recording of all the relevant incidents the local authority sought and obtained a care order and she made rapid progress in a foster home. The needs of her mother were not met. She had never experienced her social worker as helpful. As a result, her feelings about her own situation, the violence she was enduring, and her grief at giving up her child permanently were never addressed.

CATEGORY 6   (11% of cases)

Child protected	NO
Child's welfare enhanced	NO
Needs of primary carer met	NO

The cases in this last sad category represent the worst outcomes in the study. In four of them *professional intervention had had little effect on the outcome*, and in the remaining one the effect had been negative.

Most of the cases in this group concerned physical abuse with just one of sexual abuse. There was a high level of violence and concerns about poor parenting standards in these families. Both boys and girls were involved, and the ages of the children varied from 10 months to 15 years. What all the cases had in common was a failure of assessment and of treatment.

From beginning to end there was a lack of clarity about how these cases should be handled. At the initial conferences there were gaps in the available information, doubt about the assessment of risk, and uncertainty about what treatment should be offered. Sometimes there was no agreement between professionals about what had *happened*. In one case where a child was burnt, for example, there was no firm judgement at the conference as to whether or not the injury was deliberate. In another case of bruising to a baby there was no admission on the part of the parents and therefore no certainty as to who the abuser was. As a result of these uncertainities, the work that was offered lacked a clear focus and the difficulties in these families eluded help, even though the parents were often desperate for assistance with their children. The needs of the children and their parents were not met because there was too little service to them, and what little was on offer failed to deal with the problems.

Although each of the children in these cases was registered because of a specific allegation of abuse, there was a background of secondary concerns in all the families. There was also a high level of disturbed behaviour among the children. The patterns of family interaction were extremely complex, and the children might have benefited from a more dynamic analysis of the problems at the initial case conference, rather than the documentation of accumulating concerns or a preoccupation with the attribution of responsibility. In each case the floating concerns came to rest on the mother, who took responsibility for the children and generally felt blamed for inadequate child management or failure to provide protection. Our evidence showed, however, that in all these households the mothers were the *victims* of violence. In particular there was violence from aggressive partners and ex-partners, whether married or cohabiting. One lone mother was also a victim of neighbourhood violence, during the period of the study. As in the previous category of outcome, there was risk to the index child from marital conflict and from conflict between other adults, as well as from deliberate injury. Sometimes there was serious violence among *children* in the family. (One child threw an axe at his older sister.) During the course of the follow-up, all the children in this group suffered injuries at the hands of their parents or siblings, although in only two cases were the children separated from the abuser as a result.

Another feature of these cases was that, although the parents had clear views and insights which could have aided progress, these were accorded little importance. Consequently, the planning process was denuded of an important source of information; and at the same time the parents were discouraged from participation because of persistent suspicions about them.

In spite of the generally negative experience that the mothers in this group had of the child protection system, individual social workers were valued for the help or friendship which they offered. In one case where the outcome was obviously unsatisfactory, the mother said that she liked the social worker and found her supportive. Her one complaint was that she did not see her more often. The social worker, on the other hand, was extremely busy and also felt unsupported within the agency.

The situations in this outcome group echoed certain difficulties in case management that we have already noted. In particular, supervision for social workers was lacking in both quantity and quality. One social worker in this group freely admitted that she had lost track of where she was going, and another was hampered by feelings of stress and anxiety with which she received no help. Inter-agency working in these cases was largely restricted to the initial conference. Unilateral actions by other agencies (for example by the police who summoned one child for sexual assault, and by the school which suspended another child for irregular attendance) made nonsense of treatment plans. At the same time potential options for treatment, such as psychiatric referral, were suggested by other agencies but not taken up, because the members of the social services department did not think them necessary or relevant. Many of the recommendations which were put forward at conferences and reviews were repetitious or unrealistic, and left the main burden of decision-making with the key worker.

The failure of *treatment* in these and in other cases was partly connected with the absence of suitable resources, but it also followed from weaknesses in the assessments that were made at various stages. If clear information was lacking, social workers made arbitrary decisions about what needed to be done, and they sometimes unwisely became deflected from consideration of the crucial issues. A virtual culture of violence in the family was ignored, because of a general belief that although the family was 'chaotic' it was 'safe', in the sense that the mothers were seen as cooperative. It could be argued that this exemplifies what Dingwall and his colleagues (1983) have called the 'rule of optimism'; but the social workers who were working with these families were rarely optimistic. Although some individual family members were liked, and there was usually a good deal of sympathy for the child, there was a general dislike of having to deal with such cases because of their messiness, the worrying atmosphere of uncertainty, and the deeply entrenched nature of some of the problems. Although the start of intervention was often marked by intensive activity the social workers' energy was soon dissipated, so that plans tailed off and matters were allowed to drift. As a result, they ended up offering a low level of service and their efforts to monitor the children's safety were not sustained.

A sample case from Category 6

Shane was 12 when he was registered because of the high level of violence in his family. Despite a series of interventions which included activity sessions, the violence continued unabated. There was very little social work help for his lone mother. Eighteen months after registration Shane received a black eye from his mother and was accommodated in a foster home.

The issue of family violence was not well tackled at the initial case conference, which was preoccupied with a discussion of the 'accumulating concerns'. During the assessment process the dynamics of Shane's relationship with his mother had not been fully considered. As a result, none of the services offered in this case were effective in helping him, and his behaviour at school worsened to the point where he was suspended. The mother's loneliness and depression continued as before. Her own network was too restricted to help her, and in spite of the fact that she had referred herself to social services in the beginning, her needs remained unmet.

This brief analysis suggests that there are patterns of interaction between agencies and family members, and within families, which determine the outcome in cases of abuse and neglect, and that these patterns are complex but to some extent recognisable. It also confirms that a narrow focus on protection, in child abuse cases, obscures other needs (of both children and carers) which require to be met if the long-term welfare and protection of the child is to be assured.

Summary

1. There were five variations in the relationship between intervention and outcome. In a third of the cases professional intervention had had a positive effect on outcome, whilst in a further quarter of cases both professional intervention and the assistance of others had achieved a positive effect. On the other hand, in over a quarter of cases professional intervention had had little effect on outcome, whilst in 7% of cases, although this was so, assistance from other quarters had had a positive impact. Finally, in 7% of cases professional intervention had actually had a negative effect on outcome.

2. When we combined the outcome dimensions referred to in chapter 17, six types of outcome emerged for the children in the study.

   In the best outcome group (23% of the sample) there was progress on all three dimensions – that is, the child was protected, the child's welfare was enhanced, and the needs of the primary carers were met. The families of children living at home received valuable help from social services and also from relatives and friends. It was often this combination of inputs which produced improvement. When the child was being looked after, children were placed with relatives and family links were well maintained.

3. In the largest group of combined outcomes (27% of the sample) some progress was made in terms of the child's protection and welfare but the needs of the main carers were not met. Often there was a poor relationship between social worker and parent, but the child's basic protection and welfare were assured by removal to care or the provision of direct services.

4. In the third outcome group (21% of the sample) the child was protected without any progress being made on other dimensions. Most of these were cases of child sexual abuse. Very often the abuser was out of the household, and the mother was being relied on to protect the child. The cases had been quickly closed leaving a range of needs unmet.

5. In the fourth group (7% of the sample) the child was not fully protected, although some progress was made in promoting the child's welfare and meeting the needs of the carers. Concerns had often centred on neglect, and at first, after registration, further neglect occurred. However, as time went on parenting standards improved and progress was made in promoting the welfare of the children and meeting the needs of the main carers.

6. In the fifth outcome group (11% of the sample), the agency concentrated on monitoring and service inputs, in the absence of a good cooperative relationship with the parents. There was some enhancement of the child's welfare; but the child was not protected and little was done for the parents. In all of these cases the focus of agency attention was on the mother, and in

the background there was an abusive husband or cohabitee who could not be reached.

7. In the group of cases with the worst outcomes (11% of the sample) the children were not protected, and nor were their needs or those of their parents met. These cases were characterised by a high level of violence in the family, and a range of other concerns about poor parenting standards and disturbed behaviour amongst the children. There was also a lack of clarity about how the families should be handled and little assistance for the social worker had been provided by the initial conferences or the later reviews. The problems in these families were regarded as deeply entrenched. Low levels of service were provided and efforts to monitor the children's safety were not sustained.

PART V

Conclusions

Chapter 19

Conclusions

When we review the results of our research, a number of themes and issues stand out. Of particular importance for policy and practice are the relationship between the dimensions of outcome, the presence of continuities and discontinuities over time, and the impact of gender in shaping child protection interventions.

The particular conclusions emerging from our research have, of course, been derived from intensive study of a small sample, and therefore need to be replicated in other studies. Nevertheless, the general pattern of the findings is clear, and when taken together they provide a picture of the child protection system which is in line with that of a number of recent studies of child protection, including others in this series. The relevant themes and issues are discussed below.

The interdependence between the dimensions of outcome

All the children in our follow-up sample had been placed on the child protection register because they were considered to be at risk of future harm. By the end of the 20-month follow-up period protection had been assured for 70% of them.

Children whom we deemed to be unprotected were not necessarily re-abused, since we took into account the extent to which children were protected from possible as well as actual harm. (For example, a child who is living with a known sexual offender without adequate safeguards cannot be said to have been protected.) Our finding that risk continued in 30% of the cases, and that 25% of the children were actually re-abused, is in line with the findings of other studies of children in high risk situations (Barth and Berry, 1987; Farmer and Parker, 1991). It is also very close to the 31% re-abuse rate found by Gibbons, Conroy and Bell (1993) in their six-month follow-up of children placed on registers in eight local authorities, to the 26% re-abuse rate found by Cleaver and Freeman (1993) in their two-year follow-up of children whose parents were confronted after suspicion of abuse arose, and to the 28% repeated abuse rate found by Corby (1987) in his two-year follow-up study of 25 registered children.

The most important element in protection was *physical separation*. Where children were effectively protected, this result was achieved by total separation from the abuser in 45% of cases. Another 29% were separated from the abuser for part of the follow-up period. It was interesting to find that only

26% had remained safe while living continuously with the parent who was alleged to have abused them.

Our findings show that the lessons of the major child death enquiries, such as those concerning Jasmine Beckford and Tyra Henry, have been well learned by social services departments, inasmuch as the child's protection was regarded as the first priority in case management. The few exceptions to this are worth noting. The dangers to children were occasionally played down by social workers who had had long-term involvement with a family. This happened either because the social workers' commitment to keeping the children in the family led them to underestimate problems, or because the workers had come to accept low standards of child care and to believe that continuing risks to the children were inevitable. These children were usually from families which were well known to social services departments and in which there were longstanding concerns about poor standards of parenting, material deprivation, behaviourally disturbed children and family violence.

There were two other groups of children who were often poorly protected. One was children who experienced sibling or peer abuse, whether physical or sexual. The other consisted of the siblings of a registered child who, although sometimes also subject to registration, were nonetheless not the prime focus of professional attention.

As far as the immediate protection of the children was concerned, the figure of 70% represents a notable success. However, in our examination of the outcomes for children we wanted to move beyond the question of their safety to see how far the wider issues of their welfare had been addressed. To do this we evaluated the outcomes for the children in the study not only according to whether they had been protected but also according to whether the children's welfare had been enhanced and the needs of the primary carer had been met. Our interpretation of Department of Health documents suggested that these are the three principal objectives of child protection interventions.

Our analysis of the children's welfare shows that in 68% of cases the registered children made gains during the follow–up period. Sometimes, however, these gains were small. Improvements resulted from a change of placement, skilled social work intervention or a combination of family support and services such as day care, activity groups or welfare assistance at school. The provision of such services was often linked to the aim of monitoring children when there were continuing concerns about abuse or neglect; but they also had positive benefits for children. In contrast, we found that the needs of the primary carers were met in only a third of the families studied. Clearly this was an area which was accorded a low priority in child protection work.

How did this situation arise? Sometimes the needs of the parents and children were considered to be in conflict, and the child was either removed or was provided with direct services which excluded the parents. At other times the needs of different carers went unrecognised, were not sufficiently differentiated or were not seen as connected to the risk of abuse. (This applied particularly in cases involving marital violence, cramped housing conditions and social isolation.) In addition, some parents were too alienated by child protection interventions to be easily reached.

Our study confirms that the focus of the child protection system is firmly on investigation and surveillance to ensure the protection of children rather than on treatment and reunification (Howe, 1992). However, the research has also shown that the needs of parents and children cannot be compartmentalised in this way. Neglect of parental needs at both the personal and structural level had an adverse effect on the child's welfare. In addition, neglect of the welfare of both parent and child contributed to the risk of further harm. Although short-term protection for many of the children in the study was achieved during the period of registration, it was frequently precarious; and long-term protection could not be ensured if there were unresolved difficulties in the aftermath of the abuse.

There were a number of ways in which the future protection of children was placed in jeopardy by lack of attention to welfare issues. First, when children were removed under child protection procedures, little attention was sometimes paid to the maintenance of family links and as a result the relationships between parents and children were impoverished. It may be that issues of contact are viewed less favourably when the child has been removed for reasons of abuse or neglect; but children who were denied access to important family members suffered unrelieved feelings of loss or guilt, and were inclined to seek a swift return home to a situation which might well be abusive.

Secondly, when children were maintained at home an exclusive focus on the child's immediate protection could mean that if concerns about their safety diminished after registration their other needs were not seen as requiring service in their own right. Children's disturbed behaviour or even a family's impending homelessness, if not considered as integrally connected with the child's safety, could be interpreted as beyond the worker's remit. In some of these cases the mother was being relied on to do whatever was necessary to protect the child. She could well find this an impossible burden which led her to seek the support of a partner, and this sometimes increased the risk that the abuser would return.

Thirdly, if the focus was on protecting children from immediate risk rather than on assisting them to recover from the harm they had suffered, the treatment needs of abused children could be overlooked. The continuing high levels of disturbance and depression among the sexually abused children who received no treatment suggest that this is an area which requires more attention and the provision of specialist resources, such as those which were occasionally provided by a diminishing number of child and family guidance clinics. Clearly issues of protection as well as welfare are involved. We must be concerned, for example, about the highly provocative behaviour of some children who have been sexualised prematurely, and who were therefore at risk of further abuse outside the family or outside the foster home. In the absence of treatment which would increase the child's capacity for self-protection, there was no way in which a concerned adult could guarantee that the child would remain protected, even when the original risks had been removed.

Lastly, the child's long-term development and welfare seemed likely to be affected unless attempts were made to counteract the effects of the abuse in terms of life opportunities. It was noticeable that sexually abused adolescents tended to drop out of school, partly because the abuse had damaged their self-confidence, partly because the anxiety and the upset which followed disclosure had impaired their concentration, and partly because the teasing of their schoolmates could make social relationships intolerable. Under-achievement in the school system was likely to lead to poor employment opportunities, and in some cases a renewed confinement to the home environment which had caused so much distress. These children were not, in the widest sense, 'protected' as long as such deficits remained.

The links between decision-making, intervention and outcome

Given that procedures are intended to ensure maximum continuity between the plans made at one stage and their implementation at another, we would expect to find considerable continuity in the child protection system. How far were these expectations borne out in practice? We found that major continuities did exist, although not all were due to the procedures. In the first place, there were links between the professional decisions and actions taken during the investigation and the decisions taken at the initial case conference. The views formed by the investigating professionals largely determined the way in which the risks to the child were construed at the case conference and these in their turn fed into decisions about registration. In addition, the discussions at initial conferences could have an enduring effect on the way in which risks to the child were later interpreted. It was rare for a review to question a prevailing assessment once it had gained general acceptance, and later information about risk might only be taken seriously if it fitted the preconceptions already formed.

The initial conference was expected to have a major influence on subsequent intervention by means of the child protection plan and it emerged that this was true in terms of the child's subsequent protection. In 82 per cent of the cases where a comprehensive plan was made for the child's protection the child's safety was secured. On the other hand, in 50 per cent of the cases where the initial plan was deficient the child was subsequently re-abused or neglected. The initial plan also had an impact on later interventions when recommendations were specific, feasible and tailored to the needs of the child and other family members. There was an increased chance that abused children would receive treatment if it had been recommended at the initial case conference, both because the recommendations emphasised the importance of such interventions and because they made it more likely that other agencies would release the required resources. It should also be noted that the protection plan had the most enduring influence when the social worker was *new* to the case at the time of registration, whether or not the case was previously known to the social services department. In such situations more thorough protection plans were made and key workers felt more responsible for carrying out the mandate of the initial conference, unencumbered by a history of prior involvement.

The deliberations of the initial case conference were especially important because once a pattern of case management had been established it was usually endorsed at subsequent reviews, even when it was deficient in providing for the child's protection or the needs of the child and other family members. Review meetings tended to be reactive and often failed to identify major gaps in provision. Since it is important that reviews reassess risks and respond to new information, our findings suggest that those who are about to chair review meetings need to prepare carefully and to make their own assessment of the outstanding needs of the family members . Moreover, when unacceptable risks to children are identified, the chairperson needs to have access to a line manager who will ensure that the management of the case is reappraised.

The tendency for early impressions to persist was not limited to professional decisions. There was considerable evidence of continuity for family members too. In as many as 70 per cent of the families the investigation and case conference had a negative impact on the parent figures who frequently felt marginalised and badly treated. Feelings of anger and violation persisted for two-fifths of these families and social workers were kept at arm's length. However, three-fifths of the alienated families changed their views and came to welcome the services provided, and this was usually made possible by a change of worker. It was often necessary to break into a pattern of alienation, and a change of worker made it possible for the family to have a fresh start with a practitioner who was not associated with the earlier painful events.

In view of the continuities, there are strong arguments in favour of reconsidering the way in which investigations and conferences are conducted in the first place, particularly as the handling of the investigation had often influenced the alliances formed between family members or between family members and professionals. In the face of an external threat, families had sometimes closed ranks and concealed potentially discrediting information. There is likely to be less alienation if careful attention is paid to informing and involving parents and children at every stage, and to intervening strategically in order to try to strengthen the support given to the child. This will often mean strengthening the alliance between the non-abusing parent and the child, and providing help for non-abusing mothers to enable them to give their children understanding and assistance. It is also important that professionals who refer a family to the social services department inform the family of their actions. Whilst child protection investigations are always likely to be stressful, some of their worst consequences could be ameliorated by such changes in practice.

Given the enduring influence of the child protection plans made at initial case conferences, there is also a need to improve the quality of the plans themselves. The plans were limited because the concentration on risk left little time for fashioning effective interventions. In addition, the information presented to conferences was mostly about possible risk rather than about need, and did not always shed light on the possible causes of the abuse or neglect. It was therefore difficult to make good decisions about the kinds of service which would be most helpful and it was often unclear how the protection plans related to the risks to which children were exposed (see also Gibbons *et al.*, 1993). Finally, since parents and children had rarely been involved in making the plans, a vital source of information was missing. It would help if parents were fully involved in discussions about the services which they and their children need and if the reports brought to the conference dealt fully with these issues. In addition, if a time limit were placed on the discussion about risk and registration, a greater proportion of the conference could be spent in planning services jointly with children and parents. The potential for continuity could then be used to greater advantage.

The balance of power

Why was it that although the majority of children were successfully protected, a small number were not? The answers appear to lie in the shifts of power which occurred at critical points of intervention within the child protection system, and in the limitations of a service which aims to protect children by regulating women.

During the stage of the investigation and initial case conference the balance of power had rested firmly with the official agencies. The investigation of a situation where there were allegations of harm, the threat of criminal proceedings, the court-like atmosphere of the conference, and the involvement of a number of agencies, were intimidating for parents. This was also a critical point for intervention. When children were removed at these early stages because of abuse or anticipated risk, they were particularly likely to stay away. Other children who were generally believed to be unsafe were not removed but were marked out for official surveillance. Attentive recording of subsequent risks led to the removal of some of these children at a later stage. However, for most of the families whose children remained with them after the initial case conference, the balance of power shifted towards the parents (see also Farmer and Parker, 1991). Subsequent intervention depended on the cooperation, or at least the compliance of the parents, and had to be negotiated with them by the social worker. Even opportunities for surveillance were dependent on access to the child's home.

However, after the case conference social workers were in the unenviable position of carrying responsibility for children's safety at a time when opportunities for forming effective working relationships with parents had often been severely jeopardised. This was because the balance of power has been heavily weighted against parents in the initial stages of child protection interventions and they had been excluded from crucial parts of the process. Both the abusing and non-abusing parents were left feeling hostile and alienated. This was the situation in which social workers contrived to fashion ways of working which would offer support to family members and at the same time monitor potential harm to the child.

As we have seen, the children who were the least well protected were those who remained at home with an abusing or neglectful parent where standards of care were poor. Professionals were working almost exclusively with the mothers of these families, whilst the dangers were principally from their male partners. Often there were high levels of secrecy and the extent of domestic violence and substance abuse was concealed from the agencies. As a result, the structure of power within these families was not well recognised, and interventions which were directed at mothers made no impact on the men at the heart of the difficulties. Social workers felt helpless and their opportunities to intervene were limited. In addition, as time wore on, it became increasingly difficult to initiate action about circumstances which had implicitly been endorsed for some time, unless there were unequivocal signs of renewed abuse (see also Farmer and Parker, 1991).

Another factor which was capable of shifting the balance of power away from social services and affecting the outcomes for children, either positively or negatively, was the reconstitution of families. At the beginning of child protection intervention, children were removed or abusers bailed away if there was a high likelihood of repeated abuse or neglect. As time went on, though, agencies had decreasing influence on the membership of the households in which children lived. Family reconstitution could lead to a reduction in risks to children when an abuser left the household; but in other cases the risks could increase as, for example, when an alleged abuser or a Schedule One offender joined or rejoined a family. In these situations and in others where social services departments ran out of options and returned children home from unsatisfactory care placements, children could be exposed to continuing risks at a time when the activity of the monitoring agencies was actually being reduced. Needless to say, attempts at coercive interventions, short of care proceedings, were unlikely to succeed if they were made in a situation of conflict when the balance of power was not in the department's favour.

The gendered nature of child protection intervention

The focus on mothers pervaded all aspects of the child protection system. Mothers were the single largest group to initiate a child protection referral but when they sought help in this way, either because they suspected intra- or extra-familial abuse or because they had difficulty in controlling children, they often became subject to interventions in which they themselves came under suspicion. In most cases of neglect and emotional abuse there was a general assumption that mothers were responsible for all deficits in the care of the children. When mothers were seen as responsible for physical abuse, the child's name was more likely to be placed on the child protection register than when a father or male partner was responsible. It also seemed that social services departments were more willing to intervene in lone-mother families than in two-parent households, or perhaps were more unwilling to intervene when the man was seen as uncooperative or threatening. It may also have been assumed that in a two-parent household where there was a male abuser the mother would be able to protect the child.

This different treatment of mothers was also a feature of case management after registration. It was mothers who mediated with the outside world both by representing the family at the majority of case conferences and by maintaining the contact with social workers and other professionals which their male partners shunned. Lone mothers whose children were registered stood a greater chance of having children permanently removed from them than did couples. In addition, mothers whose male partners sexually abused their children tended to be treated as secondary perpetrators – guilty until proved innocent – rather than as secondary victims of the abuse. However, when mothers in cases of sexual abuse were able to demonstrate to the authorities that they had taken steps to protect their children from their partners, their reward was usually to find that the case was quickly closed, leaving them with the full responsibility of coping with the after-effects of the abuse and its consequences for them and their children.

In the registered cases in our follow-up sample, all the perpetrators of sexual abuse were male and physical abuse was inflicted in equal proportions by men and women. In spite of this, the demands that children should be protected were primarily directed at women. In cases of physical abuse by men the attention of professionals quickly moved away from the men and came to rest on the mothers who were seen as more amenable and available for intervention. This move seemed to be pragmatic, but it left women in the position of trying to regulate the actions of their partners. Mothers frequently tried to protect their children from their violent or unpredictable partners and they sometimes attempted to use registration as a deterrent to these men, for example by taking every bruise for inspection to the doctor. It should be noted that most of the children with the worst outcomes were living in families where there was continuing violence by the man towards his female partner. This violence was sometimes concealed from the authorities or was considered by professionals to be peripheral to their concerns.

It is clear that in future the risks to children need to be disaggregated, and that practice needs to take more account of the distinction between children who are at risk from a father figure, a mother, a sibling or a combination of family members or others. The relentless focus on mothers in the child protection system is all the more surprising when we consider that it is men who have been responsible for the majority of well-publicised child deaths. The link between domestic violence and child abuse also requires greater recognition if more effective interventions are to be developed.

Child protection work with minority ethnic families

When the ten cases involving minority ethnic families were compared with others in the sample as a whole, several common features were observed. The official investigation and case conference seemed to follow a similar pattern and were generally experienced as stressful. The difficulties were compounded by language problems, in addition to differences in the cultural value-base, and a high number of investigations ended in uncertainty. This gave the ensuing intervention a somewhat diffuse focus.

It was clear that many black families did not have access to services which they needed. It was therefore particularly unfortunate if the first contact with social services was by way of the child protection system. As has been pointed out by other authors (Phillips and Dutt, 1991; Jones, 1993), over-rigid use of the official guidance on assessment can result in the scapegoating of black people, since material deprivation and low educational achievement are associated with child abuse and neglect (Department of Health, 1988 b). Yet for many black people, success in our education system is difficult to achieve and low economic status is not unusual. It is important to focus on the strengths of black families:

> '. . . strengths rooted in cultural traditions, in the survival of gener-ations in spite of discrimination and the disadvantages of the stresses of migration and sometimes persecution' (Ahmed et al., 1986).

Nevertheless, the death of Tyra Henry reminds us that it is dangerous to rely on positive stereotypes as a substitute for adequate assessment in child protection cases, and that over-reliance on the coping ability of black carers in poor circumstances can result in their resources being over-stretched (London Borough of Lambeth, 1987).

Should workers and clients be carefully matched? As far as social work intervention is concerned, our study suggests that there is much value in 'experiential affinity' – the link of shared experience between worker and client which ensures that the latter's experience of hardship or oppression will be adequately understood. Our results underline the importance of racial and ethnic matching, wherever possible, in the allocation of workers; but they also emphasise the importance of other issues, such as gender and class, which must be seen and understood in the racial and cultural context. Gender matching was particularly important in households where the woman as well as the child was a victim of male abuse.

Concern has been expressed by some authors (for example, Montalvo and Gutierrez, 1984) that families may 'use their cultural heritage as a mask, a justification for curtailing needed problem-solving', and that traditional gender assignments may cover up exploitation and spousal abuse. These are real fears. As in the rest of the study, we found that male abusers who presented risks to their children or partners tended to opt out of social work involvement, and as a result their problems were not directly addressed. Nevertheless it was noticeable that when the child was living at home, an alliance between professionals and the main caretaking parent – who was usually the mother – was frequently beneficial to the child. In the study as a whole we found that the child's welfare was likely to be enhanced, and the risk of re-injury reduced, if the needs of the caretaking parent were met. With minority ethnic clients the same principles applied; but the degree of parental satisfaction was generally higher, and the progress of the child was correspondingly better, when there was successful matching across the three dimensions of race, gender and ethnicity. Out of the four cases where complete matching occurred, three seemed to be progressing well; but in the six remaining cases there was only one which was satisfactory.

Should racial matching be a matter of policy? Probably, yes; but in spite of the positive research findings about matching, it has to be admitted that there are problems with the notion of 'experiential affinity' in both casework and research. Apart from the difficulties involved in catering for the needs of different family members, it is too easy to make the assumption that groups have fixed sets of characteristics, and that 'membership of one oppressed group offers a passport to understanding all other experiences of oppression' (Boushel and Fisher, forthcoming). There were a few cases in the study which bore witness to cross-cultural difficulties in the parent-worker relationship –

difficulties which existed when racial matching was crudely made and was therefore more apparent than real.

Amongst the social workers interveiwed there was a laudable absence of attempts to see cultures in terms of fixed characteristics, but the attempt to dismantle stereotypes without building a more reliable conceptual framework led to some difficulties. In spite of (or perhaps because of) considerable sensitivity in their perceptions, a few workers were somewhat overwhelmed by the number of factors which appeared to be relevant in minority ethnic cases and they had difficulty in combining them – especially if culture, race and ethnicity were seen not as the total context for intervention but as factors to be added at the end of a lengthening list.

The main deficits in these cases, however, were not attributable to social work actions or attitudes but to the disadvantaged circumstances of many families and the limitations of the services which were available to them. Even though involvement in the child protection system was seen as highly stigmatising, and some families contrived to keep the official agencies at bay, the intervention could be seen as a valuable source of help – particularly by isolated mothers whose problems were concerned with troubled children and violent partners. As in the rest of the study, there were wide variations in the extent to which they felt that they were consulted about their needs. Nonetheless, the importance they attached to the agency response should not be underestimated.

The involvement of parents

The 1989 Children Act has given considerable impetus to the practice of informing and involving children and their parents in agency processes. There are real dilemmas when powerful professionals try to involve parents in a voluntary relationship, within what is basically a coercive system (Owen, 1992). Nevertheless, our findings underline the impact that a lack of involvement can have on participants, the resentment towards professionals which can build up, and the risk that in some cases a wedge may be driven between children and important family members. Exclusion from decision-making can also leave children fearful and uncertain about what will happen to them.

Our research emphasises the importance of eliciting the views which parents hold, not only about the incidents of concern to the professionals but about risk and harm to the child. Parents harboured justifiable resentments when they were not given a chance to express their views. Their concerns about the welfare of their children were often different from those of the professionals, but they had a right to serious consideration. For example, in a number of cases of physical abuse to teenagers, parents saw the central issue as their difficulty in controlling the child, with the abuse as a by-product. They felt powerless and humiliated in the face of acts of disobedience. Professionals, on the other hand, had seen the issue of control as secondary to that of abuse.

Time spent discovering parents' and children's views about their requirements will be repaid later. It was these understandings which were needed to inform decision-makers before, during and after the case conference if viable plans were to be made. Even when disagreements between parents and professionals about the abuse endured, it was still possible to find common ground to fashion a plan of intervention which addressed the needs of the child and parents.

The involvement of parents and children in child protection conferences is one part of this dialogue. Whilst greater parental involvement might lead to more disagreement being aired at conferences, this is likely to be beneficial in the long run. There are a number of ways in which practice in this area could be improved. The study shows the crucial importance of parents attending the whole conference wherever possible. It also shows that the parents' anxieties about attendance are somewhat eased if arrangements are made so that they can be settled before the professionals start to arrive. An informal chat with the chairperson before the conference is likely to prove helpful. Tokens of welcome such as the offer of a cup of tea are appreciated, and full advance briefing is needed for parents about the conduct of the conference, their role in it and who will attend. A copy of the agenda should be provided. The use of nameplates giving name and profession will help family members to identify individual participants, and they may have to be encouraged to bring a friend, relative or advocate to give them support.

It is also important that clear explanations about the reasons for registration are given to parents and children. The *Working Together* guidelines (Home Office *et al.*, 1991) now specify that simple written factual information about registration should be made available. This could correct some of the current misconceptions about the reasons for registration and the length of time that children will stay on the register. Written information when de-registration takes place would also be useful, as would information about parents' rights in the context of registration.

The interviews with parents showed that the relationship with the social worker was of central importance in creating a feeling of involvement, but it was frequently precarious. There are a number of possible ways in which this could be made easier. At the time when a key worker is allocated, as previously mentioned, more consideration could be given to the choice of a suitable person. A change of social worker may be indicated, not only when the investigation has been experienced as a very negative intervention but also when the goodwill of the current worker or of the family has been exhausted, or during subsequent intervention when it is clear that the worker has become so identified with the parents that continued abuse or neglect of the child are being tolerated. Referral to other agencies such as a family centre or child guidance may be important, in order to separate the 'coercive' and 'helpful' agencies in the parent's mind. There may also be a case for separate workers for the child and parent, when their needs are in conflict.

Of course, social work intervention did not stand alone. Other agencies and other people were also involved to varying degrees in the lives of parents and children. In a third of cases (34%) intervention by official agencies appeared to have had a definite positive effect, and in another quarter of cases both agency intervention and the actions of other people were responsible for a good outcome. In many of these cases registration acted as a catyalyst which called forth increased resources from within the wider family. In the remaining 41 per cent of cases, agency intervention appeared to have had little effect on the outcome for the child, or more rarely had had a detrimental effect. Nevertheless, it is clear that extremely good results can be achieved when there is a meshing together of agency intervention and family or community support, ensuring that the needs of parents and children are met from a number of coordinated sources.

The experiences of the children

The interviews with children demonstrated the complexity of service provision which is sensitive to their needs. During the initial investigations children felt that their disclosure, or the discovery of the abuse, had unleashed a process over which they had no control. They had rarely been consulted or even informed about what to expect. Children who had been removed directly from school worried about the enforced publicity, and if they had been taken from school at the end of the afternoon they were concerned about their parents' reactions when they did not return home at the expected time. They wanted to know why the investigation was being held and what its implications were. The presence of a familiar figure, whether a social worker, a friend or a trusted parent could do much to alleviate the intense anxiety created by the investigative interview. The exclusion of the non-abusing parent deprived some children of a much-needed source of support. Although the skill and sensitivity of most investigative interviewers was appreciated by children, the process of talking about abuse, especially sexual abuse, was usually extremely painful.

Throughout the investigation and thereafter children were preoccupied with concerns about the impact that their exposure of the abuse would have on their families. The fact that they had agreed to reveal details about the incidents to the authorities meant that they frequently felt responsible for subsequent events, and indeed they were often held responsible by family members. Children harboured strong feelings of self-blame for the occurrence of both sexual and physical abuse. They often viewed the expulsion of the abuser with guilt or felt that their own move to a care placement was a punishment. In these situations, there was a clear need for someone to provide children with repeated reassurance that the perpetrator had been responsible for the abuse. In addition, children needed help to develop an understanding of past and present events which could form the basis for their recovery.

Most children wanted their feelings about responsibility for the abuse to be understood and not simply denied. Adolescents whose behaviour had been a contributory factor in physical abuse, for example, were often very conscious of the interactions between themselves and their parents. A non-blaming approach combined with a genuine exploration of the children's views and feelings was helpful in treatment. With support from social workers, some non-abusing mothers or foster carers could take on part of this role, and children were also very grateful for direct counselling about the abuse.

Some children did not distinguish clearly between investigation, assessment and therapeutic interviews. It seemed as though they regarded all these events as *'talking about the abuse'*. Children who had to undergo care proceedings were questioned by a variety of adults including police, social workers and the guardian *ad litem*. By the time this process was over they could feel that they had done enough 'talking about the abuse' and when, as was usually the case, therapeutic work was made to await the outcome of legal proceedings, it might be started too late to be acceptable or effective.

As we have seen, half the sexually abused children received no direct help in dealing with the effects of the abuse. By the end of the 20-month follow-up period a number of them continued to feel that they were to blame for what had happened and some actually regretted having told. This was particularly likely when the consequences of having disclosed the abuse had significantly worsened their position, as happened when abused young people had to leave their families and consequently felt blamed and excluded.

The children who had been physically or sexually abused frequently felt love and loyalty towards one or sometimes both parent figures, as well as feelings of anger, reproach and hatred. When they left their families they tried from a distance to repair relationships with family members and worried about the safety of their siblings. Social workers who were preoccupied with the child's immediate safety sometimes underestimated the importance for children of their links with family members and their desire to return. Children also had to deal with the insidious spread of *gossip* about their situation and the attendant bullying and teasing at school which further reduced their circle of friendship and support. Tighter curbs on the amount of information which is released when parents are prosecuted could have safeguarded some children, since the children could be identified when details about a parent were released. Children also needed advice about what to tell their friends, and help in developing a 'cover story' would have been appreciated.

Social workers had generally tried hard to build up relationships with the children, but the attempt was usually ineffective if they failed at the same time to build an alliance with the parent figures who were important in the children's lives. The social workers who managed to maintain positive contact with both the child and other significant family members were greatly valued by the children and provided an important source of continuity for them.

Some young people also received succour and sustenance from trusted friends, from relatives, from health professionals or from the kindness of school staff. Nonetheless, it was clear that by the end of the study period some children were still in distress. A few children had returned home to find continuing levels of violence or rejection and regretted leaving care. Others were struggling with unresolved issues about their abuse and its consequences, which were affecting their personal adjustment and future life chances through their impact on peer relationships, school attendance, and further training. Advice and information about how to refer themselves for further help would have been of great assistance. Information in schools about confidential sources of counselling, or indeed the provision of a counselling or referral service in schools, would be a useful extension of the schools' own system of pastoral care.

In spite of the emphasis on separation as a means of protection, most young people did not want to be separated from their families. They wanted the abuse to stop, but they wanted their family to remain intact. There is no easy solution to these dilemmas, but it is important that children's wishes are taken fully into consideration, even when their views are rather different from those of child protection professionals.

The costs and benefits of the child protection system

The current child protection system in England and Wales stems directly from that devised after the inquiry into the death of Maria Colwell (Secretary of State, 1974) although, as we saw in the introduction, its historical roots extend much further back. It has undergone a series of changes since the 1970s, notably those related to the greater specification of procedures and to the inclusion of sexual abuse within its remit (Secretary of State, 1988; Department of Health and Social Security, 1988). The emphasis has been on the establishment of a set of reliable procedures which will identify children at risk and maximise inter-professional coordination to protect them.

The child protection system is therefore about the management of risk but it is also about the management of anxiety. Public opprobrium has pursued social workers who were considered to have done too little too late (see for example, London Borough of Brent, 1985; London Borough of Lambeth, 1987) or too much too soon (Secretary of State, 1988). At the time of this study, social workers generally welcomed the conference and review system for its role in spreading the awesome responsibility of carrying child protection cases. However, child protection work is very stressful for social workers and this has costs which were evident in our study both at the personal level and in terms of the work which was offered, unless good quality supervision was made available. We found that the amount and quality of supervision available to social workers was very variable.

The successes of the child protection system are set out in chapter 18, and it is clear that for some children and families there were considerable benefits. Nevertheless, in its current form the system has clear limitations. The system is 'front-loaded', in that inter-agency responses and resources are concentrated on the identification of risk; that is on the phase of the investigation and initial case conference. The majority of subsequent work is undertaken by the key workers alone, with support from health visitors in the case of children under five. Few agencies apart from social services are routinely involved in offering treatment or other interventions (see also Corby, 1987; Gough *et al.*, 1989). The priority given to identifying situations of risk leaves little time for considering the methods of intervention and the resources which will be best suited to the needs of the child and family. Arguably if more attention was given to identifying these, better use would be made of the costly time of the many professionals who attend child protection conferences. Indeed, these issues may become more prominent if the increasing number of fund-holding GPs, hospital trusts and opted-out schools leads to concerns about who should bear the cost of child protection and its procedures (Hallett, 1993).

The inclusion of sexual abuse within the child protection system has had the effect of emphasising the search for evidence in support of a prosecution. It has therefore cast the police in a central role during the investigation stage. The introduction of video-recorded interviewing of children (Home Office, 1992) has further accelerated this process. This shift is in line with Parton's views (1991) on the move towards increasing legalism and a more socio-legal basis for intervention. It was clear that the practices which have emerged have had a number of adverse consequences for children and their parents since their needs have sometimes been subordinated to the desire to collect evidence. The withholding of therapeutic help for children until the completion of prosection or care proceedings is but one example. Since few prosecutions are successful these practices warrant serious reconsideration.

Attention also needs to be given to how best to deal with Schedule One offenders who appear or reappear and join families with children. There was evidence in the study of attempts by social services departments to intervene in these cases, but social workers lacked clear policies about what they could or should do. The response of the probation service varied from an acute awareness of the dangers presented by these offenders to a blinkered focus on the offenders themselves, which sometimes resulted in the risks they presented to children being denied. If children are to be protected, a register of offenders would be useful, especially if the probation service had accompanying responsibilities to alert social services departments to their movements. Consideration might also be given to the situation of mothers whose children have been abused and who wish to have some way of checking whether a prospective new partner has a record of relevant offences.

At present the system is geared to the protection of young children. Among children who were registered, there was evidence that some adolescents who were living at home were poorly provided for. Whereas careful monitoring was provided for children under five with the help of health visitors and day-care services, and there were determined attempts to establish permanent placements for young children who were looked after, the variety of problems presented by adolescents in difficulty seemed to bear no easy solution (see also Farmer and Parker, 1991). Young people who had suffered violence from parents or siblings were sometimes held as partly to blame, and even when they were placed on the register, assistance was not always forthcoming for the parents – particularly the stressed mothers – of these adolescents. Once again we are reminded that child protection is concerned with relationships between family members, and that factors such as age and gender play a part in determining who receives benefit, or alternatively on whom the costs fall.

Registration and the Children Act

The introduction of the Children Act 1989 provides an opportunity to review the place of the child protection system within it. It is clear that section 1(5) of the Act prohibits formal intervention by the making of a court order unless it is shown to be better for the child than making no order. There are therefore questions about how registration will be used if fewer children are committed to care. It may be that registration will be used more often, as a diversion from care. On the other hand greater use of registration could act as a net-widening exercise (Masson, 1992) and for this reason among others it is likely to be avoided. On the evidence of our study there is no doubt that registration has become part of a notional 'tariff' of penalties for inadequate parenting, the end point of which is compulsory admission to care.

The emphasis on the provision of support to families, and the partnership model of care which is embodied in the Children Act, is in stark contrast to the stigmatising framework of registration, which is often accompanied by the possibility of criminal proceedings. In cases of serious abuse in the study there was little doubt about the action which was necessary; but some of the children who were drawn into the child protection system would have been better served if they had been treated as 'children in need' under section 17 of the Children Act. This applied particularly to cases where vulnerable mothers were trying to cope with demanding children in impoverished circumstances and where the issue was poor parental care rather than danger to the child. It also applied where concerns centred on the mental health of parents or on adolescent behaviour. However, if more children were to be directed away from the child protection system a satisfactory process of gatekeeping or diversion would be needed. A mandate would have to be given to personnel, preferably at management level within social services departments, to under-take this role.

Diverting children away from the child protection system also raises the question of resource allocation. Scarce resources are easier to obtain for children who are on the register. Any diversion of children away from the system would only be successful if similar resources were available without it. Nevertheless, the high cost of the child protection system in emotional as well as financial terms makes such a move worth considering.

Reference has already been made to the death of Maria Colwell, as a result of which the notion of children's rights gained currency in the mid-1970s and the present arrangements for protecting children were initiated. It seems appropriate to conclude with a quotation from one of the popular writers who made a radical contribution to that debate, since he expresses succinctly some of the ideas which emerged from our research interviews. The work is John Holt's *Escape from Childhood*, and this extract is from chapter 15, which is entitled 'What children need, we all need'.

> 'We all have a right to feel that we are not just what other people, even experts, say we are – not just this race, or size, or colour, or occupation, or income level, or position, or I.Q., or personality profile – but that there is an essence which is much larger, more unknowable, and more important. And it is a delusion to believe that even if this right is denied to us it may somehow be given to children, that they may have a right to dignity and a unique and inviolable identity where no-one else does.'

The evidence from our study suggests that an intense focus on children's protection sometimes leads to a neglect of the wider needs of children and other family members. There is a danger that the lessons learned about child care in general are being lost in the drive towards child protection. In the interests of children's future welfare, it is important that we get the balance right.

Bibliography

Adams, D. (1988), 'Treatment models of men who batter: a pro-feminist analysis', in Yllo, K. and Bograd, M. (eds), *Feminist Perspectives on Wife Abuse*, Sage.

Ahmed, S., Cheetham, J. and Small, J. (eds) (1986), *Social Work with Black Children and their Families*, London, Batsford.

Allen, N. (1990), *Making Sense of the Children Act 1989*, Harlow, Longman.

American Academy of Pediatrics Committee on Child Abuse and Neglect (1991), 'Guildelines for evaluation of sexual abuse of children', *Pediatrics*, 87, pp. 254–60.

Amulree (1932), *The Report of the Royal Commission on Licensing (England and Wales), 1929–31*, Cmd. 3988.

Anthony, G. and Watkeys, J. (1991), 'False allegations in child sexual abuse', *Children and Society*, Vol. 5, No. 2.

Bagley, C. and King, K. (1990), *Child Sexual Abuse,* London, Routledge.

Baher, E., Hyman, C., Jones, C., Kerr, A. and Mitchell, R. (1976), *At Risk: An Account of the Work of the Battered Child Research Department, NSPCC*, London, Routledge and Kegan Paul.

Baldwin, J. and Oliver, J. (1975), 'Epidemiology and family characteristics of severely abused children', *British Journal of Preventive and Social Medicine*, Vol. 29.

Barn, R. (1993), *Black Children in the Public Care System*, London, Batsford.

Barrera, M. (1981) 'Social support in the adjustment of pregnant adolescents: assessment issues', in Gottlieb, B. H., *Social Networks and Social Support*, Beverley Hills, Sage.

Barrera, M. (1985), 'Informant corroboration of social support network data', *Connections*, 8 (1), pp. 9–13.

Barth, R. P. and Berry, M. (1987), 'Outcomes of child welfare services since permanency planning', *Social Services Review*, Vol. 61, pp. 71–90.

Behlmer, G. K. (1982), *Child Abuse and Moral Reform in England, 1870–1908*, Stanford University Press.

Bentovim, A., Elton, A., Hildebrand, J., Tranter, M. and Vizard, E. (eds) (1988), *Child Sexual Abuse within the Family: Assessment and Treatment: The Work of the Great Ormond Street Team*, London, Wright.

Berliner, L. (1991 a), 'Treating the effects of sexual assault', in Murray, K. and Gough, D. A. (eds), *Intervening in Child Sexual Abuse*, Edinburgh, Scottish Academic Press.

Berliner, L. (1991 b), 'Interviewing Families', in Murray, K. and Gough, D. A. (eds), *Intervening in Child Sexual Abuse*, Edinburgh, Scottish Academic Press.

Bhaduri, R. (1988) 'Race and culture: the invisible consumers', in Allen, I. (ed), *Hearing the Voice of the Consumer*, London, Policy Studies Institute.

Borchorst, A. (1990), 'Political motherhood and child care policies', in Ungerson, C. (ed), *Gender and Caring*, Hemel Hempstead, Harvester Wheatsheaf.

Boswell, J. (1989), *The Kindness of Strangers: the Abandonment of Children in Western Europe from Late Antiquity to the Renaissance*, Penguin.

Bottoms, A. E. and McClintock, F. H. (1973), *Criminals Coming of Age: A Study of Institutional Adaptation in the Treatment of Adolescent Offenders*, London, Heinemann.

Boushel, M. and Fisher, M. C. (forthcoming), 'What kind of people are we?: Anti-racism and social welfare research', *Social Work and Social Sciences Review*.

Boushel, M. and Lebacq, M. (1992), 'Towards empowerment in child protection work', *Children and Society*, Vol. 6, No. 1.

Bowker, L. H., Arbitell, M. and McFerron, J. R. (1988), 'On the relationship between wife beating and child abuse', in Yllo, K. and Bograd, M. (eds), *Feminist Perspectives on Wife Abuse*, London, Sage.

Bridge Child Care Consultancy Service (1991), *Sukina: An Evaluation Report of the Circumstances Leading to her Death*.

Brock (1933), *Report of the Departmental Committee on Sterilisation*, Cmd. 4485.

Brown, C. (1984), *Child Abuse Parents Speaking: Parents' Impressions of Social Workers and the Social Work Process*, School for Advanced Urban Studies, University of Bristol.

Brown, G. W. and Harris, T. (1978), *The Social Origins of Depression*, London, Tavistock.

Browne, K. D. (1993), 'Violence in the family and its links to child abuse' in Hobbs, C. J. and Wynne, J. M. (eds), *Bailliere's Clinical Paediatrics: Child Abuse*, Vol. 1, No. 1, London, Bailliere Tindall.

Browne, K. and Saqi, S. (1988), 'Approaches to screening for child abuse and neglect', in Browne, K., Davies, C. and Stratton, P. (eds), *Early Prediction and Prevention of Child Abuse*, Chichester, Wiley.

Bullock, R., Little, M. and Millham, S. (1993), *Going Home*, Dartmouth.

Burns, L. (1991), *Partnership with Families: A Study of 65 Child Protection Case Conferences in Gloucestershire to which the Family were Invited,* Gloucestershire County Council Social Services.

Calam, R. and Franchi, C. (1987), *Child Abuse and Its Consequences,* Cambridge University Press.

Central Council for Education and Training in Social Work (1991), *One Small Step Towards Racial Justice,* CCETSW.

Cleaver, H. and Freeman, P. (1993), *Parental Perspectives in Suspected Child Abuse.* Report submitted to the Department of Health.

Conte, J. and Schuerman, J. (1987), 'Factors associated with an increased impact of child sexual abuse', *Child Abuse and Neglect, II,* pp. 201–11.

Corby, B. (1987), *Working with Child Abuse,* Milton Keynes, Open University Press.

Corby, B. (1990), 'Making use of child protection statistics', *Children and Society,* Vol. 4, No. 3.

Corby, B. (1993), *Child Abuse. Towards a Knowledge Base,* Milton Keynes, Open University Press.

Cornwell, J. (1985), *Hard Earned Lives,* Tavistock.

Creighton, S. J. (1984), *Trends in Child Abuse, 1977–82,* London, NSPCC.

Creighton, S. J. (1992), *Child Abuse Trends in England and Wales 1988–1990,* London, NSPCC.

Creighton, S. J. and Noyes, P. (1989), *Child Abuse Trends in England and Wales 1983–1987,* London, NSPCC.

Croft, S. and Beresford, P. (1992), 'The politics of participation', *Critical Social Policy,* Vol. 12, No. 2.

Curtis (1946), *A Report of the Care of Children Committee,* Cmd. 6922.

Dale, P., Davies, M., Morrison, T. and Waters, J. (1986), *Dangerous Families: Assessment and Treatment of Child Abuse,* London, Tavistock.

Dempster, H. (1993), 'The aftermath of child sexual abuse: women's perspectives', in Waterhouse, L. (ed), *Child Abuse and Child Abusers: Protection and Prevention ,* Research Highlights in Social Work, No. 24, London, Jessica Kingsley.

Department of Health (1988 a), *Inspection of Cleveland Social Services Department's Arrangements for Handling Child Sexual Abuse,* Social Services Inspectorate.

Department of Health (1988 b), *Protecting Children: A Guide for Social Workers Undertaking a Comprehensive Assessment,* London, HMSO.

Department of Health (1989 a), *Survey of Children and Young Persons on Child Protection Registers, Year Ending 31 March 1988, England.*

Department of Health (1989 b), *Report of Inspection of Child Abuse Services in Cumbria Social Services Department*, Social Services Inspectorate.

Department of Health (1990 a), *Child Protection in London: Aspects of Management Arrangements in Social Services Departments*, Social Services Inspectorate.

Department of Health (1990 b), *Children and Young Persons on Child Protection Registers, Year Ending 31 March 1989, England.*

Deparment of Health (1991 a), *Child Abuse. A Study of Inquiry Reports 1980–1989*, London, HMSO.

Department of Health (1991 b), *Children and Young Persons on Child Protection Registers, Year Ending 31 March 1990, England.*

Department of Health (1992), *Children and Young Persons on Child Protection Registers, Year Ending 31 March 1991, England.*

Department of Health (1993), *Children and Young Persons on Child Protection Registers, Year Ending 31 March 1992, England.*

Department of Health (1994), *Children and Young Persons on Child Protection Registers, Year Ending 31 March 1993, England.*

Department of Health (draft report), *Child Protection: A Guide to self-monitoring and inspection*. Now published as Department of Health (1993), *Evaluating Performance in Child Protection: A framework for the inspection of local authority social services practice and systems*, Social Services Inspectorate.

Department of Health and Social Security (1970), *The Battered Baby*, CM02/70.

Department of Health and Social Security (1974), *Memorandum on Non-Accidental Injury to Children*, LASSL (74)13.

Department of Health and Social Security (1980), *Child Abuse: Central Register Systems*, LASSL(80)4, London, HMSO.

Department of Health and Social Security (1982), *Child Abuse: A Study of Inquiry Reports 1973–1981*, London, HMSO.

Department of Health and Social Security and the Welsh Office (1988), *Working Together: A Guide to Arrangements for Interagency Co-operation for the Protection of Children from Abuse*, London, HMSO.

Dingwall, R. (1989), 'Some problems about predicting child abuse and neglect' in Stevenson, O. (ed), *Child Abuse: Professional Practice and Public Policy*, Harvester Wheatsheaf.

Dingwall, R., Eekelaar, J. and Murray, T. (1983), *The Protection of Children: State Intervention and Family Life*, Oxford, Blackwell.

Dominelli, L. (1989), 'An uncaring profession? An examination of racism in social work', *New Community*, Vol. 15, No. 3, April.

Donnison, D. V. (1954), *The Neglected Child and the Social Services*, Manchester University Press.

Donzelot, J. (1980), *The Policing of Families*, London, Hutchinson.

Eekelaar, J. (1984), *Family Law and Social Policy*, Weidenfeld and Nicholson.

Ely, P. and Denney, D. (1987), *Social Work in a Multi-Racial Society*, Aldershot, Gower.

Faller, K. C. (1989), *Child Sexual Abuse: An Interdisciplinary Manual for Diagnosis, Case Management and Treatment*, London, Macmillan.

Farmer, E. (1993 a), 'The Impact of Child Protection Interventions: The Experiences of Parents and Children', in Waterhouse, L. (ed), *Child Abuse and Child Abusers: Protection and Prevention*, Research Highlights in Social Work, No.24, London, Jessica Kingsley.

Farmer, E. (1993 b), 'Going home – what makes reunification work?' in Marsh, P. and Triseliotis, J. (eds), *Prevention and Reunification in Child Care*, London, Batsford.

Farmer, E. and Parker, R. (1991), *Trials and Tribulations: Returning Children from Local Authority Care to their Families*, London, HMSO.

Finkelhor, D. (1986), *A Sourcebook on Child Sexual Abuse*, Sage.

Fisher, M., Marsh, P., Phillips, D., with Sainsbury, E. (1986), *In and Out of Care: The Experiences of Children, Parents and Social Workers*, London, Batsford.

Ford, D. (1955), *The Deprived Child and the Community*, Constable.

Frothingham, T. E., Barnett, R. A. M., Hobbs, C. J. and Wynne, J. A. (1993), 'Child sexual abuse in Leeds before and after Cleveland', *Child Abuse Review*, Vol. 2, pp. 23–34.

Gibbons, J. with Thorpe, S. and Wilkinson, P. (1990), *Family Support and Prevention: Studies in Local Areas*, National Institute for Social Work, London, HMSO.

Gibbons, J., Conroy, S. and Bell, C. (1993), *Operation of Child Protection Registers*, Report to the Department of Health, Social Work Development Unit, University of East Anglia.

Giller, H., Gormely, C. and Williams, P. (1992), *The Effectiveness of Child Protection Procedures. An Evaluation of Child Protection Procedures in Four ACPC Areas*, Cheshire, Social Information Systems.

Goddard, C. and Hiller, P. (1993), 'Child sexual abuse: assault in a violent context', *Australian Journal of Social Issues*, Vol. 28, No. 1, February.

Goffman, E. (1963), *Stigma: Notes on the Management of Spoiled Identity*, Prentice-Hall, reprinted Penguin 1990.

Gomes-Schwartz, B., Horowitz, J. and Cardarelli, A. (1990), *Child Sexual Abuse: The Initial Effects*, Beverley Hills CA, Sage.

Gordon, L. (1989), *Heroes of Their Own Lives,* London, Virago Press.

Gough, D. (1993), *Child Abuse Interventions. A Review of the Research Literature*, London, HMSO.

Gough, D. A., Boddy, F. A., Dunning, N. and Stone, F. H. (1989), *A Longitudinal Study of Child Abuse in Glasgow*, Social Paediatric and Obstetric Research Unit, University of Glasgow.

Gough, D. A., Taylor, J. P. and Boddy, F. A. (1988), *Child Abuse Interventions: A Review of the Research Literature. Part C. Intervention Studies: Treating Abuse,* Report to the DHSS, Social Paediatric and Obstetric Research Unit, University of Glasgow.

Graham, P., Dingwall, R. and Wolkind, S. (1985), 'Research issues in child abuse', *Social Science and Medicine,* Vol. 21, No. 11, pp. 1216–28

Hague, G. and Malos, E., (1993), *Domestic Violence: Action for Change*, New Clarion Press.

Hallett, C. (1993), 'Working together in child protection', in Waterhouse, L. (ed), *Child Abuse and Child Abusers: Protection and Prevention*, Research Highlights in Social Work, No.24, London, Jessica Kingsley.

Hallett, C. and Birchall, E. (1992), *Co-ordination and Child Protection: A Review of the Literature*, Edinburgh, HMSO.

Hallett, C. and Stevenson, O. (1980), *Child Abuse: Aspects of Interprofessional Co-operation*, London, Allen and Unwin.

Harter, S. (1985), *The Self-Perception Profile for Children*, University of Denver, Denver.

Harter, S. (1987), *The Self-Perception Profile for Adolescents*, University of Denver, Denver.

Hearn, J. (1990), 'Child abuse and men's violence' in Violence Against Children Study Group, *Taking Child Abuse Seriously*, London, Unwin Hyman.

Higginson, S. (1992), '*Decision-making in the assessment of risk in child abuse cases*', M.Phil thesis, Cranfield Institute of Technology.

Holt, J. (1975), *Escape from Childhood*, Harmondsworth, Penguin.

Home Office (1923), *Report of the Work of the Children's Branch.*

Home Office (1926), *Report of the Departmental Committee on Sexual Offences Against Young Persons*, Cmd. 2561.

Home Office (1938), *Report of the Departmental Committee on Corporal Punishment*, Cmd. 5684.

Home Office (1990), Circular 6/90, HMSO.

Home Office, Department of Health, Department of Education and Science, Welsh Office (1991), *Working Together Under the Children Act 1989*. A guide to arrangements for inter-agency co-operation for the protection of children from abuse, London, HMSO.

Home Office with Department of Health (1992), *Memorandum of Good Practice on Video Recorded Interviews with Child Witnesses for Criminal Proceedings*, London, HMSO.

Home Office, Ministry of Health and Ministry of Education (1950), *Joint Circular on Children Neglected or Ill-Treated in their own Homes*, 31 July.

Hooper, C. (1991), 'Child sexual abuse and the regulation of women: variations on a theme', in Smart, C. (ed.), *Regulating Motherhood*, Routledge.

Hooper, C. (1992), *Mothers Surviving Child Sexual Abuse*, London, Routledge.

Howe, D. (1992), 'Child abuse and the bureaucratisation of social work', *Sociological Review*, 40, 3, pp. 491–508.

Hughes, M., Parkinson, D. and Vargo, M. (1989), 'Witnessing spouse abuse and experiencing physical abuse: a double whammy?', *Journal of Family Violence*, Vol. 4, No. 2.

Ingleby (1960), Home Office, *Report of the Committee on Children and Young Persons*, Cmnd. 1191.

Jaffe, P., Wolfe, D. and Kaye, S. (1990), *Children of Battered Women*, Sage.

Jones, A. (1993), 'Anti-racist child protection', *Race and Class*, Vol. 1, No. 35.

Jones, D. N., Pickett, J., Oates, M. R. and Barbor, P. (1987), *Understanding Child Abuse*, Basingstoke, Macmillan.

Kempe, C. H., Silverman, F. N., Steele, B. F., Droegmueller, W. and Silver, H. K. (1962), 'The battered child syndrome', *Journal of the American Medical Association*, No. 181, pp. 17–22.

King, M. and Trowell, J. (1993), *Children's Welfare and the Law*, London, Sage.

Kovacs, M. and Beck, A. T. (1977), 'An empirical clinical approach towards a definition of childhood depression' in Schulterbrandt, J. G. and Raskin, A. (eds), *Depression in Children: Diagnosis, Treatment and Conceptual Models*, New York, Raven.

London Borough of Brent (1985), *A Child in Trust*. The Report of the Panel of Inquiry into the Circumstances Surrounding the Death of Jasmine Beckford.

London Borough of Greenwich (1987), *A Child in Mind: The Protection of Children in a Responsible Society*. The Report of the Commission of Inquiry into the circumstances surrounding the death of Kimberley Carlile.

London Borough of Lambeth (1987), *Whose Child?* The Report of the Panel Appointed to Inquire into the Death of Tyra Henry.

Lynch, M. and Roberts, J. (1982), *The Consequences of Child Abuse*, London, Academic Press.

Lyth, I. M. (1988), *Containing Anxiety in Institutions*, London, Free Asociation Books.

Macleod, M. and Saraga, E. (1988), 'Challenging the orthodoxy: towards a feminist theory and practice', *Feminist Review*, No.28.

Marsh, P. and Allen, G. (1993), 'The law, prevention and reunification – the New Zealand development of family group conferences', in Marsh, P. and Triseliotis, J. (eds), *Prevention and Reunification in Child Care*, London, Batsford.

Martin, F. M., Fox, S. J. and Murray, K. (1981), *Children Out of Court*, Edinburgh, Scottish Academic Press.

Masson, J. (1992), 'Managing risk under the Children Act 1989: diversion in child care? *Child Abuse Review*, Vol. 1, pp. 103–22.

Mayer, J. E. and Timms, N. (1970), *The Client Speaks*, London, Routledge and Kegan Paul.

Mazumdar, P. M. (1992), *Eugenics, Human Genetics and Human Failings: the Eugenics Society, its Sources and its Critics in Britain*, Routledge.

McCann, W. N. (1949), letter to *The Times*, 12 Dec. as Director of the NSPCC.

McGloin, P. and Turnbull, A. (1986), *Parent Participation in Child Abuse Review Conferences. A Research Report*. London Borough of Greenwich.

Melton, G. B. and Flood, M. F. (1994), 'Research policy and child maltreatment: developing the scientific foundation for effective protection of children', *Child Abuse and Neglect*, Vol. 18, Supplement 1, pp. 1–28.

Miller, L. B. and Fisher, T. (1992), 'Some obstacles to the effective investigation and registration of children at risk. Issues gleaned from a worker's perspective', *Journal of Social Work Practice*, Vol. 6, No. 2.

Monckton (1945), *Report on the Circumstances which led to the Boarding-Out of Dennis and Terence O'Neill at Bank Farm, Minsterley, and the Steps Taken to Supervise their Welfare*, Cmd. 6636.

Montalvo, B. and Gutierrez, M. (1984), 'The mask of culture', *Family Therapy Networker*, July-Aug edition, quoted in McAdoo (ed) (1993), *Family Ethnicity: Strengths in Diversity*, Sage.

Moore, J. (1985), *The ABC of Child Abuse*, Gower.

Murphy, P. M. and Kupshik, G. A. (1992), *Loneliness, Stress and Well-Being*, London, Routledge.

NSPCC (various dates), *Research Briefing: Child Abuse.*

O'Hagan, K. (1989), *Working with Child Sexual Abuse*, Milton Keynes, Open University Press.

Owen, M. (1992), *Social Justice and Children in Care*, Aldershot, Avebury.

Owusu-Bempah, J. (1994), 'Race, self-identity and social work', *The British Journal of Social Work*, Vol. 24, No. 2, pp. 123–36.

Parker, R. A. (1986), 'Child care: the roots of a dilemma', *Political Quarterly*, Vol. 57, No. 3.

Parker, R. A. (1990 a), *Away From Home: A History of Child Care*, Barnardos.

Parker, R. A. (1990 b), *Safeguarding Standards*, Joseph Rowntree Memorial Trust and the National Institute for Social Work.

Parker, R., Ward, H., Jackson, S., Aldgate, J. and Wedge, P. (1991), *Looking After Children: Assessing Outcomes in Child Care*, London, HMSO.

Parliamentary Debates (Commons) (1948–49), vol. 467 col. 1740, 22 July and vol. 470 col. 2431, 12 Dec.

Parton, C. (1990), 'Women, gender oppression and child abuse', in Violence Against Children Study Group, *Taking Child Abuse Seriously*, London, Unwin Hyman.

Parton, N. (1989), 'Child Abuse' in Kahan, B. (ed), *Child Care Research, Policy and Practice*, Hodder and Stoughton.

Parton, N. (1991), *Governing the Family: Child Care, Child Protection and the State*, Basingstoke, Macmillan.

Phillips, M. and Dutt, R. (1991), *Towards a Black Perspective in Child Protection*, Race Equality Unit.

Pitcairn, T., Waterhouse, L., McGhee, J., Secker, J. and Sullivan, C. (1993), 'Evaluating parenting in child physical abuse', in Waterhouse, L. (ed), *Child Abuse and Child Abusers: Protection and Prevention*, Research Highlights in Social Work, No. 24, London, Jessica Kingsley.

Pollock, L. (1983), *Forgotten Children: Parent-Child Relations from 1500 to 1900*, Cambridge.

Public Record Office (a), MH 102/1966.

Public Record Office (b), BN 29/489.

Quinton, D. and Rutter, M. (1988), *Parenting Breakdown: The Making and Breaking of Intergenerational Links*, Aldershot, Avebury.

Richardson, A. (1983), *Participation: Concepts in Social Policy 1*, Routledge and Kegan Paul.

Rose, J. (1987), *For the Sake of the Children*, Hodder and Stoughton.

Rose, L. (1986), *Massacre of the Innocents: Infanticide in Great Britain, 1800–1939*, Routledge and Kegan Paul.

Rosenberg, M. (1965), *Society and the Adolescent Self-Image*, Princeton University Press.

Rowe, J. and Lambert, L. (1973), *Children Who Wait*, ABAFA.

Rowe, J., Hundleby, M. and Garnett, L. (1989), *Child Care Now: A Survey of Placement Patterns*, British Agencies for Adoption and Fostering.

Rutter, M., Quinton, D. and Liddle (1983), 'Parenting in Two Generations' in Madge, N. (ed), *Families at Risk*, Heinemann.

Rutter, M., Tizard, J. and Whitmore, K. C. (1970), Education, *Health and Behaviour*, Longman.

Sainsbury, E. (1975), *Social Work with Families,* London, Routledge and Kegan Paul.

Sainsbury, E., Nixon, S. and Phillips, D. (1982), *Social Work in Focus: Clients' and Social Workers' Perceptions in Long-Term Social Work*, London, Routledge and Kegan Paul.

Secretary of State for Social Services (1974), *Report of the Committee of Inquiry into the Care and Supervision Provided in Relation to Maria Colwell*, London, HMSO.

Secretary of State for Social Services (1988), *Report of the Inquiry into Child Abuse in Cleveland 1987*, Cm 412, London, HMSO.

Select Committee (1975), *Report from the Select Committee on Violence in Marriage*, Session 1974–75, HC 533, HMSO.

Select Committee (1977), *Report from the Select Committee on Violence in the Family*, Session 1976–77, HC 329, HMSO.

Shahar, S. (1990), *Childhood in the Middle Ages*, Routledge.

Sharland, E., Jones, D., Aldgate, J., Seal, H., Croucher, M. (1993), *Professional Intervention in Child Sexual Abuse*, Report to the Department of Health, Department of Applied Social Studies and Social Research, University of Oxford.

Sheldon, B. (1987), 'The Psychology of Incompetence' in *After Beckford? Essays on themes related to child abuse*, Dept of Social Policy and Social Science, Royal Holloway and Bedford New College, University of London, published Bedford New College.

Shemmings, D. and Thoburn, J. (1990), *Parental Participation in Child Protection Conferences: Report of a Pilot Project in Hackney Social Services Department,* Social Work Development Unit, University of East Anglia.

Smith, J. and Rachman, S. (1984), 'Non-accidental injury to children II: a controlled evaluation of a behavioural management programme', *Behaviour Research and Therapy*, 22, pp. 349–66

Stanley, J. and Goddard, C. (1993), 'The association between child abuse and other family violence, *Australian Social Work*, Vol. 46, No. 2, June.

Starr, R. H. (1982), *Child Abuse Prediction*, Cambridge Mass, Ballinger.

Straus M., (1979), 'Family patterns and child abuse in a nationally representative American sample', *Child Abuse and Neglect*, 3, pp. 213–25.

The Times (1949), 6, 8, 25 July, 12 Dec.

Thoburn, J. (1980), *Captive Clients: Social Work with Families of Children Home on Trial*, Routledge and Kegan Paul.

Thoburn J. (ed) (1992), *Participation in Practice – Involving Families in Child Protection*, Social Work Development Unit, University of East Anglia.

Thoburn, J., Lewis, A. and Shemmings, D. (1993), *Family Participation in Child Protection*. Report to the Department of Health.

Thomson, J. (1993), 'Children's hearings: a legal perspective after Orkney', in Waterhouse, L. (ed), *Child Abuse and Child Abusers: Protection and Prevention*, Research Highlights in Social Work, No. 24, London, Jessica Kingsley.

Vernon, J. and Fruin, D. (1986), *In Care: A Study of Social Work Decision-Making*, London, National Children's Bureau.

Ward, H. (1990), *The Charitable Relationship: Parents, Children and the Waifs and Strays Society*, PhD thesis, University of Bristol.

Watson, D. (1982), 'Recommendations, decisions and rubber stamps', *The Hearing*, Bulletin of the Panel Training Resource Centre, Issue No. 7.

Women's Group on Public Welfare (1948), *The Neglected Child and his Family*, OUP.

Wyatt, G. E. and Mickey, M. R. (1988), 'The support by parents and others as it mediates the effects of child sexual abuse: an exploratory study', in Wyatt, G. E. and Powell, G. J. (eds), *Lasting Effects of Child Sexual Abuse*. London, Sage.

Index

Parental Perspectives in Cases of Suspected Child Abuse
Hedy Cleaver and Pam Freeman (The Dartington Team)
HMSO, 1995, ISBN 0 11 321786 2

Child Protection Practice: Private Risks and Public Remedies
A study of decision-making, intervention and outcome in child protection work
Elaine Farmer and Morag Owen (The University of Bristol Team)
HMSO, 1995, ISBN 0 11 321787 0

The Prevalence of Child Sexual Abuse in Britain
Deborah Ghate and Liz Spencer (Social and Community Planning Research)
HMSO, 1995, ISBN 0 11 321783 8

Development After Physical Abuse in Early Childhood: A Follow-Up Study of Children on Protection Registers
Jane Gibbons, Bernard Gallagher, Caroline Bell and David Gordon (University of East Anglia)
HMSO, 1995, ISBN 0 11 321790 0

Operating of Child Protection System
Caroline Bell, Sue Conroy and Jane Gibbons (University of East Anglia)
HMSO, 1995, ISBN 0 11 321785 4

Inter-agency Coordination and Child Protection
Christine Hallett (The University of Stirling)
HMSO, 1995, ISBN 0 11 321789 7

Working Together in Child Protection
Elizabeth Birchall (The University of Stirling)
HMSO, 1995, ISBN 0 11 321830 3

Paternalism or Partnership? Family Involvement in the Child Protection Process
June Thoburn, Ann Lewis and David Shemmings (University of East Anglia)
HMSO, 1995 ISBN 0 11 321788 9

Messages from Research
HMSO, 1995 ISBN 0 11 321781 1

Printed in the United Kingdom for HMSO
Dd301681 12/95 C10 G3397 10170